Notes from Indian Country Volume I

Tim Giago
Nawica Kjici (Defender)

Photographs by Tom Casey
(Unless otherwise credited)

Publisher
Keith Cochran

© Tim Giago 1984
Library of Congress Catalog Card Number 84-91699

Printed at State Publishing Company
Pierre, South Dakota

Tim Giago

Books by Tim Giago:
The Aboriginal Sin
Notes from Indian Country, Volume I

This book is dedicated to the greatest natural resource of Indian Country: the children. It is especially dedicated to Timmy Giago (*Walking Thunder Man*), my four-year-old son, and to Marie Therese Giago (*She Stands in the Four Directions*), my two-year-old daughter, two Lakota children faced with the prospect of preserving the Lakota Nation.

Forward

What Tim's Professional Associates Say

Bill Hosokawa, Editorial Page Editor,
The Denver Post, Denver, Colorado

Almost from the beginning our society has created an aura around the image of the American Indian, more lately to be known as the Native American. At first it was Pocahontas, the Indian princess who pleaded with Powhatan to spare the life of John Smith, and the kindly tribesmen who fed the Pilgrims in Massachusetts until their first crops were harvested. The romantic and often saccharine aura of the noble, nature-loving redman, the fearless warrior and the doe-eyed maiden was immortalized in Longfellow's *Hiawatha*, and countless other pieces of literature read avidly by generations of Americans.

In more modern times that image has crumbled and the aura is more likely to be of the impoverished reservation Indian stubbornly refusing to accept "the American way of life," and the whiskey-sodden derelict who stumbled while in search of it. Or, equally demeaning, the stolid and brutish savage of persistent Hollywood epics.

Of course these images are excessively simplistic and we all know it. (We also know that the continent "discovered" and settled by Europeans was already peopled by natives who lived in harmony with the land.) The truth is that Native Americans are individuals and they should no more be categorized or stereotyped than white Americans. Yet, in the absence of many strong, eloquent voices to tell the Indian story and express the fears, frustrations and aspirations of this American minority, it is difficult to project a more human picture.

One such voice belongs to Tim Giago, a Lakota born on the Pine Ridge Reservation of South Dakota and educated in an Indian mission school. Giago also has been on the "outside." During service with the United States Navy, he became interested in journalism. He developed writing skills to complement his natural powers of observation. He could have done very well in the world of the white man.

But he chose to go back to Pine Ridge to found a weekly newspaper, *The Lakota Times*. In it he writes a personal column *Notes from Indian Country*, which also is published by several non-Indian newspapers. The column is a platform from which Giago observes America and American society from a Native American point of view. That, it goes without saying further, often is substantially different from that of the U.S. majority.

But Giago is no tomahawk-wielding extremist. I use the metaphor advisedly. He does not hesitate to criticize those who, figuratively, would return to the era of the Indian-cavalry wars. Once he nearly had his newspaper plant burned for his pains. In the best tradition of American journalism, he vowed his voice would not be stilled.

Some of Giago's columns are reprinted in this volume. You will find them of more than passing interest. Giago, in his gentle way, is telling us things we should know about some of our fellow Americans, matters we should be thinking about.

Jim Kuehn, Vice President and Editor,
The Rapid City Journal, Rapid City, South Dakota

Notes from Indian Country by Tim Giago has become a fixture since its inception in the *Rapid City Journal* in October, 1979.

I'm convinced a growing number of readers look to Tim's column for a point of view that is not otherwise available in the traditional press in South Dakota. Tim's message may one time be aimed at his Indian peers, another time at the white majority or another at officialdom, bureaucracy, the white press or even basketball referees. Whatever, Tim pulls no punches when criticizing or lecturing.

Rarely has Tim missed the mark. Most often he has clearly and correctly illuminated a subject.

Tim has enabled our newspaper to offer some hard-to-find information plus insight that is otherwise difficult for us to cultivate or claim. I recommend his column to friends and fellow journalists not only to read the opinion of an informed and energetic Indian citizen, but to enjoy the writing skills of a columnist who has steadily grown in the art of communication.

Jerold Johnson, Managing Editor,
Farmington Daily Times, Farmington, New Mexico

Every issue has at least two sides; most have more. It is the journalist's job to present all sides of an issue, recognizing that different views may be equally valid. The goal of the professional journalist is to enlighten his readers so that, collectively, the people are able to intelligently accept or reject any view. Tim Giago is true to his profession.

Introduction

As the editor of a weekly newspaper in Custer County in southwestern South Dakota, I welcomed the opportunity to present the Indian point of view to readers of that newspaper when Tim Giago began the column, *Notes from Indian Country*. I have been pleased to observe the acceptance of Tim's column in other newspapers, not only in South Dakota, but also in New Mexico and Colorado.

Subscribers to the *Custer County Chronicle* have commented to me that Tim's objective approach to controversial subjects and his fairness in writing about them have increased their awareness of Indian lifestyles and kept them reading his columns whether they agree with him or not.

There has long been a dearth of intelligent journalistic writing, untainted by serving a special cause, about modern Indians and reservation lifestyles. Tim's contributions are filling that void.

Giago has the talent to temper hard-hitting concepts with humor and provides penetrating glimpses into the lives of some of the most interesting and finest people on earth—the Native Americans.

His achievements in the communications field have opened the door for aspiring young Native American journalists, and, indeed, for all Native American youth who want to succeed in any field of endeavor. His accomplishments give testimony that it is possible to attain a successful career on the reservation.

Since beginning his weekly column, *Notes from Indian Country*, Tim has been involved in being a consultant to a television crew, in establishing the first privately Indian owned newspaper on any reservation, in running for office on the Pine Ridge Reservation, and in being recently elected the first president of the newly formed Native American Media Association.

Most of the first four years of columns written by Giago are the content of this book, grouped by subject matter. Although progress in human relations has been made over the past few years and although some of the people who are the subjects of some of these columns are no longer alive, the columns have been reproduced as they were written to maintain the perspective of the years from 1979 to 1983. Columns to be published in subsequent books will update the information in this book and provide a continuing base of study for those interested in modern American Indian history, influences on it, and the people who develop it.

Jessie Y. Sundstrom, Former Publisher
Custer County Chronicle, Custer, South Dakota

Table of Contents

CHAPTER I—COMMUNICATIONS

General

TV Mini-Series Based on *Hanta Yo*

Radio and Television

CHAPTER II—CULTURE

CHAPTER III—EDUCATION AND ATHLETICS

CHAPTER IV—GOVERNMENT

Economy

Elections

Federal

Natural Resources

State

CHAPTER V—HEALTH

CHAPTER VI—HUMOR

CHAPTER VII—LITIGATION

Chapter 1 — Communications

2   Communications

Communications
General
Indian Affairs Aid to Communication

There are several important things one learns from writing a column such as mine. Let there be no mistake that my column is an advocacy column. It is written from the Indian point of view and it supports the beliefs, opinions and ideologies of the Indian people. In that respect, it is a one-sided column.

From a white perspective, my column could be classified as liberal; but from an Indian point of view, it would probably be categorized as conservative.

Since man first set up a printing press in this region and began to publish newspapers, there has been almost only one point of view: the publisher's or someone else's in the management. It is common knowledge to all of us that most of these publishers, then and now, were not Indians. Doesn't it make sense to you that news and opinions printed in these journals about the Indian people were one-sided for a couple of centuries?

The most important lesson learned by every journalist is responsibility. Never will I ever consider myself a "spokesman" for the Indian people. Indians are their own spokesmen, and they will speak out on the issues as individuals. There is always the possibility that, because the white society places great stock in "spokesmen," my column may be misconstrued as "spokesman-like;" but nothing can be further from the truth.

However, in the event that the opinions of the Indian people, which are expressed to me daily, can be misconstrued as my own, then it is my responsibility to see that those opinions are presented with the utmost accuracy, and in the very best light.

The responsibility of this column is a very serious matter to me. The editors of the Farmington, New Mexico *Daily Times* are progressive and realistic people. As Bob Dylan said in his song, "Times, they are a-changing," and the people and institutions must keep abreast of these changes if they are to move forward. My editors realized, because of the very large Indian population in this area, there was another point of view that needed to be heard—the Indian point of view.

There are those, perhaps, who may, vehemently, disagree with the opinions expressed in my column. Because they disagree with me, they may even cast aspersions upon my integrity or veracity; but please let my critics rest assured that I have spent most of my adult life on the other side of the counter experiencing the research that has gone into my columns.

Admittedly, there are white journalists who are very capable of writing articles about Indians, but, all too frequently, they set themselves up, in their own minds, as "Indian experts" after acquiring a few years of experience in this field. In my opinion, there is no amount of experience that can be gained as that which is acquired from looking at the dominant society through the eyes of a member of the minority

Another lesson that I have learn.. d while writing this column is that I never use my column to strike out at my critics. I must always consider the fact that, if any column I have written induces comment, criticism, praise, rage or any other human emotion, perhaps it will lead to better communications beteen Indians and non-Indians.

As my editors have said to me on more than one occasion, "We may not always agree with what you write; but we enjoy your columns because they do present another point of view."

I've said it before, and I will continue to say it as long as I am able to write about it: "Communication is the key to progress, and to understanding." Until we bridge that communication gap between Indians and non-Indians, we will always have troubles between us, and if my columns can provoke thought, create an atmosphere of objectivity, or make a small dent in the walls of misunderstanding and prejudice that have divided us for too many years, I will feel that I have succeeded.

Media Manipulated in Some Instances

(First of two articles)

Last week I received a most interesting letter from Window Rock, Arizona. The writer closed his letter by asking, "Have you ever done a column on the freedom of the press on Indian reservations?"

Let me answer that question by starting with an area of South Dakota and expanding upon this concept from this point. The Pine Ridge Reservation is the second largest reservation in the United States, next to the Navajo Nation. There is no newspaper on this large reservation. The only news vehicle serving the tribe is a small, college paper which publishes periodically, and which keeps its nose out of tribal politics.

There is a tremendous interest in the news, as it occurs on the reservation; and so it is not because of a lack of interest that there is no newspaper. Given the political climate on the Pine Ridge Reservation, I do not believe that a tribally controlled newspaper could survive. There are far too many diverse points of view, and as a result, no tribal administration since Dick Wilson's, in the early 70s, had the courage to print a tribal newspaper.

Choosing Sides

A strange thing happened during the occupation of Wounded Knee in 1973. This occupation occurred during the Dick Wilson administration. The members of the news media flooded onto the reservation and set up camp. Most of the journalists were from back East, and saw a cause with which they could align, and by choosing sides, they threw their objectivity out the window.

Before long, words such as "dictator" or "goon squad" were being flashed across the wire services to describe Chairman Wilson and his staff. The members of the American Indian Movement occupying Wounded Knee had found their fall guy, and by cleverly manipulating the news media, attempted to destroy his administration.

This was an entirely new experience for the outside press, and it had absolutely no knowledge of the structure of tribal government, the control exerted over it by the Department of the Interior, nor did it make an effort to learn about these things.

News people converged upon the Pine Ridge Reservation to pursue a cause, to sensationalize a news event, with little regard for the cause, the cure or the outcome. Granted, Chairman Wilson could be very abrasive at times, especially when confronted by the hostile press, but he was caught up in the middle of an historical event. A town on the reservation was being illegally held, and as the chief law enforcement officer of the reservation, he had no choice except to try to restore law and order.

Atmosphere of Hysteria

Given the atmosphere of hysteria at the time, reinforced by an uninformed press, the most sainted of men would have been made to look like an uncouth villain. Dick Wilson was no exception!

Do not misunderstand what I have tried to say here. I was not part of Dick Wilson's administration, nor do I believe that all of the criticisms directed at him were wrong; but the same thing could have happened to any tribal chairman, and Wilson just happened to be in the wrong place at the wrong time.

To this day, if you travel around the reservation, you will find more friends supportive of Wilson, than you will find enemies. The news media abandoned the Pine Ridge Reservation in droves after the excitement died down and, of course, they all forgot to mention the fact that Dick Wilson ran for the office of president of the Oglala Sioux Tribe against the man who led the occupation of Wounded Knee, Russell Means, and soundly defeated Means. This happened after the occupation of Wounded Knee.

Funds Cut Off

Up in Browning, Montana on the Blackfeet Reservation, there used to be a newspaper called *The South Piegan Drum*. An incident occurred in which the tribal chairman became involved in a ruckus with his next door neighbor. A violent confrontation ensued, and the combatants ended up before the tribal council. *The Drum* reported this story, sparing no details, nor playing any favorites.

At the next session of the tribal council, the funding needed to support this tribal newspaper was cut off. The staff of the newspaper circulated a petition among the members of the tribe and secured over 400 signatures asking that the paper be refunded.

In this case, freedom of the press did not prevail. *The South Piegan Drum* has ceased publication because the tribal council refuses to fund it again. I consider this to be very wrong, but please let me reiterate, the "hatchet job" the outside press did to the administration of the Oglala Sioux Tribe during the occupation of Wounded Knee was also very wrong.

Freedom of Press Reservation Issue

(Second of two parts)

A writer from Window Rock, Arizona asked about freedom of the press on Indian reservations. In my last column I touched on the subject of newspapers on two reservations, the Pine Ridge Reservation in South Dakota and the Blackfeet Reservation in Montana.

Most news editors in off-reservation communities will tell you that they exercise complete control over what news is printed and what is not. They will tell you that the management of the newspaper never interferes with news content, and in most cases, this is probably true; but there are exceptions to every rule. The refusal of a large California newspaper to print stories about the corruption in its city government is a case in point.

Many Indian tribes in this country have tribally funded newspapers. For the most part, these newspapers are allowed to print the news as it happens, and editorial control is not exercised by the tribal government. My last column pointed out one exception on the Blackfeet Reservation in Montana. The editorial staff printed a news story unfavorable to the tribal chairman, and, as a result, the funding to support the newspaper was cut off, and the newspaper was forced to go out of business.

Tribal Funding

Tribally funded newspapers, as a whole, are only as strong as their staff or their editors. They usually try to stay out of reservation politics and out of any controversial events involving tribal politicians. Because so much bad news has been printed in the bordertown newspapers about their people and reservations in years past, many tribal newspapers attempt to compensate for this by swinging the pendulum in the opposite direction. They try to print only the good news and ignore the bad news.

Several weeks ago I wrote a column about the *Jicarilla Chieftain* of Dulce, New Mexico and I suggested that this newspaper is one of the best reservation newspapers. My opinion has not changed. This small newspaper tries to print the news as news, and its editorials are objective and succinct. This is a tribute to an open-minded editor, Mary Polanco, who has refined the art of incorporating a little common sense into the tribal publication.

When a newspaper owes its existence to tribal monies, and owes a certain allegiance to the incumbent administration, there are times when it is forced to skate on very thin ice. If the tribal administration is a competent one, with an eye toward the future, and confidence in its ability to govern fairly, the job of the news editor is made much easier. But, if the tribal administration is incumbent and hence, open to criticism, things can get very sticky for the news editors and their staffs.

Some Self-Supporting

Large tribal newspapers, such as the *Navajo Times*, have the capability of selling advertising to such an extent that they can, and often do, become self-supporting. It is common knowledge that the *Navajo Times* is not without its critics. But, like many enterprises on the Navajo Reservation, or on any large Indian reservation, these endeavors often suffer from growing pains. As these enterprises expand, they will, of course, make many mistakes. The object is to ride out these mistakes, learn from them, and try not to repeat them.

I alluded to the fact that the success or failure of tribal newspapers depends, to a large extent, upon the strengths of the editor and the staff of the newspaper. Let me add that much of this success is directly related to the objective support of a strong tribal chairman and administration. This holds true for many tribally owned enterprises.

Incumbents Promoted

It is inevitable that tribal newspapers often promote the interests of the incumbent administrations. These are the people who are making the news at the time, and this is the news that will end up being reported. This is a fact of life off the reservation as well.

As long as the tribal newpapers allow the voices of the dissenters to be heard, unpopular or not, they will be doing their job. The minute they refuse to print an item submitted to them because it is critical of the tribal administration, then they are practicing censorship. This is where the common sense of a Mary Polanco is so very important. Criticisms which are blatantly profane or libelous must be carefully considered before a decision on whether to print them or not is made.

Tim Giago taking pictures for **The Lakota Times**

Correspondent Starts Paper

One of the main reasons I began to write a weekly column is because I believe the Indian people do not have and have not had a voice in the media to reach the general public.

For too many years, everything written about Indian people was from the white point of view and I felt that we, as Indians, needed to get our point of view across. I'm not talking about a radical point of view that is hardly indicative of the majority of Indians, but a point of view that is too often and too easily overlooked because it is a point of view which does not make sensational headlines.

It is that silent majority of Indians who are the backbone of the reservations and urban centers of this country. The jobs they are doing do not make good news copy because they are humdrum, every day, essential jobs, and yet, it is these quiet people who are carrying the load, creating the jobs, and trying to make things a little bit easier for the generations of Indians to follow.

Real Communities

Reservations are communities in every sense of the word. They are tribal governments with federally recognized constitutions and bylaws, an organized court system, tribally controlled law enforcement, schools and hospitals. Reservations are much like sovereign nations within a nation.

Because most reservations are far from the metropolitan areas, and they are often comprised of large land masses covering many thousands of square miles; this remoteness and size make them almost inaccessible to the media. Stories of every day people doing every day things are not sufficient, in many instances, to warrant a costly trip to the reservation.

Just like other communities, reservations have social happenings, sporting events, school plays, community functions, meetings, governmental activities and so on. Because these activities are of interest to residents of the reservation only, in most cases, there is little effort made to cover them by the off-reservation news media.

The complexities of the tribal government, the unfamiliarity of the language and the geography, and the general distrust of the outside media by reservation residents make the job of collecting news on the reservation ten times as difficult for those who are not too keen on covering it in the first place.

Reservation Papers

While living in the Southwest, I was very impressed with the weekly newspaper of the Navajo Nation. The twice-per-month publication of the Jicarilla Apache Tribe also provides an important service to that small reservation just as the Navajo newspaper does for that gigantic reservation, the largest in the land.

These two newspapers provide news of importance to the people of their respective reservations. The newspapers are published with this idea in mind and as a result, the quality of the newspaper does not suffer because the news content is peculiar to a specific segment of the population.

It is because most Indian reservations are like separate nations, complete with different languages, customs, religions and laws, that any newspaper designed to serve this unique population be situated locally, on the reservation it is designed to cover.

New Venture

With all of these problems in mind, a former classmate of mine and I decided to start a newspaper to serve the second largest reservation in the United States. Our first edition of *The Lakota Times* hit the streets of the Pine Ridge Reservation on the 9th day of July (1980).

Our newspaper is in no way connected to the tribal government. It is a privately-owned, fully commercial, Indian-oriented newspaper free to praise or criticize the tribal administration as it sees fit. In this respect, *The Lakota Times* is unique in Indian Country. Even the *Navajo Times* is under the control of the tribal administration. This means the editor must adhere to many of the guidelines set down by the elected officials of that tribe.

For subscriptions or more information about the newspaper, write to: *The Lakota Times*, P. O. Box 318, Pine Ridge, SD 57770.

Communications Gap Discussed

Writing a weekly column for several newspapers and serving as editor of a weekly reservation newspaper sometimes requires that I wear two hats.

Most of the columns I write are read by many non-Indians residing in communities far from the Indian reservations, but the editorials I write for our newspaper, *The Lakota Times*, are read, primarily, by residents of the Pine Ridge Reservation.

A letter I received at the newspaper office last week made me pause to reflect on the diversity of writing for the reservation community as opposed to writing for a largely non-Indian readership. Is the communications gap between the two real or imagined?

The letter reads, "I moved to the reservation in September of 1981. I have been a faithful reader of your newspaper ever since. I was upset to notice in your recent editorial that you feel only Indian people might be concerned about certain problems and should write to the Secretary of the Interior.

"Might it not also do good to know that there are non-Indian people living and working on the reservation who also agree and are concerned? I know I speak for more than myself (non-Indians) in wanting to see changes made and problems solved. So, please, don't leave us out when seeking solutions."

White Perspective

For more years than many of us would care to remember, the Indian had no voice at all in the press. Articles appearing in newspapers were written from the white perspective and fashioned to emphasize the differences between the two races. This was due, for the most part, to the geographical isolation of the Indian tribes, and a decided lack of knowledge about Indians by non-Indian journalists.

Many Western states have very large Indian populations, and yet, if you go back through the archives of many newspapers bordering reservations, you will find very few articles about the Indian people in general, and almost none of Indian people as individuals. I'm talking about newspapers published twenty-five or thirty years ago.

Invisible Spectators

I always get a strange feeling when I read newspapers located in the border towns of the reservations that have a section called "Thirty Years Ago," etc., and I am forced to come face to face with the fact that Indians did not exist, for all intents and purposes, in those days. We were truly the invisible spectators at the media table.

Yes, maybe there are many non-Indians residing on our reservations who are concerned about our problem, and have a genuine interest to help us solve them.

But I must ask them this question: Why didn't you ever write letters to the non-Indian press asking them why they never made an effort to include the Indian people in their newspapers? Perhaps, the situation is a little different to find yourselves on the outside looking in, just as we have been for many, many years.

Then, perhaps, because we have been excluded from providing input into the local newspapers, I am over-compensating by inadvertently excluding non-Indians. If this be the case, the exclusion is not intentional.

However, I am of the opinion that we, and we alone, as Indians can solve our problems. For too many years, we relied upon the integrity and benevolence of non-Indians to assist us in this department, and we have paid dearly for extending this trust. The losses we have suffered at the hands of the white man have severely restricted our openness and trust.

Points of View

Our reservation newspaper and my weekly column give us the opportunity to express our personal points of view from an Indian perspective, and clearly that perspective is an advocacy for Indians. This isn't something that happened overnight. How many years has it been since the Indian reservations were considered too remote to provide adequate news coverage?

We have never asked special treatment from the news media. Time and time again I have advised the off-reservation newspapers that we are a large population that reads what is written by the press and we do enjoy reading about the good things being accomplished by our people. We are sick and tired of mostly bad things being printed about us.

The Indian population is not going to dry up and blow away. We are not the invisible people of twenty years ago. We are here to stay and we are growing. This is a fact of life that must be faced squarely by the non-Indian press.

In helping bring about these media changes, I hope that I never make the mistake of excluding non-Indians simply because they are non-Indians. If I allow this to happen, I will be doing the very same thing to them that has been done to us by the non-Indian press for hundreds of years.

Rhetoric of "Indian Experts" Should be Put on Back Burner

News reporter David Freed of the *Rocky Mountain News*, Denver Colorado, made his journalistic sojourn in Indian Country, staying a few days (just long enough to become an "Indian expert"), and then returning to his metropolitan home base to transcribe his unerring impressions of the Black Hills Claim Settlement, the Great Sioux Nation, and the redneck rabble-rousers into a feature story for the "city folk."

Statistics, as compiled in the mind of Mr. Freed, are intended to shock people. For instance, he writes, "Seventy percent of the population of Pine Ridge are unemployed." He adds, "Only half of the Oglala homes have electricity. Estimates of alcoholism run as high as 60 percent." And, of course, Freed uses the standard description of Pine Ridge made popular by social workers and proposal writers, "the desolate, windswept reservation."

If there is a genuine statistician who provided these grossly distorted figures and percentages to our visitor from Denver, I would certainly like to visit with him or her and verify the sources and the validity of these preposterous assumptions.

The article I am referring to appeared in the Sunday, September 28, 1890 edition of the *Rocky Mountain News*. The photograph accompanying the article was one of Mount Rushmore and the caption reads: "Mount Rushmore's great white fathers oversee the Black Hills of the Sioux." After reading this caption, I was sorely tempted to either roll up my trouser legs or put on some rubber boots, because I knew that the stuff was going to start getting real deep.

Robert Fast Horse, right, addressing meeting at Pine Ridge; left, Russell Means and Newton Cummings

Nellie Red Owl, grandmother, from Wakpamni Lake at Tenth Anniversary of Wounded Knee, 1983

14 Communications

Freed then quoted from a story written by Charley Najacht of Hot Springs, South Dakota for the *Star* which said, "If the Indians still think they are a sovereign nation, then perhaps it is time to go to war again and beat them again." Taken out of context, this sounds like a declaration of war by Najacht. In all fairness to Charley, he writes a column called "For What It's Worth," and he is the editor of the *Hot Springs Star*. Charley's column is intended to be a tongue-in-cheek, written-in-jest feature, and in most cases, this is the way it turns out. The one mistake Charley made in this particular column is that he should have repeated several times within the body of the article that "this is just a joke." Most residents of the Pine Ridge Reservation find very little humor in the loss of the Black Hills or in the pittance that is being offered as compensation. There are some thing in this world that one does not make jokes about.

Freed continued his pilgrimage to South Dakota with a trip to Pierre and a visit with Attorney General Mark Meierhenry. This is usually an important part of the standard tour package itinerary for visiting journalists. Here are a few excerpts from that enlightening interview and a few impressions of the Pine Ridge Reservation as provided by the attorney general: "Meierhenry believes Sioux leaders should forget about owning the Black Hills and encourage their young to leave the reservation and get into mainstream America. 'There is no hope for the Oglala who insist on living at Pine Ridge,' he said. Meierhenry continued, 'It's a terrible, nothing place. It's so damned bleak there. The kids are programmed for poverty.'"

Of course, no report on the Black Hills would be complete without a quotation from one of the American Indian Movement leaders. Freed fulfilled this obligation by speaking with Ted Means who said, "Since the Wounded Knee takeover, AIM has adopted a less militant attitude, devoting its efforts to educating tribal members on the tribe's battle in court. Should all legal avenues fail, AIM wouldn't rule out the possibilities of violence in the fight for the Black Hills."

Now, you take that whole concoction of an article, you mix in a few homilies from the outraged, white businessman, and you've got a real humdinger of a story. Where better to start than in the community of Keystone, nestled at the foot of the Shrine of Democracy?

The *Rocky Mountain News* article goes on to say, "The road is dotted with billboard signs that advertise such attractions as the Life of Christ Wax Museum, Reptile Gardens and the Sitting Bull Crystal Cave." It continues, "Businessmen in the tourist town of Keystone say they aren't afraid of the Oglalas' demands."

Gene Jelliffe, who for ten years has run a souvenir shop called "The Indians" is quoted as saying, "Even if the court found in the Indians' favor, the government would never have the power and the money to uproot all the people who live here. They'd have to buy out my inventory, which is in excess of $500,000, to move me."

In my opinion, I think that all of the rhetoric and nonsense should be put on a back burner, and that the people of the State of South Dakota, the federal government, and the members of the news media should give the Indian people the right to have their day in court. That's all we ever asked for, and that is all we expect! Isn't that the American way?

Way Titles Used Not Always Fair

How many times have you picked up a newspaper and read the heading of an article which began "Indian leader says . . ." or "Indian expert believes . . ."? Let's take a long, hard look at these two captions from another point of view— the Indian's.

Several years ago I was speaking with a young Oglala man named Gerald Clifford. Gerald was the president of a consulting firm based in Boulder, Colorado and held the unique distinction of graduating from the South Dakota School of Mines & Technology in Rapid City with a degree in engineering at the tender age of 19. This was accomplished about twenty years ago and it is a record that stands to this day.

Gerald had placed an advertisement in a newspaper seeking business for his consulting firm and the ad writer had taken it upon himself to include in the ad, "Indian experts," in referring to Mr. Clifford's firm. Gerald was quite perturbed and asked that it be withdrawn immediately.

He explained to the ad writer that this sort of advertising would cost him more business in Indian Country that it would gain him. He said, "Many years ago government agents and missionaries who worked among Indian people were given the title of "Indian expert."

Gerald continued, "Can you imagine how ridiculous it would appear if Indian people who worked among the white people for any length of time gave themselves the title of "white man expert"?

The point is that most non-Indians can only judge a culture different from their own by making comparisons.

Those people who become proficient at drawing these comparisons so that these alien concepts could be categorized by virtue of similarities, either with their own culture or an already identified and documented culture, became "Indian experts."

The sad part about this approach was that the cultural contribution was diminished because the emphasis was always placed on the "difference" rather than on its merits as a useful addition to the invading culture.

Indian Leaders

A few weeks ago I was reading a news article written by an Associated Press writer. The story concerned Dennis Banks, a member of the American Indian movement, who then resided in California enjoying the hospitality of Governor Jerry Brown who refused to let the State of South Dakota extradite him to face a prison sentence in that state for the riots at the Custer County Courthouse incident. The heading of the article began, "Indian leader says . . ." And therein lies the error.

By using the "Indian expert" method of comparison, one could say that an article about the Grand Dragon of the Ku Klux Klan should be headed, "White leaders says . . ."

It is unfair to the Indian people to take one person whose opinion may be as diverse from the majority as yours might be from that of the Grand Dragon of the Ku Klux Klan and give him the title of "Indian leader."

I am not comparing Dennis Banks to the Grand Dragon by any means; but the reasoning behind the media's habit of giving titles of leadership to Indians whose opinions do not reflect those of the many is arbitrary, selective and patently unfair.

When one considers that there are approximately 300 different Indian tribes in this country, each with distinct customs and languages, it becomes apparent why the use of headings such as "Indian expert" or "Indian leader" is a ridiculous assumption by the news media and a practice that most Indian people would like to see brought to a halt.

Criticism Hits Home for Tribal Officials

Several weeks ago, I wrote a column which questioned the overall effectiveness of tribal government, and I suggested that much of the money intended for the poor grassroots people of the reservation had a tendency to disappear before it ever was filtered down to the really needy Indian people.

This is a common problem on many reservations, and the article written by me was of a general nature, and did not name any specific reservation but, instead, concentrated upon the many. Well, it apparently struck pretty close to home with some officials of the Navajo Nation.

Not too long after that article appeared, I received a phone call from Window Rock, Arizona and was told that some of the tribal officials took exception to such allegations, and a letter to the editor of the Farmington *Daily Times* would soon be sent severely reprimanding me for such audacity. To the best of my knowledge, the letter was never sent. As the old saying goes, "Where there's smoke, their's fire."

Apparent Dissatisfaction

There is, apparently, some dissatisfaction with the way things are being run by the tribal government of the Navajo Nation. Witness the recent meetings held by several chapters seeking to unite enough of the people to secede from the central, Arizona-based government, and form a separate government composed of the New Mexico chapters.

Many tribal governments have become miniature replicas of the federal government. They have taken to treating their people like numbers, compiled for the benefit of the funding branches of the various agencies of the federal government. The people have become statistics on a piece of paper, statistics needed to justify programs and increase appropriations. Of course, this is all a big part of the bureaucratic game, and if the tribal governments are to survive, they must learn to play it with the best of them.

Every funding proposal is replete with "statistics " and these proposals have become a way of life. Are the Indian tribes sovereign nations, or are they also statistics on someone else's chart? British statesman Benjamin Disraeli once noted that there were three kinds of lies: "Lies, damned lies and statistics." Tribal officials would do well to file these words away for future reference.

Public Broadcasting

There is an indication that many of the radio stations totally dependent upon federal monies and contributions for their survival may soon be in big trouble. Hard times nationally, will be one of the major reasons federal dollars will be cut for these projects. Already there is talk of Pacifica Radio, a federally subsidized network with a liberal point of view, as being a target for the new right.

According to Howard Phillips, head of the Conservative Caucus, "The federal government must stop subsidizing policy advocacy by liberals." This sort of talk contributes to the fears of such organizations as the Corporation for Public Broadcasting and National Public Radio because they are so dependent upon federal dollars.

There has been a feeling among conservative politicians for many years that the federal government should not be in the business of competing against commercial broadcasting enterprises. The handwriting was on the wall over two years ago, and several public broadcasting facilities have begun to cut back on programming and expenditures to survive the trend.

Unfortunately, 99 percent of the radio stations now operating, or in the planning stages, for Indian reservations are non-commercial, and will be hard pressed to secure funds each year in order to stay on the air. The pinch is real, and some of the radio stations already on the air have had to make drastic cutbacks and sacrifices in quality programming in order to survive.

Correspondent Gets Severe Criticism

There is an old saying that was intended to be applied to some organizations. But, in this case, I will apply that saying to Indian tribes, because as governments seeking self-determination and independence, they must be considered as governmental organizations.

The saying goes like this:

"Somebody has said that the membership of every organization is made up of four kinds of bones.

"There are the wishbones, who spend all their time wishing someone else would do the work.

"There are the jawbones, who do all the talking but very little else.

"There are the knucklebones, who knock everything everbody else tries to do.

"And, finally, there are the backbones who get under the load and do the work!"

One More Type

To these four types of bones I would add one other: There are the neckbones, who are unafraid to stick out their necks, take the risks, take an unpopular stand because it is right, knowing full well that there are those people only too willing to chop off that neck.

I wrote an article for a South Dakota newspaper recently in which I criticized the American Indian Movement for its role in the Fairchild Plant takeover. (See article titled, "Loss of Fairchild Plant Hurts Navajo People," page 296). It was my contention that one does not "burn down his barn in the middle of the winter, until he has found a new shelter to house his livestock." In other words, I felt that more harm was done to the people of Shiprock, New Mexico by this takeover than good, because no sensible, alternate plan had been worked out in the eventuality the plant was shut down.

Harsh Criticism

Russell Means, of the Dakota American Indian Movement, responded to this article by blasting at me, personally. He was extremely harsh in this criticism, and I thought about it for several days before I responded. I summed up my response by saying, "There is a narrow path between self-righteous indignation and despotism, and it is a path that any self-proclaimed Indian idealist should survey with extreme care, lest he stray from it and begin barking at shadows."

In 1975, AIM was about as popular in South Dakota as the bubonic plague. Two FBI agents had been killed in the village of Oglala on the Pine Ridge Reservation, and several members of AIM were being sought by the authorities in connection with this incident. I was producing and hosting a weekly television show for the ABC affiliate in Rapid City, South Dakota, and it was my very strong belief that every Indian man or woman with a story to tell should be given the opportunity to appear on that show, whether I, or the majority of the people agreed or disagreed with their opinions. I felt, and still do, that if I would deny them the right to express their opinion on a public forum, simply because it was an unpopular view, I would be doing the same thing to them as the media there had done to us for years.

Right to Express

The time came when AIM requested the time on my show to express views to the public. I knew that if I decided to put them on the air, I would be roundly criticized, and stood a good chance of having my show removed from the air. Given the intense and volatile climate of that time, I was also well aware that physical harm could come to me or my family.

However, it was my feeling then, and it is my feeling now, that freedom of the press, and freedom of expression should be available to all factions within the Indian community. I felt that I was on the air to present the news as it occurs, not to shape it to coincide with my own personal philosophies. AIM went on the air!

There is no place in the traditional Indian way of life for those who would use threats and intimidation against people who do not agree with their views; and whenever I see wrongs being committed against the Indian people whether by an organization or a tribal government, I will continue to speak out against these wrongs, but once again, as the old saying goes, "I may not agree with what you say, but I will defend to the death your right to say it."

Spokane Story Draws Criticism

The article appeared in the *Los Angeles Times, Newsweek Magazine* and many other publications.

It was datelined Spokane, Washington, and was written by Lena F. Reed for the Independent News Alliance. I could readily see why it was not reprinted in Indian Country, particularly in the newspapers serving the Great Sioux Nation.

The story began, "An eight-year-old boy named Little Sun Bordeaux is the new hereditary chief of the Teton Sioux. He is the grandson of the late Dallas Chief Eagle Bordeaux and the direct descendant of Chief Crazy Horse, and his tribe considers him the reincarnation of that famous warrior. And he is Jewish."

It is very difficult to write a column critical of this particular news story because there are those who will assume I am speaking badly about a man who is no longer with us. But the point is, if Dallas Chief Eagle were alive today, would he permit his name to be used in such a way as to bring discredit to the Lakota people? I think not.

Double Minority

Keep in mind the young man of the article named Little Sun had to have been born around 1973. Mentioning his mother, Armalona, the story says, "Her double minority family have good memories of their tepee life in the Dakotas." Little Sun's mother is married to an Army sergeant named Russell Richardson, a Tuscarora-Cherokee from North Carolina and they live in Spokane, Washington. His unit is being transferred to Butzbach, Germany, and Armalona and Little Sun will be moving there also.

Mentioning this move, the article continues, "The Sioux tribe is saddened that Little Sun will be out of the country for three years, but the elders agree that it is important for him to be with his mother and continue his education. Little Sun, although chief now, will assume his full tribal powers when he is 19."

The article mentions a vision in which a child "with the blue eyes and light brown hair of Chief Crazy Horse" would be born and was destined to be the next tribal chief. Someone apparently believed in the description given of Crazy Horse by the novelist, Mari Sandoz, in the book, *Crazy Horse.*

Perhaps author Sandoz felt that only a man with the blood of the white man flowing through his veins could perform some of the prodigious feats attributed to Crazy Horse. Since there is no portrait available of Crazy Horse to dispute Sandoz, her description has been accepted as fact by many historians.

Description Disputed

Speaking with some of the direct descendants of Crazy Horse, including Dave Long of the Oglala Sioux Tribe, the "blue eyes and light brown hair" description supplied by Sandoz is strongly disputed. According to Long, neither Crazy Horse or his family ever set eyes upon a white man until he was already a young man. I would believe the argument of Long before Sandoz because the oral history of a tribe or clan has proven to be unerringly accurate time after time by historians.

Shirley Bordeaux, the wife of the late Dallas Chief Eagle Bordeaux, is angered by the whole story. She lives at Mission, South Dakota, on the Rosebud Reservation and she said, "Almost everything in that article is a pack of lies. About the only thing in it which was true is that Little Sun (his real name) is my grandson. He lived with me when he was little because his mother, Armalona, did not want him at that time. As a matter of fact, I had him baptized a Catholic."

The article said Little Sun "spoke Sioux before he spoke English" and the vision by Chief Eagle Bordeaux predicted he is "the reincarnation of Crazy Horse." Mrs. Bordeaux refutes this adamantly, saying, "In the first place, Little Sun did not speak Lakota. If my husband ever had a vision, he would never reveal it in this way because it is not the Lakota way to do that sort of thing publicly, and it's just not true."

As a result of this nationally circulated article, so full of errors and inaccuracies, the Bordeaux family has had to defend itself in many ways. Even the kidding it must endure at Mission has become unbearable.

Understandable Anger

Mrs. Bordeaux, who is seriously considering a lawsuit against the Independent News Alliance and the publications which carried the story, is understandably angry. She said, "Why is it that the white press thinks that they can write anything they want about Indians, without checking the facts, they can portray us as a primitive people, still living in teepees and insult our intelligence by making us the butt of the white man's jokes?"

As a journalist, it strikes me as somewhat irresponsible of the media to reprint a story such as this without verifying its authenticity. I had very little trouble locating Dallas Chief Eagle Bordeaux' wife, the grandmother of Little Sun, and it is an insult to every journalist that large publications such as the *Los Angeles Times* and *Newsweek* could not have done so as easily.

I would hope we all learn something from the predicament the *Washington Post* found itself in when it was awarded a Pulitzer Prize for a feature story which proved to be a hoax perpetrated by one of its reporters, Janet Cooke.

Media has to be Watchdogged

Watchdogging the non-Indian news media is a full time job. At times I feel as if I am on a treadmill going nowhere. No sooner is there a degree of sensitivity developed with news writers and broadcasters than they move on to other pastures, and a whole new bunch moves in to replace them, and the process begins all over again.

There is so much ignorance and misinformation to contend with as regards Indian people and so much myth has been accepted as fact by the media in general that the facts are seldom checked when news stories on Indians are being prepared.

Most news reporters are products of their education and environment. Their viewpoints of Indian history were shaped by erroneous history books built around the "Pocahontas-Sale-of-Manhattan" concept of fictionalized, romanticized versions of Indian history.

A few years back, *Time* magazine did a story on the use of feathers by Indian tribes. A cartoon illustrating the article depicted an Indian with a live chicken tied to the top of his head. In this case, the reporter and the illustrator failed to understand the religious significance of feathers, particularly eagle feathers, to many Indian tribes.

Would this particular reporter write an article ridiculing the yarmulke of the Jewish faith or artifacts sacred to the Black Muslims? Eagle feathers are as sacred to many Indian tribes as the artifacts of the Catholics, Protestants or any other religious organization. Is it because the Indian population is so small in numbers, with little financial or political clout, that news reporters feel they can hold our religious artifacts up to public ridicule with assured impunity?

After several letters of protest to *Time* outlining my outrage at such total disregard of religious artifacts associated with many Indian religions brought no satisfaction, I did the only thing I could do: I canceled my subscription.

Next came the "Reincarnation of Crazy Horse" story that appeared in *Newsweek* last year. According to the article, a young Indian boy, originally from the Rosebud Reservation, and a member of the Jewish faith, was thought to be the reincarnation of Chief Crazy Horse and the heir apparent to the chieftainship of all the tribes of the Great Sioux Nation.

A simple telephone call to the family members of this young man, who still reside on the Rosebud Reservation, would have pointed out the absolute fabrication behind this ridiculous little article. No such telephone call was made, and the story ran nationally as factual.

Once more, I protested an article in a national magazine with letters. Some of you may recall, I also wrote an article of protest in my weekly "Notes from Indian Country" column. In due time, I did get a half-hearted attempt at apologizing by an obscure editor of *Newsweek*; but no public apology or revocation of this fictitional story, printed as fact, ever appeared in that magazine.

A news service based in Washington, D.C., relies heavily upon self-serving Indian organizations located in that city for verification of facts included in news releases about Indian tribes. I wrote an article about one such news release I considered to be filled with errors, and sent the article, along with a letter of protest, to the editor of the news service. For my troubles, I received a curt reply from the editor dissecting the journalistic structure of my article and taking me to task for the grammatical mechanics of my composition. He never did address the issue brought up in my article or letter.

Struggling to correct erroneous articles by national magazines or news networks is a frustrating but necessary task. Someone has to let them know that the stories they are doing about Indian people are being read and monitored. There should be no such problems with newspapers, wire services, or television newscasts originating in geographical locations with large Indian populations. Right?

As I said at the beginning of this article, each and every time a batch of new reporters is trained in the area of sensitivity to Indian issues, they move on, and in comes another batch with little or no interest in learning about Indians. The educational process begins anew, and the frustrations grow.

In states with large Indian populations such as South Dakota, Arizona and New Mexico, why isn't there a media organization set up to meet with members of the Indian media, to discuss the problems of sensitivity to Indian issues?

It seems to me that just one meeting per year would do wonders to educate the non-Indian reporters and news directors or editors to many extremely sensitive things to look out for in stories involving Indian people or issues. The news media located in cities with large black populations set up such forums which yielded immediate and positive results. One of the first steps to take is to admit to yourselves that you don't know it all when it comes to Indians, and take it from there.

Public Relations Work Important

There are some jobs that are difficult to gauge in terms of effectiveness. The question can always be asked: Has this position contributed to productivity or progress? They are positions that are, in effect, intangible.

Probably the most under-rated job in any company is that of the public relations officer. This job is often described as "human relations" or 'customer relations' but it is a job that requires conveying a good impression of the company to the general population.

When Lee Cannon first went to work for the Navajo Nation as public relations officer, he drew a lot of criticism from many people. First of all, they said, his salary was too high; secondly, he was not a member of the Navajo Tribe; and thirdly, he was not even an Indian.

Criticism

A letter to the *Navajo Times* (June 12, 1980) said, "This man, Cannon, is supposed to paint a bright and cheerful picture of the Navajos to the rest of the outside world. I imagine he is also supposed to portray a few egotistical officials as tribal heroes . . . these officials using tribal money for a very expensive portrait of themselves."

The writer continued, "The *Navajo Times* had an article recently coming down to the local press, saying that most of the stories published have attempted to place the Navajos in a bad light. I disagree. Most of the stories have been on the government, a government not entirely elected by the people or a government which has lost sight of what it means to be a government for the people."

Mary E. Gorman of the Navajo Nation, Window Rock, Arizona, answered the charges brought up in the letter by expounding upon the experience and dedication Cannon had brought to the Navajo Nation, and of the unselfish support he had given to the Navajo Code Talkers and the tribe for over 13 years without pay. She added, "Cannon is considered one of the best informed men in the country on the work of the Navajo Code Talkers. He is frequently invited to speak on that subject. Whenever he is paid a fee, he has the check made payable to the Navajo Code Talkers Association."

Expertise Needed

Mrs. Gorman summed up her defense of Cannon by saying, "But more importantly, he understands the hopes and aspirations of our people. He was asked to share his knowhow and enthusiasm with our young professionals. His is an expertise that is sorely needed by every American Indian tribe."

Based on personal experience, I know that the job of public relations is too lightly regarded by most Indian tribes.

I served the Oglala Sioux Tribe of South Dakota in that capacity for over two years. I wish I could remember how many times I heard, "It is so nice to be able to call an agency on the reservation and to get the information we are seeking, or to be assisted in finding the right person, if you do not have an answer by the various news media serving the reservation."

Important Service

Public relations is more than creating good images for tribal officials. It is scheduling press conferences, it is issuing press releases, it is meeting with visiting dignitaries and escorting them about the reservation, it is making arrangements with newspapers, radio stations and television stations to cover events occurring on the reservation.

But the most important service provided by public relations of any Indian tribe is supplying the various news media with information about the reservation that is accurate, concise and reliable, and that does not constitute a disservice to the Indian people.

Yes, the work of the public relations officer is intangible; but it is a job that should be filled on every Indian reservation in the United States.

'Public Relations' Benefit to Tribes

Every major corporation, most governments and many federal agencies have officers attached called public relations officers. In a recent column I dealt briefly with public relations on the tribal level.

Lee Cannon is the public relations officer for the Navajo Nation. Because of the adverse reaction by many of the tribal members to his appointment to this position, and the negative reaction to the title, "public relations," the title of his position was changed to "executive assistant."

A few years back, I was appointed to serve as public relations director for the Oglala Sioux Tribe of South Dakota. In my case, perhaps, I did not face as much of a controversy as Cannon because I was a member of the tribe, and was born and raised on that reservation. The difficult part of that job was getting the point across to the tribal council members, program directors, and district representatives the importance of establishing a good, working relationship with the various news media serving the reservation from the border towns.

Common Complaint

I had heard so many complaints from the reservation community and the urban population about the bad press given to Indian people. One of the most common was, "There are so many good things happening in our community, but all the press is interested in are the negative things."

There was some truth in that statement; but like everything else involving the media, the main reason for the negativism was brought about by the lack of communication between the news directors and the tribal governments.

"Press Secretary"

The one major drawback to the job, I discovered, is that one ends up being the "press secretary" for the tribal president. Too often, I found myself writing speeches, coaching the president for radio or television appearances, which had been arranged by me, and writing press releases which had a tendency to keep his name before the public.

Because you are on the payroll of the tribal government, it is impossible not to become involved in tribal politics. As most reservation people know all too well, tribal politics can be very vicious.

But, the job of public relations is a subjective position no matter where it is located, or whether it is representative of a major corporation or governmental agency. Public relations means establishing a good working relationship with the general public. It's as simple as that!

Some Drawbacks

Admittedly, there were some drawbacks, as I have pointed out; but the good things that resulted far outweighed the bad. For instance, all of a sudden the people of the reservation began seeing stories in the paper, on television or heard them on the radio about positive things that were happening in Indian Country. I mean the entire national Indian community, not just the local community.

One thing that non-Indian people find hard to understand, particularly non-Indian news editors, is that Indian people are starving for news about all Indians, not just their own tribe. They take great pride in the achievements of other Indians; but above all, they recognize the fact that what happens on other reservations, can, and often does, affect their own lives.

I don't envy the task Lee Cannon has undertaken. It is a job that fits the adage of "damned if you do, and damned if you don't" to a T.

Every tribal member should keep in mind that the lack of information has caused far more problems in the past than an abundance of information. Keeping the news media informed about the positive things in the Indian community is an important function.

Whites Should Read about Indian Affairs

Not long ago, the managing editor of a daily newspaper said to me, "You'd be surprised at how many local, non-Indians complain to me about your column, or that we are giving too much space in our newspaper to Indian affairs. Maybe they just don't want to hear some of the things you are saying, or maybe they just don't want to learn about Indian people, even though they have lived right next to them all of their lives."

He went on, "I always tell these complainers they are just going to have to face the fact that Indian people make up a very large portion of this community, and they can't go on pretending that they don't."

For many generations Indian people have been forced to learn all about the white man. We have had to learn his language, his history, as seen through his eyes and recorded from his point of view, and we have had to learn to adjust to his way of life. And yet, with all of this education about the white society foisted upon the Indians, I have never heard an Indian claim to be a "white man expert."

Just the opposite has been true of the white man. He had no interest whatever in learning about the ways of the Indian. The Indian culture did not fit into his scheme of things to come, so it was shunted aside as inconsequential, and ignored. The object was to make the Indian over in the white man's image, at whatever cost, and if this couldn't be done, eliminate the problem by extermination, or remove the Indian to a remote part of the country where he would not interfere with the so-called progress of the white race. "Out of sight and out of mind" became the solution to the "Indian problem."

Blunt Assessments

Many non-Indians I have spoken to while persuing news stories have been very blunt in their assessments of their relationships with the Indian people. One non-Indian said to me, "Whenever I see an article in the newspapers about Indians, I just skip over it, and I guess that I do this because I really don't want to learn about the problems of the Indians, and I'm really not that concerned."

"Why do you suppose that is?" I asked him. He replied, "Well, I guess it's because most of us consider the Indian problems to be the responsibility of the federal government. They've always taken care of those things, without any help from us, and so we just don't want to know anything about it."

This attitude has, apparently, carried over to the media in areas with large Indian populations and it has been very difficult for educators to get young Indian students interested in seeking a career in this field of endeavor.

Job Interview

One Indian man, with a very good background in communications, thanks to the U.S. Army, applied for a job at a television station. He said to me, "I was put through a one-hour session of very grueling questions, many of them of a very personal nature. In fact, the interviewer even had the nerve to ask me if I was a member of the American Indian Movement." He continued, "Even if I was, or had been, a member of AIM, I didn't feel that this was relevant to my ability to do the job."

Recently, I spoke with a former news director or news editor about the problem.

"Of course, I am aware of the fact that the person I am talking to is Indian or not . . . Oftentimes, I find myself sizing up this person and making mental comparisons of him to white people."

Looking for Replica

"What it amounts to," he added, "is that I am screening out the differences, and seeking out the similarities. In other words, I am looking for a replica, or mirror-image of myself." He concluded, "One other thing I find myself doing is trying to determine if this Indian will have a tendency to make us look good in the eyes of our larger, white audience. If I decide that he will not, then he is out."

The problem facing the media hierarchy is, first of all, to admit to themselves that a problem does exist, and then to use their resources, their ingenuity, their sensivity, and above all, their sense of fair play in solving this dilemma which has proven to be an embarrassment on the American scene.

Things Are Not Always What They Seem

Several years ago, I had a weekly television show on a station in Rapid City. The show, "The First Americans," dealt with a variety of issues of concern to Indian people.

One week my guests who were particularly venomous toward former Oglala Sioux Tribal Chairman Dick Wilson, labeled him everything from a henchman to a goon.

Coincidentally, about a week later, one of the news reporters from the station was assigned to go to the Pine Ridge Reservation and do a story on the political situation there. One of the first stops he made was at the home of Dick Wilson.

Our knock on the door was answered by Wilson, himself. He looked at me and said, "Giago, you've got to be gutsy or crazy to come to my house after what was said on your TV show last week." I answered, "Well, Dick, I'm probably a little bit of both." Wilson laughed and said, "Come on in, then. I've got a fresh pot of coffee brewing."

Much to the surprise of the news reporter and me, Wilson turned out to be an engaging, serious individual who had some real concerns about the many problems on the reservation. He was bluntly candid and did not mince his words on any topic. The reporter and I left Wilson's house with a different perspective of the man.

I relate this story to you because it leads us into the subject of journalism as it was practiced shortly after the Occupation of Wounded Knee in 1973. During those hectic days on the Pine Ridge Reservation, journalists, print and electronic, converged upon a place they labeled "the tiny hamlet of Wounded Knee." Most of them came from the eastern United States or other metropolitan areas and had little or no knowledge about Indians or reservations.

In my opinion, many of these journalists were liberals looking for a cause. They found just what they were looking for at Wounded Knee. In order to support a cause, it is almost essential that you find a villain.

Dick Wilson had the misfortune to be elected chairman of the Oglala Sioux Tribe at the time. He was faced with a situation in which he was damned if he didn't act and damned if he did. A trading post was being illegally occupied. This was against the law of the tribe and of the federal government. He opted to uphold the laws of the Oglala Sioux Tribe.

From that day forward, anything he tried to do to assuage the situation became fodder for the press. He was called a goon and vilified in the cruelest possible way. I have read articles written in those terrible days and published in nationally respected magazines and newspapers that are a disgrace to every objective journalist. I remember one article in particular which I still have on file and refer to whenever I want to refresh my memory about subjective reporting, in which every single person interviewed was anti-Wilson. No effort was made by the writer to get the other side of the story.

"They never wanted to hear the tribal government's side of anything back then," Wilson said last week. "They came to our reservation with their minds made up, and began to write stories that only added wood to the fire." Wilson admitted that he wasn't very polite to the press, and probably angered them. "But, by God, I was tired of trying to get them to see both sides of the issue," he said.

After all was said and done, the reporters packed up their typewriters and cameras and went back to wherever they came from and left the people of this reservation to clean up the debris.

In the wake of their departure, a deep division occurred within the tribe which has taken all of these years to mend. Labels become commonplace. For many years, there was no middle ground. One was either for or against the occupation.

A lot of mud was tossed around, and as is usually the case, some of it found its mark and stuck. But, as the adverse publicity subsided, so, too, did the animosity and factionalism.

This is the anniversary of the Occupation of Wounded Knee, and although there are many scars from those days, most of the wounds have healed. The Oglala people have chalked it up to a bad experience and are trying to put the pieces back together.

There are still those who bring up the old hatreds and try to make political hay of them, but even they are beginning to disappear from the landscape.

People on both sides of the controversy made blunders and I'm sure they would do things differently if given the opportunity. But that's hindsight, and as the politicians are fond of saying, "Hindsight is no sight."

I guess that one of the genuine ironies is the fact that Dick Wilson and the man who served as his vice president following Wounded Knee, Joe American Horse, are opposing each other for the presidency of the Oglala Sioux Tribe this year (1982).

Because of the extreme emotionalism surrounding anything having to do with the occupation of Wounded Knee and the dark days that followed, I was very reluctant to tackle this subject in my column, but there are certain things that must be said. Sometimes it is better to talk about a painful experience rather than sweep it under the rug as if it had never happened.

Watt's Comments Become Opportunity for Indians

"Every dark cloud has a silver lining," or so the saying goes, and perhaps the quotes attributed to Secretary of the Interior James Watt about "abolishing the Indian reservations" will serve to give the Indian nations the national media exposure they need to get across their points of view.

Like most people living out on the reservations, my information is second hand. Listening to radio broadcasts in the aftermath of Watt's alleged statement, I was left with the distinct impression that Watt was referring to the severe problems faced by the Indians living on reservations, and was not suggesting a cure for those ills.

I am not trying to defend Watt, not by any stretch of the imagination, but what he had to say about the effects of socialism on the reservation made a lot of sense. Abolishing our reservations, however, is not the solution.

Watt made the comments on a program called "Conservative Counterpoint," broadcast on the Satellite Program Network on January 19, 1981. At one point in the interview, Watt accused the Congress of tolerating the government's abusive actions against Indians. He said, "I try to liberate them and get squashed by liberal Democrats in the House of Representatives."

What bothers more tribal leaders about such comments made by one entrusted with assisting the Indian nations is the fact that every Indian living on a reservation knows all about the many problems. We don't want to hear a rehash of our many problems. We want to hear some new ideas for curing the problems.

The local news media should take a lesson from ABC's "Nightline" presentation last Wednesday. This national television show chose to go directly to the duly elected tribal chairmen of three Indian reservations for comments. The fourth party interviewed was the executive director of the National Congress of American Indians, "Tatoo" Andrade.

This is a refreshing change and a large step forward. The local media usually go to the spokesmen of radical organizations, or to the local spokesmen they have created. At least the national media was wise enough to know that there are elected officials of legal tribal governments who speak for all of the people of their respective reservations because they have been elected by a majority vote of the people to do just that.

Following the "Nightline" show, I spoke with Kathy Anderson of ABC's Network News, one of the people responsible for the guests interviewed on the show. She said, "I believe that this show, though put together rather hurriedly, brought up far more questions than it answered. I believe we have whetted the natural curiosity of our viewing public about Indian reservations, tribal governments, and their relationships to the United States government." Miss Anderson suggested that another "Nightline" show is in the planning stage to deal with more specific questions.

Perhaps the voracity for the shocking treatment displayed by Secretary Watt has, in its own inimitable way, caused a reverse reaction by the general public. Indeed, their interest piqued, they may demand "the rest of the story," as Paul Harvey is so fond of saying.

The fact that this media exposure was foisted upon us by the adverse comments of Watt is the "silver lining." It is now up to the tribal leaders to exploit that national forum to their utmost. Watt has been painted the villain by the media, and the Indians are the "good guys." The opportunity for our tribal chairmen to grab the microphone and express themselves from a reservation perspective has never been better.

For once, we have been handed the opportunity to take the offensive. Usually, when tribal officials are given national television exposure, they are defending themselves. Either that, or they are busy attempting to define our problems. Now, they may have the golden chance to offer some suggestions about how to cure the problems.

We can only hope our tribal leaders speak with words of foresight, integrity, and wisdom, and we also hope these words reach all the way to the White House. Are you listening, President Reagan?

Creative Authors, Artists Show Indian Strength

There is a quiet movement beginning to take place in Indian Country.

It is being spearheaded by those Indian authors, journalists, and artists who have lived through the dark ages of racism, termination, assimilation, acculturation, and ridicule. Whether living on an Indian reservation or in the urban centers, they have experienced the worst and the best of two worlds, two cultures.

They learned many years ago that progress, according to the white man, meant the destruction of a way of life. They have also learned that, left to their own devices, progress would take on a whole new meaning to the Indian people, themselves. The day an Indian fashioned a spoon from the horn of a buffalo, that was the beginning of a new era in progress.

From the windows of the reservation, or from the Indian islands floating in the urban centers, surrounded on all sides by the "dominant society," these individuals have observed the world around them, mindful of its many changes. Oftentimes, they have watched in silent anger as the bungling bureaucracy wreaked havoc upon their people.

An education, to them, became a means to an end. Whether they completed their studies and earned a degree, or just remained long enough to hone the natural talents they already possessed, they all had one thing in common. Never did they lose sight of their "Indianness" or of the mission they hoped to pursue.

Although many of them accepted it reluctantly, most of them acknowledged the common language of English that allowed them to communicate. Whether they were Laguna, Blackfeet, Crow, Otoe, Ponca, Pueblo, Comanche, Kiowa or Sioux, it was the common language, English, which allowed them to break down the language barriers.

At conferences and conventions, they gathered in small groups to exchange ideas and information. They compared notes and then returned to their own reservations and homes in the urban centers to ponder what they had learned about each other.

The fruits of these ideas were harvested in the works of art produced, poems written, and books published. They discovered they did not need the white writer to transcribe their thoughts and hopes. They found that they were prefectly capable of doing it themselves, and, along the way, they discovered they did not lose the meaning or intent of their ideas as so often happens when interpretations are funneled through a third party.

From these artists and writers there began to emerge an artistic and literary concept that was pure Indian. Perhaps the educational processes leading to their creations were gleaned from the white world, but the finished product came deep from the heart and sould of the Indian.

Like a young fawn, taking its first steps on unsteady legs, the movement began less than ten years ago—one decade—a blink of the eye as the Indian marks time.

In the beginning, probably because they were so few in numbers, the initial form of communications between these writers and artists was usually via a complimentary note or a telephone call. What began as a mutual admiration society began to assert itself as a meaningful movement as the results of their work began to bring out changes and break down previously insurmountable barriers.

Although the people involved are real enough, the movement itself is presently unencumbered by labels or titles. It is made up of a collection of voices clamoring to be heard. Whether through a painting, statue, poem, or book, the story of the Indian people is beginning to emerge as told by the Indians, themselves.

The messages of the emerging movement can be found in the books of James Welch, a Blackfeet Indian, in *Winter in the Blood* or *The Death of Jim Loney*. They can be found in the works of art by Fritz Scholder, Vic Runnels, Robert Penn, Ed Two Bulls, or Jaune Quick to See. The interpretations traverse time from the traditional to the contemporary scene.

They speak of a new beginning, an awakening. They are saying to their own people and to the non-Indian: "Open your ears, your eyes, and, above all, open your minds. Hear us, see our works of art, read the words we write, and learn." Through their combined works, they are showing the strength of the Indian in its purest form.

In the novel, *Ceremony*, by Leslie Marmon Silko, a Laguna Indian, she writes about a Navajo medicine man named Betonie. Betonie is describing to his listener the story of how the white man stole the land. He points to a mountain sacred to the Pueblo Indians and says, "They only fool themselves when they think it is theirs. The deeds and papers don't mean anything. It is the people who belong to the mountain." It is in this fashion the Indian story unfolds.

An informal gathering of writers and artists is in the planning stages. If you are interested in obtaining more information, please drop a note to Juane Quick to See, Drawer F, Corrales, NM 87048.

Wounded Knee Tenth Anniversary Will Return Media to Scene

Next month will be the tenth anniversary of the 1973 Occupation of Wounded Knee. I have no doubt in my mind that the Pine Ridge Reservaion will be inundated with off-reservation journalists and television reporters.

I would advise those journalists visiting our reservation to make a list of negatives and positives. For instance, did the Occupation bring unity to the Lakota people? Did it make life better for the people of the reservation? Who benefited from it?

Wounded Knee 1973 is as much a part of our history as any other event that had a profound impact upon the Lakota people. The ensuing division, anger, and bitterness have taken almost ten long years to dissipate.

When I was a young boy, I lived at Wounded Knee. My father was a clerk in Clive Gildersleeve's store. The store is no longer standing. It was burned to the ground. The museum at Wounded Knee is also destroyed, as is most of the village. The Catholic church was burned to the ground, but has since been rebuilt. What did the destruction of a reservation community prove?

No doubt, there will be some sort of remembrance ceremony held at Wounded Knee. At a time in our history when common goals are a prerequisite for the survival of the Lakota Nation, those celebrants at Wounded Knee should talk about the future of the tribe and put all of the bitterness behind them. What's past is past! Today is a new day and we must get on with our future.

If the off-reservation media chooses to open up the old wounds, so be it. After all, haven't they always been able to come onto our reservation, get news stories, print them, or televise them, with little or no concern for the aftermath of their journalistic endeavors, and then return to the safety of their homes in the urban centers?

Where has the off-reservation media been for the past ten years? It is a common sight to see them here on our reservation every two years at election time, but where are they in between those times?

While these non-Indian journalists are visiting our reservation, it would be nice if they took at stab at clearing up some of the myths and misconceptions about Indians.

For instance: No, all Indians do not receive monthly checks simply because they are Indian! No, all Indians are not entitled to a free college education! No, all Indians are not on welfare! We are not all drunkards, lazy, dirty, unable to hold a steady job, nor do we still live in tipis.

These journalists might also point out to their readers and viewers that, just like the federal government and state government, we have a duly elected tribal government. We have a presidential and a tribal council elected by the people to initiate legislation. We have our own tribal courts, police department, and educational system. The State of South Dakota does not have jurisdiction of any kind on our reservations.

Maybe our tribal government doesn't always function in the best interests of all the reservation people. But do the federal and state governments? After all, we have had a governmental system for less than fifty years, while the United States government is more than 200 years old. Let me clarify that. Although our system of self-government is much older than that of the United States, it was not until 1934, under the Indian Reorganization Act, that we were permitted to practice a semblance of self-government, and that, under the benevolent, paternalistic, baleful eye of the Interior Department through the Bureau of Indian Affairs.

One of the positives that came out of the Wounded Knee Occupation is almost intangible. The effect it had upon the tribal government is quite subtle. It made the people out in the districts more cognizant of whom they put in office. And it made the elected tribal officials more responsive to the demands of the reservation voters.

Tenth Anniversary of Wounded Knee II, 1983

Cattle graze below pine-clad bluffs on Pine Ridge Reservation

The Occupation also focused national attention upon the ineptitudes of the BIA and the Interior Department. It caused the Indian people themselves to demand changes within these bureaucratic structures, and it served to put these entrenched bureaucrats on notice that their actions would not go unquestioned, ever again.

Yes, for a few weeks in 1973, the spotlight of world attention focused upon the Pine Ridge Reservation. When that spotlight was extinguished, it was the reservation people left behind who had to cope with the dark void of the aftermath. It was they who had to pick up the pieces and get on with the business of living.

The media event was over. Notebooks and cameras were put away for the flight home, and the reservation people were left to mull over what had occurred, and to try to find answers and solutions to the problems left in the wake of the Occupation.

As the white man measures time, anniversaries are always something to remember. So, it has been ten years—one decade—time for a media revival!

At this stage in our history, whether one was pro-occupation or anti-occupation should matter little. As Lakota people, we knew that some good and some bad came from it, and we know that we must get on with tomorrow. We learn from our history, and this has truly been a lesson—in history.

Reporters Would Help by Being Truthful about Reservations

A few weeks back, the Pine Ridge Reservation was inundated by journalists from radio, television, and the press sent here to focus nationwide attention on the tenth anniversary of the Occuation of Wounded Knee. Most of us breathed a sight of relief when they packed their bags and departed.

We won't attempt to comment upon the journalistic endeavors of most of these once-in-a-decade invaders. Let it suffice to say that most of their "eyewitness accounts" were filled with exaggerations and inaccuracies.

I'm sure these news junkets have given birth to a new generation of so-called "Indian experts" who spent all of three or four days learning all there is to know about Indians.

One of these erstwhile reporters, Lea Donosky, outdid all of the others in depicting the Lakota Indians as helpless welfare cases with little hope for the future. I would like to critique some of the half-truths and inaccuracies in her article which appeared in the Chicago *Tribune* February 28, 1983.

In describing the arrests following the 1973 Occupation of Wounded Knee, Donosky writes, "More than 400 Indians were arrested, but fewer than a dozen went to prison." To be precise, 617 people were arrested during and after the occupation. Of these, 120 were indicted in federal court. Fifty-one percent of those indicted were not Indians at all. Most of them were college students from many different states. FBI records will verify this.

She continues, "The tug of war between the 19th and 20th Centuries is vivid here. A satellite dish sits in front of one home, bringing cable television to the reservation. Nearby, smoke rises from a fire where stones are being heated for a sweat lodge, an Indian purification ceremony similar to a Turkish bath."

The satellite is owned by Oyate Vision, the Indian-owned cable television company of Pine Ridge. Fred "Budger" Brewer, the owner, is also a practitioner of traditional religion and quite often purifies himself in a sweat lodge. Would Donosky compare a Jewish yarmulke to a beanie worn by college freshmen? The Lakota sweat lodge is an integral part of the Lakota religion.

Donosky writes, "the tribal government provides $1,500 in burial insurance for each member." A little more research would have informed her that many of the tribal members, with jobs pay annual premiums for this insurance.

"Despite the millions of dollars in federal funds that have been poured into the reservation in the last half-century, the lives of many Indians, here and elsewhere, are little changed," she writes. This is a most frequent and popular misconception. The Bureau of Indian Affairs, with its many area offices and central offices in Washington, D.C. eats up much of the money before it ever reaches the reservations. For instance, the area office in Aberdeen, South Dakota earmarks at least $7,000,000 annually for administrative purposes. And that's just one of the twelve area offices. The reservations are lucky to receive 40 percent of the $1.6 billion budgeted by the BIA for Fiscal Year 1983.

For those of us in private industry, the next comment is really a slam. Donosky writes, "The only private employers here, a moccasin and arrow factory, have both laid off workers in recent months because of the recession."

One business, dismissed by Donosky as "a supermarket," is actually a shopping center selling clothing, shoes, dry goods, etc., and it actually employs twenty-five people. Another, written off as a "gas station," is a mini-mart and employs nine full time employees. She left out more. The reservation newspaper also employs seven people, and in almost every community on the reservation, one can find Indian-owned businesses with several employees. As a matter of fact, in the heartland of the reservation, at Kyle, there is a mini-shopping mall.

There are several more inaccuracies within the article written by Donosky, but I'm sure you get the point I'm trying to make. Many reporters believe they can come to our reservation and write articles filled with inaccuracies with absolute impunity. After all, aren't we just a bunch of dumb Indians ready to jump at any form of publicity that would point out our plight?

Most native Chicagoans probably read this article over a cup of coffee, "cluck-clucked" over the "poor Indians," and then went back to munching on a breakfast roll. Maybe a few were moved enough to take out their check books and write a small check to their local Indian center.

Did these media people come out here to help us or hinder us? If they really wanted to help us, they should be asking their readers to write letters to their congressmen demanding some long-range economic development programs be initiated on our reservations to give us a shot at self-sufficiency. They should be writing to their senators to restore the monstrous budget cuts that all but decimated the Indian reservations in the name of austerity.

We do not want pity or charity. We want the financial assistance to help us determine our own destiny. In the year 1983, the federal government has managed to cut off the legs of the Indian nations, just when we were beginning to learn how to walk.

Mattheissen Book Example of Speculation and Confusion

Written by Peter Matthiessen and published by Viking Press, "In the Spirit of Crazy Horse" could well have been named "In the Spirit of Speculation and Confusion."

Matthiessen's limited knowledge of the Pine Ridge Reservation and its residents is apparent throughout the book. He implies that the Pine Ridge Reservation was divided evenly between members of the American Indian Movement and the Tribal Government and BIA "Goons." The fact that the vast majority of the people on the reservation—the silent majority—fitted into none of those categories completely escapes Matthiessen.

The author begins to show his ignorance of Lakota traditions in the introduction. He writes, "At the death of his father, John Fire Lame Deer in 1976, Archie Fire became chief." There are no hereditary chiefs in the Lakota Nation. In the old days, a man had to earn the right to be chief. Many traditional Lakotas, including Louis Bad Wound who is mentioned in the book, dismissed Archie Fire as an exploiter of the Indian religion.

Matthiessen attacks the works of sculptor Korczak Ziolkowski as "a huge and vulgar scale above the rubble of a sacred mountain." And yet, he uses a quote from Luther Standing Bear to begin one chapter, never realizing that it was Henry Standing Bear, brother of Luther, who asked Korczak Ziolkowski to carve the statue so the white man would know "we had our heroes, too." Dennis Banks was, and is, a very close friend of the Ziolkowski family. He spent many hours visiting them on the mountain called Crazy Horse.

Time and time again, Matthiessen uses the word, "traditional," to support his erroneous assumptions. At the end of Chapter Two, he writes, "More than five hundred traditional people were indicted by the FBI in connection with Wounded Knee, and one hundred eighty-five were subsequently indicted by federal grand juries." What he fails to point out to his readers is that 51 percent of those indicted were not even Indians. Are these non-Indians also considered to be "traditionals?"

Mike Anderson, a young Navajo man, who testified against Leonard Peltier at his trials, said, "he had not sworn on the sacred pipe before testifying for the U.S. government, the implication was that he felt no obligation to be truthful." Anderson said he believed "in his traditional religion." The sacred pipe has never been a part of the traditional Navajo religion.

Matthiessen has some harsh things to say about Chiefs Red Cloud and Spotted Tail. He writes about how the "greedy 'chiefs' appointed by the white men were soon selling or leasing ancestral lands that did not belong to them, in dishonest arrangements that were duly endorsed in the white man's courts." He attempts to soften this accusation with, "Despite their records as great war leaders, Red Cloud and Spotted Tail are now included among such chiefs by their own people." This is a gross falsehood.

More than once in the book, Russell Means is quoted as saying he had to get out of "that BIA concentration camp at Kyle." In reality, the BIA has less control at Kyle (the second largest community on the reservation) than at any of the other communities on the reservation. The large high school and elementary school located there is a contract school and is run by a local school board. The police and courts are contracted and are run by the tribal government. As a matter of fact, Russell's wife, Peggy, lives and works at "that BIA concentration camp at Kyle."

Edgar Bear Runner, who is mentioned several times in the book, is angry because, "I never met this Matthiessen in my life, and I don't know how he can write these things about me, and quote me, if he has never talked to me."

David Long, the great-grandson of Crazy Horse, is livid with anger. "This white man is capitalizing on the name of my great-grandfather. He is comparing Leonard Peltier to Crazy Horse all through the book and this is not right," he said angrily. South Dakota Governor William Janklow who is trying to get the book removed from the book stores because "it is an embarrassment to me and is causing anguish to my family," received a call from Long last week. Long told the governor that he would assit him in getting the book out of circulation.

Gordon, Nebraska, the town where Raymond Yellow Thunder was killed, continues to be vilified as "a red neck town." Many reservation residents will attest to the fact that Gordon has come a long way in improving race relations. Said one businessman, "We were just as upset and angry over what happened to Yellow Thunder as anyone. We have tried our darndest to improve and strengthen our relations with the people of the reservation since then."

In the spirit of subjectivity, this book ranks with the most one-sided novels ever written. No effort was made by Matthiessen to speak with any of the people labeled as "goons" in this book although many of these individuals still live and work on the reservation.

The one man who did the most to bring about unity to the reservation, former tribal chairman, Elijah Whirlwind Horse, now deceased, is dismissed by Matthiessen as "another bureaucrat who soon replaced most of the AIM people with the Pine Ridge faction, including many of the old faces from the Wilson days."

As with many of the observations in this book, the charge is unfair, malicious, and untruthful. It is because of the efforts in uniting the Lakota people by Whirlwind Horse that his book will be read, out of curiosity, and put back on the shelf to collect dust.

"Not Going to Take it Anymore!"

I don't know how many times I've heard people say, "Indians never write letters to protest wrongs against themselves." Well, over the years, I have discovered that this is partly true. We don't make too many responses to things that are written about us that are erroneous. As a result, we find ourselves fair game for any journalist with a penchant to write about Indians.

Politicians, editors and television and radio station managers are very aware of public opinion. Why else would they pay such close attention to polls and rating reports? I don't mean they bend over backwards to gloss things over in an effort to make things more palatable to the public (with the possible exceptions of politicians), but they are very aware that they have a certain inmage to project and protect.

Are those national Indian organizations based in the big cities, which are designed to assist the reservations, and indeed, receive large federal grants and foundation monies to do just that, really doing a job in our behalf? Are they really responsive to the requests and the needs of the grassroots Indian people living on the Indian reservations?

Each year, these organizations choose a different city to hold their week-long discussions to discuss our future. In the first place, how many of us can afford to travel to these distant cities to attend these meetings which help shape the policies and make recommendations to the federal government which affect the lives of every Indian man, woman and child living in the United States?

And another thing, are the tribal officials who attend these meetings in your behalf speaking out for you, or are they spending their time sitting in the fancy cocktail lounge patting themselves on the back for hanging on to a job for another two years?

If you could attend one of these posh conventions and were given the opportunity of addressing the crowd, what would you have to say? What are your goals, your dreams, your concerns, and above all else, what are your complaints? Are they being discussed?

Don't ever think that your opinion is so insignificant that it will not be heard, or that it cannot make a difference because you could be wrong. Individually and collectively, our opinions do matter! But they will not matter if they are never heard. We must get off our cans, take a pen and pencil in our hands, and write to the Indian leadership of these organizations which is supposed to have our best interest at heart, and let them know what is on our minds.

Several years ago there was a movie out called "Network" which illustrated, albeit outrageously, the power of public opinion. The film featured a television newscaster on the nightly news who became fed up and angry at world events, went slightly bonkers, and began to shout over the air, "I'm mad as hell, and I'm not going to take it any more." He exhorted his viewers to join him in this ritual, and soon voices all over the country were shouting, "We're mad as hell, and we're not going to take it anymore!"

This is a fictional and yet graphic illustration of how mountains can be moved by public opinion. If enough people make enough noise, their voices will be heard.

Can you, as Indian people, do the same thing? Why not give it a try and find out? On October 27, 1980, the National Congress of American Indians will hold its annual convention in Spokane, Washington. This is the oldest Indian organization in the country and is the one with the most influence in Washington, D.C. What would happen if each and every one of us were to sit down, now, and write a letter about the things that we are really concerned about, and ask the organization to include these things on its agenda? Would it make a difference if we said, "We're mad as hell, and we're not going to take it anymore!"?

The address is: National Congress of American Indians; 1430 K Street N.W.; Washington, DC 20005.

Try it! It can't do any harm, and maybe it will make you feel a little better just knowing that you tried.

Conference Format Seems to be Changing

There has been a perceptive change in the format of many national Indian conferences.

Over the years, I have been critical of the gala affairs staged by national organizations such as the National Congress of American Indians. Usually, their conferences were top heavy with Washington, D.C. bureaucrats and executive directors of urban Indian organizations. The grassroots Indian people were left on the outside looking in.

In June of 1982 the Native American Public Broadcasting Consortium sponsored a conference in Albuquerque, New Mexico known as the National Indian Media Conference. Reservation people and elected tribal officials were a common sight at this meeting. As a matter of fact, the president of the Rosebud Sioux Tribe, Carl Waln, was the keynote speaker.

Waln has long been an advocate of open communications between the tribal government and the people. His emphasis has been upon a channel of communication, whether radio, television, or newspaper, that would reach all of the people of the reservation emanating from an Indian perspective.

It was this kind of reservation-based support that made this particular conference so different and significant. Many of the people attending the conference represented fledgling radio stations and tribal newspapers from many different Indian reservations. The mental electricity generated by the Indian men and women from radio, television and the print media fairly crackled. The quiet force behind this subtle change in conference format is Frank Blythe, a Santee Sioux from South Dakota. Founder and president of the Native American Broadcast Consortium, Blythe has had to go through all of the bureaucratic hoops in an effort to keep his organization afloat. He had to play all of the games expected of him out of Washington, D.C. in order to secure funding each year.

All Blythe ever wanted to prove was that his organization could provide a vitally needed service to the Indian people. Patiently, he gritted his teeth and took it one step at a time. The early National Indian media conferences sponsored by his organization are indicative of the Washington influence. There was a definite chasm between the conference presenters and the largely Indian audience in attendance.

While some of the speakers from the Corporation for Public Broadcasting were speaking about "space-age and satellite" technology, many of the Indian people at the conference were trying to find out how to take the first step in bringing a radio station to their reservation. There was a definite lack of what the conference was supposed to be about—communications.

I spoke to Blythe about this problem a few years back at a conference held in Phoenix, Arizona. In so many words, Blythe asked me to be patient. He said, "Just let us get our feet on the ground and bring a few more Indians into the organization. I know what has to be done, but for now, I've got to play a lot of silly games to get there."

At times, it is hard to accept a logical, steadfast approach readily adaptable to a circuitous route, secure in the knowledge that the ultimate goals will be achieved with patience. This is doubly hard to take if you are the one who believes that all major changes should have happened yesterday! Blythe was right!

What had begun as an organization geared to radio and television, soon became a blanket company for all forms of Indian media. Blythe had guided the NAPBC through the rough waters and had achieved his objectives—an organization made up of Indian professionals from all branches of the media. He had weeded out the bureaucratic influence, and had installed a leadership geared to doing things from an Indian perspective.

Like Carl Waln, Blythe understood the desperate need for open communications on the reservations—and he also recognized the reservation land bases as the last foothold of the American Indian on this continent. In this regard, he said, "Without our reservations, there are no more Indians."

Acknowledging that Indians in the media need to be applauded for their efforts, Blythe instituted the "National Indian Media Awards" banquet to honor those Indian achievers in print, radio and television media. He knew they would receive very little recognition from the non-Indian media.

I was very proud of the award given to me by Blythe as the "National Print Media Person of the Year." First of all, I was proud because I was the first journalist living and working on an Indian reservation to receive this award, and, secondly, because it was awarded to me by my peers in the media.

This year the National Indian Media Conference will be May 15-18, 1983 in Minneapolis, Minnesota. If Blythe runs true to form, he'll pull a few surprises out of his magical hat.

Blend of Cultures, Communication Needed for Unity

Every culture must draw from its past in order to provide for its future. This does not mean living in the past to the detriment of the present.

The Indian tribes have survived because they have been able to adapt. They survived assimilation, acculturation and termination as sovereign nations through tact, diplomacy, determination and perseverance.

Isolated on reservations, cut off from the mainstream, relegated to the roles of totally dependent colonists of the United States, denied the basic human rights of freedom of religion, and saddled with an educational system designed to destroy the culture, and drive the young people from the reservation, the Indian people have come through it all—battered but unbowed.

If there are those who have run this American gauntlet of ignorance and have been subjected to the questionable attitude of superiority of the dominant society, and have come away with anger in their hearts, and a bitter hatred toward the white man—can they really be faulted?

Perhaps not! But they cannot allow their feelings or anger to dissipate into self-pity and aimless wrath. What's done is done! There is far too much constructive work to be done by the Indian people. Blind hatred can only weaken our resolve to correct the wrongs of the past and to find a better way for the future.

Before we can stand on our own as independent nations—with pride in our past and confidence in our ability to face what is ahead—we must first begin to try to solve the many problems rampant on our reservations—here and now.

It is a fine thing to have lofty ideals and to preach the rhetoric of revolution and change; but talk is cheap. If it is not accompanied by a sound, basic plan to restructure that which we already have, and clean up the mess that is keeping us in bondage as a people, slaves to our own petty bickering, and in chains, secured by the federal government and forged by an incompetent tribal government, then words become meaningless.

Racial prejudice on Indian reservations between so-called full bloods, mixed bloods and other races does exist. Alcoholism is destroying the very fabric of human dignity, and drugs are corrupting the morals of the young.

Thievery, violence and a complete lack of respect for the property of others is the cancer caused by these combinations of diseases. Wearing long or short hair—or wearing feathers or not wearing feathers—is not the solution or the cure to these runaway problems. The decision to do either is a personal choice and should never be used to cause further division amongst the people.

It was never the way of the Indian people to force a way of life upon a tribal member if that person chose not to adopt it.

In order to generate a small beginning, in an effort to confront the many problems existing on the Indian reservations, we must have meaningful dialogue between the different factions. How can we seriously discuss our differences if we cannot communicate? We cannot continue to dismiss another's opinion simply because it does not agree with our own.

We cannot continue to look only to the past for our salvation. As much as many of us would like to believe that life before the white man was a paradise, anyone versed in Indian history will tell you it was not! We had diseases, we had wars, we had famine, and we had change. Nothing stood still then and nothing stands still now. Our existence is static—everchanging—and we must move with the times in order to survive.

Indian reservations should be thought of by the people as huge ships. Every tribal member, the young and the old, the traditional and the Christian, are all passengers on this ship.

It is up to all of the people of the reservation to insure that this ship remains afloat. If the fabric of the reservation is ripped and destroyed, like a ship, it will sink into the blackness and nothingness, and all of the people will go to the bottom with it.

The future course of the Indian reservations must include the best of the traditional societies and the best of the modern societies, blended together to achieve a mixture that will pull us through these troubled waters.

The old maxim, "United we stand—divided we fall," has never meant more to our future as a people. The solutions to our problems are not going to come from without—but instead must come from within the confines of our own reservation, from within our own hearts and minds. There is no   other way.

TV Mini-Series Based on *Hanta Yo*

Hanta Yo Criticisms Apparently Justified

According to the *Los Angeles Times*, April 21, 1980, "Author Ruth Beebe Hill shot back at Sioux critics of her scheduled-to-be-dramatized novel, *Hanta Yo*, calling them 'pop Indians'."

"What's happening is that we've had pop music, pop art and now we have some pop Indians," Hill charged. "They're making a lot of war whoops for one reason: They have nothing else to rally around."

These are the kind of irresponsible statements being made by Mrs. Hill that cause David Wolper, the man slated to produce the mini-series for ABC based on the best selling novel, to wince in anguish. "I sure can't control what she says. But she has been asked to refrain from such harsh comments because it only serves to alienate the Indian people who are trying to work with us," Wolper said.

I had a lengthy conversation with Wolper this week about the series he intends to produce. Mrs. Hill was unavailable for comment—she, instead, has been directing questions to her attorney, Richard Harker of Encino, Californa.

Because of the complexities of the situation surrounding the novel, *Hanta Yo*, and the many critics involved, it is virtually impossible to do a meaningful article on the controversies in a single column. And so, I will do my impressions on this subject as a two-parter, the first part dealing primarily with the book itself, and the second part dealing mostly with the proposed TV mini-series.

Hanta Yo is the best-selling novel by Ruth Beebe Hill, published by Doubleday, that supposedly represents the life of the Lakota people from the mid-1700s to about 1835. It is loosely based upon a Winter Count kept by

Hehaka (Elk) of the Mahto Band of the Teton Sioux. A winter count was a method of reckoning time by recording on a tanned hide one outstanding event that occurred to the tribe each year.

The major objection to the book by Indian people is that it is being advertised as "factual." In the front of the paperback edition, David Wolper called the book a "masterpiece" and added that "this epic book makes every other book about Indians seem shallow and out of date."

Since Mr. Wolper has discovered just why many Indian people object to this novel as "factual," he has modified his own position by referring to the book now as "a good fictional story."

Dr. Bea Medicine, Standing Rock Sioux; Vine Deloria and Raymond J. Demallie give extensive criticisms of *Hanta Yo* in the *Newsletter of the Association for Study of American Indian Literature*, published by Columbia University (Vol. 3, No. 4, Winter, 1979). Dr. Medicine's *Hanta Yo: A New Phenomenon*, Mr. Demallie's *Ayn Rand Meets Hiawatha* and Mr. Deloria's *Hanta Yo—Super Hype* are detailed objections to the book and to its authenticity.

Apparently their objections were read by Mrs. Hill's attorney, Mr. Richard Harker. He says, "attacks on the book's authenticity are publicity-seeking gestures by some Indians or attempts to make the white man feel guilty."

Dr. Bea Medicine makes one statement in her review that says much for her as a Lakota woman. She mentions Chunksa Yuha, the Dakota Sioux who provided much of the linguistic data to Ruth Beebe Hill; a man who has been harshly criticized, maligned and denigrated by other critics, by saying, "True to Lakota ideals and respect for elders, I shall say no more—except that I hope he shares in the author's spoils—especially the monetary ones."

The majority of the book reviews on *Hanta Yo* were extremely negative.

Of all the reviews that I have read on the matter, the most concise and analytical appeared in the Sinte Gleska college newspaper at Rosebud, South Dakota, *Hanta Yo: Authentic Farce* by Victor Douville, chairman of the Lakota Studies department. Mr. Douville sums up the feelings of myself and many other critics of this laborious novel when he says, "There is much misinformation and misinterpretation of Lakota history and culture found in this book by Mrs. Hill. In fact, there exists so much that a multi-volume work would have to be compiled in order to comprehensively deal with the distorted picture of the Lakota by Ruth Beebe Hill."

Hanta Yo Filming Likely to Proceed

Saudi Arabia objected strongly to the airing of *Death of a Princess* on Public Broadcasting. The two-hour telecast was listed as a "dramatized documentary" and dealt with the execution of a married nineteen-year-old Saudi princess and her lover.

The Saudi Arabian government protested that the presentation was "completely false" and warned that it could "undermine the internationally significant relations" between the United States and its largest oil supplier. In a letter sent to Acting Secretary of State Warren Christopher, Saudi Ambassador Faisal Alhegelan described the TV presentation as "offensive to the entire Islamic world." But he added, "we recognize your constitutional guarantees of freedom of speech and expression, and it is not my purpose to suggest any infringement upon those rights."

Without wishing to appear resigned or fatalistic I would like to make a point by asking this question: If a government such as Saudi Arabia, with its billions of dollars in oil revenues to back it up, and with the club of an oil embargo as its chief weapon, could not dissuade this government from airing a show uncomplimentary to it, how can a small "ad hoc" committee of Indian people stop a major television network from airing a profit-making venture such as *Hanta Yo?* There is a great difference in being fatalistic and realistic. In my opinion, the production of *Hanta Yo* will proceed as planned, and there is precious little that Indian people can do to stop it.

Not Like Book

According to David Wolper, executive producer of this show, "It is important to judge the project on the scripts and not on the book. A bush may have many thorns and yet produce a beautiful flower. It is foolish for people to be objecting to a TV show having never read the script," he added.

Wolper is adamant that "only about ten percent of the book will be used in the TV production. You must remember that many Indian readers believe that there is a very strong core to build from and once the parts that are objectionable to the Lakota people are carved away, we have the foundation for a very meaningful and beautiful story."

"I can understand the apprehension of many Native Americans because of the many false promises made to them for many years, but I also have a reputation to protect. Over the past thirty years, I have produced more than six hundred films and won well over two hundred awards," Wolper continued.

Outside Review

He said that for the first time in television history, a major television network, ABC, will be willing to submit all of the scripts for review from an outside source, the Lakota Nation. "We will look to the tribe to check the scripts for accuracy and to comment on all aspects, ranging from the visible ones of costumes, props, songs, ceremonies and rituals to the more important invisibles: religious and spiritual beliefs," Wolper said.

In a letter written to Louis Bad Wound of the Lakota Treaty Council, Wolper states: "One of the things which attracted us to the story was the fact that we can present a non-stereotyped depiction of the Native Americans. We are dedicated to presenting on American television screens a fresh and positive portrayal of the Oglala Lakota, one that gets away from the standard cliches. The emphasis in our scripts is on one family, surrounded by the greater family

Tim Giago and Louis Bad Wound researching material for **The Mystic Warrior**

of the Mahto, surrounded by the even greater family of the Oglala Lakota. We hope to show these people in terms that will appeal to all viewers: as husbands and wives, fathers and sons, wives and daughters, grandparents and children and grandchildren. . ."

Sensitive Man

It is my opinion that the production of Hanta Yo has been placed in the hands of a very sensitive and gifted man. David Wolper assured me that he would never, in his lifetime, do anything to demean or ridicule the Indian people. I feel that we should not "throw the baby out with the bathwater," but we should consider the good that can come from a well done, accurately scripted movie which can do more to open doors to communications between Indians and non-Indians than anything to date.

I have read the scripts for this production and they are far, far different from the book. According to Wolper, "There is an opportunity for the Lakota Nation to have this mini-series followed up by a history of the Oglala people from 1840 to the present."

In the history of television there has never been such an opportunity offered to the Oglala people and they should consider all aspects, pro and con, before they render a decision.

TV Mini-Series Based on Hanta Yo Will be Filmed

"Why help a woman such as Ruth Beebe Hill make more money on her book by letting her sell the television rights? Why help her increase her book sales at our expense? There are plenty of good, Indian authors in this country, so why further the career of a non-Indian woman who writes about Indians?" These were some of the questions directed at me by some individuals after my two-part series on the novel, Hanta Yo. I might add that one of my loudest critics failed to read either of my articles; but instead based his criticisms on hearsay.

Let me refresh the memories of my readers on the subject. A few months ago the novel, Hanta Yo, was being widely discussed in this area. The first article I wrote on the subject agreed with most of the critics of the book, that it was inaccurate, deceptive, and contained erroneous information which was purported to be authentic.

The second article stated that the filming of the suggested mini-series, based on the novel, would proceed, and that, try as we might, we could not stop this production. In the light of this inevitability, I suggested that the national criticisms of the novel had been heard by the producers of the show, and that the script had been drastically altered to eliminate those portions of the novel found to be objectionable.

Tremendous amounts of money had already been spent by the American Broadcasting Company for the rights to do this mini-series, and huge corporations such as ABC do not spend money without a purpose. They will proceed with this production despite the many protests of the Indian people.

As so often happens in situations such as this, the national protests over the book did more to promote the sales of *Hanta Yo* than the advertising agency used by Doubleday Publishers could have done in twenty years. One person, who owns several book stores, told me that *Hanta Yo* was dead on the shelf. He couldn't give the books away. Then "all of a sudden the Indian people started to get a lot of publicity in newspapers and magazines. In fact, one article even appeared in *Time* magazine. After this, we couldn't keep the book in stock. It sold like crazy."

Let me go on record as saying, once more, that I do not support the planned TV mini-series or the novel. What I stated before, and I will repeat, is this: "If we cannot stop the production of this television program, then let's continue to fight to get the best possible deal for the Lakota people that we can."

Under pressure, the producer of this show, David Wolper, has agreed to several concessions. He has guaranteed that immediately following the final segment of this mini-series, a panel of Indian people will be given the opportunity to address complaints aimed at the novel and the TV show to an audience of approximately twenty-five million people. In a single night, the Lakota people can say more against the exploitation and inaccuracies of this book than they could have said in a lifetime of random protests.

He has hired a staff of Lakota people to research the accuracy of the TV mini-series, and has stated that he will abide by their final decisions and incorporate their findings and suggestions into the show. He has stopped all advertising suggesting that this novel or mini-series is, in any way, the "roots" of the American Indian. His advertising will stress that the movie is based upon a "fictional novel" and that the scripts have been rewritten, with the assistance of many Lakota people, to insure that the movie will be accurate, and in no way, will be embarrassing or degrading to the Lakota Nation.

The national protest movement spearheaded by JoAllyn Archambault did have an impact. The protest sent out the message, quite clearly, that the Indian people are not going to sit idly by and allow this sort of thing to happen again. By standing up, and speaking out against this treatment, people from the Pine Ridge Reservation, such as Hildegarde Catches (Red War Bonnet Woman) and Lyman Red Cloud have let it be known that the days of the "dime novel" and the "shoot 'em up Western movie" are over. The Lakota people will not tolerate these abuses, ever again.

Just as the revised version of *The Godfather* took such great pains to let the audience know that they did not intend to malign, or defame Italian-Americans or any other "ethnic group," so, too, will future movies about the Indian people use discretion and sensitivity in dealing with the treatment of the American Indian.

I spoke with movie actor Will Sampson, Creek Indian (*One Flew over the Cukoo's Nest*), this week and he said, "You know, Tim, over four years ago, when I was on your TV show, we both lashed out against books like *The Last Portage* and movies like *They Died with Their Boots On* but nobody was listening. If people would have listened to us then, such a thing as the controversy over *Hanta Yo* could never have happened. It would have been stopped before it started."

Novel *Hanta Yo* Situation Updated

Now that the confrontations over the novel, *Hanta Yo*, have subsided, and the initial hysteria has been placed on the back burner, pehaps it will be possible to do a brief update on the overall situation.

The loose coalition of Indian people who organized against the book objected to the fact that the novel was being touted as a parallel to *Roots*. It was being billed, as a matter of fact, as "The Indian Roots." Considering the fact that there are approximately 280 different Indian tribes in this country, how can one do a single novel about the "roots" (supposedly) of one tribe, and give it the general title, "Indian roots"?

Other objections had to do with the graphic descriptions of certain "sex acts" and ceremonies involving the birth of a child. Here again, there is a strong possibility that the comparisons were being made by present-day morality, as opposed to "what-might-have-been" back in the years prior to 1750.

Medicine Men

I have spoken at length with medicine men of the Lakota Nation (the tribe of record in the book) and have drawn different answers about the authenticity of the ceremonies depicted. Some say, "No;" others, "Maybe." The most frequent answer is, "I don't know."

One of my main criticisms of the novel was, and still is, that it is a boring, tedious, and sing-song sort of novel that leaves you counting cadence in your head as you laboriously read each and every sentence. If you remember your school days, there were those novels you "had to read" for book reviews, and such, that you approached with trepidation.', and read with martyr-like determination.

Picking up that assigned novel to begin your review became a daily challenge. You knew that you had to stay with it, through thick and thin, in order to come up with a good grade for your efforts. Now, reading that sort of novel is an obligation, not a pleasure. Such a book is *Hanta Yo.*

Earlier Review

In a two-part series written by me several weeks ago, I did a review on this novel and a separate column on the proposed TV mini-series based on the book. My review of the novel was in general agreement with most of the critics of it, and I suggested other sources of criticism. However, I separated it from the criticisms on the television presentation.

The biggest gripe that has reached me on my column about supporting the television show is this: "Why in the heck help a woman such as Ruth Beebe

Hill (the author) make more money on her book by letting her sell the television rights? Why help her increase her book sales by having a TV mini-series advertising her novel?" There was little criticism about the television script for the mini-series because it had been drastically altered, and would use only about 25 percent of the novel as a foundation for the show. The other complaint was: "There are plenty of good Indian authors in this country; why further the career of a non-Indian woman who chooses to write about Indians?"

Biggest Gripes

As a journalist, myself, this has been one of my biggest gripes in life. I get very tired of non-Indian writers capitalizing upon the Indian people. If the writing is good, that's different, but so much of it is pure trash, it hurts the Indian people by supplying more myths and misconceptions to minds already trained by society to expect the worst of Indians.

Unfortunate as it might seem, the national hoopla raised by the chief critics of the novel, *Hanta Yo*, had the opposite reaction. The sales of the book jumped like crazy!

Now, I supported the TV mini-series for one reason: The producer of the show has guaranteed that immediately following the final segment of the series, a panel of Indian people will be given the opportunity to voice their complaints about the novel, *Hanta Yo*, and other literature that is defamatory or inaccurate.

Never, in the history of television or movies, have the Indian people had an opportunity to act as critics of a major novel before an audience estimated to be 25 million plus. In a single night, Indian people can say more against this book than they could in a lifetime of protests. My feelings are, if we can't stop the production of this mini-series, why not try to get the best possible deal for the Indian people? I believe this has been accomplished.

Few Stir Turmoil Around Production

Though few in numbers, there are still those people around who are trying to stir up the controvesy surrounding the movie production, *The Mystic Warrior*, taken from the novel by Ruth Beebe Hill, *Hanta Yo*.

About two years ago, I was called by Stan Margulies, one of the producers of the project, and asked if I would assist them in researching some of the things written into a brand new script by Jeb Rosebrook.

Since that time, I have used what little expertise I have accumulated over the years as a professional journalist to help David Wolper and his producers (and Rosebrook) verify many of the scenes from the soon to be filmed, made for television, five-hour production.

Personal Gain

One individual has already attacked me publicly, saying that I know nothing about the Lakota religion and culture, that I am in it for personal gain, and that I am a self-styled Indian expert.

Well, I am not about to become involved in a name-calling contest with those who are opposed to the movie. In the first place, if they are true, traditionalist Lakota, as they profess to be, they would not be using non-Indian media to insult another Lakota. Everything I have ever reserached in this particular area tells me that Lakota people did not insult each other publicly. In so doing, they would have been insulting all Lakota people.

Anyone who has ever read anything I have written over the past several years will understand that I have never claimed to be an expert on the Lakota, or any other Indian tribe. My involvement in this production is to research the scenes in the scripts with the many elders and other Indians on and off the reservation and, by so doing, come up with a general consensus of thought from the Lakota people, themselves.

On Reservations

I live and work on the Pine Ridge Reservation. Any payment I will receive for my involvement in the film will be put back into the economy of the Pine Ridge Reservation. It will go into my newspaper, *The Lakota Times*, which serves the reservation by providing a weekly news forum, and provides jobs for six Lakota people who would otherwise be unemployed. As far as I can determine, we have the only self-supporting, independent, Indian-owned, and Indian-staffed newspaper in the United States.

The movie, *The Mystic Warrior*, is not, even remotely, identifiable with the novel, *Hanta Yo*. The script has been completely rewritten by Rosebook, a most gifted writer, and is built around the family that apeared in the novel. It depicts the Lakota people as individuals who laugh, love and have respect for themselves and their families. It is a tribute to the Lakota of the early 1800s.

The biggest complaint voiced by those opposed to the production is that, after the film is aired, people will rush out and buy the novel, and will get a source of information filled with negatives and misconceptions. Have you ever rushed out to buy a novel after you have seen the movie?

Every Effort

Much to the credit of David Wolper, he has made every effort to get input from the Lakota people in making the scripts as authentic as possible. Any suggestions I have made to him, based upon the objections of the Indian people I have interviewed, he has followed to the letter. Countless times he has said, "If the Lakota people don't like this particular scene, remove it from the script!"

There are many good Lakota people who have supplied me with information and given me sound advice. Many of these people wish to remain anonymous because they fear the controversy their participation might precipitate.

It is my belief that the movie will be one of the most beautiful movies ever done on Indian people. There are scenes in the script that are lighthearted, exciting, sorrowful and joyful. I am firmly convinced that there will be very few Lakota or non-Indian viewers with dry eyes during the course of the production.

Utmost Faith

I have the utmost faith in the director, Richard Heffron, and location producer, Paul Freeman. They realized from the outset that there were objections from the Indian people about this movie, and when they became actively involved, they set out to find out what was causing the turmoil, and then they corrected the problems.

From past experience, I know that Indian people have a hard time agreeing upon anything 100 percent. I certainly respect the rights of those who disapprove of this movie, and I hope they respect my right to approve of it.

There is one thing I reaffirmed in my mind while doing some of the research on the script. Oftentimes, if you ask five Lakota people one question about the authenticity of a certain event, you get five different answers. It has been my job to correlate these answers, and to put them into perspective.

Preview of TV Mini-Series Goes Welll

Getting lost on a Los Angeles, California freeway at night in a blinding, driving rainstorm, in a rented car with bad windshield wipers, pushed along by what seemed to be 10,000,000 motorists driving with the "pedal to the metal" will age you considerably. This "white-knuckle" experience is what stress is all about.

At the behest of movie producer David Wolper, my wife, Doris, and yours truly flew from the relative tranquility of the Pine Ridge Reservation to the wet, smoggy and mad confines of LA to view the rough cut screening of *The Mystic Warrior*, an ABC mini-series taken from the book, *Hanta Yo*, by Ruth Beebe Hill.

This was my fourth trip to Los Angeles in connection with my work as "script consultant" to the producer. Over the past two years I had become very close to the script and to the many fine people involved in the production. Because I needed a sounding board, an impartial point of view, and an unbiased critic to let me know if all the good things I felt about the production had merit, I asked Doris to come along. A Lakota woman with a sixth sense of knowing a good story from a bad one, and a woman with the courage of her convictions, I knew that she would not mince words about this movie production.

As we entered our motel room, Doris exhaled with delight as she darted about the room looking at the beautiful bouquet of flowers, a basket of mixed fruit, and a basket full of nuts. A card, attached to the flowers, from producer Paul Freeman, welcomed Doris to sunny California. A bottle of California champagne, chilling in a bucket of ice, beckoned from a corner table.

Early the next morning we met with Freeman at his office in "the glass building" at Warner Brothers, and braved the intermittent rain squalls to get across Warner Boulevard to the screening room. Producer Freeman told us that we were the only people not working directly with the post-production of the film, to be allowed a special screening. Producers Wolper and Stan Margulies had seen the rough cuts the day before.

The screening room itself was like a mini-theatre with captain's chairs. It was equipped with chrome, floor ashtrays and clipboards with lights attached for note taking. Freeman explained to us that the music was temporary as the musical score had not been written as yet. He said there was some editing to be done and the lights and darks had to be corrected in the film itself. He also explained that the "optics" or special effects had not been added, but he would tell us which scenes would contain these effects.

The mini-series is a five-hour production. It will, in all probability, air on ABC this fall. It would have caused considerable strain to the eye and the posterior to sit through five solid hours. We viewed the first three hours in the morning and then broke for lunch. David Wolper joined us and took us to the dining room on the lot of Warner Brothers for lunch. He questioned us about our reactions to the film and was pleased to see that we both enjoyed the first three hours immensely.

On a previous trip to Los Angeles, I had met, and had dinner with, Ruth Hill and Chunksa Yuha, the Dakota man who had interpreted much of the material for *Hanta Yo*. I must admit that I was reluctant to visit with them because of the adverse publicity they had received, but my curiosity as a journalist overcame my trepidation.

Mrs. Hill has spent thirty years of her life researching the book and during those years had become very close to many elders of the Lakota and Cheyenne people. She named a few of the elders she had worked with in compiling statistics for the novel and I was delighted to discover that each and every one of these elders had nothing but the deepest respect for Mrs. Hill and Chunksa Yuha.

Chunksa, himself, is a Dakota man nearing eighty years of age. He is a modest, softspoken, yet eloquent Indian man. Speaking with him, I could not help but be a little angry at the disrespect and derision shown to him by some of the urban Indian people who protested this book. True Lakota people do not treat their elders in this manner. Chunksa is a true linguist, well versed in the archaic Dakota. He is the grandson of Wapasa, a Mdewakantonwan Dakota.

Mrs. Hill and Chunksa Yuha have been much maligned by those who have never met them or taken the trouble to sit down and speak with them. In Ruth Hill I found a woman who had the deepest respect for the Lakota people. She said, "There are no finer people on the face of this planet than the Lakota people. It has been one of the greatest pleasures and experiences of my life to have met so many of them and to have shared their meals and slept in their lodges."

After viewing the final two hours of the movie, Paul Freeman, his beautiful wife, Barbara, and their precocious son, Michael, took Doris and me out for dinner. We discussed our meeting earlier in the day with Wolper, and went over some of the changes suggested by Doris and me for the movie. It was at this dinner that Paul drew the easy map to get us back to our motel in Burbank which culminated in our getting lost.

Paul and I were both dying to know what Doris thought of the film but we both hesitated to ask, hoping that she would volunteer the information. She didn't. Finally, in desparation, Paul asked, "Well, Doris, what did you think of the production? I know how I felt about it. I thought it is the best movie production ever done on Indians." Doris thought for a minute, and then said, "It makes you proud to be an Indian."

Producer Paul Freeman's eyes lit up like two Roman candles.

Radio and Television
Prejudice Shows in Lack of News Coverage

Does the local news media (newspapers, television and radio) contribute to the erroneous impressions of Indian reservations in this state? Are Indian people inadvertently singled out, and identified as "Indian" in crime-related stories?

In answering the second question, I would have to say that in many cases it appears to be an unavoidable fact of news reporting that Indians involved in criminal activities stand out like sore thumbs. First of all, if they have a name that is obviously Indian, they are immediately identified as Indian. Secondly, if they are involved in an incident which requires medical treatment, they are usually taken to the Soo San (Rapid City Sioux Sanitorium), and this also serves to identify them as Indian. And thirdly, if they are involved in an accident which takes place in Lakota Homes district of Rapid City, this also serves to single them out as Indian.

Each and every time a crime is committed on any of the reservations, or if the perpetrator of the crime is identified as being from one of the reservations, the fact is clearly established that an Indian was involved. Granted, much of this background data is essential to the story, but not all of it.

According to Debbie Condit Calvert of KTOQ Radio, "I don't think that the Indian people are being given a fair shake by the local news. It just seems to me that we often create an image of the Indian which is not true. She added, "Too often, we pick up stories off the wire service, and repeat them, without really knowing the source, or checking the accuracy."

Debbie feels that the local media could do a lot to improve the race relationships between Indians and non-Indians if they would try to do more stories of a positive nature. "I'm sure that there are a lot of good new stories," Debbie concluded, "stories that deal with good things that are happening on the reservations or in the Indian community. We have to get out and start looking for these things, and not wait for them to come to us."

Here is a case in point. Recently, I had a lengthy conversation with a longtime Rapid City resident, a businesswoman. It should be noted here that she was not an Indian. Our conversation turned to real estate. She asked, "Do you think that you will be buying a home in the Rapid City area in the near future?" I replied, "No, my wife and I are considering building a home in my home town, at Kyle." The lady had sort of a puzzled expression on her face, and she said, "Isn't that very dangerous? I mean, isn't there an awful lot of crime on the reservation?"

Of course I asked where she had formulated this idea. She replied, quite seriously, "Well, that's all you ever read about, or see on television, I mean, about all the crime, murders and things, so I just assumed that it was a terrible place to want to live."

Case in point No. 2: There is a non-Indian gentleman I know who drives a delivery truck to various and sundry places on the Pine Ridge Reservation. He said to me, "I always enjoy reading your column because I think it shows us a side to the Indian people that you don't see in the local press." He continued, "For instance, whenever any white person finds out that I make my living by delivering goods on the reservation, they are really shocked. They can't understand why I am not afraid to go down there." He wanted to make one thing very clear when he said, "Most of the people I meet on the reservation are the nicest people you'll find anywhere in the world. In fact, I feel safer on the reservation than I do in Rapid City."

Jim Carrier, News Editor of the *Rapid City Journal*, feels that, "There is a lack of sensitivity to the differences between Indians and non-Indians, and I believe that this is an area that we at the *Journal* have long neglected." He continued, "There seems to be a history of distrust by Indians of the power structure which controls the press. I think that we need more Indians to report on the news and in this way, we can get more of a first-hand point of view, because it is really hard to get the news by remote control. In fact, it just doesn't work."

"When I attended a seminar on journalism at Wolf Creek School in Pine Ridge," Carrier stressed, "one of the first questions I asked was 'How many of you would be interested in a career in journalism?' and not a single hand was raised." He added, "Perhaps, this is because they do not have local access to any media they can relate to, and maybe that's why they haven't developed an interest in this career."

Carrier concluded, "I feel that the reservation should be covered as routinely as Rapid City. We are trying to change. But it is disappointing that some of our news efforts on Indians, whether on the death of a fifteen-year-old or a change in leadership at the Rapid City Indian Service Council, have met with almost as much criticism as good comments."

The news media in Oakland, California, a city with a 50 percent black population, got together and held a series of sensitivity seminars for newsmen and black and other minority people in order to correct a bad situation. I'll never forget a remark made by Huey P. Newton as he addressed the various news reporters: "If you want to get a good look at unconscious prejudism, check your Sunday newspaper society pages." He admonished,

"How many black faces do you see? Don't you think that blacks ever have weddings?"

News Media Should Reflect All Segments of Population

"I would have to say that our coverage of Indian news is adequate, in comparison to what we do on any other specific group," volunteered Marci Christensen, news director of KEVN-TV. "It would be very difficult for us to devote a lot of time to this because we are a small station, only five years old, and we really don't have the finances yet," she added.

Marci stressed, "We are probably lacking in the area of insight into the problems of Indian people, but then so are most of the other forms of media in this area, and this makes it difficult to know what really goes on behind the scenes in Indian affairs. But even when we do a lot of Indian news, we are sometimes criticized by non-Indians for having too much on Indians."

This sounds like a good spot to place the old cliche: "Damned if we do and damned if we don't."

"When we do stories on water rights or on the Black Hills Claim," Marci emphasized, "these are stories that should be of interest to all of the people of South Dakota, not just the Indian people, because everyone is involved. But these stories are very depressing to the non-Indian population and they just don't want to hear them."

Once again we must deal with "insight" or "sensitivity" as regards Indian people. Last week a movie called *Trial of Billy Jack* aired on KEVN. The promotion for this feature mentioned the "half-Indian" star. I spoke with Joy Benson of KEVN and asked her this question: "If the star of *Billy Jack* had been half-French or Greek, would this fact have been pointed out in the promotion?" She answered, "Probably not." It seems that the promotion had been done by CBS and had not been checked for content before airing. An oversight or a lack of sensitivity? Probably a little bit of both, but nonetheless, very objectionable.

In fairness to the media, the Bureau of Indian Affairs is as guilty as anyone for promoting this stereotyped image of the American Indian. Blood quantum played an important role in establishing enrollment for the different Indian tribes, and so the terms "full-blood," "half-breed," and "quarter-breed" were hung upon the Indian people, and their use encouraged. Have you ever heard a pure-blood German refer to himself as a "full-blood" or a half-French-half-Irish called a "half-breed?"

Orville Salway (Paha Ska) works in Keystone, posing with tourists and their children for photographs. Attired in his native costume, with headdress and war paint, he is a fearsome sight. He said to me, "There are many, many white children who are really frightened of me. One time I reached for this young boy in order to sit him on my horse for a picture, and he became hysterical with fear."

Where have these children developed this terrible fear of the Red Man?

Probably the worst culprit of them all in demeaning Indian people is the grade B Western movie. Many of these dime-a-dozen Westerns, mass-produced in Hollywood by movie moguls with little or no understanding of the Indian people, are being re-run on TV to show to a new generation of children. These movies promoted racial prejudice in the past, and they are serving up the same pap of misconceptions, causing the vicious cycle of ignorance to continue unabated.

Recently, the ABC news program, "Nightline," did a special show on the Black Hills Claims Settlement. Attorney General Mark Meierhenry appeared in behalf of the State of South Dakota. Vine Deloria, Jr., a Standing Rock Sioux (and attorney) appeared in behalf of the Oglala Sioux Tribe. What is wrong with this? First of all, Vine Deloria was selected by ABC because he is "nationally known," never mind that he has not been a participant in preparing the case for the tribe, and had no knowledge of the information contained in the tribe's legal briefs. Secondly, Deloria resides in Tucson, Arizona and is pretty far removed from this case.

Louis Bad Wound of the Lakota Treaty Council reacted to this by asking, "If ABC was looking for "nationally known" figures, why didn't they get F. Lee Bailey to represent the State of South Dakota on this show?" He answered his own question with, "Because F. Lee Bailey didn't know a damned thing about the state's case, and from our point of view, neither did Vine Deloria know anything about our case." He added, "It would have been unthinkable for ABC to use this sort of logic with any other minority in the country."

One comment made by Marci Christensen is memorable because it smacks of dreamers with their heads conveniently immersed in Utopia.

She said, "When I interview employees, I never notice whether they are men, women or Indians: I only consider their qualifications." It is this kind of illogical logic that has proven to be the biggest barrier for Indians interested in breaking into the television news business and has made a complete farce of affirmative action and added a new meaning to the word, "sensitivity."

Whenever I have an occasion to visit Washington, D.C., San Francisco, California or Albuquerque, New Mexico, I cannot help but be amazed at how the nightly television newscasters reflect the racial mixture of the community. According to the Census Bureau, Indians make up 14 percent of the population of western South Dakota. It is projected that by the year 2000, this will increase to almost 30 percent.

It is my belief that the news media must begin to reflect this segment of the population now, not somewhere in the distant future. The Indian people are asking to become participants and not continue to be considered outside observers. The message is quite clear: "Communications is the key to understanding, and sensitivity is the door."

Tribes Make Gains in Communications

The movement to improve communications on Indian reservations began in earnest about 1970. Many tribes began to establish or improve upon existing newspapers; but the real venture into mass communications was in the efforts made by several tribes to bring radio stations to their reservations.

Radio stations on Indian reservations is a story unto itself, and I will not go into that subject in this particular column, but instead, I will in the next few columns, attempt to explain why so many Indian tribes felt it necessary to establish their own radio stations.

Some tribes brought the outside world a little closer by bringing cable television to their communities. One tribe that is in the process of doing this is the Navajo Nation.

Paul Haws is employed by NCC Systems, Inc., a subsidiary of the Great Southwest Telephone Corporation of Grandview, Texas. His firm is working through its Washington, D.C. attorney, Dean Hill, to get a "waiver request" approved by the Federal Communications Commission that will allow the firm to proceed with the program of bringing cable television to many of the remote communities on the vast Navajo Reservation.

Tremendous Undertaking

"When we were first approached by the Navajo Tribe, we figured that it was a tremendous undertaking," Haws said, "but, we decided that it was a worthwhile project and even though no other company the tribe approached would consider doing it, we decided to give it our best effort."

Tuba City is the only major community on the reservation that the NCC Systems will not serve. A cable firm called Individeo, Inc. has the franchise to bring cable to Tuba City and it has been bringing programs out of Phoenix, Arizona to that community. The franchise agreement between the Navajo Tribe and the NCC Systems, Inc. stipulated that they would not attempt to go into Tuba City.

According to Haws, there was only one petition of protest filed against having the waiver request approved. "Under federal law a telephone company such as the Navajo Communications Company is prohibited from having a cable system also, and that is why we had to file a petition with the FCC to get this ruling waived," Haws stated. "Apparently this company, called the National Cable Television Association, felt that our franchise gave us too many communities or was too broad, so they filed a petition opposing our request," Haws surmised.

Receiver Near Shiprock

Each major community on the reservation will have a "head-in" or "earth receiver" (dish) to receive the signal from the four Albuquerque channels. The main receiver will be located on the top of Ruth Butte, a 10,000-foot mountain southwest of Shiprock in New Mexico.

Haws continued: "Right now, we are negotiating with Home Box Office and Showtime to see if we can come up with equitable agreements to bring this sort of entertainment to our cable customers. We feel that there should be special consideration given to the people who are located in such isolated and sparsely populated areas as you find on the Navajo Reservation.''

If the release is given within the next few weeks by the Federal Communications Commission, there is a possibility that the cable system can be installed and operable in Window Rock and Fort Defiance by the end of this year.

The financial returns to the Navajo Tribe will be three percent of the amount collected from the cable customers.

"Right now, the bottleneck is at the FCC in Washington, D.C.," Haws concluded. "And, as soon as they give us the go ahead, we will start to roll.''

Better Business Practices Would Benefit State and Tribe

The possibility of a fulltime CBS television station in Rapid City, South Dakota—being proposed by Midcontinent Broadcasting of Sioux Falls, and being watched closely by KOTA-TV and KEVN-TV—is also interesting to the people of the Pine Ridge Reservation.

Under the proposal, a UHF television translator would repeat the signal from KPLO-TV in Reliance, South Dakota.

The concept of a UHF frequency in Rapid City to carry CBS programming was first suggested in a proposal to the FCC in 1978 by the Oglala Sioux Broadcasting Company, a tribal enterprise. While the tribe was applying for an allocation of UHF-22 for the reservation, it was also considering applying for UHF-15 in Rapid City to serve the reservation as a satellite station.

Tribal officals talked to CBS Network affiliate executives about such a possibility, and the CBS people were very receptive to the idea.

On September 29, 1979, UHF-TV frequency Channel 22 was awarded to the Pine Ridge Reservation. Several funding sources were available for constructing and equipping a very modern facility at Allen, Pass Creek District, on the reservation. Unfortunately, for the people of the reservation, this very attainable project, a first for Indian tribes in this country, was delayed indefinitely by tribal politics.

There are several people on the Pine Ridge Reservation who have been working very quietly, behind the scenes, to keep this project alive. Tribal Attorney Mario Gonzalez has worked with the divisive factions in an effort to patch up the differences and to "get on with a vital project."

For a long time, his pleadings fell on deaf ears. But there is a strong possibility that his fence-mending will succeed and that the television project will begin anew in the next few months.

If tribal officials can unite behind this project, the next step for the tribe would be to complete the ascertainment studies required by the Federal Communications Commission, and then file an application for a license to construct and operate a television station.

A project that was "scoffed at" as impossible by many critics, is, indeed, a very strong reality.

Costs of Lawsuits

In my article of last week I wrote about the jurisdictional struggles that are taking place between states and tribes across this country. An interesting question was posed to me by an employee of the legal office regarding this. He asked, "Have the tax-conscious people of the State of South Dakota ever stopped to figure out how much money is being spent to take tribal governments to court month after month? Do they realize that it is their tax dollars that are being spent?"

One case that involved jurisdiction cost the citizens of this state $20,000, according to William Janklow, as quoted in the *Rapid City Journal* on March 9, 1978. The case was Oliphant vs. Suquamish Indian Tribe.

Another case that has drawn fire from all sides is the one involving licensing of businesses to do business on the reservation without a proper license. C. Hobart Keith, former tribal judge, brought the case against the various businesses this year. If one would sweep away all of the muck and mire, and just look at the issue, set personalities aside and review the facts, it is a very valid legal question. Most businesses must acquire a license to operate in a city, county or state. These licenses provide revenues for the licensing agency. Why should the Oglala Sioux Tribe not do likewise?

Skilled Help Needed for Tribal Stations

The problems that most Indian tribes are experienceing in attempting to establish tribally-owned radio stations on their reservations are varied.

Skilled technicians with First Class FCC licenses are a rarity; and locating engineers to assist in the initial planning, constructing and equipping of the facilities has often meant bringing help from outside the reservation at great expense to the tribe.

However, bringing a radio station to an Indian reservation that can help bridge the vast communications gap between the tribal government and the grassroots people who reside far out in the chapters of the districts, has proven to be well worth the investment.

What about finding qualified broadcasters to staff the station after it goes on the air? Most tribes are determined to have members of their respective tribes fulfill the duties of on-air personnel and have undertaken different training programs that would provide these trained Native Americans.

Papago Experience

In square miles, the Papago Reservation located in Southwestern Arizona, is the second largest Indian reservation in the United States. Because of its vast size and scattered, sparsely populated districts, communication is almost nonexistant between the government in Sells, Arizona and the people in the outlying area. Tribal government officials began a step-by-step program to solve this problem.

They worked out a Department of Interior contract with the University of Arizona to train four Papago students at the university's KUAT station in the fundamentals of broadcasting, production and management. Three of the original four students made it through the yearlong course and during the training period, began broadcasting a weekly radio show from KUAT to the Papago Reservation. Two brothers, Mel and Dennis Ortega, and a very tenacious young woman named Berni Felix now form the backbone of the crew that will soon staff the radio station that is in the planning stages for the Papago Tribe of Arizona.

Up on the Rosebud Reservation in South Dakota, radio station KINI went on the air in 1978. In the Lakota language, KINI means "new beginning."

Father Joseph Gill, a Jesuit priest assigned to St. Francis Mission at Rosebud, was the prime mover behind the project. By a quirk of fate, a mission benefactor, Mrs. Aileen A. Van Skike, died and left a will giving enough money to St. Francis Mission to construct the radio station. This badly needed money materialized at the very moment Father Gill had exhausted his last possibility for funding.

First Class License

Program director for KINI Radio is Lorna Smith, a Rosebud Sioux, who graduated from Brown Institute of Broadcasting in Minneapolis, Minnesota and carries a First Class FCC License.

KINI begins its broadcast day at 7 a.m. each day with a recording of the Sioux National Anthem and at the top of each hour, news is broadcast in Lakota and then in English.

When KINI first went on the air, there were very few FM radios to be found on the reservation. But after the initial acceptance of the station, long lines could be found at the department stores in Winner, South Dakota, fifty miles northeast of the reservation, formed by people from Rosebud who were purchasing FM radios.

As I stated earlier, the problems confronting Indian tribes attempting to secure FCC licenses to construct radio stations are many, and I will go into this in the next column.

Tribal Runners Supplanted by News Media

The Papago Reservation is located on the extreme southcentral section of Arizona on the arid Sonoran Desert. Although the population is smaller than that of the Pine Ridge Reservation, the land mass within its borders makes it the second largest reservation in the United States (The Navajo Nation is the largest.).

Four young Papagos had a dream. They wanted to improve the communications on their vast reservation. The four, Mona Jose, Bernie Felix and Dennis and Mel Ortega, started by getting a weekly radio show on station KUAT-TV, Tucson, Arizona called "Desert Voices" which enabled them to broadcast news and public service announcements to the reservation community. This weekly broadcast was the forerunner of the radio station they planned to construct for the O'Odham people (the traditional name of the Papago Tribe).

In order to keep the tribal people informed about the progress of their project they began to prepare and distribute a letter which they called *The Papago Telecommunications Newsletter.*

Their October, 1979 *Newsletter* said it best: "The environment, animals and people, need to communicate in order to survive. Every day birds and animals communicate among themselves by the sounds they make. The seasons (spring, summer, fall and winter) of the year, the wind, sun, moon and stars talk to us in different ways through air, heat, rainstorms and eclipses."

The newsletter continued, "One of the main forms of communications is talking, whether in Papago, Spanish or English. Therefore, one of the many ways to improve and preserve the knowledge of our O'Odham ways and traditional culture is through communications." This ability to communicate is found in many lifestyles, whether at home, in the office, at district meetings or at tribal ceremonies."

The *Newsletter* continued: "The work of this project is to help the people, tribal departments, and the tribal council improve and increase their current means of communications. The immediate goal of the project is improving communications by utilizing equipment already available on the reservation. The long-range goal of the project is to build a radio station on the reservation. The dream for the future can only come true if the people, the tribal leaders and the project members communicate with each other in order to do what is best for everyone."

Because of the perseverance of these four visionaries, the radio station is no longer a dream, but is becoming a reality. The Papago Tribe acknowledged their support by providing funds, office space and logistical support for the telecommunications project. The overall funding to construct and equip the radio station has been provided by the Economic Development Administration.

Modern methods of communications are only a part of the many changes that are taking place in Indian Country. From Arizona to South Dakota, survival of the tribes is the common goal. Just as the ancient tribal runners used to carry messages from village to village in order to keep the people informed, tribally-owned radio and television stations will replace those runners.

I have had the pleasure of working with the four young Papagos as an advisor to their project. Their dedication and determination has enabled them to overcome many roadblocks that have been placed in their paths. The progressive nature of their tribal government has been their main source of inspiration.

Bernie Felix, one of the four, spoke for the entire Papago Tribe when she said, "In order for this to have happened, we all had to decide to make it happen, and all of us had to be willing to take an active part in making the dream of a radio station for our people come true."

Navajos Planning for Radio-TV Use

Over the past few days, my columns have dealt with the efforts by the various Indian tribes in this country to bring mass communications to the reservations by applying to the Federal Communications Commission for licenses to operate tribally-owned radio stations.

It is a complex situation because of the relationship of Indian tribes to the federal government; but many of the projects are succeeding beyond the wildest dreams of the tribal innovators in spite of the many roadblocks strewn in their path by an over-protective bureaucracy.

The Navajo Nation is preparing itself for the eventual construction of radio stations in quite a different way. Nora Amasa Louis is the executive director of the Navajo Film and Media Commission located in Window Rock, Arizona. She holds a bachelor's degree in communications from Brigham Young University and has extensive experience in the fields of radio-television broadcast and broadcast management.

She is an attractive young woman who is fluent in her native Navajo and is very optimistic that the Navajo Nation is on the threshold of some exciting breakthroughs in the area of communications. "We hope that in the very near future we will be able to form a 'Navajo Mass Communications Center' on the reservation," Louis emphasizes, "which will bring all communication matters under one umbrella."

Radio Network

Within the Navajo Film and Media Commission is the Navajo Nation Radio Network. A prodution facility at the NFMC office in Window Rock allows the tribe to tape news broadcasts and keep the people informed of upcoming events. The tapes are distributed to nine radio stations located in towns that border the reservation (Gallup, Farmington, Flagstaff, etc.) and are a part of that station's daily programming. The broadcasts are entirely in the Navajo language.

Recently, two floor-model, black and white TV cameras were donated to the Navajo Tribe by CBS. According to Lewis, "There are a few adjustments and equipment repairs that must be made before the television production becomes a reality; but this is being done and we hope to be able to produce our Navajo Nation Report at this facility in the near future."

Presently, the Navajo Nation Report is broadcast on two stations.

The NFMC was organized in 1971 to regulate and monitor the movie companies that visited the reservation. "There is one important thing that I should mention," Louis concluded. "It is important that people from the movie and television industry who wish to film or tape on the Navajo Reservation stop at our offices in Window Rock and get a permit to do so; and there is a fee for the premit which begins at $50."

Reservation Radio Funding Important

Thus far, every Indian tribe that has filed a petition with the Federal Communications Commission for radio stations had opted to go with non-commercial status. This has presented them with the very real problem of obtaining financing through governmental agencies, such as the Economic Development Administration or with the Bureau of Indian Affairs. It is very difficult to get funded by private lending institutions when you are operating a tribally-owned, non-profit corporation.

Once the funding has been secured to equip and construct a station, the battle to get on the air has just begun. Each and every year, the tribe must find different sources to finance the day-to-day operation of the station. Some of the very large tribes can include the radio station on their annual budget; but even those tribes that are able to do this find that operating a radio station is an expensive proposition and can create quite a drain on the financial resources of the tribe.

One possible solution to the funding problem would be for the FCC to allow Indian tribes to operate their facilities as profit-non-profit organizations. This would allow tribes to seek out funding through federal agencies and foundations as usual; but it would also permit them to solicit advertisers in the towns that border the reservations.

Increasing Sales

There are many towns bordering Indian reservations that do a very large percentage of their business with customers from the reservations and it has been my experience that many of the businesses in these towns would be more than happy to advertise on Indian-owned stations as a means of increasing retail sales.

When you consider that Reservation Indians often spend millions of dollars annually in border towns for trucks, automobiles, furniture, appliances, groceries, etc., it would make good sound business sense to be able to reach these potential customers with advertising that will bring them into one's place of business. What better way to do this than on a radio station that is located on the reservation and reaches large numbers of the reservation inhabitants?

The difficulty in getting this point across to the commissioners of the FCC is that you are dealing with a Washington, D.C. based bureaucracy that believes one rule should fit all situations. Also, other radio stations that are not located on reservations may feel that since they were not given any special consideration, Indian tribes should be treated similarly.

If you consider that any revenue garnered by profit-non-profit reservation radio stations would reduce the amount of federal dollars necessary to support such a venture, it becomes obvious that fewer dollars would come out of the taxpayers' pocket.

Tribal Politics

Tribal politics has also played an important role in hampering the tribes in the development of radio stations. On reservations where there are diverse opinions and radical political differences, the warring factions have often been their own worst enemies.

One tribal offical on the Pine Ridge Reservation in South Dakota commented recently, "If you took a member of the American Indian Movement and a member of the tribal council into different rooms, and listened to each one separately about the things they are attempting to do to help their own people, you would probably find that they are both saying the very same thing; the only difference would be in the methods they use to achieve these things."

As more and more Indian tribes acquire radio stations (There are approximately twelve tribally-owned radio stations at this time.), they eliminate one other major problem: the lack of expertise in dealing with the Federal Communications Commission. Many of its confusing rules and regulations were designed for the urban or metropolitan areas or for wealthy business corporations and not comparatively poor Indian tribes located on reservations who are trying to form a better life for themselves through communications.

Radio Deregulation under Consideration

The Federal Communication Commission is considering a petition filed by the broadcast industry to "deregulate" radio. The petition has run into strong opposition from church groups and minorities.

Deregulation means that there would be no restrictions placed upon radio stations in the number of commercials they could air in a broadcast hour. It also means that serving the needs of the community would be at the discretion of the radio station. A station could eliminate all religious or minority programming if it chose to do so.

At the present time, any group that wishes to apply for a license for a radio or television station must submit to the FCC a study on the makeup of the community it serves, and of the special needs of the community. This is accomplished by meeting with different segments of the community such as farmers, ranchers, unions, colleges, minorities, etc., and setting up a list of priorities known as the "Ascertainment Requirement."

Percentages List

FCC regulations require that once this list of priorities or "Ascertainment List" has been established, a certain portion of the broadcast day, week or month, must be utilized to fulfill that requirement. This is usually done by breaking down the list and establishing the percentage each segment makes up within the community. For instance, farmers, 60 percent; miners, 20 percent; Indians, 15 percent, etc., is the method that is used by many radio and television stations. Once this list has been established and approved by the FCC, it must be adhered to because it is one of the regulations requiring fulfillment before a license will be granted to any group or individual for a radio or television station.

Now here is the kicker: if a group within the community feels that it is being neglected by the broadcast facility, and it has made a concerted effort to remedy the situation without success, it can file a petition with the FCC requesting that the station's license be revoked at license renewal time.

This might appear to be an insurmountable task, but it has been attempted and successfully accomplished. Several years ago, in Jackson, Mississippi, a group of black people began a campaign to get more programming to serve the very large black population of that community. At the same time they attempted to get more black employees hired at the station. Their efforts to sway the station management proved to be futile, and so when the station's license came up for renewal, a petition was filed with the FCC to have it revoked.

Challenge Successful

Not only were they successful in having the license revoked, but they managed to have the license awarded to a group made up of many black people.

These FCC rules and regulations were written to include all radio and television license holders. As more and more Indian tribes file for and are granted licenses to operate radio stations on their reservations, they will find that this is not a one-way street. The same rules and regulations will be applied to them. In other words, if an Indian tribe is granted a license to operate a radio station on a reservation, it must serve all of the people of that reservation or its license can be challenged by any group residing on that reservation that feels that it is being excluded from the station's programming.

Reverse Discrimination

There have been rumors that Hispanic radio and television stations that broadcast entirely in the Spanish language will be challenged in a reverse discrimination case, much like the Bakke case in which the Supreme Court abolished the quota system in medical schools. A broad interpretation of the FCC ascertainment requirements makes this a distinct possibility.

I do not want to be an alarmist. I am merely suggesting that any Indian tribe that files for a license to operate a radio station consider this possibility when it schedules its daily programming so that it is not guilty of doing the very thing that has been done to many Indian people by other broadcast facilities for so many years. Two wrongs will never make a right.

Editorial Discretion Needed;
Government Has Cake and Eats It, Too

Where do editors draw the line on what is news and what is not? On May 13, 1981 a front page article by Gordon Johnson, a staff writer for the *Rapid City Journal*, displayed a picture of a 1974 Jaguar which was to be used by the Bureau of Indian Affairs for undercover drug operations. By running this story, the *Journal* effectively negated the usefulness of the vehicle.

The detailed story went on to tell where the vehicle would be used and for what purpose it had been purchased. Many residents of the several reservations in South Dakota who read that article were incensed. They know that the drug problems on the reservations have been growing with each passing year and they would like to see more stringent law enforcement efforts undertaken to help solve this situation. Were these very concerned Indian people taken into consideration when the news editor made the decision to go with the story?

Coincidentally, the very next day, the *Journal* front page blared out the headlines of a major drug bust resulting in the arrest of more than twenty drug dealers. The bust was the culmination of several weeks of effort by many city, state and county law enforcement agencies who had worked undercover, in many instances, to bring about this major bust.

The reservation residents are asking these questions. Would the *Journal* have published the pictures of the undercover vehicles being used by the law agencies involved in this drug operation? If so, what would the official and public reaction have been? Did the fact the vehicle is being used by Indian law enforcement officers on distant reservations influence the news editor and the reporter involved to proceed with the story? Printing the angry reaction of BIA official Loren Farmer in the article hardly excuses the lack of responsibility exhibited by the news editor.

If an article is going to hamper the efforts of law and order, cancel a planned undercover operation, and endanger the lives of the officers assigned to carry out the operation if the BIA proceeds, is not editorial discretion essential to fair play and journalistic responsibility?

Having Your Cake and Eating It, Too

The U.S. government decided it wanted the Black Hills of South Dakota because of the wealth located therein. After the tribes of the Great Sioux Nation annihilated George Armstrong Custer and the Seventh Cavalry at Little Big Horn, the Congress of the United States was inflamed with anger. They acted swiftly and decisively, for one of the few times in their history, and illegally confiscated several million acres of land from the tribes of the Great Sioux Nation.

They hardly expected the tribes to hire attorneys and to fight for the return of the land. Faced with this unexpected turn of events, the federal government, totally disregarding the provisions of its own constitution—"land can only be taken for public purposes, with due process of law, and just compensation must be provided" as written in the Fifth Amendment—, attempted to block the tribes from legally protesting this illegal act by refusing to give them a means to be heard.

For more than 100 years, the Sioux tribes fought tenaciously for the return of the land. The U.S. government held all of the cards. It set the price per acre it wanted to pay for the land; it refused to allow for any compensation other than monetary; and it provided the court systems and the judges to hear the claims of the Sioux tribes.

The U.S. Supreme Court finally ruled that the land had been taken illegally, and awarded $17 million for the land's value in 1877, and $88.4 million for interest accrued at five percent for 103 years.

One tribe, the Oglala Sioux Tribe, refuses to take the money awarded and wants the return of the land. It challenged the rights of attorney Arthur Lazarus to represent it, claiming his contract had expired in 1977, three years before the ruling.

Now, to add insult to inujry, the U.S. Court of Claims has awarded Lazarus and his Washington, D.C. law firm $10.6 million in attorney's fees for representing the tribes of the Sioux Nation.

The Sioux tribes have had to fight their legal battle in the government's back yard, play the game by their rules, accept whatever they wanted to give them, and pay one-tenth of any money awarded to them to an attorney they had to hire to get back the land the government admitted was taken illegally by themselves in the first place. Now that's what I call having your cake and eating it, too!

'Public Affairs' Air Time FCC-Required

There is an Indian man hosting a television show near a large reservation who is identified by his peers as "assimilated." His television shows reflect this assimilation and, according to his detractors, are programmed for a white audience.

He is further accused of ignoring the issues that are pertinent but controversial, and concentrating on "artsy-crafty" or "Christian oriented" types of shows which do not reflect the attitudes of the majority of Indians living on the nearby reservations or in the urban communities the television station serves.

After tolerating this TV show for the past two years, several reservation residents decided they had reached the end of their patience. They had said nothing for such a long time because they hoped that the show would change, and also because they were afraid of losing the only show on television in their part of the state.

Finally, a committe was formed and a petition began circulating on the reservation requesting that this show which "does not reflect the sentiment or cultural values of our people" be removed from the air.

Prefers None

One petitioner said, "I would rather have no show at all on the air, than to have one that distorts our views and is an insult to our intelligence as Indian people."

The issue is far from being settled, and the reservation residents are hoping for a meeting with the general manager of the TV station so they will be able to give their views and air their complaints. There is even talk of boycotting the sponsors of this station if their demands are not discussed and if drastic changes are not made or if the offensive show is not removed from the air.

Programs such as the one under attack are carried on television stations as "public affairs" programs. They are usually carried by the station to fulfill certain requirements of the Federal Communications Commission called "ascertainment requirements," usually to meet the special needs of a minority or special segment of the community.

No Exception

Every television station operating under an FCC license, and that includes all of them, must broadcast to reflect the racial, cultural, governmental or whatever makeup of their respective viewing audiences. There is no exception to the FCC rule. This regulation is a vital part of the application which each station manager must submit to the FCC before a license will be granted.

Too often, station managers take the easy way out. Rather than take the time to seek out those individuals within the minority commuity who are attuned to the needs of their own people, they install replicas of themselves in these positions designed to broadcast minority shows, and in this manner, they fulfill their obligations to the FCC. One might call this an attitude of "No muss, no fuss."

More Harm

At a time when the Indian people are striving to change the many erroneous attitudes and eradicate the many myths and misconceptions about their own people, these TV shows can do more harm than good.

In reality, they often serve to confuse or confirm foregone conclusions already formulated by a prejudiced majority, rather than define or clarify the realistic point of view.

It is no longer necessary for Indian people to suffer in silence over this form of selective bias. The FCC is trying to stop this practice to the best of its ability, and it is reviewing petitions of complaints in an effort to solve some of those long-standing problems.

The important thing for the Indian people to keep in mind is that television stations and radio stations have an obligation to devote a certain amount of "public affairs" time to different segments of their viewing audience. They do not do these shows out of generosity; but because they are required by law to do so. Don't let any station manager convince you that he is doing you a favor by having any programming on Indians at all because, as I stated, he is only fulfilling his legal obligations.

Complaints may be sent to Federal Communications Commission, 1919 M Street, N.W., Washington, DC 20554 or telephoned to (202) 632-7000.

Newspapers

Column Written to Give Indian Viewpoint

Two years ago, news editor Jim Carrier of the *Rapid City Journal* in Rapid City, South Dakota called me and said he had read an article I had written for the Indian magazine, *Wassaja*. He asked me to come to Rapid City, have lunch with him and discuss the possibilities of doing some form of writing for the *Journal*.

A few weeks later, we got together and discussed a variety of subjects. At the time, we had no idea of how we were going to go about arranging my writing for the *Journal*. Finally, I suggested the idea of writing a weekly column. Jim cautioned me about the extreme difficulty in creating a weekly column and being able to present fresh, new stories every seven days.

Having hosted a weekly television show for almost two years, I knew there was a variety of subjects in Indian Country and all I wanted was the opportunity to present them. This in itself had presented somewhat of a problem in helping Jim make up his mind about using me as a writer. He had checked with some of the people who had been acquainted with me during the time I did the television show called "The First Americans" and several of them had not been too enthusiastic about my writing a regular column.

Television is a demanding format, and too often the host of a television show is identified with his guests. My show had made its debut during the hectic days in 1975 following the death of two FBI agents at Oglala, and the feelings of hate, fear and animosity permeated the reservation. Any guest whose point of view was extreme, either to the left or the right, caused an immediate response from those who chose the middle road, or from those who were opposed to a particular viewpoint.

Hosting and producing a show of the nature of "The First Americans" did not make me a contestant for Mr. Popularity. The old cliche, "damned if you do and damned if you don't," was never more applicable. Many times, the opinions of my guests were mistaken for my own simply because they expressed them on my show. I received many blistering phone calls because of the comments of my guests, or because of the organizations they represented.

Jim and I reached an understanding on this point because it was, and is, a touchy one, but one that is all too familiar to any newsman. The following week my first column, "Notes from Indian Country," began appearing in the *Rapid City Journal*, and more than 100 columns later, it is still a regular feature.

One of the things I promised myself I would never do in my column was to be identified as a "spokesman" for Indians. The Indian people are their own spokesmen, and I have tried to let my columns reflect those opinions. The white man places great stock in "spokesmen" and often identifies any Indian willing to speak out on an issue as "an Indian spokesman."

Another issue I have tried to tackle is the media's habit of giving any Indian willing to stand up on a soap box and pontificate the title of "Indian leader." This has been an uphill battle.

I object to the media selecting an Indian with national views, making a media darling out of him, and then falling all over itself every time their creation opens his mouth. There are elected tribal leaders who represent many thousands of Indians who get little if any news coverage because they are not as colorful or as radical as some of the media Frankensteins.

One question every reporter worth his salt should ask any self-appointed spokesman for the Indian people is, "Who do you represent?" After you ask this question, check out the answer given, and find out who and how many Indians this individual is supposedly representing. Isn't this the standard procedure used when interviewing other non-Indian radical spokesmen?

I am going to repeat something I have said in other columns because I believe it is important. If there is a single reader who can prove to me, and to the Indian people, that the state and federal government are not trying to impose their wills upon Indian people by abolishing treaties and terminating the reservations out of existence, then I will stop writing this column.

But as long as these problems exist in this country, and as long as the editors of the newspapers who carry my column feel that an Indian point of view is needed, I will continue to write.

Perhaps, over the past two years, this column has caused a non-Indian to stop and reflect upon the things I have written about, and in so doing, he has come away with a different point of view. If this column has changed one mind for the better, or has created dialogue between Indian and non-Indian, the reasons for Jim Carrier giving me the opportunity have been justified.

Constructive Criticism Gives Proper Perspective

Perhaps in the process of publishing a weekly newspaper and writing a weekly column from a reservation setting, one has a tendency to allow his thinking to become polarized.

The immediate hardships and needs of the people living on the reservation become the major concern, and although news from an international or national level is included in the weekly menu, the day-to-day concerns of the reservation take precedence over all other forms.

A letter signed by several Lakota residents of Rapid City reminds me of this shortcoming. The writers pointed out my use of the terms "urban Indian" and "diploma Indian." Although the words were not coined by me, they are words that can be taken as offensive.

I wrote the columns in which these terms were used in an effort to describe certain individuals of Indian descent. There are several who fit the descriptions. Fortunately, there are also many Indians living in urban settings,

Doris and Tim Giago set last-minute headlines for **The Lakota Times**

who hold degrees of educational accomplishment, who do not fit into this category.

The use of this terminology makes it appear that I am lumping all of these poeple together, the good along with the bad. I will be the first to admit that generalizing can be harmful, and to those people who signed the letter written to me, I offer my apologies.

Many Indians moving to the cities did so because the opportunities available to them on the reservation were very limited. They moved to pursue a higher education and to seek employment. And there are those who returned to the reservation, Indians with very good educations, who soon became disillusioned by the inefficiency of tribal government and by the grossly exaggerated role played by tribal politics in every facet of everyday life on the reservation.

Many highly skilled people found themselves on the outside looking in after a change in administrations. They disovered that individual politics was more important in securing a job than qualifications. Unable to get a job on the reservation because of adverse politics, many Indians moved to the cities.

It would be well to point out that the people who sent the letter to me are correct in offering constructive criticism about things I have written. Their tendency to include excerpts in their letter of a personal nature accomplish very little.

I will be the first to admit that my life has not been one of perfection. Like the people who signed the letter, I have made many mistakes in the past, and will probably make many more in the future. We should all keep in mind that people have an opportunity to change, and often, the circumstances of their professions dictate that change.

Granted, I have many things to learn about the ways of the Lakota people and about the traditions of the tribe, but I have never professed to be an expert, or a spokesman, for the people of the Pine Ridge Reservation. Each day that I live on the reservation is a learning experience to me. The wisdom offered to me by many of the elders who come into my office each day is accepted in all humility.

Many of the columns I write are but reflections of the opinions and thoughts of the many people I speak with each day. The concerns they bring to me are real. The fears they express are genuine.

Of all the columns I have written, the one that drew the most favorable comment from the people of the reservation was the one I wrote about the "diploma Indian." Many Indians with a coveted diploma agree wholeheartedly with my observations on the subject. Many said, "We have all met those Indians with degrees who look down upon us because we do not have their credentials." This was their opinion based on years of experience. That particular column did not come to me out of the clear blue sky, but through conversations with many Indians.

Differences of opinion are what make the world go round, and all I can do is reiterate the fact that I did not intend that column to be offensive to those hardworking people who pursued higher education. It was intended for those who use their education as a club to advance their own personal ambitions.

If my writings tend to favor the people of the reservations, it is because I have chosen to make the reservation my home. It is where I live now, and by the grace of God, will continue to live for all the days of my life.

I hope I have brought back to the reservation the ability to perform a task that is important to the future wellbeing of the entire tribe. It should go without saying that I was taught the skills of the journalistic profession in the urban centers of this land, but rather than pursue that career in the city, I chose to use these talents to assist the people of the reservation.

A letter such as the one written by the Indians from Rapid City is needed at times to put things in perspective. We must never lose sight of who we are, what we are, where we have been, and where we are going. Constructive criticism can be a great benefit when taken in the right way. It tends to keep things on an even keel.

To my critics, I say: Thank you for keeping me on the straight and narrow.

Column is for Indians First

When you read the columns written by a George F. Will, William Safire, or a Russell Baker, you immediately identify the writer as liberal or conservative. The bottom line is that we realize the columnist is expressing personal opinions he has garnered through years of experience and living.

Many of the newspaper editors who carry my column, "Notes from Indian Country, " refer to the column as "our Indian column." And therein lies the dangerous habit of the national media to categorize opinions into neat little slots. If the columnist is black, for instance, there is the strong possibility of creating a journalistic spokesman for that minority.

To begin with, a columnist of Indian background, born, raised, educated and still residing on an Indian reservation is an extreme rarity. How many others can you name? Although the things I write about are from an advocacy position for Indian thought, rights and problems, I do not consider myself a spokesman for the Indian people.

I am constantly appalled at the total ignorance about Indians that is commonplace in the large society. For instance, in writing my column I am held to using the word "Indian" to identify an ethnic group although that word, in itself, is a misnomer. Traditionally, we referred to ourselves by identifying our tribal affiliation, such as Lakota, Navajo, Nez Perce or Kiowa.

When writing in a much broader concept, especially when a single article might encompass many different Indian tribes, the terms Native American, American Indian, or just plain Indian, then become necessary tools to avoid confusion. I have seen many non-Indian journalists refer to an Indian tribe as, say, Apache. To most Indians the question immediately arises, which Apache Tribe? There are several tribes of Apache background: the Jicarilla, White Mountain, and the Mescalero immediately come to mind.

The same can be said of the word Sioux. This name was put together by the French using a combination of two Algonquin words mixed with Dakota, and used almost exclusively in the beginning by the Ojibwa (Chippewa) and was akin to the word "snake." The people called Sioux identified themselves by the dialects spoken: Lakota, Dakota and Nakota, names meaning "allied." The names were further broken down to identify the tribes within these groups, such as Oglala, Hunkpapa, Miniconjou, etc.

It was this fundamental ignorance so often displayed by the non-Indian through television, movies, and novels that prompted me to write this column as a weekly staple. I hoped that by writing about the Indian in a contemporary setting, or by focusing upon some of the most common misconceptions and stereotypes, I would be able to make a small dent in the national ignorance about Indians.

Finding subjects to write about each week is no problem. There are so many things happening in Indian Country today that, at times, I could write three or four columns per week. The next problem is in trying to write about things that are of interest to a large cross section of readers. I found this to be almost impossible. I decided, early on, to write for an Indian audience. I believed that it was very important that the Indian readers of my column have something in the non-Indian newspaper they could identify with, something they could use as a point of reference.

By the same token, I hoped that non-Indian readers would be curious enough to read my column with an open mind, and even if they vehemently disagreed with the things I wrote about, being intelligent enough to understand that in their Anglo-Saxon world, there is another point of view—the Indian's.

Over the years I have discovered that whenever I have pointed out the tarnish on heretofore sacred cows, the reaction from the non-Indian community has been swift and angry. I see this as a good thing. I see this as a way of opening up a line of communications between the Indian and the non-Indian. Since my column is published primarily in areas with large Indian populations, I believe that dialogue, even from divergent perspectives, is a step in the right direction. Isn't that what communication is all about?

Above all else, I have made it a point to listen to the people of the reservations. I have listened with respect to our elders from many Indian nations, and, hopefully, I have learned. I have listened to the anger and the anguish of our young, and it is through these voices, voices expressing the concerns, fears, dreams, and hopes of the Indian people that I draw my ideas for the subjects I write about.

I have always considered myself to be a sounding board for the voices that have never had forum in the non-Indian media. Go through your newspaper and see how many weekly columns reflect Indian thought and perspective.

Writing a column that is read by thousands is an awesome responsibility. Even though I do not now, nor have I ever, considered myself to be a spokesman for the Indian people, many non-Indian readers will assign me this task. One editor asked me if I felt a sense of loyalty to his newspaper. I replied that my first sense of loyalty was to the Indian people I write about. All else is incidental.

Interests of Tribes Frequently Overlap

While visiting with Carey Vicenti, assistant editor of the *Jicarilla Chieftain*, a newspaper published every other Monday by the tribe, I could not help but notice the shelves on one wall that were stocked with newspapers from national Indian organizations and other tribes. It brought to my mind the fact that the tribal newspapers throughout the United States are faced with the problem of collecting news from other reservations, no matter how often they go to press. One of the quickest and easiest ways to solve this problem is to subscribe to other Indian publications, and use this information to keep your tribal members informed.

National Issues

Our conversation turned to national issues, such as the Supreme Court decision on sales taxes to non-Indians for cigarettes purchased on Indian reservations. This subject, in turn, brought us around to a discussion of the tax rights of Indians. One landmark case that is winding its way to the Supreme Court involves the Jicarilla Apache Tribe, and just as most decisions concerning litigation on Indian lands affect many other Indian tribes, this Jicarilla case will probably set a precedent.

The decision handed down by the Tenth Circuit Court of Appeals states that, "The Jicarilla Apache Tribe of New Mexico has the power to impose a severance tax—a tax on the value of the oil and gas removed—as an inherent aspect of its sovereignty. This right is not diminished by the fact that the state may also be able to tax the resource," ruled the court. One attorney working on the case said, "It's a significant victory because it affirms the right of Indian tribes to tax commercial activities of non-Indians within reservation boundaries."

Mutual Concerns

My conversation with Carey Vicenti reaffirmed the fact that news from one reservation is also very important to most of the other reservations.

There has been a plethora of lawsuits brought by Indian tribes and state governments against each other, or against the federal government, in the past few years. Many of the decisions handed down in these cases have had a profound effect upon the states and the Indian tribes as a whole. In many of these cases, state governments have given moral, as well as financial, support to the states where the litigation was taking place in hopes of influencing the decisions handed down by the high courts, and thereby getting rulings favorable to states' rights.

Not to be outdone, many Indian tribes are now filing writs of amicus curiae (friend of the court) in support of other Indian tribes involved in litigation that could affect their own legal positions. This gives the tribes the opportunity to advise the court in respect to some matter of law that directly affects the case in question.

The discussion between Carey Vicenti and myself pointed out the importance of exchanging information between different tribal governments and building unity between different tribes.

Indian Newspapers

Finding a source that will provide Indian news on a national level is very difficult. As I stated earlier, the only alternative is to subscribe to dozens of tribal newspapers and become a voracious reader in hopes of consolidating all of this digested information into a concise report.

One monthly publication that filled this gap for many years was called *Wassaja*. The word was a Yavapi Apache word meaning "signal" or "beckoning" and was taken from one of the first Indian newspapers published in the United States by Dr. Carlos Montezuma on the Fort McDowell Reservation in Arizona in the early 1900s. Dr. Montezuma was himself a Yavapi Indian and his newspaper, *Wassaja*, ceased publication upon his death in 1928.

In 1930, *Wassaja* was combined with a quarterly magazine published by The Indian Historian Press, Inc. and was renamed *Wassaja—The Indian Historian*. The first issue was delivered in April.

Requests for subscriptions to the magazine can be sent to: The Indian Historian Press, Inc.; 1451 Masonic Avenue; San Francisco, CA 94117. It is a professionally done, well-written magazine that can keep you informed about national Indian happenings.

Erroneous Stories Widely Circulated

A few weeks back, an Associated Press news relese from Denver, Colorado told about the new Secretary of the Interior and some of his plans for the future. He was quoted as saying that he would create a new position called Assistant Secretary of the Interior and this office would work closely with the Indian tribes.

Most Indians know that there already is such a job position and that it is a cabinet level function. And yet, this erroneous story went all over the United States and was corrected by only one newspaper (to the best of my knowledge), and that paper was the Farmington, New Mexico *Daily Times*.

Other newspapers situated deep in Indian Country, such as the Rapid City, South Dakota *Journal*; the Sioux Falls, South Dakota *Argus Leader*; and the Denver *Post*, carried this release without change. The *Times* assumed that it was wrong, attempted to verify this error, and then ran a corrected version in that day's paper. I applaud reporter Scott Sandlin who questioned the AP release, and then did something to correct it.

Guess Work

There is a news service organization known as the Medill News Service based in Washigton, D.C. It has a correspondent by the name of John Legg who writes many articles about Native Americans. This, in itself, isn't bad, but the fact that many of his articles are a patchwork of guess work, and are often blatantly erroneous, is very bad.

Just as the erroneous news release by AP was picked up and run in hundreds of newspapers, so are the articles furnished by Medill News Service. Recently, I was asked by a local newspaper in South Dakota to review one of John Legg's articles, a three-part series on Indian education. By the time I finished making corrections, there was very little left of the original story.

Now my point is this: these articles on Indian education were sent to areas of the country with large Indian populations. How many newspapers actually carried the series? How many readers are now left with false impressions of Indian education because of these stories?

Mohawk Not Lakota

One paragraph of this series by Legg included an interview with a Tom Cook, identified as a Mohawk Indian from New York and a member of the Lakota Treaty Council. Whoa!! If Cook is a Mohawk, he could never be a member of the Lakota Treaty Council because one has to be a Lakota in order to be a member of that council.

This is a small mistake, but I bring it out now because it is one fact that could have been easily checked by a simple phone call. If errors of this type, simple to verify, can become a part of an important series affecting Indian schools and funds to Indian schools, how many major mistakes can be found in the articles? As I have said time and time again, "With friends like this, we sure don't need enemies."

Speaking of Indian education, I would like to review a point which is often overlooked. Senator Edward Kennedy said, "The Constitution and the Supreme Court's interpretation of the equal protection clause clearly permit the redress of Constitutional violences. Separate educational facilities foster inferior education and result in disparate burdens upon certain members of society. The abolition of busing as a remedy would serve, in many instances, to abrogate the guarantees of the 14th Amendment."

Assumption

If one were to assume that protection under the Constitution meant protection for all citizens of the United States, one would have to assume the American Indian would be included within this statement.

Can you imagine the hue and cry which would arise in the Western reservation border cities of this land if Indians suddenly demanded to be included in the school busing because of the inferior educational facilities on reservations?

Fortunately for the federal government, in this instance, Indian people do not want to be bused to the cities to achieve racial balance in school systems near large Indian populations. We only wish to receive equal funds for the improvement of the facilities on the reservations, and for the the training of more Indian teachers to instruct our children.

Paper Ownership Questioned

A situation arose two weeks ago involving the *Navajo Times*, the tribal administration and a question of who owns the newspaper.

Does the tribal administration own the *Navajo Times*, or do the people of the Navajo Nation own it?

I have received letters in the past complaining that the tribal administration believes the *Navajo Times* is a promotional tool for the administration. It has also been said to me that the newspaper will tolerate only one point of view—the tribal government's.

The *Navajo Times* is in the Division of Resources of the tribal government which is headed by Ray Lancer. Much of the money needed to run the paper is gained by newspaper advertising, encouraging the Navajo people to shop at certain places on and off the reservation. It is said by some Navajos that the money accumulated by the Division of Resources is really the people's money since it is drawn from them in several ways. Who does own *The Navajo Times?*

Competence Not Questioned

This column is not intended to question the competence of the *Navajo Times* editor, Jim Largo. He is a professional who cut his teeth on a major, commercial newspaper in Albuquerque and knows what freedom of the press is all about. He has done an outstanding job since taking the helm of the newspaper. However, Jim is a tribal employee, and as such, he must acquiesce to the whims of the tribal administration.

A few weeks back, an informal meeting was called by several tribal officials in Window Rock, Arizona to discuss the contents of the columns carried on the editorial page of the *Navajo Times*. The discussion concerned the possibility of doing away with the columns written by Ray Baldwin Lewis, John Redhouse and Largo. One other column which appears regularly on the editorial page is written by the tribal chairman, Peter MacDonald.

During this "informal meeting" it was decided all columns on the editorial page, except Chairman MacDonald's, would no longer be carried. After much discussion, it was finally decided that the only column to be discontinued by the newspaper would be the one written by John Redhouse.

Administration Critic

Redhouse has been classified as a nonconformist by some tribal officials, and his columns have been critical of the tribal administration. He has been a strong supporter of the Shiprock Chapter's resolution refusing to accept the $14.8 million award for confiscated lands around the Navajo Reservation, and has advocated the policies of the Oglala Sioux Tribe and the Western Shoshones in refusing to accept monetary compensation and, instead, asking for the return of the land.

When discussing the First Amendment of the Constitution of the United States with tribal governmental officials, one can get into some very murky waters. Tribal governments have their own constitutions and, as dependent sovereign nations, they are not restricted to the letter of the U.S. Constitution. Many flag-waving Americans find this hard to believe, and some find it downright heretical.

Nonetheless, this is the way things are on the many Indian reservations of this country. The tribal constitution and the tribal laws, even the traditional laws, are the laws the Indian people follow.

Redhouse is a very gifted writer. Editor Jim Largo has the opinion Redhouse was the finest writer on his staff. His column, "Dissenting Opinion," will no longer be published by the *Navajo Times*. In the name of tribal unity, does the silencing of a critical voice take precedence over the Navajo people's right to know? In an effort to create an atomosphere of harmony on the reservation, is there no room for a different point of view?

Private Enterprise Only Way for Reservation Newspaper

An interesting letter crossed my desk this week. Sent to me by the enterprise manager of another tribe, the letter wanted my views on "tribal management" versus "private management" of a reservation newspaper.

The writer asked about "influence of tribal politics," and "to what degree and how should the tribe be involved if it is a tribal newspaper?"

For one, I firmly believe in the theory that reservation newspapers should be published by Indian persons, preferably members of the tribe where the newspaper is located. I believe that tribal members have much more insight into the affairs of the tribal government, and no outsider could have more in-depth knowledge of the people of a particular reservation than the one who was born and raised on that reservation, and who continues to live there and share the lifestyles and hardships.

Tribal politics, on many reservations are incomprehensible. Because of the power wielded by any incumbent administration to give jobs, housing, and many, many other services, when placed in the wrong hands, tribal government can become a chain around the necks of the grassroots people, or of those who are the real or considered political enemies.

The constitutions of most Indian tribes try to combat the awesome power of each administration by outlining the powers of the tribal council and the chairman. In most cases, if the constitutions are followed religiously, they do contain foundations for a solid tribal government.

It is the nature of most tribal governments to exercise total control over tribal enterprises. If the salaries of a newspaper editor and his staff are being paid by the tribal government, it stands to reason that the newspaper will reflect the views and opinions of those people paying the bills.

The editor of the *South Piegan Drum*, a tribal newspaper of the Blackfeet Tribe of Browning, Montana, found this out the hard way. He reported an incident involving the tribal chairman and a member of the tribe which resulted in physical violence. The editorial was an objective one, giving both sides of the argument.

Coincidentally, it was budget renewal time on the reservation. To no one's great surprise, the *South Piegan Drum* was deleted from the tribal budget, and for all intent and purpose, ceased to exist as a newspaper on the reservation.

On the other hand, there are tribally-owned newspapers such as the *Navajo Times*, with a circulation of more than 14,000 weekly newspapers, which has had several confrontations with the tribal administration, and has gone through several editors in the past few years, but has continued to play an important role on the Navajo Reservation.

Originally designed to return a profit to the Navajo Nation as a tribal enterprise, the *Navajo Times*, with its vast commercial potential, has never really capitalized on the financial opportunities available. Last year, the *Times* showed a $50,000 deficit and the tribal administration fired editor Jim Largo, a Navajo man, and is trying to turn the profit picture around or face the possibility of losing the newspaper altogether.

Despite these negatives, I believe that there can be a successful marriage between a newspaper and the tribal government. Like any marriage, it would require a lot of give and take on the part of the publisher and the tribal administration, but I believe it could work for the mutual benefit of both parties.

For one, the tribe has tremendous financial clout, if it is a large tribe such as the Navajo Nation or the Oglala Sioux Tribe; and if the tribal administration could develop the advertising potential available through the many business people who are willing to return those advertising dollars back to the tribe in exchange for their share of the market, the prospective profits to the tribally-owned newspaper can be quite lucrative.

The problem is that most tribal governments do not realize that it is possible to use the huge financial clout they possess to their own benefit. Until profit motivation becomes second nature to tribal governments, and this is happening on many reservations as the bureaucratic wells dry up, tribally-owned newspapers will continue to be a financial drain upon the economy of the tribe.

If it cannot, private enterprise is the only way to go with a reservation newspaper.

Jicarilla Newspaper Refreshing, Reliable

The motto of the *Jicarillo Chieftain*, the newspaper published by the Jicarilla Apache Tribe, is: "Independent in Politics, Optimistic in Disposition, Impartial in Religion," and the paper advertises itself by adding, "Published so that the Jicarilla Apache Tribe may have a spokesman and a champion."

The newspaper is a small one, ten pages or so, and is published on a weekly basis, on Mondays, put together by the *Chieftain* staff, and the actual publication is done by the Pagosa Springs *Sun* in Colorado. The editor of the *Chieftain* is Mary F. Polanco; the assistant editor is Carey Vicenti.

Polanco writes a column each week called "Mary Mix-Up" and she usually sprinkles each column with homilies and humor. For instance, she says, "An expert is someone who can take something you already know and make it sound confusing." In one of her columns, she told a joke that went like this: "Some years ago, a medicine show passing through a rural area was exhibiting what was reported to be the skull of Geronimo. A doctor who happened to be in the audience one night objected, 'Geronimo was a large man with a good-sized head and that skull is too small to be his.' 'Oh, I know that,' replied the quick-thinking spieler, 'but you see, this was his skull when he was a child.'"

Pow Wow

Most of Polanco's column of July 14 was devoted to the Little Beaver Pow Wow. Her sense of humor came shining through when she described the many good things to eat: "There was plenty of good and well-prepared Native American food at the pow wow over the weekend. Oink!"

Assistant Editor Vicenti is a young man with a sharp mind, and an easy-going approach to life. He has that special ability that is so essential to good news writers. He can read volumes of technical documents and difficult-to-read federal directives, sort through most of the pompous rhetoric, and condense the entire works into a readable, understandable and enjoyable article. This is, indeed, a special gift.

As a tribal newspaper, the *Chieftain* is well-written, informative and well-researched. As a subscriber to several tribal newspapers, I find it particularly gratifying to find such an outstanding news vehicle on a small reservation. Tribal newspapers are not, usually, a "cup of tea" to publish. Quite often, there is political interference which can, and on some reservations, does, make news writing "hazardous to one's health."

Topical Stories

The *Chieftain* carries news stories that are topical, historical and educational. It keeps important breaking news from the national Indian scene in front of its readers as a constant reminder that "what happens on other reservations can affect our reservation."

There is some advertising in the *Chieftain*, which helps to defray a small amount of the operating cost, but most of the revenues needed to publish this unique newspaper are provided by the tribal government. Yearly subscriptions are $6 and the address is: *Jicarilla Chieftain*, Dulce, NM 87528.

I was very interested by the progress and economic development on the Jicarilla Apache Reservation, and I believe that an informal tribal membership has had a lot to do with that progress. When one from a reservation environment sees this kind of positive progress, one can only compare the situation to his own reservation, and wonder aloud about a remark he has heard so many times: "When in hell are we going to get our act together?"

Consider this: The Oglala Sioux Tribe of the Pine Ridge Reservation in South Dakota has a population four times that of the Jicarilla Apache Tribe, and yet it does not have a newspaper to serve the people.

Wendell Willkie, a man who ran against Roosevelt in 1940, had a favorite saying hanging on his office wall which every elected tribal official of every Indian tribe should memorize: "Informed people make wise decisions."

Officers of the Native American Media Association: Loren Tapahe, publisher, **Navajo Times Today**; *Anita Austin, editor, National American Indian Rights Fund* **Newsletter**; *Mary Polanco, editor,* **Jicarilla Chieftain**; *and Tim Giago, publisher,* **The Lakota Times**. *(Photo courtesy of* **The Lakota Times***)*

Edition of Indian Newspaper Printed in Washington

When the "Prototype Edition" of the newspaper hit my desk, I anxiously cleaned up all of the work stacked in front of me so I could sit back, relax and check it out.

Managing Editor Richard La Course, a Yakima Indian, had talked to tme about his ambitious plans to publish a full-sized national Indian newspaper to be based in Washington, D.C. As I scanned the evidence of his labors from cover to cover, all I could say was, "Bravo!"

La Course has said, with conviction, "There is presently no comprehensive weekly reportage of national Indian concerns and events from the capital—the administrative and policy center of the federal trust responsibility to American Indian tribes."

One of the few professional Indian journalists in the nation, a man with unquestionable newspaper experience and impeccable credentials, La Course emphasized, "There is presently an almost insuperable and sometimes dangerous time-lag in conveying significant and critical information to both the tribal leadership and tribal communities. But that gap can be bridged."

The prototype newspaper, which hit the newsstands this week, is designed with dual purposes in mind: to test potential advertisers and funding sources. La Course believes that his newspaper can, "convey the accurate contexts and perspectives of Indian history and law, reflect the real voices of contemporary Indian people rather than the stereotypes purveyed by the majority media."

La Course hopes to test the market to determine if a national, weekly Indian newspaper can be commercially productive. Long-range goals are to publish a totally self-supporting newspaper, and the field of advertising is the essential and only ingredient in financial self-support. He said, "We want to test all potential advertisers, both Indian and non-Indian, by providing regular weekly printed access across Indian America."

Printed by the *Northern Virginia Sun*, Alexandria, Virginia, the initial press run was 10,000 copies mailed out from a collection of hodgepodge mailing lists compiled by La Course over the years.

Most newspaper editors say that in order for a weekly newspaper to make a profit, it should contain at least fifty percent advertising. The first edition of CERT Report (named for the Council of Energy Resource Tribes, the prime funding agency) contained 36 percent advertising within its 32 pages. Not a bad start.

The preview edition of the CERT Report (a tentative name, hopefully) was well-written and well laid out. The articles inside covered the environment, business, law, Congress and such vital Indian issues as water rights litigation. The ads were attractive. Most of the ads were placed by Indian organizations, law firms and consulting offices.

The subscription rates were categorized for non-profit organizations ($35 annually) and profit-making institutions ($87 annually) with no rates listed for individual subscribers. At the reservation level, these rates are quite high. As most publishers will tell you, one does not make it on subscribers in this business. Newspaper profits come from the advertising. We hope La Course decides to drop his subscription rates considerably.

Newspapers serving Indian country have had a high mortality rate in these hard times. Tribal governments seem to place a very low priority upon the printed word. As the drastic budget cuts took their inevitable toll on the reservations of this land, some of the first tribal projects to be scratched from the budgets were the tribally-funded newspapers.

The Bureau of Indian Affairs publishes an informative sheet called "Indian News Notes," from Washington, D.C., but these are mostly capsule reports heavily slanted to be pro-BIA.

Publishing a weekly newspaper is no easy matter, even on a local level. My sympathies and my hopes go out to Richard La Course and his staff. The national path they have chosen is strewn with the bodies of editorial dreamers. The fact that his project has been well thought out, well-planned, and is being brought along slowly and carefully is indicative of La Course's years of accumulative journalistic experiences and speaks favorably of his chances at success.

I would encourage individuals, tribal leaders, and newspaper editors to subscribe to this informative publication.

Write: The CERT Report; 1140 Connecticut Ave., N.W.; Suite 310; Washington, DC 20036; phone (202) 887-9155.

Chapter II—Culture

Iktomi's Traits Adopted by Attorneys

Iktomi is a Lakota word that means "spider," but it is much more than that. Iktomi is the equivalent of a fabulous creature such as the fox in English literature and folklore. Ikotmi was the central character in the parables that educated and entertained the young long before Aesop. He was adverturous, mischievous and comical; but he always reflected a lesson in moral values.

Charlotte Black Elk is the great-granddaughter of Black Elk, who was immortalized in the novel, *Black Elk Speaks*. She lives on the Pine Ridge Reservation at Manderson. Charlotte was educated at Manderson and Oglala Community Schools. She holds a Bachelor of Science Degree from the University of Colorado where she majored in Molecular Cellular Developmental Biology and Radical Political Economy. She shares her experiences with "Iktomi" then and now:

"As a young child growing up in my Grandma's log house, I can remember the hours of story telling every night. After blowing out the kerosene lamp, we would listen to Grandma telling us about Lakota customs and beliefs; religious, social and governmental practices; animal stories; historical events; name histories and our favorite—the Ikotmi stories. So our education consisted of learning about being civilized at the Bureau of Indian Affairs school during the day, and learning about being Oglala in Grandma's monolingual Lakota house during those long nights on White Horse Creek.

"In adulthood, my reflections of the stories told by Grandma indicate that there are some remnants of traditional Lakota culture still existing. Many are in 'pidgin' form; such as the practice of having a dinner one year after the passing of a relative, which replaces the traditional keeping and releasing of the spirit or the now casual attitude regarding the 'hunka' or Indian custom of adoption.

"Some reservation era social structures have been replaced with corrupt versions of their predecessors. In pre-reservation Lakota government there was a system of truth-bearers, advisors, deciders and enforcers composed of men who earned respect through a lifetime of respectable, responsible example and behavior. There is now a 'democratically' elected Tribal Council whose members gain leadership by proposing themselves to the people, usually as the lesser incompetent among a field of incompetents. This has led to a tenet of compromise that contributes to the loss of individual and institutional integrity. The traditional concept of tribal leaders turning their entire face to the people is gone and can only be learned at the knee of grandmothers on storytelling nights.

"Incredibly, the one traditional structure that has survived the transition is the system of Iktomi. However, Iktomi has undergone a marked physical evolution. Unlike the Iktomi of old, who entertained and educated, he has become flesh and blood. He has taken the role of advisor, the most respected Lakota institution. The role of advisor in pre-reservation days was to gather information from tribal individuals whose integrity was beyond question, and based upon that information, provide advice for a course of action that would insure the welfare of all of the people.

"Today Iktomi has become a lawyer or attorney and from that position has assumed the role of advisor to government. Consequently, the law in present Lakota society has changed from a system of social restitution based upon the principle of justice tempered with mercy, to a convoluted maze of technical precedence. This system of precedence or 'what happened to the other guy' has become justice based on loopholes that are written into the text of the law. Whatever happened to the traditional values of what is good, what is right and what is honest?

"From a mischievous manipulator, Iktomi has become an advisor to the lawmakers who then have the audacity to turn around and interpret the laws. This has allowed Iktomi's influence to permeate the tribal governmental structure and, unfortunately, is changing our system of life from one based on Lakota values to one based on an Iktomi value system."

Tight Schedules Not Always Best

The other day I had the opportunity of sitting in on some classroom sessions at the Navajo Academy located in Farmington, New Mexico. The instructor was an Oglala Sioux man by the name of Patrick Lee. Pat has a degree in law, and is one of the most skilled people in Indian law anywhere in this country. On this particular day he was talking to his students about the Dawes Act of 1877, which divided the reservations of this country into allotments of land. He said to his students, "Did you know that this act diminished the Indian lands by over 90 million acres?"

Pat went on to explain to the students that by dividing the reservations into allotments, because of the small population of the reservations at that time, many acres of land were left over, so to speak, and this land was declared surplus lands by the federal government, and opened up to the general public for homesteading. This act diminished the size of the reservations considerably.

As I sat in that classroom and listened to the lecture by Mr. Lee, I could not help but think of my days spent at an Indian mission on the Pine Ridge Reservation, and reflect on the fact that we were denied so much of this vital information and we had to learn most of the things which these students take for granted, by research. In many cases we had to approach further education on Indian law on a hit or miss method.

The Navajo Academy is located on the campus of the Navajo Methodist Mission and the overall concept of a merger between a mission school and a school fully supported by the Navajo Tribe and the federal government is, indeed, an innovative one.

Pros and Cons

Operating under a single administration, one curriculum, one staff and one student body, the merger of these two distinct schools has come about at a time when many of the Indian missions were having a difficult time continuing operation. There are several pro and con attitudes to the merger, and it is a situation which needed to be explained in depth. This column does not give me the space to do this effectively, so if you'll follow the Farmington *Daily Times* over the next few days, you will read an article which I wrote for the *Times* of delving into the reasoning behind this merger. I think it will answer many questions about this new concept in Indian education.

I suppose that the final irony of my visit to the Navajo Academy was the fact that Patrick Lee and I were classmates at the Holy Rosary Mission, located on the Pine Ridge Reservation in South Dakota. It struck me as ironic because Pat and I spent many hours together as boys playing the games that mission boys play, and sitting in mission classrooms listening to the lectures of the Jesuit priests who served as our instructors.

Now, here he was, standing in front of a classroom of Indian students, lecturing to them about Indian law, and here I was, sitting at a desk, preparing to write an article about him and the school. Small world, isn't it?

'Indian Time'

For those people who are very punctual, attending a meeting on an Indian reservation, or a function chaired by an Indian official, can sometimes be very frustrating.

They run into a method of marking time called 'Indian time.'

Many times I have observed members of the news media busily setting up their TV cameras, or newsreporters nervously chewing on their ball point pens, anticipating the start of the meeting. For the life of them, they cannot understand why the Indian officials are not busily going about trying to get the meeting started at the advertised time.

The old adage that "Time is money" is very apparent when this happens. Perhaps, this is one of the problems with members of the dominant society. Have they become so wrapped up keeping their lives on a well-defined, tight schedule that when they are confronted with a culture which does not place the same importance on a schedule, they become nervous and upset?

Relaxed Approach

Maybe, in this day of stress and strain, hustle and bustle, get up and go, there is a place for a more relaxed approach to life. One time there was a man busily working away in his office located high on the tenth floor of a shiny new building. It was evident from the look of anxiety that he was very upset. His boss, observing this, went up to him and said, "John, why don't you take a few days off, and just go home and relax for awhile? Heaven knows, you've been putting in a lot of overtime, and you look like you can use a good rest." The man looked at his boss and said, "Gee, I sure would like to, but if I don't get this work done, it will never get done."

His boss took him by the arm and led him to the window. He said to him, "John, take a look across the street and tell me what you see." "There isn't anything there except an old gaveyard," the man replied. "Well, John," said the boss, "in that graveyard, are buried many, many men who felt that they could not be replaced."

The moral is that perhaps we place too much value upon our own importance. Whether we're here today and gone tomorrow is of small consequence in the overall scheme of things. The world will still go on its merry way without us.

New Interpretation of Theory Offered

Oftentimes, differing cultural attitudes precipitate discussions between Indian and non-Indian which become arguments for the sake of argument. These discussions are no-win affairs because both sides are firmly set in their minds that they are right, and neither really listens to the other's point of view.

It is like discussing Darwin's Theory of Evolution as opposed to the Biblical version of creation. Science has taken a theory and expounded upon its merits for so long, and so loudly, it has come to be accepted as fact.

One theory, which in the minds of many, has been proven as factual, is the Great Land Bridge Theory. Most books on the history of man will tell you that a bridge existed across the Bering Strait, between Asia and Alaska. All of the inhabitants of this continent came across this bridge. Or so say those who would proclaim this theory to be fact.

Anthropologists and archaeologists have never been able to document this theory of the land bridge. And yet, in the light of this inconclusive evidence, the theory is still accepted by many as factual.

Cultural View

Now, if an individual is arguing the point, from his cultural point of view, that we are all immigrants to this land, he invariably invokes the land bridge theory to support his argument. He will say, "We are all immigrants to this country because, after all, the Indian's ancestors came across the land bridge from Asia."

First of all, assuming there was a land bridge, and this is still a theory, connecting two continents, why did it have to be considered a one-way bridge? Wouldn't it be reasonable to assume this supposed land bridge could provide two-way traffic?

If you look at the argument in this light, then you can argue that perhaps, the Indian originated on this continent, and then migrated to Asia. Why must we continue to believe the land bridge would attract people headed only in one direction?

Not Idle Speculation

This is not idle speculation on my part. Witness the fact that scientists have recently unearthed the remains of a horse and rhinoceros in Kansas which have been carbon dated to a time of well over 40,000 years ago. Each new archaeological dig in this country moves the date of man's appearance on this soil back far beyond the original 10,000 years first accepted as fact. Actually, the latest estimate of man on this continent almost pre-dates man on any continent on this sphere.

When the white man first came across the ancient "mounds" of the eastern United States, this discovery led to wild speculation of a super race. The attitudes of the times could not, or would not, credit the American Indian with having the know-how to create such spectacular projects. In order to do this, the early settler would have to admit he was dealing with an intelligent human being.

Conjecture Grows

Soon the conjecture led to the myths of crediting the earthen mounds to the survivors of Atlantis, or to Egyptians and Phoenicians who had wandered far from home to this continent.

America's first metropolis north of the Rio Grande, according to the *National Geographic Magazine*, December 1972 edition, was "12th Century Cahokia, supporting a community of 30,000." The magazine goes on, "Today, in sight of St. Louis' soaring Gateway Arch, flat-topped Monk's Mound remains, its rectangular 16-acre base surpassing that of Egypt's Great Pyramid."

Even in New Mexico, it was believed that the North American Indians were not capable of constructing anything as spectacular as Chaco Ruins. As a matter of fact, so sure of this belief was the white man, that the Aztec Ruins are a misnomer to this day. It was assumed that these dwellings were built by the Aztec Indians instead of the Pueblo Indians of this country.

Every day we're making new discoveries which would indicate that the American Indian is one of the oldest races of man on this earth. Perhaps, someday soon, we will determine that the Indian is not, and never has been, an immigrant from the Asian continent; but indeed, could be the progenitor of all mankind.

Report Incorrect

The report prepared by Harry Tome, tribal council delegate from Red Valley, concerning the prosposed $14.8 million settlement for Navajo land claims, was not totally correct.

In his report, Tome referred to the lawsuit brought by the Oglala Sioux Tribe on the Black Hills claims settlement, and he said, "It failed because the federal courts do not have the power to hear such lawsuits." This is erroneous information. The dismissal of this lawsuit has been appealed by the Oglala Sioux Tribe to the Eighth Circuit Court of Appeals in St. Louis. It is scheduled to be heard in about six weeks.

Columnist Responds to Recent Criticism

The old slogan, "My Country, right or wrong" is not dead. In the present, it is more of an attitude of the subconscious, but it is there. It is almost as if the super patriots are saying, "Yes, we were wrong in our treatment of minorities in the past, but please don't criticize us for it."

First of all, let me make one vital point. Most Indians are not trying to pique the conscience of the white man, and so the defensive posture assumed by the non-Indians when they are criticized is hardly warranted. What Indian people are saying, matter of factly, is, "You have tried enough governmental experiments upon us and they have all failed. Now, get out of our lives and let us decide our own future."

I bring out these points because of the letters of recent critics of my column which have been printed in the Farmington, New Mexico *Daily Times*. When one writes a column such as mine, he becomes very visible, and hence, he is fair game.

Point Missed

Let me quote from a letter by Jim Hassell of Farmington. In the third paragraph of the letter, he says, "Perhaps I miss the problems facing the Indian tribes," and as the rest of the letter would indicate, yes, he did miss the point.

Mr. Hassell's ancestors came to this country as immigrants. If they chose to surrender their Norweigian ancestry, and become bubbles in the supposed "melting pot" of this nation, that was their prerogative. No one coerced them into doing this. Not so with the American Indian. He was not an immigrant, but the original inhabitant of this land. In the attempt to assimilate him into the general society, his institutions, his religion and his culture were systematcially destroyed.

But, much to the chagrin of the dominant society, the Indian survived. His culture withstood all attempts of destruction made upon it and over the past few years, it has grown stronger.

Motivating Factors

Perhaps in the white society, individual success is a part of the "Great American Dream," but in the Native American Society, survival as tribes with independent identities , the preservation of "Mother Earth" and a place in our land as "sovereign nations" are the motivating factors. Most Indians do not say "Me," but instead, say "My people."

Mr. Hassell continues, "It is unhealthy for individuals to lose their identity under such fabrications as tribe, clubs, political groups, connection with tribes with self-realization of one's own abilities." To compare the feelings for one's tribe with the feelings one might have for a club or group shows more clearly than I ever could Mr. Hassell's penchant to "miss the problems facing the Indian tribes."

Most Indian people do not consider their tribes "fabrications" but as the source of their being. We are Lakota, we are Navajo, we are Jicarilla first; we are American second. When the white man can grasp the fact that we, as Indians, are not impressed with his way of life; but would prefer to live according to our own traditions, then maybe, we can begin to communicate.

Another Response

While I am on the subject, let me respond to another critic. In reviewing a foreward of the novel, *Hosteen Klah*, I did, indeed, feel that an attitude of superiority crept into the comments. In no way did I cast any aspersions upon the integrity of Mrs. Bloomfield or the author. As a matter of fact, the attitude displayed is one that was very prevalent at that time. One only need read some of the works of the early Catholic and Methodist missionaries to find such terms as "uncivilized," "savages" and "heathens" used in referring to Native Americans.

It was an attitude that was wrong, and this superior attitude has been at the root of many of the problems existing between the Indian and the white man, to this day.

Well, as one of my readers from Shiprock, New Mexico said in a recent conversation, "At least, your're getting their attention."

Indian Reservations: The Only Land We Know

"The Indian reservations are nothing but concentration camps!" The young woman addressing the largely non-Indian audience was raised on the Navajo Reservation, but now resides in Los Angeles, California.

She acknowledged my raised hand. I asked her if she really meant what she had just said. Replying in the affirmative, she said quite sadly, "I still have family and friends living on that reservation."

My mind immediately flashed back to the war movies that saturated the market during World War II. The Gestapo interrogator, rawhide quirt in hand, looms menacingly over his victim and says, "You still have relatives living in Cher-many?"

"Aren't your friends and relatives free to leave any time they wish?" I asked. The non-Indian crowd murmured indignantly.

For the life of me, I can't comprehend why many Indians who have left the reservations and selected the urban way of life would malign their former homes, the lands of their ancestors. Do they do it for sympathy? For drama?

One so-called militant Indian, well-known across the land, uses this tactic unabashedly while seeking donations from the college audiences he frequently addresses. In the midst of his tirade against "neo-colonialsim and the miltinational corporations," he will usually add, "The reservations are nothing but government-controlled concentration camps!" The shock waves this comment generates through the malleable mind is something to behold.

During the days when the Bureau of Indian Affairs was shipping Indian families to the ghettos of the urban centers under the guise of "Relocation," (now euphemistically called "Employment Assistance), thousands left the reservations with uncertainty and fear, believing the promises of a better life. Many remained in the cities, but many more, disillusioned by the traumatic change in lifestyles, and lonesome for the "uncis" and "tunkasilas" (grandmothers and grandfathers) they had left behind, returned to the lands of their birth.

Many of those who remained became assimilated into the mainstream, addicted to the easy conveniences of city life. Many who returned to the reservations came home angry at a federal government that would use human beings as guinea pigs in an ill-fated experiment.

The bureaucracy, in its infinite wisdom, has created two classes of Indians— the reservation Indian and the urban Indian. Never able to learn from their mistakes, the federal government attempted to divide the meager funds earmarked for Indian programs between the cities and the reservations. Subsistence on the reservation was already below poverty level, and to further dilute the funding available by allocating portions of it to the urban Indians caused anger and division.

From the sprawling ghettos of the inner cities arose the militant Indian factions. Like a burning prairie fire, militancy spread across the reservations. The anger that fed the prairie fire soon burned itself out and the reservation Indian, shaken by the tumultuous wave, backed off to assess the damage and evaluate the rapid change.

During the ensuing years, there has been a terrible "brain drain" of talent snatched from the reservations and planted in urban centers. Many educated Indians found the large salaries and the modern conveniences of city life much more inviting than the poverty and hardships of reservation life.

After it became fashionable to be Indian, feathers and braids became more commonplace in the cities than on the reservations. The urban Indians "out-Indianed" the reservation Indians.

Through it all, many Indians with vocational skills and college educations have returned to the reservations. They have set aside their personal ambitions, and have rejoined "the tribe," working toward the common goal of all the people.

Eager for immediate change, they have learned patience. They have discovered that the reservation people will change in their own way, and in their own time, if they decide to. What is progress to the white man isn't necessarily progress to the Indians.

Reservations have become the Mecca for urban Indians, the land base that bespeaks what lies ahead. Without the reservations, there will be no more Indians.

It is something the traditional, reservation Indian has always known. Our past, present and future is embedded in the lands of our ancestors. How can a Sacred Land ever be called a concentration camp?

There are no walls to contain us, or chains to bind us. We stay on the reservation because it is home, it is the land we love, and it is the only thing that gives purpose to our lives. In short, it is the only land we know!

Whites' Religion and Law Enemies of Indians

Over the centuries, two of the most dangerous enemies of the Indian nation have been the white man's law and the white man's religion.

A system of jurisprudence organized under the strict standards of uniformity leaves no room for difference. It did not matter that justice under aboriginal law did not fit, nor could ever fit, into the accepted interpretation of Western European justice as adopted by the United States government.

For instance, some common sentences for wrongful acts under Indian law included restitution, banishment or death. In some cases a murderer was sentenced to make restitution while a liar was sentenced to death, if the lie endangered the entire tribe.

The early white settlers could not and did not want to understand a system of laws culturally different from their own. Furthermore, they believed that any system of justice contrary to their own had to be inferior. Because the white man's religious and legal beliefs often intertwined, the ecclesiastical concept of law made Indian law totally unacceptable and became the basis for the theory of "manifest destiny."

The principles of manifest destiny made it possible for the white man to totally disregard any prior laws governing Indian tribes as mere obstcles to be pushed aside by the supposed superior laws of his own. If the Indian resisted what the white man conceived to be inevitable, the Indian was destroyed with God's full approval. Might makes right!

Because the white man's law took precedence over all others, he made no effort to understand the prior laws of the Indian. Instead, the white man considered them to be paganistic or heathen laws. This made it impossible for him to allow Indians the basic freedoms that he professed and enjoyed.

A simple, but deadly, solution was found to remedy these differences. The white man reasoned that if he could pass laws forbidding the practice of Indian religion, he would, eventually, destroy him. Those who refused to accept Christianity as their new religion would be eliminated, and those who chose to be indoctrinated would be spared and assimilated.

Eventually, this solution became a joint venture of the federal government and the Christian churches. It is ironic that a fledgling government, one that prided itself on the separation of powers between church and state, could set aside this philosophy in favor of expediency. And so it happened that for the first and only time in the history of the United States, the federal government and the Christian churches joined hands in a unified effort to acculturate and indoctrinate a race of people.

And so the immigrants, who came to this country seeking freedom from persecution for their religious beliefs, began to impose their own brand of religious suppression upon a culture alien to their own. They completely forgot or ignored the lessons they had learned so painfully. Suppression did not work in their case, but indeed, made their beliefs that much stronger. What possessed them to believe they could destroy religion by forbidding its practice?

The foundations of insensitivity toward Indian law and the failure to understand or accept any religion different from their own were laid down in those early days. The sad part is that it exists down to this very day. The white American has never learned from his past mistakes, but continues to trample upon the rights of people whose beliefs and religions are different from their own. The very laws he creates leave little room for difference.

Ten years ago there was only a handful of Indian attorneys. All of the complex cases dealing with Indian land rights and past injustices were handled by white attorneys. They did not, and could not, really understand the deep feelings the Indian has for the land. They believed that monetary compensation was an acceptable solution. And so this is how they approached the courts when dealing with issues involving Indian lands.

But as the Indian tribes became more aware of the tremendous losses they were suffering because of misunderstandings and outright greed, often on the part of the lawyers representing them, they saw a dire necessity to send their young to the law schools of the white man, and make an effort to save their land base by fighting fire with fire.

Because the land and their religion were often inseparable, the Indian tribes began an uphill fight to regain lands, charging the federal government with a direct violation of their First Amendment rights under the U.S. Constitution—interfering with their basic rights to practice their religion.

It was then discovered that the pursuit of justice can be effectively blocked by laws that are selective, and yes, even discriminatory.

Who Came First?

For generations archaeologists have been conditioned to follow the theories taught to them in classrooms and reinforced by the many books written by their mentors.

In seeking the origins of man, they have allowed this "mind-set philosophy" to control their thinking. Totally ignoring the oral history of the Indian tribes, they pursued the theory that man originated everywhere except in the Americas.

Countless bits of evidence to the contrary have been overlooked simply because they got in the way of accepted theory. In any endeavor, it is difficult to seek out new ideas and concepts if one is afraid to wander from the path of accepted theory. Perhaps modern archaeologists subconsciously feared the upheaval that would follow if the theories as presented by Western European thinkers were questioned and proven to be wrong.

As I have said in columns written more than one year ago, the Bering Sea Land Bridge theory is just that—a theory. No one can prove that the traffic on that bridge was one-way traffic. No one can prove in which direction it flowed.

When I expressed these thoughts last year, I was relying upon the religious teachings of the Lakota people and of the Hopi Indians. Several archaeological digs had turned up evidence of man's existence on this continent far beyond the 12,000-year theory of the land bridge crossing accepted by most modern academicians.

At long last, a book has come along written by an archaeologist, Jeffery Goodman, *Indians, the First People on Earth*, which would support some of the theories I expressed. I have learned of the book while reading *The Blackfeet Tribal News*.

The book was reviewed for the *Blackfeet Tribal News* by Harvey Knight, who wrote: "Archaeologist Jeffery Goodman presents startling new evidence combined with Indian oral history to come to the astounding conclusion that modern man first appeared in the Americas as early as 170,000 years ago. This puts America's first citizen much further back than the Old World's first modern man (the Cro-Magnon), who appeared 35,000 years ago in Europe. This could then place the biblical 'Garden of Man' in the Americas."

According to Knight, Goodman verified his finding using radiocarbon dating from at least twenty-eight very recent archaeological excavations in both North and South America which have turned up a large number of bones and artifacts.

Goodman expresses the theory that the American Indian is of great antiquity. According to Knight, "Goodman set out to prove ancient migrations over the Bering Land Bridge, in glacial times, happened in the reverse. Indians traveled across the Bering Land Bridge and populated Asia and Europe, taking with them major cultural and technological achievements to the rest of the world."

Goodman believes that this "reverse migration" could account for the sudden appearance of the Cro-Magnon Man in Europe more than 35,000 years ago.

Whenever the subject of land ownersship—especially that in the Black Hills of South Dakota—is brought up, the first argument put forward by non-Indians is: "Who did you steal the land from?"

Is the theft of land such an integral part of the history of the white man that they must assume that every race acquired their lands in the same fashion?

The white man has been creating theories for hundreds of years to show that the Indian is a late arrival on the North and South American continents. When evidence to the contrary is presented, a jumble of religious and archaeological evidence is brought out and dusted off to refute the obvious—even if it means the archaeologists must go against their own elaborate theories.

After several archaeological digs began to turn up evidence of a very superior lifestyle dating back thousands of years, many hsitorical purists, unable to accept the fact that they might be wrong, began to theorize that extra-terrestial beings had inhabited North and South America, and the evidence now being collected had either come from outer space, or the technical knowledge to create the artifacts had been taught to "ignorant savages."

Does it really matter how long the Indian has populated this continent? In the long run, title to land is established by the ownership at the time of the taking of the land. By formulating treaties and agreements with the different tribes of North American continent, the United States government recognized the tribes as owners of the land.

Whether the federal government was dealing with the Navajo, Shoshone, or Lakota, they were making agreements with the tribes they considered to be the legal owners of the land in question.

So, please, spare the Indian people from the inane theories of "Who came first—the chicken or the egg?" Read the legal documents of land ownership and you will understand that the United States government dealt with the various Indian tribes of this continent as sovereign nations.

Of Jailhouses, Conference Confusion and the Name Game

Throughout the year, I hear stories that are of interest, or I attend meetings where small happenings occur; but, in themselves, these events and stories are not large enough to build a full-scale column around, so I file them away and keep telling myself that someday I'll put a few of these stories together and write a sort of "potpourri" column. So here it is!

Dedication

The dedication of the new correctional facility in Pine Ridge last Thursday brought out a large crowd of people, and former U.S. Senator James Abourezk. Jim was out stumping for Senator George McGovern, and he had in tow congressional candidate Ken Stofferahn.

After all of the speech-making and kudos had run their course, a meal of buffalo stew, wojapi and fry bread was served to all of the guests. At the urging of Abourezk, Stofferahn got behind the serving tables, along with several Pine Ridge police officers, and with ladle in hand, pitched in to dish up the buffalo stew to the people in the long line. It earned him the applause, and a handshake from the large Indian gathering.

Dawson No Horse, Pejuta Wakan, led the crowd in prayer, but before he started, he added a little humor to the occasion. Dawson said, "I was just inside visiting the new facility, and let me tell you that it is really beautiful. In fact, this new jailhouse is so pretty that I think I'll come down and move in for a few days. It's a lot nicer than my home."

Confusion

If I were to select a single word to describe the Great Sioux Nation Conference held the last week of September in Pierre, I would use "confusion." A huge portion of this confusion should be laid at the doorsteps of the United Sioux Tribes. In fact, many tribal officials were under the impression that the meeting had been canceled (Oglala Tribal President

Stanley Looking Elk was told this.) and as a result, many never showed up. The date of the meeting, the last weekend in September, was also a poor selection because all of the tribes are on an October 1 to October 1 fiscal year, and they are about at the end of their funds one week before that date.

The press stories and news releases coming from that meeting also contributed to the confusion. Each time I heard a newscast which stated that "the Great Sioux Nation meeting failed to reach a decision of whether to decline or to accept the money offered by the federal government," I immediately called and corrected that erroneous assumption. The fact that this meeting was not being held for that purpose, but was to be used as a fact-gathering session, was never made clear to the media, and this caused further confusion.

The legal representatives for all of the tribes involved in the Black Hills Claims Settlement were invited to attend this meeting to answer the questions of the audience. Only one attorney was present. Mario Gonzalez of the Oglala Sioux Tribe stood alone on the podium to answer these questions. Every single tribe attending that meeting has paid huge sums of money to their legal representatives for many years on this case. Why was it that none of these highly paid attorneys were there to answer to the people? Robert Fast Horse, legal assistant to Mario Gonzalez, summed up the thoughts of most of the people present with, "If the claims attorneys won't come to the meetings such as this when they are invited, and they continue to refuse to communicate with you, the people they represent, then I say that it's about time we got rid of them."

Name Game

The low point of the meeting occurred when Crow Creek Tribal Chairman Ron Kurkie took the floor and said, "Who is this Mario Gonzalez? Sounds like a Mexican name to me!"

Gonzalez, who was on the podium at the time, answering the questions of the audience, answered this ridiculous statement with, "You know, Ron, there are a lot of you Indians sitting in the audience with English or French surnames. Does anyone ever accuse you of being English or French? There are a lot of Indians with Mexican or Pueblo last names also."

Perhaps Councilman Kurkie would also like to know that the Mexican-Americans did not come to this country on the Mayflower or with the millions of boat people since that time; but they are native to this continent and are of Indian descent. The sooner we put this kind of thinking behind us, the better off we will all be.

Special Buffalo Feed

A buffalo feed to honor the elderly of the Indian community will be held at Mother Butler Center in Rapid City, South Dakota on February 25 beginning at 12 p.m. I have been asked to be Master of Ceremonies for the event. Guest speakers will include Tribal Attorney Mario Gonzalez, former tribal president

Enos Poor Bear and a member of the Lakota Treaty Council, Louis Bad Wound. Everybody is encouraged to bring his own dishes for the traditional feed.

Legend Sustains Black Hills Treaty Claim

The non-Indian has always taken pride in his ability to make land purchases and to negotiate deals for land through treaties and leases.

Therefore, many Lakota people find it puzzling why so many non-Indians continue to ask who owned the Black Hills of South Dakota before it became the property of the Great Sioux Nation.

When a non-Indian purchases a piece of real estate, is he concerned about who owned the property before the man he purchased it from, or is he only concerned with the legality of the present ownership?

In 1868 the United States Congress entered into an agreement with the several Indian tribes of the Western Plains at Fort Laramie. It was the intent of the Indian leaders signing this treaty that certain lands be deeded to the United States, and the Indian tribes retain certain lands.

It is a common, but erroneous, assumption that the tribes of South Dakota were given reservations to live upon. This is not the case at all. The tribes retained lands they already had title to, and deeded lands to the United States. In other words, it was the Indian tribes who did the giving in this instance.

The 1868 Fort Laramie Treaty is a legal document approved by the Congress of the United States. This treaty recognizes the tribes of the Great Sioux Nation as the legal owners of the Black Hills. The document was signed by members of the concerned tribes without consideration of prior ownership. Just like any agreement between two sovereign nations, the negotiated agreement is a legal and binding document. This is a historical and legitimate fact.

Bringing ridiculous arguments into the discussions of legal ownership, such as who was here first, or which way the traffic flowed on the so-called Great Land Bridge between the North American shores and the Asian land masses is, at most, a nefarious attempt to cloud a rather simple, clear-cut treaty agreement between two nations.

It should not matter one iota who was on this land first. The fact of the matter is the final treaty agreement bearing the signatures of the two consenting parties of people involved, is a legal document which takes precedence over all others.

If the case presented to the federal courts in behalf of the Oglala Sioux Tribe by attorney Mario Gonzalez did not have merit, it would have been thrown out of court last year. The fact that it is still being mulled over in 1981 by the entire panel of judges of the Eighth Circuit Court of Appeals in St. Louis, Missouri, must say something about the case and its complexities.

When we attended schools on the reservations of the land and learned about the world outside of our homes, from books supplied to us by the white man we were taught that this is a nation of laws. We were taught the Constitution protects all people living within the boundaries of the United States.

And yet, when an Indian tribe questions the illegal actions of the government for taking lands outside of the guidelines set down by that Constitution, we are considered to be troublemakers and ingrates. Isn't this why we spent so many years in school—to learn the Constitution is for all people—not just for the non-Indians?

Just as the Holy Land is sacred to the Christian and Mecca is sacred to the Moslem, so the Black Hills are sacred to the Lakota and Dakota people. Why is it so difficult for the white man to understand that there are other religious beliefs besides his own, simply because he cannot comprehend them?

The white man believes, for the most part, in the prophecies and miracles documented in his religious books. Because it is in writing, does it have more religious significance than the oral teachings of the Lakota?

In the *Annual Report of the Bureau of Ethnology* published by J. W. Powell in 1888-1889, a revelation was made by a Lakota man named Brown Hat, called Battiste Good by the white man, which I will translate verbatim for you here. There are many interpretations about the meaning of this revelation, and so I will leave it up to you to draw your own conclusions:

The revelation as told by Battiste, about a woman speaking to him, reads, "I am the Eagle-Woman who tell you this. The whites know that there are four black flags of God; that is, four divisions of the earth,. He first made the earth soft by wetting it, then cut it into four parts, one of which, containing the Black Hills, he gave to the Lakotas, and because I am a woman, I shall not consent to the pouring of blood on this dwelling place, the Black Hills. The time will come when you will remember my words; for, after many years, you shall grow up one with the white people."

Black Hat continued, "She then circled round and round and gradually passed out of my sight. I also saw prints of a man's hands and horse's hooves on the rocks, and two thousand years, and one hundred million dollars ($100,000,000). I came away crying, as I had gone. I have told this to many Lakotas, and all agree that it meant that we were to seek and keep peace with the whites."

Some Lakota people interpret this to mean that if they accept the $100,000,000 plus for the Black Hills, they will be terminated as a tribe by the year 2000.

History Will Judge Indian Unity

I wasn't the first one to say it, by any stretch of the imagination, but I have repeated it so often over the years in hopes that we, as Indian people, would take a hard look at ourselves and end the internal bickering that is tearing us apart. The saying is, "Indians are their own worst enemies."

Too often, the issues causing the division between members of Indian tribes are blown out of proportion. Charges are made, followed by countercharges, and before you know it, a full-blown disagreement ensues. Communications between the warring factions, along with a little common sense, would seem to be the easy way to end disagreements at the outset.

Perhaps, by disagreeing about almost everything we—as Indians—are expressing our fierce independence, but we must draw the line somewhere. Time has never been our ally, and in these days of diminishing reservations, shrinking budgets and an impersonal attitude toward our unique problems by a calloused federal government, the sands of time are slipping rapidly through our fingers. Only through a united, common effort by all Indian tribes and people can we salvage our future as Indian nations.

How difficult can it be for us to sit down and negotiate with each other with open minds? Are we so determined to go our separate ways that we would idly stand by and watch our nations perish rather than meet each other halfway?

There is absolutely nothing wrong with having differences of opinion. Long before the advent of the white man, we had our disagreements, but in the days of our ancestors, time was on our side. In those day, the overriding consideration in solving all disputes was the survival of the clan or tribe. Survival was the common goal of all Indians and it could not be achieved without unity of action and thought.

Once more, we are faced with exterior and interior threats to our survival. The dangers are as prevalent now as they were two hundred years ago. If our ancestors had succumbed to the challenges of their day, we would not be here today to carry on the battle, and if we succumb, their victories will have been in vain.

History is often a cruel judge of human errors, and just as sure as the sun will rise tomorrow, history will record what we do today to salvage a tomorrow for our future generations. The ability to control our destiny is really in our own hands, and as long as we continue to shape that destiny through disunity, we are seriously eroding the chances of our survival for our descendants.

One of the most difficult statements to make, in any language is, "I forgive you. I believe that it is harder to say this than to say, "I'm sorry." But in order for us to mend our fences and to stop the tide that is engulfing our reservations, these are the things we must say to each other.

Now, more so than at any time in our history, our tribal leaders need our support, not our antagonism. Our leaders will only be strong when they have the people behind them making them strong.

Every time our Indian nations have faced extinction, great leaders stepped forward to guide us through the troubled times. Those leaders are here, in our midst, even today. It is up to us, the tribal people, to seek them out. Our salvation will not come from without; it must come from within. It must come from those leaders who have chosen to live out their lives on the lands of their ancestors. They, and only they, know from the recesses of their hearts that, without our reservation, we will cease to exist as a people.

Our only hope of survival, as a people with a unique culture and tradition, must come through our efforts to maintain ourselves as a sovereign nation. It is only through total sovereignty that our future can be assured. The only way to attain sovereignty is to put aside our petty differences, put an end to the factions that are creating internal division, and to face those who would terminate our reservation, as one, united people.

Now, here is the question we must ask ourselves. Are we big enough, in our hearts and minds, to meet the challenge? Can we rise above our own penchant to self-destruct and set aside our pettiness for our future generations so that, someday, they can look back on our generation as the one that generated the salvation of the Indian nations?

History will be our judge, and it is up to us, the Indian people of 1982, to guarantee that history will treat us with kindness. If we fail this crucial test, there will be no more Indian nations. I know one thing for sure: if we continue on our present course, after awhile we won't have anything left to fight about.

Elders Ask Respect for Life

Last week in June of 1983, at the Santa Clara Pueblo of New Mexico, a group of Indian elders met for the eighth consecutive year. They represented many tribes. They call America "The Great Turtle Island." The things they had to say are frightening. They are culled from the ancient teachings of many Indian nations. This week's column will be used to repeat what this "circle of elders" has said for generations.

"The prophecies and visions of our grandfathers are upon us. The Chief of Trees, the Maple, is dying from the top down as we were told would happen. This is from the industrial poisons that rain down in the Northeast. The rivers are runnning backwards as was foretold. This is from the dams on our rivers, the lifelines for all living things.

"The children are leading the parents and they grow up on their own without proper instructions or guidance. They grow up without love from their families, and the families are scattered like ashes in the wind, as we were told would someday come about.

"These are just a few of the devastating things reported to the Elders Circle. Our people have reported that our grandfather, the Wind, has continued to increase his force and destruction. Tornadoes have multiplied and visited the four directions now occupied by our white brothers. Etenohah, the Earth we call Mother, has tears running down her face and great floods and rains are everywhere and people are suffering.

"The Earth has shaken herself and rumbled in the Four Corners of the Great Turtle Island. The mountains are stirring, smoking, and sending their powers over the land and its inhabitants. These are warnings clear and direct. These are the powers the Great Spirit has put here to work in harmony with people through prayer, ceremony and respect in how we live. We have failed and we are being warned.

"How did this happen and who is responsible?

"The forces of the military are once again raising their faces to the powers of creation, the natural world. The judicial system is being used to suppress the spiritual power of the Four Directions. The leaders of some countries have deputized runners of destruction and exploitation. They have been given instructions to find all natural resources and remove them from their ancient habitats and deliver them to the industrial complexes that gird for war. Leaders of industrial nations throughout the world confront each other with ideological dogmas that speak of peace, but mean war. All of this is being done without regard to the consequences that will be visited upon our children.

"Our white brother, whose gift from the creator was invention, has used this gift to unleash the ultimate power of the atom. This was done in the Sacred Mountains of New Mexico, mountains which have held these forces within their protection since we were planted here by the Creator.

"Sacred sites are being desecrated and destroyed despite the protest of our spiritual leaders. Poisons have been unleashed upon the land, in the waters and springs that we need for survival. By destroying the sacred mountains and burial sites, man has destroyed the prayer sticks and sacred places that hold the dust of our ancient ones, those put there to work with the Creator for our welfare.

"The holders of these objects have now become the experts and they tell the Indian people what they mean without knowledge or respect. They exercise a cultural arrogance they claim was manifest by God to be their destiny. Indian nations have suffered death, destruction, forced removal from the land, and we have witnessed the desecration of our dead. It continues to this day under the guise of education, even going to far as to use our own people against us. It is this blindness that is so dangerous. We have failed and we are being warned.

"We must heed the warning being visited upon the earth. We must make the connection between the warnings and the desecration of the earth. The drumbeat of our hearts will cease and we shall have destroyed that which we have sworn to protect. There will be no life or future for our children.

"Our elders, who carry the ancient instructions and teachings, stand in a circle praying for the land and life. The ceremonies are sacred and the instructions are sacred. They must be treated with respect and conducted by the proper authorities in the Four Directions.

"As long as we hold fast to this, our life will continue and there will be a future for all people. We look to other people in other lands to recognize this and stand with the Circle of Life."

It was in the Kiva, the prayer circle, of the ancient Pueblo of Santa Clara, that the people gathered to pray and reflect upon the many bad things happening on this island called earth. The elders are afraid for the future of all people. They know of the ominous predictions spoken over the campfires for thousands of years, and they want all people to heed the warnings.

The meeting ended in a sacred way. The end was signified with "Wo Wa Tse Woegah Nah Keh Wiat" which mens, "Finished with respect for life."

Tribe Comes Before Personal Interests

South Dakota State Representative Ron Volesky, Republican of Huron, claims to be the only Indian in the South Dakota Legislature. Volesky allegedly was born on the Standing Rock reservation.

A tongue-in-cheek resolution honoring the great Oglala leader Crazy Horse was presented to the legislature for approval. Before voting in favor of the

Honor guard for a tribal policeman's funeral, Pine Ridge Reservation

resolution, Volesky said, "There are a lot of truly great Indian leaders besides Crazy Horse who could have been recognized, who did not come from such a warlike background. He never accepted the white man's way of life or the white man's culture."

One observer said that the hesitation of Volesky to vote in favor of the resolution "drew a round of laughs from the lawmakers." The fact that a commemorative postage stamp is being issued by the U.S. government to honor this Oglala leader probably prompted the state legislators to join the parade, belatedly and half-heartedly.

In all fairness to the Lakota people, I cannot let the remarks of Volesky pass without comment. In order to make the non-Indian and Volesky more fully understand the point I am trying to make, I must dwell on two American words: patriotism and assimilation.

During World War II, after the German army had driven to the gates of Moscow and had been stopped at Stalingard, the patriotism of the Russian people, who were ready to give up their lives rather than surrender their homelands, became evident.

Led by Georgi Zhukov, among others, the Russian people drove the German army from their country. Surprisingly, these patriotic people were not recorded in history books as "warlike" nor was their great general, Zhukov, criticized for being unwilling to accept the German way of life or the German culture.

History has always regarded those people and individuals who are willing to lay down their lives in defense of their homelands as patriots. Why then, is Chief Crazy Horse labeled warlike and hostile for wanting to defend the lives of his people and to protect his homeland from invasion? Does Volesky truly believe that, if a man is of the red race, he is "warlike" if he chooses to fight for his family and home, and, if he is white and does the very same thing, he is "patriotic?"

If Volesky has become totally assimilated into the "white man's way of life," the choice to do so was his to make. But if, in acquiescing to assimilation, he has decided to replace his Indian heritage with that of the white man's, in criticizing our Oglala leader, Crazy Horse, he is then speaking as a white man, not as an Indian, and his comments should be regarded as such.

There are many Indians living on the reservations of South Dakota and in the cities, who are mentally capable of making it in the white man's world. But these people do not think of themselves as "the only Indian" doing this or that. Instead, they think of themselves in relationship to their association with the tribe. They exist as distinct members of an Indian tribe, and their individual efforts are sublimated to the goals of the entire tribe.

Indians such as the late Edwin Fills the Pipe epitomize this unique separation of cultural beliefs. Fills the Pipe had the education and the determination to "make it" anywhere in the white man's world. If personal gain had been his only goal in life, he would have been a very successful man, according to the standards of the white man. Instead, he chose to return to the Pine Ridge Reservation and put the education and talents he had acquired from both

Edwin Fills the Pipe

cultures to work for his own people, his own tribe.

Fills the Pipe is what is known as a tribal man. He placed the interests and the future of the Oglala Sioux Tribe ahead of his own.

There are many Indians like him who gave up the conveniences of the white man's world in order to return to the Indian reservations of their birth and to put their individual efforts to the task of helping the tribe. The tribe then became their motivation, not the state, the federal government or personal ambition.

Almost every Indian tribe on this continent had tribal names which referred to themselves as "the people."

It is this unique ability to place the tribe first, ahead of self, that has sustained the Indian people. It is one of the main reasons that most Indian tribes have not become assimilated into the great melting pot after more than four hundred years of assaults upon their cultures and beliefs by the United States and other governments that have tried, in vain, to achieve this goal.

An elder I have much respect for told me one time, "If you decide to live in the white man's world, as a white man, and give up your reservations ties to the land, I will still respect you, but I will no longer consider you an Indian; but if you return to the reservation and live as we do, and use your talents to help your people, I will respect you much more, because like me, you will always remain an Indian."

1980s Pose Problems, Promises for Tribes

It is very difficult for most reservation residents to look upon the 1970s without some anxiety. The 1970s were a time of strife, turmoil and grief that, at times, pitted brother against brother, and sister against sister. The occupation of Wounded Knee, the death of two FBI agents at Oglala and the subsequent violence and unrest that followed have not been forgotten on the Pine Ridge Reservation. These events have been firmly etched into the minds all law-abiding Indians.

The lessons from these events have been quietly accepted, and the consensus is that they will not be repeated. Talk to any elderly person on the reservation and you will be told, "Violence breeds more violence," and "we cannot afford to let it happen again."

Perhaps it is a blessing that there is little time to dwell on the past. With the beginning of the new year, the 1980s are upon us and have been heralded by Navajo author, John Redhouse as "The Last Indian War—a war which we will inevitably lose if we enter the forthcoming decade unprepared."

Dagmar Thorpe Shaw wrote an article for the *Native Nevadan* that brings into focus many of the problems facing Indian tribes in the 1980s. She wrote: "Development of political strategy necessitates identification of the major political issues which we as Indian people face in the next decade. Reservations are the so-called "last frontier" of remaining natural resources, land and water in the United States. As America rushes to consume the last of her resources, tribes are viewed as an impediment."

Dagmar goes on to mention some of the factors impacting on tribal survival. She mentions, "the increasing trend toward political conservatism, tax reform, the increasing competition for energy and water, and the general attitude toward Indian people that our rights as sovereign nations are dispensable as 'minority interest must cede to majority demand.'"

The article continues, "This struggle is epitomized by the 'Sagebrush Rebellion,' an alliance of twelve western states seeking to transfer federal lands to state dominion. The reality of 'anti-Indian backlash' is becoming legitimized through mainstream political movements like the 'Sagebrush Rebellion.' Although specifically united behind the federal lands transfer to the states, the western coalition provides a political bulwark which will eventually encompass all of the concerns of the western states, including tribal-state relations."

She concludes, "If the western states do not fear tackling the politically powerful U.S. government, what will prevent them from attacking the politically vulnerable tribes? Honor and justice will not insure our survival in the face of unparalleled greed. We are not faced with the alternative of sitting back and hoping that disaster will not strike our people. Indian leadership has no alternative except to develop the initiatives for political organization and strategy."

Travel anywhere on this vast reservation and talk with the people in any community or district and you'll hear many of the same wishes expressed. Most people would like to see more jobs, better housing, better schools and better hospitals. They would like to see the lands on the reservation developed for the future of the tribe. They would like to be assured that the legacy to their grandchildren will be a secure future on their own reservation lands.

Above all, you will meet an optimistic people who look forward to the challenge of the 1980s. There is a religious fiber that has become woven into the day-to-day lives of the people that is hard for non-Indians to comprehend. There is a quiet reserve and dignity that can only be described as pride.

An elderly man in Wounded Knee said it best, "We have endured and 'Wakan Tanka' has never deserted us. Can what lies ahead be any worse than what we just now left behind? 'Wakan Tanka' will guide us and protect us."

Gerrard's Successor

The resignation of Forrest Gerrard, Assistant Secretary of the Interior, has presented a problem to many Indian tribal leaders in this country. They would like to be included in the selection process of the new secretary by consultation, but they fear that by insisting upon sharing in this selection process, they could run the risk of losing the position of assistant secretary altogether.

Interior Secretary Cecil Andrus has named Sid Mills, an Oglala Sioux, as the acting assistant secretary, but he has let it be known that he favors attorney Tom Fredericks, a Mandan, who is presently serving as associate solicitor for the Division of Indian Affairs. Fredericks was the executive director of the Native American Rights Fund, a legal organization based in Boulder, Colorado before he reported to work in Washington, D.C.

There are several other candidates in the running for this high office. Dr. Joseph Exendine (Lumbee), Franklin Ducheneaux (Cheyenne River Sioux), Sid Mills (Oglala Sioux) and Mel Tonasket (Colville) have all submitted applications for the job.

The way things are in Indian politics, no matter who is chosen, there will be controversy. According to one prominent tribal leader, "I don't think anyone in the Indian world—and I'm being realistic—can come up with an ideal candidate that everyone likes."

Deals, Doctors and Designations

The Billings, Montana *Gazette* reports that the Crow Indian Tribe rejected a multi-million dollar coal mining agreement with Shell Oil Company in March of 1980 by a vote of 281-156 at the tribe's quarterly council meeting. The proposed agreement would have brought the tribe as much as $12 million before the first coal was dug. It also offered a joint venture opportunity to the tribe. Shell has been trying unsuccessfuly to work out a deal with the Crows since 1975.

Why would such a poor Indian tribe turn down such financial rewards? For over two hundred years, Indian tribes throughout the United States have seen treaties signed and broken; they have seen argeements and contracts touted as beneficial to the tribes, only to discover that they have been cheated.

There is one ingredient that has been missing from the white man's dealing with the Indian nations for two centuries. That ingredient is "trust." Until there are guarantees that the land will not be destroyed in pursuit of energy, and that the Indian tribes will have complete control over the development of these resources, the coal and the oil will stay in the ground.

The key word here is "trust."

Navajo Woman Doctor

According to the Navajo *Times*, Susan John, a Navajo woman will be the first Navajo woman physician, ever, when she graduates from the New Mexico School of Medicine in 1981.

John believes that "Navajos have a feeling that if an illness befalls a person, that person is out of harmony."

"Everything is like a circle," she said. "There is a bigger emphasis on religion, on the psyche, in Indian medicine than in Western medicine. Navajos are always aware of the people involved, not just the case. If you see a patient, it's important to understand who he is, what clan he belongs to, and who he is related to. When a Navajo person becomes ill, the entire family is involved."

John added, "When an Indian person becomes sick, there's always the decision whether to opt for traditional medicine . . . to have a sing . . . or to go to a Western doctor." Susan John feels that both could be beneficial because the spiritual and physical selves are not separate entities. She concluded by saying, "The key is to know when each is appropriate."

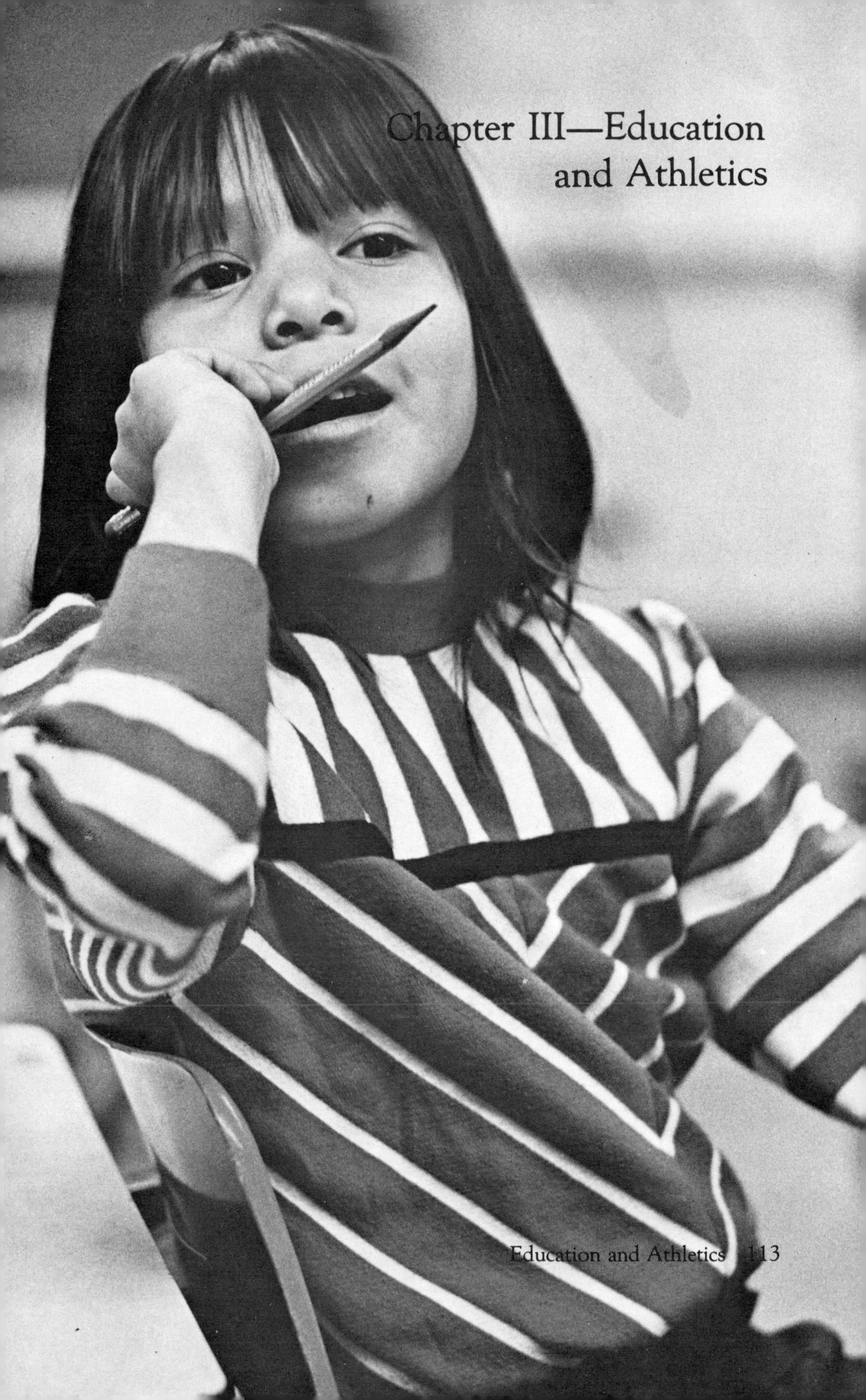

Chapter III—Education and Athletics

Chapter III—Education and Athletics

A Plot to Destroy an Indian Culture

It was Sunday morning and the campus grounds around Holy Rosary Mission were deserted and quiet. I could hear the church choir singing in the distance and the melody seemed to hang in the early autumn air.

I was walking along a dirt road behind the mission with my little eight-month-old son perched on my shoulders. As we passed the place where the old poultry building used to stand, my son started to wave wildly as he observed a fat, lazy magpie bouncing around the limbs of a nearby tree. The chattering of the bird, the smell of the grass and trees, and the old, familiar sights along the dirt road brought back a flood of memories.

As a boy, I had walked this road many times, and it struck me as ironic that I was strolling here with my own son. More than seventy years ago, my father walked this road as a Holy Rosary student.

Recently, old Jim Iron Cloud walked up to me at the store. He said, "Young Tim, your father and I were very good friends when we were boys. One time at Holy Rosary Mission, we sure got our behinds blistered for speaking our Lakota language." As he shook hands with me, his hand held onto mine for a moment, and he looked past me and shook his head, almost as if he were reliving those mission days. Mr. Iron Cloud paid me a compliment which meant so much to me because it was coming from one of the elders. He said, "Your father was a good man."

My father had already left Holy Rosary when Red Cloud Hall was built in 1921. And now, Red Cloud Hall is gone, crushed by the demolition ball and carted away in trucks. The hall had been our home. Its third floor was our dormitory, the first floor our playroom and gymnasium, and the second floor our classroom.

A bright, new building stands in its place. There are no more dormitories, only classrooms. Although the old, grey, concrete building has been destroyed, the memories are still there.

The school itself has undergone an evolution of sorts. When I see the beaming faces of the young, white volunteers (as they are called) who teach our young, I can't help but wonder why they have left their homes in the East to come here. Do they know how it used to be? Have they left their homes to do penance on our reservation, or do they really care about what happens to the young Indian children they are teaching? What are their motives?

Do they know that, not many years ago, the church and the federal government joined forces for the first and only time in U.S. history to acculturate and assimilate the Indian population into the mainstream of white society by destroying a culture?

Do they know that Indian children were taught that the only way to succeed in this life was to leave the reservation and live as the white man? When we should have been taught to stay home, work for the good of our elders, and try to make the reservations a better place for the young who were to follow, why were we encouraged to abandon our homes?

The old Holy Rosary School attended by Tim and his father
(Photos from Giago collection)

The old section of the mission was completed in 1891. It is made of red bricks. Most of the bricks were made by hand, utilizing young Indian students of that era to supply the labor force. My grandmother, Sophie, was a young girl when she helped to make these bricks in 1890.

It is as much a part of the history of the Indian people as the other events recorded in history books, and yet the harsh treatment of the Indian children, both physically and mentally, lives only in the memories of the Indians who endured and survived because of the strength deep down within themselves.

A Catholic priest, who is also a good friend, told me not too long ago, "Many of the things done to the Indian children were wrong, and we can't sweep them under the rug and pretend that the church was not a part of the conspiracy. We worked hand in hand with the government to carry out a policy that has since proven to be wrong and harmful to the people of the Indian reservations."

The severe policies of the religious orders to assimilate the Indian people were the politics of man, not God. Even though they may have been carried out in the name of God, they were steeped with human frailties, and therein lies the danger of blind, unquestioned obedience.

Reservation Pupils Learn 'Fairy Tales'

(First in a series on education)

The education of Indian children has been a hit-or-miss proposition for over two hundred years. The emphasis was usually on assimilation rather than education. The BIA boarding schools and the religious mission boarding schools failed, miserably, to accomplish this objective.

Statisticians have told us that the American Indian has one of the highest dropout rates per capita of any ethnic group in the country. Statistics are transitory and can never reveal the causes, or suggest the cures, for this national malady. Because of this fact, and because of my own personal experience with Indian education, I place little stock in statistics.

Most elementary age students on the reservations across this country were immunized, mentally, to the fact that the "Dick, Jane and Spot" readers which were used to educate us in our most malleable stages of growth, bore any resemblance to the realities of reservation life, and we were totally different in appearance from the white kids depicted in the books.

Far From Reality

The neat, white framed houses; green, manicured lawns; wide, paved streets; and the three-piece suited Father and well-clad Mother; cast in a supposedly typical American setting, were as far from our visual concept of reality as the Biblical scenes and stories from the Old Testament taught to us in our catechism classes. These social and religous classes, sternly taught to us by white teachers or white nuns, came across to many of us as fairy tales.

The lessons in history and geography were desinged (intentionally, or not) to show the American Indian as a wandering savage, without religion, purpose or a land base. The Indian lands shown in the geography books were claimed by the settlers with the approval of the Supreme Being (Manifest Destiny) and any methods required to attach the land and the resources was acceptable, including genocide and deception, because God had willed it so.

Effective to a Point

This method of acculturation through education was effective up to a certain point, and up to a certain age. It was not uncommon in reservation schools to see young Indian boys and girls stand up at a movie and cheer for the cavalry to defeat the Indians. One of the first lessons of propaganda has always been, "If you repeat a lie often enough, people will begin to believe it."

Imagine, if you will, the cultural shock experienced by many teenage Indian children when they discovered that the cliches taught to us in high school such as "All men are created equal" and "Liberty and Justice for All" and the patriotic songs and Pledge of Allegiance we committed to memory were intended for other Americans, but not the American Indians.

Humiliation

How did we discover this grim reality? Many of us would travel with our parents to the towns that border our reservations when they did their shopping and we experienced, first hand, the humiliation of being refused service in a public restaurant because "We don't serve your kind," or went to a movie theater and found out that "All Indians and Mexicans have to sit in the balcony or on the left-hand aisle," or saw the hurt look on our father's face when he was told by a white landlord, "Sorry, we don't rent to Indians," or when we sought employment off the reservation, we were told, quite unabashedly, "We don't hire Indians."

The shock was like having ice water thrown in our faces and being left with the numb realization that what we had been taught in school all of these years was a big, fat lie.

Reservation Schools Fail to Assimilate

(Second in a series on education)

The attempts to assimilate the Indian people into the great "melting pot" through the educational process failed for many reasons.

First of all, in order to convince the young people that an education is beneficial, you must offer a guarantee for the future. When many Indian children discoverd that there was no future for them, they reacted by dropping out of school. If getting an education meant being taken from family, friends and home and being isolated in a boarding school under the supervision of strict, often cruel, disciplinarians, then education was a thing to be feared.

Secondly, by isolating the Indian tribes on reservations, far away from the mainstream, the federal government insured solidarity in peer identification.

Hit-or-Miss Approach

By including the destruction of a culture into the educational process using a hit-and-run approach, the Indian child became a human guinea pig and, therefore, fair game for every well-intentioned "do-gooder" and religious despot willing to give it a try. In order for the white educators to create a new kind of Indian, in his own image, he first had to erase the Indian child's culture, religion and identity in order to have a clean, clear blackboard to write his own ideas on.

As each experiment failed, a new one would spring up in its place, and this process was repeated over and over for more than 100 years. Is it any wonder that the Indian people finally said, "Enough is enough!"?

It is as American as "apple pie" for the average citizen to serve on the PTA or the school board. Do you realize that it wasn't until the 1970s, after the passage of Public Law 93-638, the Indian Education and Self-Determination Act, that Indian parents were allowed the same participation in the education of their children?

Anger Understandable

One teacher, an Indian woman, became absolutely furious when she was told by a white school administrator that "I'm glad to see that Indian parents are, at last, taking an interest in the education of their children." Her anger was understandable to most Indians. The parents of Indian children were totally excluded, in fact, were discouraged, from sharing in the educational processes of their own children. Every aspect of education was in the hands of the BIA or the religious orders that ran the mission schools.

The school system was intended to eliminate all ties with the past, not reinforce them.

Entire families were moved to the urban ghettos of this country during the great "relocation" experiment of the 1950s and 1960s. Men and women were encouraged to attend vocational schools and "learn a trade." You will find more unemployed "welders" and "iron workers" on Indian reservations than anywhere else in the United States. After all, what good does it do to teach a person a profession or trade if there are no jobs available in the field when he returns to the reservation?

Not Ancient History

In discussing the failures of the many experiments in the education of Indian children, I am not referring to ancient history. I'm talking about my generation, and the generation that followed mine into the reservaion school system.

Last week I had a reunion with two classmates from an Indian mission on the Pine Ridge Reservation, and, as usually happens when schoolmates from the mission school get together, our conversation soon turned to other classmates.

We compared notes on the frequency of tragic incidents that were commonplace among our friends—incidents of tragic death, imprisonment, suicide or alcoholism permeated our conversation. Were these former classmates of ours victims of a misguided experiment in education? To those of us who survived this onslaught on our senses, it was a chilling thought.

Schools Contracted Under Education Act

According to former Assistant Secretary of the Interior Forrest Gerrard, "The passage of the Indian Education and Self-Determination Act of 1972 provided that certain services could be contracted by the various tribal governments." The education of Indian children came under this category.

The tribes did not start a stampede to avail themselves of this new service. It was almost as if many tribal educators and officials were imitating the old *Alphonse and Gaston* vaudeville routine of "After you, sir—No, after you."

The reservation people had seen so many experiments in education come and go that they found it almost impossible to believe that the federal government was actually going to give the grassroots people a say in the education of their children. Even when the tribal educators decided to proceed, they did so with extreme caution. In many instances they called for special referendum elections and left the final decision in the hands of the people.

Many non-Indian teachers opposed the new program. One call I received from a non-Indian teacher emphasized this apprehension. The caller feared that the 'contract school experiment' on the Navajo Reservation was a "complete disaster."

New Venture

In defense of the Navajo educators, one must consider that this is a new venture by the Department of the Interior, through its administrative arm, the BIA, and subsequently, many portions of the new program are uncharted. Several revisions will take place in administering to the different tribal governments before a workable format can be established. Do not blame the tribal educator for the initial chaos. Burdensome and often unnecessary red tape must share much of the blame.

For the first time tribal teachers and Indian school board members are supplying ideas which are actually being adopted and used by the powers that be, and this has caused the program to be constantly revised and updated.

A constant shift in policy at the Washington, D.C. level has resulted in vital funds being withheld; in disputed budgets; or in funding arriving so late that the credibility of the school officials has been severely jeopardized.

Suspicion Felt

This lack of communication has caused many reservation people to feel that the federal government is deliberately sabotaging the 'contract school'

Head Start graduate, Pine Ridge Reservation

experiment. One reservation official told me, "If the government can throw enough obstacles in our path and prevent us from succeeding, they can abolish this program with the excuse that the Indians can't handle the education of their own children, and we will find ourselves back at square one."

It is possible that the BIA is having difficulty relinquishing the responsibility of the school programs because it is a program that has, heretofore, been firmly entrenched within the bureaucracy.

Each and every reservation school that decided to go 'contract' experienced many initial difficulties. Those detractors who would like to see the program brought to an end harped on these problems and had little praise for the accomplishments.

There is an old saying that goes, "The proof of the pudding is in the eating" and in my next column we will take a look at one 'contract school' that is succeeding beyond the wildest dreams of the innovators on this reservation. They accepted the challenge, took the ball, and ran with it.

'Contract School' Developing Pride

You can see the pride in the face of the Indian men and women as they talk about Little Wound School which is located in the Pejuta Haka District of the Pine Ridge Reservation in South Dakota. Named after Lakota Chief Little Wound, the school has a board whose members have had to fight every inch of the way to survive as a 'contract school.'

Tom Allen, the executive director, can tell you about the politicians who tried to stop the progress of the school before it ever got started. He can tell you how the people of the district where the school is located had to vote down two attempts by the tribal government to get Little Wound turned back into a BIA school once more.

Sure, the people were apprehensive at first; but when they heard their children talk about the many good things happening at the school, they were amazed, and when they began to attend the school meetings and found out that they had a voice in the running of the school, they were astounded.

Credit to People

Five years have passed since Little Wound went 'contract' and the statistics in favor of the experiment are so impressive that they are a credit to the ability of the Indian people to educate their children, in their own way, if given the opportunity to do so.

The dropout rate at Little Wound, a twelve-year school, has been reduced so drastically that it is no longer a serious factor. The quality of education has been improved at all grade levels to such an extent that it is almost on a par with the other educational institutions in the state. This is a major achievement when you consider that at the beginning of this experiment the school was about five years behind other schools in the state.

The one quality that has been instilled into the student and the community, a quality that all of the federal dollars ever poured into a reservation program could never buy in a million years, is pride.

The philosophy that it taught at Little Wound inspires confidence in the students and urges them to reach for greatness.

Athletic Philosophy

Before his Little Wound Mustangs basketball team went to the State B Tournament, Coach Dave Archambault, a Hunkpapa from the Standing Rock Reservation, said, "I teach our athletes that we run and play ball for the Lakota Nation; but more specifically, for the Oglala Band of Sioux. We are trying to say to the world we are fine athletes. We are the best Native Americans in the world. We do this for the pride it will bring to our families, our community and our school. It makes our young grow up and want to do great things."

In a letter sent to the National Indian Education Association, President Jimmy Carter said, "I fully share your determination to meet the challenges of making Indian education program better and more responsive to the needs of Indian children. We can no longer tolerate inferior schools or second rate programs for these youngsters."

The passage of Public Law 95-561 on November 1, 1978, will have a strong impact upon the education of Indian children. The law has three basic ingredients: (1) it increases funding for Indian children by one-fourth; (2) school districts must insure that Indian children participate on an equal basis in the school program; (3) school districts must inform and involve Indian parents and tribes in the school program.

Giant Steps

These acts, along with the Tribally Controlled Community College Act of 1978, which provides funding to the seventeen community colleges on different Indian reservations, are giant steps in the right direction.

Keep in mind that even these small gains were not handed to the Indian people on a silver platter. It took years of unselfish sacrifice and confrontation by dedicated Indian people to gain what most Americans have always had and take for granted.

Money Worship Stirs Discussion

The three young men sat on the floor with their legs folded beneath them in the manner of the elders.

The oldest of the three spoke first. "Many of our people have found a new god to worship. You can see his face on the dollar bill, the five, the ten or any greenback. The god they worship is called money," he said.

"Hau," the two others said. The second youth spoke. "Now, it is very difficult to find a medicine man who will tend to the Sun Dance and will not ask for money to do so. This was never the way of our ancestors," he said.

All the while the first two spoke, the third youth, clearly the youngest of the three, sat silently listening and observing.

White Man's Schools

"The schools on the reservations are the white man's schools. They are teaching the young to leave the reservation instead of teaching them to stay at home, take care of the elders, and make the reservation a better place for all of the people," the first youth said.

He continued, "Why do we have a community college that is teaching us to go out into the white man's world to make money? Why do we have to have accreditation or approval from the white school system for our Indian college? Why are we becoming bad imitations of the white colleges instead of becoming Indian colleges that would use the knowledge and the wisdom of our elders or the expertise of our own educated people to improve life on the reservation?"

After a long silence, the second youth spoke once more. "It is us, the young people, who must turn the other young people away from drugs and alcohol. These are the two things on the reservations of this country that are quickly destroying us as a people. It is sad for us to see the children whose parents are such drunkards, they do not take care of them, or they kill themselves in car wrecks, or by fighting among themselves," he said.

Setting Example

"The children see these things, and these are the people who are supposed to be setting an example for them. Is it any wonder this goes on and on, from one generation to the next?"

The first young man summed it up for the others. "One time we spoke about these things at the college. Right away, many of the students said, 'Why don't you form an organization and maybe this will help you reach the people?'" He continued, "No, we do not want to form another organization and get ourselves a label as so many others have done. If we have to go door-to-door, or village-to-village to talk with the young, we will do it; but we will not need to form an organization to do this. We will speak to them as one of them—as grassroots Indians—and we will do it without asking for money or pay."

"Hou," the other two said.

Mission Experience Left Mental Scars

For the boys and girls of the Holy Rosary Indian Mission on the Pine Ridge Reservation in South Dakota, Sunday nights held a mixture of joy, anticipation and fear. It was movie night at the mission boarding school!

Built in 1891 by immigrant priests, brothers and nuns—mostly from Europe—"The Mission" became home nine months out of every year to Indian children from across the reservation.

Sundays were always kind of special days to most of us. On this one day, we got to sleep until the sun came up, and even though the Sunday Mass was a lot longer than the weekday Masses we attended each day, we knew that we would not be served our usual breakfast of yellow mush, but instead would be treated to cornflakes.

Throughout the school year, the boys went to school in one building and the girls in another. Even in church, the boys sat on one side of the aisle and the girls on the other. We even ate in segregated dining rooms!

But on Sundays, boys and girls got to go to the picnic grounds and actually mingle—under close supervision, of course. On this occasion we could visit with our sisters or our girlfriends.

And Sunday was the day the movies came to town. The movie of the week was shown in the boys' gym, and not only did the students of Holy Rosary get to attend, but many of the townspeople from Pine Ridge and other reservation communities came to the school to enjoy the popcorn and the movies.

Our trials and tribulations began about one-half hour before the movie started. All of the boys lined up by grades. Beginning with the first graders at the east end, we stood in perfect military ranks awaiting the roll call that would determine whether we could go to the movie or not.

During the week each prefect (a young white man studying to be a Jesuit priest) carried a notebook, and if he observed any infractions of the many rules and regulations set up to control our lives, he entered the name of the culprit and charged him with a certain number of demerits. On movie night, these demerits were tallied, and if there were enough of them, the youngster charged was forbidden to attend the movie.

One wall in the little boys gym was left vacant. As the name of the offenders were read out, those with more demerits were ordered to walk to the vacant wall.

As we stood in ranks, hoping for the best, the calls went out, shouted by a black-robed prefect: "Heavy" Garnett—to the wall; Aloysius Day Boy—to the wall—and on—and on! Some Sunday nights, if we had been particularly bad that week, there were more boys lined up against the wall than there were in the ranks of those who would get to see the movie.

There were usually suppressed sighs of relief from each boy as he was passed over. These sighs turned to open laughter once the fatal list had been read completely. If you were one of the lucky ones, you marched triumphantly down the tunnel that led to the gym anticipating the movie adventure ahead.

Even in our joy, we could not help but look back over our shoulders at the line of dejected boys marching silently to the stairwell that would take them to an early bedtime in the dormitory on the third floor.

Basil Brave Heart, a former mission student, said of the experience, "One time I was given enough demerits so I had to miss two movies in a row for speaking my native Lakota language. What upset me is the prefect who gave me the demerits was studying the Lakota language at this time, and he would spend many hours questioning the elders who stopped by the mission but would never ask any of the kids who knew the language because, like other Jesuits, he was trying to destroy our knowledge of the language.

"Missing two movies was bad enough, but this prefect also made me bite down on a large rubber band, and then he stretched the rubber band to its limit, and let it snap back against my lips. It was very painful. All of this punishment for speaking my Lakota language!" Brave Heart said.

Well, that was many years ago, but it did happen within my lifetime and in those days I was a student at Holy Rosary. Things have changed considerably since then, including the name of the school (It is now called Red Cloud Indian School); Lakota language and culture are actively taught.

There are no more boarders or Sunday night movies. Boys and girls attend classes in coeducational classrooms, now, and there are no more black-robed prefects skulking about with their notebooks filled with the names of students earning demerits.

Yes, that was a long time ago, but the mental scars are still carried by many of us, and I don't know if we'll ever really get over the mission experience.

Elders' Wisdom Needed by Children As Well As Education

Often we hear people on the reservations ask: "What are the priorities of the tribal government?" There is little doubt that priorities have become turned around in many cases, and the most important things have been placed last.

One elderly man told me recently, "If the tribal government would place the welfare of the young and the elderly at the top of their list, everything else will fall into place."

In order for us to plan for the future, it is imperative that our young be educated to deal with the world, for they are the future of the Indian reservations. Providing the facilities for a good education will not do it. Along with the facilities we must have good educators, educators who know about the Indian way of life, and can integrate the characteristics of generosity, humility, wisdom, and hard work in to the educational processes of the young.

Because we have been locked into an educational system which makes it a requirement for teachers to have "certification," we are adhering to an institutional concept which all but eliminates one of our most valuable educational resources—our elderly.

The state says that in order to teach the young, a teacher must have a "diploma" to prove they meet the state standards required. Certainly, it is important for our young to learn about the history of the world, about reading, writing and arithmetic, because these are tools that will help them help their own people, or if they choose to leave the reservation, and take up another lifestyle, it will help them find employment.

But, on the reservations of this land, there is much more to life than learning from books. That is the wisdom of the elders that has always been part of the traditional way of learning, a wisdom which prepared the children for a future within a tribal setting. We forget, too often, that even though we are a nation within a nation, we are also an Indian tribe, and our way of life is not always

At Oglala Community College graduation exercises an elder of the tribe ties a feather in a graduate's hair

Education and Athletics   127

identical to the lifestyles outside of our reservation boundaries.

The existing conditions on most reservations, and the bad attitude of many of our young, should prove to us beyond a shadow of a doubt, that the educational system foisted upon us by the state and the federal government is not working. Is it because we are imitating an educational system designed for an environment far different than our own?

By placing the education of our young in the hands of the state and federal government, and by adopting an educational system which has no use for the wisdom of our elders, we are contributing to the assimilation of our own children into a society far different than our own. Who is to say that in the process, we are not destroying their future, and the future of the reservation?

The education of our young is our responsibility, not the state's and not the federal government's. The time has come for us to take a long, hard look at the school system on our reservations. Granted, we need to prepare our young to compete in a modern world, but in preparing the mind, we cannot ignore the body and the spirit. This is where the elders can utilize the wisdom of a lifetime, and the oral history of many generations. The things they have to teach our young cannot be replaced by all of the certificates and diplomas in the world.

Navajo Tribal Chairman Peter MacDonald had this to say about the elderly of the Navajo Nation: "The leaves on the cottonwoods are turning yellow, and there is now a chill in the air in the early morning. All summer long, people have lived outside, moving freely about in the warmth of the sun. Now, with the encroaching cold and winter, we draw together as families, to the warmth of the home and relatives. Yet, there are many people who are alone, isolated due to circumstances and social change, and who see winter as a time of suffering and hardship."

MacDonald continued, "Many of these people are old. They are the people who had in their hearts the legends and knowledge of our land, and who understand our relationship with the natural world. Traditionally, the elders were held in high respect at all levels of society. They were involved in the decision-making process and held a position of status in the community. Their words were heeded. We taught our children never to make fun of the elderly, to be respectful and never be ashamed of them for their physical weakness."

The Navajo tribal chairman concluded: "The elderly of the Navajo Nation should not grow old alone, dependent totally upon outside support. That is not the way of the Navajo. Our way is to care for our own. Care for the elderly within the closeness of the family, for they are the backbone of the Navajo Nation. Respect the elderly, for they are our passport to a meaningful life, and to the wisdom and beauty of old age."

The elderly are the treasurers of our rich past, and if we continue to hide the wisdom of their years from the young, it will be lost for all time, and with it, a beautiful way of life. Before we allow this to happen, let us re-examine our educational system on our reservations, and bring this widom of the elders to the young.

Reservation Adults Full of Surprises

Margaret Cuny raised ten children; Clara Giago raised eleven; and Eva Witt, nine; but that isn't the only thing they have in common.

About twelve years ago they all started working as teachers' aides at schools on the reservation. They taught during the day, took extension courses from Black Hills State College at night and eventually began to attend classes at Oglala Community College when it opened.

Margaret and Eva earned bachelor of science degrees in education and Clara earned a master's degree in education from BHSC.

There have been many other Indian women following in their footsteps. Rhoda Mesteth, "Jimmy" Red Shirt, Frankie Clifford and Dorothy Gonzalez have all gone on to earn bachelor's degrees or are in the final stages of completing their college education after having worked long and hard as teachers' aides.

"You know," said Eva Witt, "my son, who is working on his college degree, told me that he heard a white teacher say that Indian parents have just recently begun to be interested in the education of their children. That really makes me mad. Don't these people realize," she continued, "that it has just been within the past few years that we were allowed to become interested in the education of our children?"

She wanted to stress that "for many, many years the Bureau of Indian Affairs and the Indian missions had complete control over the education of the children, and Indian parents were totally excluded from participating in any way, shape or form."

These women "play down" the dedication and determination that it must have taken to pursue their education after so many years as housewives and parents. They all feel that one of the strongest points of motivation was the fact that Indian teachers were needed to teach Indian children.

Delores Iron Cloud teaches at Oglala Community School and is in the process of earning her master's degree in education from BHSC. She is much younger than the women who raised all of their children before embarking on teaching careers; but she has some fine role models to emulate.

It's not just women who are returning to school. Melvin "Dickie" Brewer has just earned a bachelor of science degree at age forty-three in human service work with an emphasis on drug and alcohol abuse from Metropolitan State College in Denver, Colorado.

While earning his degree, he helped establish Alcoholics Anonymous groups on the reservation with membership of about sixty people. "Many of them have been sober for five months to three years," Dickie said.

Glen Three Stars was one of the finest athletes ever produced on the Pine Ridge Reservation. He is presently working for Project Recovery Program in Pine Ridge and is attending night classes working toward a degree at Oglala Sioux Community College. These are just a few examples of the role being taken by many reservation residents trying to improve their education.

Chicago Re-location

Enos Poor Bear is a consummate teller of stories. Whether in Lakota or English, he can weave a yarn that will keep you sitting on the edge of your chair. Poor Bear swerved two terms as president of the Oglala Sioux Tribe, and currently serves as a councilman from the Eagle Nest District.

Enos was describing the days way back when "I got off of the train in Chicago, Illinois after being sent there by the BIA on the re-location program. It just so happened that it was the birthday of Enos 'Country' Slaughter of the Chicago Cubs. The headlines for the Chicago *Tribune* said 'Happy Birthday, Enos.'" "Well," Enos continued, "I bought several copies of the newspaper, cut out those headlines, and posted them behind my desk at the office. For many months the new arrivals from the reservation who visited my office would look at those words, 'Happy Birthday, Enos,' and really think the city of Chicago was paying homage to this old Sioux."

The Oglala Indians—1936 State B Champs

How many of you remember the old Oglala Indians basketball team of 1936? There are only three memeber of that great team alive today. They are Francis "Jacks" Brewer, Dave Brewer and Sterling "Chicken" Big Bear.

The Oglala Indians defeated Belle Fourche 37 to 27 to win the Region 8 championship and then advanced to the first B championships ever held in the state. Their first game was played on Friday, the 13th, and they defeated the Region 7 champs, Tyndall, 37 to 33.

Next team to go under was Harrisburg. Oglala defeated them 36 to 33. "As I remember, this was the toughest team we faced in the entire tournament," said the man who was selected along with "Chicken" Big Bear for the All-State Team that year, Dave Brewer.

The old Rapid City *Daily Journal* said of the Oglala Indians, "The Indians exhibited the most spectacular play of the first rounds, with clever ball handling and thrilling long-range shots, but they showed a defensive weakness."

The championship game was against Bridgewater. Oglala won the title 24 to 22. The *Journal* reads, "Bridgewater outscored the Indians 9 to 4 in the final period, but the final gun halted the comeback drive of the Region 6 champs, leaving them two points behind."

Manuel Moran, superintendent of schools for the Pine Ridge Reservation, is hoping to get the three surviving members of the great Oglala team together for a long overdue honoring ceremony at the half-time of the State B Tournament which will be held in Rapid City this year, 1981.

The other members of the Oglala Indians who played on the first state B championship team and who have since passed away were Walter "Hank" Means, Irving "Boob" Jumping Eagle, Lawrence "Prunes" Ecoffey and Raymond Chief.

The old *Daily Journal* summed up the efforts of the Oglala Indians with, "The Indians nonchalantly dropped the ball through the hoop from mid-floor time after time, and executed several startling one-handed shots." For many years there was a footprint painted on the floor of the Huron Gym, where the tourney was held, marking the spot where Dave Brewer fired a one-handed shot that swished the net. It was the longest shot ever made in that gym.

1936 State B Basketball Champions

Pep Rally Boosts First Indian Team to B Tournament

The special camaraderie, feelings of pride and experiences shared which are present only on an Indian reservation flowed through the crowd at Tuesday evening's pep rally honoring the Lady Thorpes of Oglala Community High School. People from throughout the Pine Ridge Reservation cheered and wished them success in the South Dakota B Basketball Tournament in Huron Thursday.

The Lady Thorpes, the first Indian basketball team to advance to the state tournament, have a 16 and 5 record and won their last seven games, including district and regional championships.

Senior starter Suzie Pettigrew told the large audience the season and the state tournament play were dedicated to "our former teammate and friend, Kathy McLaughlin, who died in an automobile accident. She would have been a senior this year, and probably a starter on the team."

The Lady Thorpes received corsages from the Student Council on behalf of the Little Wound Mustangs, a placard from the Red Cloud Crusaders and words of encouragement from representatives of Crazy Horse High School as all of the high schools on the reservation united behind the tournament-bound team.

The auditorium was rocking with laughter by the time Tiny DeCory of the Thorpe Booster Club reached the letter "S" as she used her body to spell out the cheer "T-H-O-R-P-E-S."

Oglala Sioux Tribal Councilwoman Penny Janis of the Medicine Root District read a resolution from the council commending the team and wishing it tournament success.

Coach Jesse Mendoza introduced the nucleus of next year's team, the freshmen, sophomores and juniors, and then bid fond farewell to "the leaders of the Lady Thorpes, the senior girls who have been with me since my first day as a coach at OCS three years ago."

The audience stood with heads bowed as Oliver Red Cloud explained: "There is a long journey ahead for these girls and it could be dangerous for them, so I will pray for them in our Lakota language and wish them a safe journey because I know they will come home to the victory dance we plan to hold for them."

Indian Athletes Play for Lakota
Nation, Oglala Band and Families

"The sport of running has one important aspect that sets it apart from all others. The efforts of the team or individual cannot be diminished by the officiating. In other sports that require officiating, you constantly come up with the term "judgment call" and regardless of the integrity of that judgment, it still has a profound effect upon the outcome."

Coach Dave Archambault of Little Wound School, Kyle, South Dakota was reflecting on the successful season of his cross country running team. "At the state meet this year Wallace White Dress and Myron Ghost Bear finished one

Little Wound State B Cross County Champions

Little Wound Mustangs participating in State B Tournament

and two and Sam One Horn was ninth. We beat out Elkton, South Dakota 12-16 to win the state B championship.

"The real inspiration on our team was Bernard Little Whiteman."

Little Whiteman, a junior-varsity runner for Little Wound, is a victim of cerebral palsy. "He does everything we ask of him and runs right with the rest of the team. He never cries or complains. Bernard's an inspriation to the whole team, and deserves a lot of credit for our success."

Coach Dave Archambault is a slender man who wears his black hair long and ties it back in a pony tail. He was in a philosophical mood this night as he talked about the athletic program at Little Wound.

"We run or play ball for the betterment of the Indian people. If we perform well, we bring respectability to the Red Man. Others may look at our achievements and generalize about the Indian people, as non-Indians are prone to do; but it is a positive generalization."

It was at the half-time of the district play-offs and Little Wound girls' team had advanced to the finals against Custer. Shonna Ferguson, Little Wound's brilliant guard and playmaker, had sprained her ankle the previous night and had to watch in anguish as Little Wound lost to Custer 39-33.

Dave stood under the basket at the west end of the Oglala Community School basketball court and continued to talk about the fundamentals he stresses in his day-to-day coaching. "I teach our athletes that we can run and play ball for the Lakota Nation; but more specifically, for the Oglala band. We are trying to say to the world we are fine athletes, both men and women. We are the best Native Americans in the world.

"We run and play ball for the good that it will bring to our families, community and our school. It will bring pride to our people. It is the modern way of counting coup. It helps our young want to grow up and do great things; makes them aspire to greatness. Our doing good or being the best helps our people in many ways.

"Let me give you an example of dedication. On our way to the state cross country championships, we won six other meets. In order to do this, it takes training. I added up the total mileage our team ran in training and I came up with 2,613 miles. That's clear across the United States! Our top mileage getter was Cleveland Broken Rope with 267 miles.

"It seems that our Indian athletes receive very little recognition. They are very seldom recruited by state colleges even though Little Wound, Holy Rosary, St. Francis and Oglala Community School, from this area, have turned out many outstanding athletes for many, many years." With that parting shot, Dave turned to join his team for the second half.

While I am on the subject of Little Wound School, I heard an interesting' story the other day I will repeat. James Welch, a Blackfeet Indian, author of *Winter in the Blood* and *The Death of Jim Loney*, was in Kyle to speak last week. After his lecture, we talked him into joining us at the home of Colleen Brewer, a third-grade teacher at Little Wound, for coffee and conversation. Colleen was expounding on the creativeness of the children in her class. "One day I asked the children to write a short story on their new kites. The class had been given kites for a class project and they were very excited about it. As I reviewed their assignments, one caught my eye. It was written by a little girl and summed up all of her feelings, expectations and hopes in one short sentence. She stated very simply, "The day I got my kite—it rained."

All-Indian Basketball Tournament

On a lighter note, I would like to extend a special thank you to John Mastilir and Bob Laskowski of KOTA-TV for the efforts they made to promote the All-Indian Basketball Tournament held in Rapid City December 18-20, 1980. The announcements they made and the television coverage they gave, contributed to the large crowds and helped to make the tournament a success. Thanks, John and Bob.

Former tribal chairman,
Joe American Horse

Chapter IV—Government
Economy
Taxes on Cigarettes

There is much discussion in Indian country about the recent ruling by the Supreme Court which gives the states the rights to cigarette and sales taxes on sales to non-Indians. The ruling was made in a suit brought by the state of Washington against the Colville, Makah, Lummi and Yakima tribes of that state. It is estimated that the state of Washington was losing approximately $15 million per year in revenues because the taxes were being collected and used by the various Indian tribes named in the suit.

Who is the real loser because of this Supreme Court decision? The revenues collected by the Indian tribes were being used to defray the costs of tribal government and to make improvements on the reservations. The tax collections were also a good lesson in self-government and helped the tribes to pull away from total federal dependence by learning a little bit about the profit motive or incentive that is so important to self-determination.

Where will the money come from to fill the gap caused by these lost revenues? In the long run, who is the real loser?

Budget Cuts Would Wreak Havoc in Health Service

Guess what the Great White Father in the Office of Management and Budget has in store for the Indian Health Service. The proposals made by the all-seeing, all-knowing, faceless bureaucrats in the city by the Potomac must make tribal leaders feel like they are shoveling, and against the tide.

OMB Director David Stockman is proposing that individual Indians be required to pay for health care services they receive free from the IHS starting October 1, 1983. The National Indian Health Board reports the recommendation is part of the administration's "austere 1984 budget request for IHS that counts upon an unprecedent $70 million in reimbursements and also calls for the elimination of funds for the Community Health Representative program, urban Indian health projects, and construction of Indian health facilities."

Spokesman for OMB, Ed Dale told me that the proposal is not calling for payments from Indians for health services. "Our office is not suggesting a 'financial means test' to determine an Indian's ability to pay for health services. What we are trying to do is to have those Indian people who are capable of paying, those who are insured, have Medicaid/Medicare, or federal employees insurance programs, be charged for medical services," he said.

Dale said the article appearing in the April *NIHB Health Reporter* was not entirely accurate. "This idea is still in the planning stages and what we hope to accomplish with it is to have the Indian hospitals go through the motions of caring for patients, and those who do not have insurance coverage will not be required to pay for services," Dale said.

In 1982, 900,000 Indians received services through the IHS under a nationwide budget of $653 million. IHS realized reimbursements in the amount of $20 million through Medicaid/Medicare payments. The Stockman proposal would increase reimbursement by another $40 million. This means that the expanded collection program would collect $600 million from private insurers if the proposal is accepted.

Dale emphasized, "IHS will treat individual Indians regardless of their ability to pay. All we are doing is looking at an untapped source of revenue to to supplement IHS for losses suffered due to other budget cutbacks in health service."

NIHB Director Jake Whitecrow sent a letter to Department of Health Director Margaret Heckler condemning Stockman's proposal. "Health care provided by the IHS is part of a legal obligation to Indian people that has evolved directly from treaty and trust responsibility that exists between the United States and Indian tribes. The OMB proposal clearly represents a fundamental lack of understanding about this relationship . . . and we deplore such a callous and ill-conceived attempt to alter this relationship and turn the Indian Health Service into a welfare program," Whitecrow said.

Elmer Savilla, executive director of the National Tribal Chairmen's Association located in Washington, D.C., was equally chagrined. He said, "We are trying our darndest to get IHS out of the decision-making celler in Washington and elevate it to where these kinds of decisions are being made. We're having a hard time getting Dr. Everette Rhoades, head of IHS, to listen to us. But as far as having a say in policy that affects the Indian people, IHS is way at the bottom of the ladder."

The one program many reservation Indians dread losing is the Community Health Representative program. OMB spokesman Dale said, "They keep trying to get rid of this program, but somehow, it keeps getting approved each year. I think that it was first instituted on Indian reservations to provide jobs, or to create makeshift jobs."

On huge reservations such as the Navajo Nation and the Pine Ridge Reservation, the CHR program soon provided medical services to those Indians living far out on the reservation. Many of these grassroots Indians had no means of transportation to travel the great distance to IHS facilities. The CHR program filled a vital, often life-saving need on the reservations.

Most reservation officials have been studying the Stockman proposal and have decided on how to respond to it. Oglala Sioux Tribal Councilman, a member of the health committe, G. Wayne Tapio, said, "I think it comes down to the fact that policies are introduced and implemented from the Washington, D.C. level without ever consulting the Indian tribes. It seems that we are subject to their every whim and fancy as if our opinions don't matter at all. What the hell, it's only our lives they are playing with and talking about."

Terry Pourier, administrator for the Public Health Service hospital at Pine Ridge, said, "I hope those budget cutters in the OMB realize that none of the hospitals in this area, or in most reservation locations, have the capabilities for billing if this new policy is implemented. It would mean hiring added personnel and probably enlisting the aid of a computer in order for our office to set up a billing system to itemize the costs for insurance companies.''

Savilla of the NTCA summed up the feelings of many Indians. He said, with an edge in his voice, ''Most of the policies, and proposed policies of the Reagan Administration are nothing but death sentences for the Indian people. They are deadly—and I mean that literally.''

Marshall Plan Needed to Offset Budget Cutbacks

The official symbol for the U.S. Department of the Interior is a mountain scene, with a buffalo in the foreground. Speaking before a luncheon crowd in Tamarron, Colorado last week, Assistant Secretary of the Interior Garrey Carruthers said, ''The buffalo used to go to the left. Now it goes to the right.''

Carruthers intimated the reversal symbolized the shift in philosophy of the Reagan Administration from previous administrations. Thus far, that philosophical shift has wrought untold hardships, suffering, and a dramatic reversal of previous gains in Indian Country.

The concept of private industry picking up the slack for the loss of governmental programs, slashed to the bare bones or eliminated, has not worked on the Indian reservations of this land because, for the most part, there is no private sector on the reservation.

It is my contention that only a massive influx of funds earmarked for economic development, funds provided for long-range planning, unaffected by administrative changes, can restore the reservations and fulfill the obligations and the intent of the many hundreds of broken treaties.

Such a plan, known as the Marshall Plan, designed to set Europe back on it feet after it had been devastated by World War II, was suggested by General George C. Marshall on June 5, 1947 in a speech delivered at Harvard University.

The Foreign Assistance Act, which laid the foundation for a four-year European recovery program, was signed into law in April of 1948 by President Harry S. Truman. The Economic Cooperation Administration, headed by Paul G. Hoffman, the president of the Studebaker Corporation, administered the program. Halfway through the four-year plan, $10 billion had been invested into the economy of Europe.

The beauty of the Marshall Plan was that it allowed the affected nations to formulate the plans and yearly budget needed to carry out the enormous tasks of economic recovery. The heads of the European nations knew the customs, the goals, the limitations and the potential of their own people, and they were given the financial assistance and the freedom to work within an economic recovery structure designed by themselves. A prosperous Europe is evidence of the success of the Marshall Plan.

Quite often, people who claim to be friends of the American Indian turn out to be our worst enemies. Last year, a visitor from Europe shook his head in obvious sadness when he listened to members of the Oglala Sioux Tribe talk about economic self-sufficiency. It was almost as if he imagined that the false images he had garnered about the American Indian from history books would be forever destroyed by the talk of economic progress.

The American Indian has been locked into a historical vacuum. While other nations have been allowed to progress with the times, the Indian has been relegated to the role of a museum piece, not quite extinct, but well worth preserving in his natural state. A victim of massive misconceptions, stereotyped by books, movies and television, the contemporary Indian has had to live in the dark shadows of his illustrious past.

A close friend of mine owns a store near a large Indian reservation. He told me tourists often stop at his place of business and ask, "What time do they open the gates to the reservation?" He assured them that there are no gates to keep the Indians on the reservation, or to keep the tourists out. "Well, we want to see some Indians," they responded. He told them, "I am an Indian." Usually they look at his modern attire, his short haircut, and listen to his flawless English and say with ignorant conviction, "No, we want to see some real Indians." They actually believe that time has stood still for the American Indian.

President John F. Kennedy said, "The Indian is the most misunderstood, and the least understood of all Americans." The images of a few radicals shouting slogans as they occupy buildings or land is far more newsworthy than the quiet lifestyles of the vast majority of Indians who are trying to bring about change and progress within the framework of constitutional law.

The day an Indian fashioned a spoon from the horn of a buffalo, climbed aboard his first horse, or picked up his first rifle—that was progress. The American Indian has overcome tremendous odds and restrictions place upon him by a paternalistic bureaucracy in order to forge ahead. While retaining the best of our cultures, we have never remained static.

Without ever consulting the Indian himself, every administration since George Washington's has initiated "new Indian programs" designed to assimilate us into the mainstream. We have been the subjects of more experiments than laboratory guinea pigs. Churches flocked to our reservations to Christianize us, usually at the expense of our older, traditional religions. Never mind that for one of the few times in the history of this country the church and federal government worked hand in hand, financially and fundamentally, to destroy a race of people.

We are not relying upon the guilt complex of American society to rectify past wrongs. We are asking the American people to bring pressure upon those people in the Congress of the United States to honor the treaties they signed with the Indian nations.

Allow us, the Indian people, to solve the Indian problem that has plagued the federal government for more than two hundred years. We are not very high on the priority list of federal goals. This was made quite obvious when President Ronald Reagan remained silent while Secretary of the Interior James Watt inadvertently insulted more than one million American Indians, and yet spoke out clearly in the defense of a rock group, the Beach Boys, when Watt talked about banning them from a Fourth of July celebration to be held in

Washington, D.C.

The bottom line is: We do not want pity or charity. We want the United States of America to act like a nation with honor, and give us the same opportunity to restructure our economy as it gave the nations of Europe and Japan after her armies had devastated those countries. We want an "American Indian Marshall Plan."

High Cost of Government Told Pine Ridge Residents

Myron Rock was elected to the office of Treasurer of the Oglala Sioux Tribe on April 10, 1980. He was elected over incumbent Ivan Bettelyoun by a 14 to 12 vote of the new tribal council. He made one of the strongest speeches to the council that I have ever heard.

He said, "For too many years there has been an abundance of waste on this reservation that has seen the funds that should have been used to help the grassroots people instead of being eaten up by extravagant administrative costs."

Rock continued, "Why is there so much secrecy in tribal government? Doesn't the administration want to let the people know what they are doing with their money? Why must each administration operate secretly, behind closed doors?"

Apparently his speech struck a few responsive chords with the new council because they voted him into office for the next two years.

The cost of administering to the needs of the people of the Pine Ridge Reservation is outlandish. The president, the executive committee and the tribal council are paid over $500,000 in salaries each year. This says nothing for the various tribal administrators and their staffs. When you consider that most tribal administrators receive salaries in excess of $18,000 and their secretaries start at $10,000 and up, you can readily imagine the tremendous cost of operating the tribal government. The total cost of salaries for administration last year was $731,848.

The one cost to the tribe that seems to grow each year with no end in sight is that of travel expenses. In 1979 the tribe expended $64,000 in travel funds. The cost to operate the various tribal offices (printing, utilities, office supplies, etc.) was $144,212.

One cost to the tribe that will continue to grow because of the rise in fuel prices is the expense of operating the tribal vehicles. Last year it cost the people of this reservation $31,000.

The legal and accounting costs to the tribe were $97,756 which included $50,000 to the Washington, D.C. legal office of Fried, Frank, Harris, etc.

This brought the total cost to the tribe from the general fund to $1,394,720!

The main concern to the new treasurer, Myron Rock—and it should be the chief concern to all tribal officials—is that the new austerity program enacted by the Carter administration will begin to be felt over the next few months.

The Comprehensive Employment and Training Act (CETA) alone will be reduced by approximately $1 million this fiscal year.

In addition to the legal services purchased by the tribe from the firm in Washington, D.C., there are also three full time attorneys on staff at the reservation who draw salaries of $30,000 apiece plus expenses.

I am not telling tales out of school by relating these costs to you because they are public knowledge and I feel that Rock hit the nail on the head when he referred to the monies in the tribal treasury as belonging to the people. I believe that they have a right to know how it is going to be spent.

It is not my intention in this column to ridicule the financial shortcomings of the Oglala Sioux Tribe. Instead, it is my intention to inform the people of the reservation of some of the costs that can, and should be dealt with as a tribal people. Unless you have specific knowledge of how the funds on the reservation are being misspent, business will continue as usual.

Until the people of the Oglala Sioux Tribe are fully informed of what is happening in tribal government, and only then, will they be able to help solve the many problems that are facing the Indian nations across this country in the 1980s.

Tribes Flirting with Financial Chaos

Time and time again the Interior Department has pulled the various Indian tribes from financial disaster with myopic short-term measures.

These patchwork methods caused a constant state of financial insecurity because they rewarded fiscal incompetence, encouraged dependency and caused the tribes to exist on a year-to-year basis.

This misplaced, paternalistic approach by Interior has contributed mightily to the dilemma most Indian tribes face. The inflationary spiral, budget cuts and tribal excesses have caused many tribal leaders to realize they are on the verge of financial chaos.

Rosebud Sioux Tribal Chairman Norman Wilson said, "We can no longer afford the cost of maintaining thirty-three tribal council representatives under Reagan's budget cuts. We can either reduce the size of the council or reduce their per diem rate of $800 per month." Wilson favors a council of seven.

On the Pine Ridge Reservation, the twenty-seven tribal council members of the Oglala Sioux Tribe draw annual salaries of $15,000 each. Combine this with the exorbitant salaries of the five-member executive committee (president, vice president, secretary, treasurer and a fifth member) and it is evident the elected officials cost the tribe $524,000 a year.

Add to this the thousands of dollars the tribe has borrowed to finance tribal economic enterprises, such as Angler Products and the Agriculture Enterprise, which have defaulted on tribally-guaranteed loans of $75,000 and $594,000, respectively, and throw in a few more enterprises on the verge of collapse, and it is apparent a drastic change in fiscal management is in order.

One Pine Ridge councilman had some suggestions. I hope he makes these on the council floor, also, and not just to me. He said, "If we reduce the number of council members from twenty-seven to nine, cut the council salaries in half, reduce the number of executive committeemen to three by eliminating the position of the fifth member and combining the offices of secretary and treasurer into one, cut the president's salary by one-half, and, finally, eliminate most travel expenses for the council, we can save the tribe a whopping $443,000 per year as starters."

This is only the tip of the iceberg. Every Indian tribe in the United States should apply the scalpel to reservation programs. Carve away the fat, layer by layer, and they will find that they can save the Indian people millions of dollars.

Although much blame for the tribes' problems can be laid directly on Interior, some of it must be shouldered by incompetent tribal leadership.

All of the signs indicating severe reductions in financial assistance to the tribes have been aparent for many years. The administrations of tribe after tribe were shaken by charges of mismanagement, incompetence and outright theft of tribal funds and resources. Many grassroots, reservation-based Indians knew that it was just a matter of time before the tribe's day of reckoning arrived.

At at time when spiraling inflation was forcing extreme austerity upon many Americans, most tribal governments conducted business as usual. The airways and highways were still filled with tribal leaders traveling to distant, expensive meetings being held in plush, metropolitan hotels. Many tribal people complained that these meetings could have been conducted for the cost of an 18-cent stamp or a $3 telephone call.

On many reservations, tribal leaders drawing salaries of $20,000 still drive tribally-owned vehicles to and from work, charging all expenses, including gasoline, to the tribe. It isn't uncommon to find offices on reservations where secretaries have secretaries.

Many high-salaried program directors and tribal officials work whenever they feel up to it. Using the outdated excuse of operating on "Indian time," this lackadaisical attitude is passed on to employees of these so-called leaders. Tribal offices are often closed at the drop of a hat with no interruption in wages.

If the reservations are going to be run like the giant corporations they are, it will require a magnitudinal change in the thinking and attitudes of elected tribal officials. The well is almost dry. It is up to the people themselves to seek out the leadership needed to save the tribes from extinction. Old prejudices must be set aside for the common good of all the people of the reservation.

The only people capable of destroying the Indian tribes are the Indians, themselves.

Archaic Thinking Hampers Development

Just what is the unemployment situation on the Indian reservations of this country?

The largest reservation in the United States, the Navajo Nation, estimates a 60 percent unemployment rate, while the second largest reservation, the Pine

Ridge Reservation, estimates an 80 percent unemployment rate.

After President Reagan took office, his administration began a massive budget cutback program. The heaviest ax fell upon the social programs and governmental agencies. About 90 percent of all jobs on Indian reservations are provided by governmental and social programs.

Utilizing the theory of supply-side economics, the Republican administration predicted that many of the jobs lost through these drastic budget cuts would be picked up by the private sector. It should go without saying that most of the people basing their hopes on this theory had never been to an Indian reservation. If they had, they would have realized that there is no private sector on an Indian reservation.

And so, to the people living on Indian reservations, the budget cutbacks were just that—budget cutbacks. In the lands of consumptive poverty, we were being forced to tighten our belts when there was no more slack.

For many years, the federal government had not developed an economic development program for the Indian reservations to cushion the effects of drastic budget reductions. Instead of assisting the tribes to develop economic self-sufficiency, the government, in its infinite wisdom, had kept the Indian nations securely tied to its ample apron strings.

Without considering the devastating effects of its actions, the government swept aside the obligations of many of the treaties signed in good faith with the Indian nations as so much pulp, and began the final phase of our destruction.

It was never the ambition of the Indian tribes to be totally dependent upon the federal government. Far from it! As a matter of fact, the paternalistic programs designed to keep the Indian nations subservient to the federal government were hatched in the minds of the bureaucrats from their ivory towers in Washington, D.C.

Consultation with the Indian tribes about "what it is they wanted to do to develop their reservation economics" was unthinkable. The concept of the Indian nations being "wards" of the federal government was, and is, firmly embedded into the archaic thinking of the federal bureaucrats. The policy of keeping the Indian tribes totally dependent upon the doles of the federal government was the government's idea, not the idea of the Indian tribal leaders.

The appalling unemployment rates and the stresses of poverty have not dampened the spirits of the Indian people. On the contrary, the abrupt actions by Uncle Sam have served to strengthen the resolve of the Indian people to become self-sufficient. Most Indian officials realize that this is only the beginning and that in order to survive as sovereign, independent nations, the Indian tribes must begin to develop the economic, industrial, tax and natural resource base in a way that will best serve their reservations.

There is one thing that sets the Indian people apart from all of the other minorities in this land. We have the largest land base of any minority. Our reservations comprise this land base. Most Indian land is marked by clearly defined borders and boundaries.

Upon these lands live a people who are considered to be residents of the United States, and citizens of the state in which their reservations are located. But more than that, the Indian people are also citizens of their reservations.

What is more, it is estimated that more than one-third of the remaining mineral wealth of this land is located on Indian reservations. Many of the Indian tribes, especially the larger ones, were not "given" reservations to live upon. Instead, their reservations are lands they lived upon from time immemorial, and these are lands they retained in treaty agreements. In fact, while retaining these lands, it was the Indian nations who gave up portions of this land to the white man for various reasons.

There is one question asked over and over on the reservations. If the federal government can pour millions of dollars in the economy of foreign countries in order to make them self-sufficient, why can't it do the same thing for the Indian people, the first Americans, the true landlords of this country?

Don't punish us for the past excesses of Washington, D.C. We were not a party to those excesses. In fact, we continue to be the poorest of the poor in the land we once owned.

As one tribal leader put it, "You can keep your perpetual handouts, but don't cut our feet out from under us when we are just beginning to learn how to stand on our own two feet."

Population, Budget Cuts, Taxes are Topics of Week

The Associated Press news story outlined the makeup of the state's population by race. The headline attached to the news release by the *Journal* staff read "Racial makeup of South Dakota is little changed." According to the 1970 census, Indians comprised 32,365 of the total state population. The 1980 census showed an increase to 45,101 for the Indian population.

Now, if my figures are correct, that is an increase of about 30 percent for Indians. If this increase is indicative of "little change," it boggles my mind that it would be considered an insignificant increase.

According to the Bureau of Indian Affairs, Indians have the youngest median age of any racial group in the state. Per capita, we are the fastest growing minority in South Dakota. This rapid growth for the Indian population holds true in every state with large Indian reservations. The fabled "Vanishing American" is making an amazing comeback.

Reagan Budget Cuts

At first glance, the $161 million proposed budget cuts from the BIA and the Indian Health Service portend an ominous trend for Indian tribes across this country. This is not necessarily so, according to President Ed Driving Hawk of the National Congress of American Indians. In Driving Hawk's opinion, these cuts represent "taking from the bureaucrats and giving to the poor."

Driving Hawk clarifies his startling deduction saying, "Despite millions of federal dollars that have been designated for Indian tribes over the past century, the actual benefit to the Indian tribes has been minimal. When one considers that 91 cents of every dollar allocated for Indian programs in the BIA remains within the department for administrative costs, and only 31 cents of every dollar is earmarked for Indians, it is readily apparent that the primary beneficiary of these federal monies has been the federal bureaucracy itself."

The direct funding approach to Indian tribes, called the block grant program, is supposed to circumvent the middleman, and by escaping the filtering process, put larger sums of money directly into the hands of tribal governments.

There are plenty of Indian administrators who would be very capable of budgeting and disbursing block grant funds for the benefit of all tribal members. The question I and many other tribal members would have is this: Will these capable Indian people be given the opportunity to administrate, or will the same incompetents, who believe in spending and more spending for their own benefit, be handed these funds?

Under the block grant concept, budgetary bungling by the tribal administration would become intolerable. If the tribal administration cannot live within its budgetary means, there would be no more "going back to the well" for additional funds to cover up these fiscal blunders. With the awesome responsibility of sound financial management placed directly upon the back of the tribal adminsitrators, their ability to cope with the complexities of fiscal management could spell the beginning of a new day for the Lakota people; or if they are not up to the challenge, it could mean the self-destruction of the Pine Ridge Reservation as we know it.

Monumental Decision

There is a case to be heard before the U.S. Supreme Court on March 30 which could have a profound impact upon every tribal government in this country. The case involves an Indian tribe's sovereign right to levy severance taxes. This hearing involves the Jicarilla Apache Tribe of Dulce, New Mexico.

The severance tax case, as it is called, arose after the Jicarilla Apache Tribe passed an ordinance placing a tax on oil and gas "severed" from tribal lands. Oil companies responded to the tax by charging the tribe had no right to levy such a tax. The oil companies further charged the tribe with placing an unfair burden on interstate commerce by forcing the oil companies to pay taxes which had already been paid to the State of New Mexico.

This is an important case for all Indian tribes because the outcome will strike at the heart of tribal sovereignty. It is a direct confrontation between state and tribal governments. The question to be answered is this: Can tribal governments levy taxes in order to raise revenues for self-support? The tribal government's ability to levy taxes is the crux of tribal sovereignty. Self-government is not possible without the ability to raise revenues to support it.

Difficulties Fail to Kill Spirit

The winter wheat is beginning to show tiny, green sprouts in the fields of the Pine Ridge Reservation. The melting ice on the dams and ponds dotting the reservation tells us that the long, hard winter is almost over.

There were times this winter when everything came to a complete standstill for several days. The cold winds whipped the snow around in such a fury that, at times, visibility was limited to just a few feet.

Working one day in the Pine Ridge Post Office, garbed in a heavy coat due to a heating malfunction, Postmaster Nancy Akers said, "Oh, I'll be so darned glad when this winter is over. I'm just getting sick of it."

Adding fuel to Nancy's anger was the cutback in working hours given to her employees because of "Reaganomics." Mrs. Akers said, "They just don't realize that there are no home deliveries around here. Almost all of the people on the reservation come to the post office to pick up their mail."

Complaints Heard

The cutbacks have caused her to close down the post office windows from 9:30 to 10:30 a.m. so her staff will have the time to put all of the day's mail in the post office boxes used by so many of the reservation residents. "People are really mad about this, but they just don't write letters to complain. We hear the complaints all day long, but what can we do?"

The rising cost of fuel has created many hardships on this reservation. Many of the residents are complaining about the inefficiency of the "Low-Income Energy Assistance Program" that is administered by the Tribal Government through the State of South Dakota.

Dave Long, an elder of the tribe and a former tribal vice president, said, "They make these forms so complicated that many of the poor people, who should be getting this assistance, are just getting by the best way they can. I have gone to them to complain many times, but I am still fighting to get the assistance my family needs."

Ramon Bear Runner, director of the Tribal Tax Office, said, "You know, when unemployment reaches 10 percent in the United States there is a near panic. And yet, on this reservation, we are right at 80 percent unemployment, and nobody seems to give a damn."

Jobs Lost

The single largest employer on the reservation is the federal government. The tribal government survives by federal funds, and the Bureau of Indian Affairs employs many reservation residents. When President Reagan reduced, and all but eliminated, the Comprehensive Employment and Training Act fund, more than 800 reservation jobs went down the tube.

Even the once secure jobs with the BIA are not sacrosanct any more. Several dozen BIA employees are looking at short lay-offs (one or two months) because the funding for their salaries has been reduced.

At a time when Indian people are saddled with the poorest housing in the United States, funding cutbacks in the Housing and Urban Development Program have eliminated the construction of all new housing, and funds to maintain and repair existing housing have been reduced so drastically that many houses are literally falling apart. Drive anywhere on this vast reservation and you will see homes with cardboard windows or old newspapers jammed into cracks in the walls to keep out the bitter South Dakota winter.

Wasuduta (Red Hail), who is employed by the state Food Stamp Program, is visibly angry. "How can this country send billions of dollars to buy guns for other nations and yet leave its own people, the first Americans, to wither and die?" he said one day last week. "My God, the cost of one jet airplane would build nice warm houses for the more than 2,500 homeless people on this reservation. Where are the priorities in Washington, D.C., when it comes to their own Native People?" he asked.

The Oglala Sioux Tribe exists on funds provided on a year-to-year basis. There are no long-range funding programs set up to enable the tribal officals to learn about long-term construction and budgeting. It is almost as if the federal government is afraid to make long-term agreements with tribal governments in order to keep them in costant fear of termination.

"They keep us on pins and needles year after year," said Tribal Attorney Mario Gonzalez. "Every time a new administration comes in, we have to worry about what their 'Indian Policy' is going to be, and whether they will be antagonistic or sympathetic to our existence as sovereign peoples."

The bitter cold winter of 1981-82 brought many hardships to the long-suffering grassroots people of this reservation. And now, with the smell of spring in the air, optimism can be seen in the faces of the Lakota people. Said one elderly woman, "They have done everything possible to ruin us already and they have failed." With a beautiful smile and a shrug of her shoulders, she added, "What more can they do to us?"

Elections

Columnist Begins Weekly Series with Election Information

(Editor's note: This is the first (October 26, 1979) of a weekly column of Indian news by Tim Giago, Jr., a Sioux author from Pine Ridge Reservation in South Dakota.

The column will be run each Friday in the Rapid City, South Dakota *Journal* and contain news and features about Indians.

Giago is a former public relations spokesman for the Pine Ridge tribal government and is the author of the book, *The Aboriginal Sin*. He is a former TV talk-show host on KEVN-TV, Rapid City, and now broadcasts Indian news on KSDZ, Gordon, Nebraska.

Your comments on this column are welcome. Giago can be reached at Box 925, Pine Ridge, SD 57770, or write Jim Carrier, News Editor, *Rapid City Journal*, Box 450, Rapid City, SD 57709.)

Tribal elections are held every two years on the Pine Ridge Reservation.

Many people think it is too often, because the cost to the tribal government is almost $50,000, the price of preparing and monitoring the balloting.

Next March 11, 1980, the offices of the president, vice president and twenty-six council seats will be up. Some on the reservation feel that in two years, these office holders hardly have time to familiarize themselves with their respective jobs, learn the hard lessons of serving and get acquainted with the various officials in Washington, D.C. who are the umbilical cord to the reservation.

And yet there are those who fear increasing the terms of office to four years because of the political atmosphere that is a part of every waking moment. If they are on the "outs" with the "in" administration, they would rather be unemployed for only two years, rather than four. Many also feel that they would rather have only two years of a bad administration and hope for the best instead of being saddled with the possibility of a questionable four years.

It was with these questions in mind that the Tribal Council met in Kyle, South Dakota in the Medicine Root District last week to discuss the ordinances and a timetable for the upcoming elections.

Severt Young Bear is chairman of the election committee. He and his committee had put together a calendar, marking all of the appropriate dates on huge calendars in red, yellow and green, Then the council went to work and dissected the schedule, making the changes they felt were necessary.

Here are the results of that meeting and the important new dates for all candidates.

In order to qualify, each candidate must meet all of the requirements of residency, enrollment and have the required number of signatures on a petition that is issued to them by the election committee; twenty-five signatures from their respective districts for council and one hundred signatures from each of the nine districts for vice president and president. These petitions will be issued December 17. The primary election will be held February 5; the general election, March 11; and the inauguration will be April 8, 1980.

Will eighteen-year-olds be allowed to vote? Not this time! The Council tabled this recommendation after a lot of discussion.

Russell Means took the floor and reminded the council that a ruling had been made by the Eighth U.S. Circuit Court, making it legal for eighteen-year-olds to vote on the Cheyenne River Reservation.

He said Judge Fred Nichols had ruled originally that the tribe could decide the question of eighteen-year-olds voting under their constitution (which set the age limit at twenty-one).

But Means said the ruling was overturned after a suit was brought against the tribe, and eighteen-year-olds were given the right to vote.

"Who would ever have thought that I, Russell Means, would ever stand before the governing body of the Oglala Sioux Tribe and ask them to uphold the Constitution of the United States and be rejected?" Means said after the meeting.

Elijah Whirlwind Horse, the current tribal chairman, who has served one term, hasn't indicated yet whether he'll run for re-election.

The next Tribal Council meeting is scheduled to be held in Pine Ridge Village October 25 and 26.

A district meeting on the Pine Ridge Reservation

Indians Cannot Turn Backs on Elections

There's an old saying: "If you don't want to get into arguments, never discuss religion or politics."

Well, I'm going to stay away from religious discussions, for the time being, but, because this is an election year, I cannot avoid politics.

We, as Indian people, cannot turn our backs on national or state elections any longer. We have political clout in South Dakota and it's about time that we begin to realize it.

Whether we like it or not, those politicians who are elected to serve in the Congress or the Senate of the United States are our representatives, also. The way they vote on issues pertaining to Indian tribes in this state can have a profound impact upon our lives, and what is worse, upon the lives of our children. We no longer can afford the luxury of complacency when the future of our children and our reservations are at stake.

Where would the Indian tribes of the United States be today if it had not been for the mighty efforts of former Senator James Abourezk? Can an Indian in this country deny the fact that he risked his political career to champion the cause of the Indian people? He stood up on the Senate floor and spoke up for the Indians when it was political suicide to do so and this is an undeniable fact.

Perhaps we will never again see the likes of Abourezk, because he was truly one of a kind, but we must maintain a constant vigilance over Washington, D.C. to protect our basic rights. In order to do this, we must decide which senatorial candidate will give us the best representation.

Before I discuss the merits of the two candidates running for the Senate, I will urge every Indian man and woman of voting age to register to vote. On election day, November 4, exercise your rights as a citizen of the reservation upon which you reside, get out and vote, and let your vote be your expression of sovereignty.

Independent candidate Wayne Peterson of Holabird, South Dakota has not, to my knowledge, taken a position on Indian issues but it would take ten columns to review the voting records of Senator George McGovern and Congressman James Abdnor on issues involving Indian concerns. But keep one very important point in mind when considering either of these candidates—Indian people comprise more than five percent of the total population of this state.

I called Barbara Walking Stick of the U.S. Census Bureau in Denver, Colorado and she sent me the figures from the 1970 census for twenty-three counties west of the Missouri River in South Dakota. Did you know that Indian people make up 13.95 percent of that population?

The reason I wanted these figures is that I have yet to see or hear either of these senatorial candidates address themselves to issues important to the Indian people. In fact, most of their TV commercials are conspicuous by the absoute absence of Indian people and Indian issues. Is it because these issues are best left untouched in an election year? Because Indian people make up almost 14 percent of the West River population, doesn't it seem plausible their votes would be actively sought by these two senatorial candidates?

Even though Senator McGovern has been most timid, at least in South Dakota, about speaking out for Indian legislation or rights, he has never to my knowledge, done anything while in the Senate to bring harm to the Indian people.

On the other hand, Congressman Abdnor co-sponsored a bill with Jack Cunningham of Washington to abrogate the treaties of all Indians in this country. Indian tribes found this piece of legislation so detestable that in 1978 they started what has become known as "The Longest Walk" which culminated on the steps of the Capital Building in Washington, D.C. This bill drew sharp criticism and attacks from every Indian organization and federally recognized tribe in this country.

If Senator McGovern chooses to extend his political career by assisting Indian tribes from inside a closet of anonymity, it is a sad reflection upon our times.

As I said, perhaps we'll never have another James Abourezk, and perhaps, we found out too late, what a courageous man he was on the Senate floor. But time marches on, and we have to make a decision to cast our ballots for the man who will fight for us, albeit from behind the curtains.

No matter, we must as concerned Indian people, get out and cast our votes in solid unison so that in future elections major candidates will not write off our votes as the kiss of death or as a slap in the face.

Minorities Vote in Blocs to Protect Themselves

A recent editorial in the Farmington, New Mexico *Daily Times*, located in the four-corners area of New Mexico, Colorado, Utah and Arizona, deserves some attention from an Indian perspective.

The editorial mentioned a voter drive about to be kicked off in San Antonio, Texas, aimed at registering Hispanic voters. According to a news story from the Southwest Voter Registration Education Project in San Antonio, the goal of the drive is to increase the 3.4 million Hispanics registered in 1980 to 4.4 million in time for the 1984 presidential election.

The editorial read, "We subscribe to any program designed to increase the number of citizens who participate in the electoral process. It is somewhat difficult, however, to endorse an effort having the announced intention to sign up members of a particular ethnic group with the assumption that they will somehow vote as a bloc in future elections."

It continued, "At a time when millions of Americans of all races, religions, colors, ethnic backgrounds and economic conditions are striving for equal treatment for all, it seems somewhat counterproductive to launch a program that has the appearance of preferential treatment for one segment of our population. People should not be encouraged to vote on the bais of their ethnicity—they should be encouraged to vote because they are Americans."

Yes, it would be nice if the white population of this country would accept all ethnic groups living there as "Americans." But, unfortunately, this is the real world, not an imaginary Utopia. If ever there was a line reading "Do not cross" painted between the white population and the minorities of this land, it was not the minority people who put it there.

As a matter of fact, in many cases it was the white political candidates who made it a point to make a distinction between races. How many of you can recall Governor George Wallace standing in the doorway of the University of Alabama and confronting the U.S. Marshalls in an effort to prevent a black student from enrolling?

In the State of South Dakota, it required federal intervention to force the all-white legislative body to reapportion the voting districts that gerrymandered the Indian reservations so that the Native Americans of the state would be able to elect representatives. Even though Indian people comprised as much as 85 percent of some counties, the voting districts were apportioned in such a way that many of these all-Indian counties had never been able to elect representatives.

It wasn't until January of 1982 that the reapportionment took place, and that fall, for the first time in the history of South Dakota, Indian people were elected to serve in the house and senate. No, you didn't misread the year—I said it was 1982!

Where were the bold newspaper editors of this state while the largest minority residing within their borders was being selectively and maliciously discriminated against? Why didn't the press exercise some of the freedom they are always clamoring about and speak out to bring an end to such an unfair system?

What many people fail to understand is that Hispanics and Blacks are seeking to become integrated into the social system of this country. They are looking for equality in hiring, education, the political process, housing, lending, and many other areas. Indian people are not looking to be integrated into the mainstream. We do ask to be treated as equals in all of the areas mentioned above.

The one thing that makes Indians different from all other minorities is the fact that we have a land base. We live on reservations with clearly defined borders and boundaries. We are a self-governing people with our own judicial, law enforcement and governing bodies. We are striving for total sovereignty. This means total independence, not total integration.

It is a fact of life that certain political candidates play off of the attitudes, racial and otherwise of their constituents. Too often, these attitudes are reflected in the legislation they introduce, and if their constituents have a negative attitude toward a certain minority, that attitude can be expressed through the introduction or perpetuation of laws designed to hold back, or infringe upon the freedom of that minority. This is a political reality, like it or not.

The one way that minorities can protect themselves is by electing officials who are sympathetic to their problems and will make an effort to help them. Although Indians, as a group, do not with to become assimilated into the mainstream, we must still be realistic enough to know what outside forces set into motion by state and federal legislators can, and do, have a profound impact upon our lives.

When congressional candidate Clint Roberts of South Dakota made a brash statement that was construed by many Indians of the state to mean that he intended to introduce legislation to "terminate" the Indian reservations if he was elected, it set off a tide of opposition to him that eventually led to his defeat. The eventual winner, Congressman Tom Daschle, won the election by less than 15,000 voters. Native American poll watchers estimate that the majority of the 15,000 to 20,000 Indian voters of the state voted against Roberts.

As long as there are candidates who would use ethnic differences to gain votes, minorities voters must vote in a bloc in order to protect themselves and their vested interests. It is a sad fact of life.

Tribes Must Implement Good Election Procedures

In too many cases, the transition between newly elected tribal administrations and the old, is not an easy one.

Most tribal councils fail to understand the extremely important role played in the tribal elections by the Election Board. It is the duty of this board to screen candidates, issue petitions, set up an easily understandable election ordinance, conduct the actual elections, count and validate the election results, and respond to challenges of discrepancies concerning the candidates or the conduct of the election.

Too often, the appointees to the election board are political. People are put on the boards because they have been on the board in the past, with little or no consideration given to their involvement in previous election fiascos. Or their appointment becomes a popularity contest. Little consideration is given to the qualifications of the appointees.

Almost every single problem which may arise in conducting an election, could have been nipped in the bud by an astute election board long before it ever became a problem. It should be their job to sort out and solve the election problems before the election, not after the fact. The high cost of conducting an election should preclude repeating a district, or reservation-wide election due to the incompetency of the election board.

Time after time candidates are issued petitions and allowed to run for tribal office without establishing residency, or without proving they have not been convicted of a felony. Most tribal constitutions and election ordinances spell out, quite clearly, the residential requirements, and the criminal conviction limitations that would eliminate prospective candidates. It should be up to the election boards to screen these political candidates BEFORE they are issued petitions to run for office, not after.

How many times, on how many reservations, have we heard of incumbent tribal councils refusing to recognize the results of an official election, and refusing to seat newly-elected candidates? When this occurs, the incumbent council usually calls for a new election.

A case in point is the recent election held on the Lower Brule Reservation in which the incumbent council refused to accept the results of the election, refused to seat the winners, and declared the election invalid. Once again the Election Board was caught in the middle and charged with discrepancies over how they conducted the election.

To make matters worse, the acting superintendent of the Bureau of Indian Affairs, William Gipp, along with the Acting Aberdeen Area Director, Donald Dodge, concurred with the incumbent council, and refused to recognize the newly-elected winners. As a result, DeWayne Goodface, Winona Long, Charles Langdeaux, Patrick Spears and William Ziegler, the winners, have hired a lawyer to appeal this decision, and seek a court decision resolving the election dispute.

Following the recent elections in Navajo Country, where Peterson Zah unseated incumbent tribal president (four terms), Peter MacDonald, the fur is still flying. His last day in office, MacDonald stored one hundred four boxes containing what he claims are "personal mementos of my twelve years as tribal chairman" at the Defiance Trading Post. Claiming the boxes may contain tribal property, Zah ordered a raid on the trading post and confiscated the boxes.

Former MacDonald aide, Samuel Pete, called the raid "Gestapo tactics" and accused the Zah administration of repeated efforts to "harrass, intimidate, degrade and smear" MacDonald. At last report, there may be a few lawsuits arising over this election transition incident.

Is it any wonder that certain white politicians attack tribal government by saying, "If they are claiming to be sovereign nations, they better start acting like sovereigns."?

The obnoxious arrogance of the BIA and the Department of the Interior to interfere with tribal elections further shackles the efforts of tribal governments to become self-sufficient. "How can we claim to be a sovereign nation when we run crying to the BIA every time an election doesn't go our way?" asked one disgusted Lower Brule resident.

All in all, the continued disputes brought about by the heated political climate on most Indian reservations must be addressed by cooler heads. Unless this is accomplished in the very near future, tribal governments will continue to be the laughing stock of white politicians and the whipping boys of an uninformed press.

Election Committee Has Tough Job

There are more than 2,000,000 acres of land within the borders of the Pine Ridge Reservation. The many treaties and laws passed by Congress, and verified by the U.S. Supreme Court (Worcester vs. State of Georgia) gives reservations the title of "dependent sovereign nations." The Indian Reorganization Act of 1934 set up democratic forms of government on many Indian reservations. Not all tribes in the United States voted in favor of the act, and it passed by the narrowest of margins on the Pine Ridge Reservation. There are those who do not recognize it, even today.

Article II, Section I of the Constitution and By-Laws of the Oglala Sioux Tribe states: "The governing body of the tribe under this constitution shall be a council which shall be composed of councilmen chosen by secret ballot by qualified voters of the tribe, which council shall hereafter be known as 'The Oglala Sioux Tribal Council.'"

The reservation was divided into eight communities or districts under the original constitution; but a ninth district was added later. Each district elects one councilman for each 500 members "or a remainder of more than 250."

Anyone who has ever tried to put together an election, whether for a student body or city representative, knows firsthand the great task he faces. In order for it to be a valid election, it requires much more effort than pulling the votes out of the ballot box and counting them.

The organization charged with this responsibility on the reservation is called the Oglala Sioux Tribal Council Election Committee. They are: chairman, David O. Brewer, and committeemen, Gilbert Mathews and Edgar High Whiteman, in 1980.

Their term in office began December 10, 1979, when they were sworn in to prepare for the coming tribal elections.

Since that day they have issued more than 140 petitions to the candidates for offices of representative, president and vice president. Each candidate had to be verified as eligible, the names on his or her petition checked for eligible voters, and ballots listing the names of all the candidates had to be prepared for the primary election on February 5, 1980.

After the primaries, the top vote-getters from each district will be placed on another ballot for the general election which will be March 11, 1980. For instance, Pass Creek has one representative; therefore, the two top vote-getters will face each other in the general election. There are more than thirty candidates running for the six positions open in Pine Ridge District. The top twelve will be selected to run off in the general election.

There are many new faces turning up at election headquarters. Bronc-buster Howard Hunter is seeking a seat as representative of the Medicine Root District. Former tribal president Albert Trimble is running for the council from the Wakpamni District; Associate Judge Hildegard Catches from the Wakpamni District; Tribal Treasurer Ivan Bettelyoun as a representative for the White Clay District; and former Executive Board Member Birgil Kills Straight is running for council from the Medicine Root District (Kyle). It seems that the candidates, this time around, are beginning to realize that the future of this tribe is in the hands of a strong council.

In order to alleviate any problems that might occur during this election, the election committee has set down some very tough guidelines for itself which have been incorporated into the Oglala Sioux Tribal Election Ordinance and has charged itself with "strict adherence to the provisions of this ordinance."

Those people who reside on the reservation and have been listed as NE's for so many years will have the opportunity of voting and running for office thanks to the effort of the tribal council which passed this motion, submitted by Councilman Eugene Rooks last week in Pine Ridge. This should solve one of the major problems faced each election by the election committee.

Most Indian people feel that the future of the reservation is at stake in the 1980s and only a strong, experienced government will be able to insure their safety. They will be taking a long, hard look at the candidates before they mark their ballots this year.

Federal

Indians Evaluate Self-Rule After Fifty Years

Nestled in the beautiful mountains of south central Idaho, the village of Sun Valley gives the impression of golf courses, tennis courts and expensive condominiums.

Sponsored by the Institute of the American West, the historic meeting held at the Elkhorn Inn was entitled, "Indian Self-Rule—Fifty Years under the Indian Reorganziation Act." Organized by E. Richard Hart, the director of the Institute, an expert on the Zuni history and ethnohistory, the meeting was intended as an educational gathering of scholars, historians, and tribal leaders to review and discuss, in depth, the good and the bad of the past fifty years of the IRA.

The IRA was a branchild of Indian Commissioner John Collier. Extensive studies by his staff had indicated to him that tribal lands were being sold off, and a general erosion of tribal structure was evident on many of this nations's Indian reservations. Collier firmly believed that if Indian tribes were given an opportunity to practice self-government, the trend could be reversed. Passed by Congress in 1934, the IRA was then sent out to the Indian reservations for acceptance or rejection. Although the majority of Indian nations became "IRA tribes," there were many that refused to approve the IRA constitutions they believed were being forced upon them.

Alfonso Ortiz, a member of the San Juan Pueblo Tribe, professor of anthropology at the University of New Mexico, talked about the participation in IRA by the tribes of the Southwest. He said that Collier had strongly supported some religious issues before Congress for the Pueblos of New Mexico, and as a result, he was deeply respected by the Pueblo Indians.

Because of this respect, the Pueblo Indians gladly accepted the provisions of IRA and three of the Pueblo Tribes adopted IRA constitutions.

Ortiz told about his tribe at the time IRA was suggested. He said, "We had herds of sheep, and we grew and traded such products as corn, red chili and wheat. Our boss farmer was called a "Kahu," which translated to mean "he who knows how to farm." The Indian agents told us that, if we did not stop having religious ceremonies involving the sun, moon and stars, we would go to hell when we died. We all laughed at this because we all knew that there were no Indians in hell. That place was not designed for Indians."

Ortiz said that some of the ideas put forth by Collier and the IRA were fundamentally different than those practiced under the traditional form of tribal government. Traditionally, our council was comprised of elders who were usually religious leaders as well. Any problems arising among the people were settled by the family or the extended family. If they could not settle their differences, it then went to a Council of Elders. This seldom happened because most Pueblo families did not want to go public with their family dispute."

Throughout the conference, arguments were presented that questioned the extensive use of anthropologists who had studied the Indian cultures and by their studies, helped to shape and formulate much of the policy woven into the fabric of the IRA. An elderly Ute Indian man from Utah asked Ortiz if these anthropologists formed their ideas of what they perceived to be important functions of the different tribes, and then shaped their findings to support these preconceived notions. This man, Frank McKinley, said, "Most of us remember the old saying about anthropologists. People used to ask how many people made up a Navajo family? The answer was: a mother, a father, the children, and an anthropologist. Kind of like one anthro per family."

Author Alvin Josephy (*Now That The Buffalo's Gone, The Patriot Chiefs*, etc.) decided to take full advantage of the accumulation of intellectuals present at the conference. He walked about with a note pad and asked some of the participants, "Did IRA give the Secretary of the Interior too much power over the Indian tribes and thereby make them more dependent?" Most of the tribal chairmen and Indian organization leaders responded to this question with a vigorous affirmative nod of their heads.

Robert Burnett, former chairman of the Rosebud Sioux Tribe, believed the conference would serve as a great source of information to the collective of writers and historians in attendance. "I hear a lot of ideas springing up from the people here and many of the tribal people, whether they realize it or not, are being hit right in the face, with these new ideas. This meeting could lead to the birth of a new, and better, Indian policy."

Elmer Savilla, the executive director of the powerful National Tribal Chairmen's Association based in Washington, D.C., mused, "IRA meant different things to different people. As we look at its implementation fifty years later, we can see some of the good and much of the bad. Hopefully, if we examine all of the papers and documents that will come from this meeting because of all the writers and historians present, we will learn from our mistakes."

Savilla, like many of the tribal officials present, regretted the fact that some of the internal tribal political problems were being hung out on the clothesline for everyone to see. "They should wait until they get back to their respective reservations before they talk about such things. These should be considered private matters. Of course, I am always bothered when some Indian officials run to the white media with problems that are made worse by the bad exposure the non-Indians give it."

All in all, this meeting at Sun Valley was highly charged with stimulating conversation and ideas. It covered much more ground than I am able to report in this small column. In my mind, much good came from this historic meeting.

Rule Changes Require Comments from Reservation

It was common practice, in years gone by, for various agencies set up to serve the Indian populations of this country, to determine policy at the Washington, D.C. level without seeking input from the Indian tribes.

Usually, these agencies relied upon the advice of such organizations as the National Congress of American Indians, or upon the advice of governmental Indians stationed in Washington known by the not-so-affectionate name of "The Washington Redskins" by tribal leaders.

Since the inception of self-determination for the Indian nations, these governmental agencies have published their intentions of changing or revising policies that have an adverse or positive affect upon the Indian tribes in the Federal Register. This maneuver is intended to solicit input from the tribal leaders.

Has this switch in governmental policy been effective? In some cases it has, but the biggest obstacle, and the cause of much concern, has been the failure of the Indian tribes to respond, in their own behalf, to proposed changes or revisions. Time after time, federal agencies have been deluged with angry letters and phone calls after the fact. When tribal leadership had the opportunity to offer meaningful input in determining policy, in many cases they sat on their hands.

One of the most important revisions in the delivery of health services to Indians is now under consideration by the Department of Health and Human Services. It was published in the Federal Register on June 6, 1983. The stir that it should have caused in Indian Country has been negligible.

When enacted, the revised policy would determine the eligibility for beneficiaries served by the Indian Health Service. What this means to the Indian tribes is that a new set of guidelines will be set up nationally to determine who is, or who is not, eligible to receive medical services from the Indian Health Service.

A synopsis of the criteria under consideration, options that are begging for tribal input, was sent to the Oglala Sioux Tribe by the Washington, D.C. law firm of Hobbs, Straus, Dean and Wilder. These tribal attorneys stress the importance of tribal input. They write, "On June 6, 1983, the Department of Health and Human Services issued the attached general notices concerning certain options under consideration to revise the eligibility criteria for persons being served by the Indian Health Service. It is the intention of HRSA to revise the present eligibility standards in order to strengthen the capability of IHS to manage its existing resources. In this regard, the HRSA is requesting detailed comments from American Indians, Alaska Natives, and Indian organizations on the options enumerated in these notices. The HRSA is also soliciting any general or specific comments on proposed alternatives, or combinations of the options presented."

The Washington law firm then goes on to list some of the specific changes under consideration. "Eligibility standards that are being considered include an option which will allow tribal governments to set their own eligibility standards, a singular requirement of membership in a federally recognized tribe. In addition, changes in eligibility standards are being considered which would affect the residency areas to be served by the IHS, and the process by which eligible beneficiaries are verified," the letter said.

The National Indian Health Board, based in Denver, is one organization actively involved in submitting input which could affect the implementation of the proposed changes. John O'Connor, public information officer for NIHB, is very concerned about the lack of publicity given this most important issue by the Indian media. He said, "We subscribe to many Indian newspapers, and I am really bothered by the lack of coverage in these newspapers. If we expect to get rule changes that are favorable to Indian tribes, we must inform our tribal leaders so they can respond on behalf of their respective tribes."

O'Connor said that the National Congress of American Indians had backed away from the issue when it was presented to them. They said that these are issues that should be left in the hands of each individual tribal council. "We are going to suggest that each tribal government be allowed to determine eligibility criteria based upon its membership. If HRSA tries to determine eligibility across the board, many Indian tribes will be in an uproar," he said.

In the event that eligibility is determined by tribal membership, O'Connor suggested that tribal identification cards could be issued to enrolled members by each individual tribe. "A disproportionate amount of health care resources (dollars) is allocated to certain areas, such as Oklahoma, where some of the eligible recipients have as little as 1/100th degree of Indian blood," said O'Connor.

The deadline for submitting proposals or comments on them was July 21, 1983. Any subsequent comments should be sent to Mr. Rich McCloskey, Director; Office of Legislation and Regulation Services; Indian Health Services; Health Resources and Services Administration; Room 6A-14, Parklawn Building; 5600 Fishers Lane; Rockerville, MD 20857.

Are Bureaucrats Winning the Battle?

June 25 is a special day to the Northern Cheyenne and the tribes of the Great Sioux Nation. It was on this day in 1876 that George Armstrong Custer and the troops of the Seventh Cavalry met their Waterloo at the Battle of the Little Big Horn. Many tribes consider this day a national holiday.

At a press conference held in Washington, D.C. last week (June, 1983), the members of the National Tribal Chairmen's Association, an organization made up of tribal leaders and one of the few that is truly representative of the Indian nations, struck at the core of the Reagan Administration and the budget cuts that have devastated Indian Country.

Many tribal leaders were optimistic when the new Indian Policy was announced by the White House in January. It promised a government-to-government policy between the federal and tribal governments. The tribal leaders were tired of trying to pierce the layers of insulation constructed between themselves and the agencies designed to serve them. Said one tribal chairman, "It is like dealing with an octopus. Every time you untangle yourselt from the grasp of one arm, another one grabs you."

The focal point of the association's complaints is the Bureau of Indian Affairs. Historically set up to assist the tribes of the United States, the BIA grew into a monstrous bureaucracy. It became "the tail that wagged the dog." Policies enacted by the BIA have wrought havoc in Indian Country in many instances.

There was a glimmer of optimism several years ago when the BIA instituted what became known on the reservations as "the honky bill." This bill gave early retirements to non-Indians working in the bureau and replaced them with Indians. Many tribal leaders believed that it would be impossible for Indians to work against their own people. They believed that the "termination" policies started in the 1950s would be brought to an end. They were wrong.

Oglala Sioux Tribal Attorney Mario Gonzalez said in a recent interview, "It's outrageous that the BIA is still promoting the terminationist policies of the 1950s. Worse yet, it is a small clique of Indians in the area offices of the BIA who are behind it." Gonzalez fears that "Indian preference in hiring" could be one of the worst things happening in Indian Country. He said, "You now have a neo-colonial situation where our own people are now accelerating termination. This is repugnant to self-determination and to our right to a landbase under federal and international law."

Newton Lamar, president of the Wichita Tribe of Western Oklahoma, and vice president of the chairmen's association said, "We are going to ask Congress to take back its traditional responsibility for dealing with Indians instead of leaving all of that responsibility in the hands of the BIA."

The association is planning to introduce legislation to create a greater congressional role in managing Indian affairs sometime in September.

The history of the Indian nations since June 26, 1876 has been a national disgrace. More than one hundred years since Little Big Horn, the Indian tribes are still fighting for recognition and survival. Our plight is recognized more by the nations of Europe than it is in our own back yard. The seat of our cultural, religious, governmental, and economic troubles continues to be located in Washington, D.C. Elmer Savilla, executive director of the chairmen's association, said recently, "We believe the handwriting is now on the wall and it reads 'termination.' We need to work together if we are to force the BIA and the Indian Health Service to work for us, not against us."

How independently powerful has the BIA become? Recent congressional efforts to restructure and redesign the BIA have proven to be virtually fruitless. As preposterous as it may sound, it is the BIA itself that is drafting a policy of restructuring itself, without input or consultation from the Indian nations it purportedly represents. In the past, this agency has thwarted, time and time again, efforts at reorganizing it to better do its job of serving the Indian people. Instead, it is the Indian people who have become servants of the former servant.

The twelve BIA area offices set up nationally to act as buffers between the BIA central office in Washington, D.C. and the Indian nations have become virtual roadblocks between the tribes and Washington. The administrative costs of operating these area offices runs into the hundreds of millions. As the salaries of these "go-between" administrators have grown, the financial services to the Indian tribes have shrunk.

To the casual observer, it may appear that there are enough dollars allocated to the BIA to serve the Indian nations. As a matter of fact, the BIA budget for fiscal year 1984 will probably top $1 billion. How much of this will actually reach the Indians of the reservations? With a little bit of luck, probably less than 40 percent.

Former President Jimmy Carter discovered, much to his dismay, that the hardest thing to move—or change—in the Nation's capital is the entrenched bureaucracy. The Bureau of Indian Affairs has become the epitome of an entrenched bureaucracy. And so, 107 years after Little Big Horn, the battle lines are still drawn. It appears the bureaucrats are winning.

All That Glitters . . .

Last month, two years into his administration, President Reagan announced his "New Indian Policy."

Anyone familiar with tribal governments will determine that the generalistic language of the new policy is based more upon idealism than practicality. Paper suggestions originating in the nation's capitol bear little resemblance to the actualities of reservation politics and lifestyles, particularly when they are submitted by self-appointed "Indian spokesmen" who have lost all touch with today's tribal leaders and have little or no contact with the grassroots people living on the reservations.

There are four basic initiatives suggested in the new policy which deserve to be implemented at the earliest possible date.

1. The Reagan Administration has requested Congress to repudiate House Concurrent Resolution 108 of the 83rd Congress. This resolution called for the termination of the federal-tribal relationship. The implied threat of this resolution has hung over the heads of tribal leaders for too long. In reality, it has prevented the efforts of long-range planning for the survival of tribal governments and has negated the government-to-government relationship between the federal and tribal governments.

2. A suggestion to move the White House liaison for federally recognized tribes from the Office of Public Liaison to the Office of Intergovernmental Affairs has been requested.

In the past, tribal governments have been lumped together with private interest groups such as veterans, businessmen and religious organizations. This move would put tribal governments on the same footing with state governments.

3. The Reagan Administration supported and signed into law the Tribal Government Tax Status Act. This will allow tribal governments the same

capability of raising tax revenues as other governments.

The one serious drawback with this Act is that a two-year limitation was placed on it. Since tribal governments have had no experience whatever in forming a tax base, reservation studies must be done, experts in the field of taxation hired, and laws initiated and implemented for the supervision and collection of such taxes. For most tribes, it will take all of the two years allotted to come up with a plan of action.

The way the law is written, it appears that the tribes will have to go back to Congress to lobby for an extension of the Tax Act or find a way to make it a permanent act.

4.Support has been offered by the Reagan Administration for direct funding to Indian tribes under Title XX social service block grants to states.

In the past, problems have arisen over the administration of certain social programs. Because of the adversary roles between state and tribe, this has been a continuous source of agitation.

As an example, in the State of South Dakota, confrontations between the state and tribe over the administration of the U.S. Commodity Program have almost resulted in violence.

By eliminating the middleman—the state government—in the administration and distribution of several social programs, most tribal officials believe these programs can be administered at less cost to the federal government and more efficiently serve the grassroots people living far out on the reservations.

Most of the problems between the tribe and state over the administration and implementation of social programs on the reservation have been due to a lack of communication and a decided lack of trust. The communications gap could probably be overcome in time, but the lack of trust felt by many Indian people for the state administrators appears to be virtually insurmountable at this juncture in our history.

Admonishing previous administrations for their paternalistic approach to tribal government, Reagan's policy reads, "Instead of fostering and encouraging self-government, federal policies have by and large inhibited the political and economic development of the tribes. Excessive regulation and self-perpetruating bureaucracy have stifled local deicison making, thwarted Indian control of Indian resources, and promoted dependency rather than self-sufficiency."

On paper, the "New Indian Policy" sounds almost too good to be true. Out on the reservations we have learned through practical experience that "all that glitters is not gold." Time after time we have had our high hopes dashed by bureaucratic mismanagement and needless red tape.

For the moment, tribal governments will take a wait and see approach to this latest Indian program. As the old saying goes, "The proof of the pudding is in the eating."

Indian Reorganization Act Worked Against Reservations

Many years ago, I had a political science professor who used to wonder aloud, "Are we shaping the system, or is the system shaping us?"

I am reminded of his words because we are in the midst of an election on the Pine Ridge Reservation and my observations lead me to believe that many of our voters are being pushed around by the system, rather than having the system work in their behalf.

At the time my political science professor was trying to pound some education into my head, I was living with my father who had been born in the Medicine Root District of the Pine Ridge Reservation in 1895, just five years after the Massacre of Wounded Knee. His first language had been Lakota, and he did not learn English until he was taught the language at the Holy Rosary Mission just after the turn of the century.

I was studying the lessons of "bossism" in relationship to the political machines of Tammany Hall. The lessons were so difficult and alien to me that I threw up my hands in total discouragement. My father, who had only a third-grade education, began to help me in his own quiet way. He said, "First of all, Tammany is taken from the name of an Indian of the Delaware Tribe who was actually known as Tammend. Because of his wisdom and pursuit of liberty, many early colonists adopted his name and his ideas in choosing democracy and patriotism."

He then began to tell me about the times before 1914 when the government was trying to install a form of democratic government on the Indian reservation. It was through him that I first learned about the Indian Reorganization Act of 1934. "There are many who opposed this act when it was first presented to us, but I knew that we had to have some form of government that would be recognized by the federal government in order to deal with our troubles on the reservation, and to save the land base," he told me.

He continued, "You must remember that this was 1934 and many of us who voted in favor of the IRA were looking for something to save our reservation. We all hoped that, as we became more familiar with the democratic system of government, we could change it to suit our own special needs ; but in those days, I don't think we really had any choice."

There were things about the system that bothered my father and he always talked about these things from a philosophical rather than a political perspective. "I left the reservation after spending the first fifty years of my life there. I left during World War II because there were no jobs on the reservation. The system was very new back then, but, instead of us shaping it to serve us, it seems that it always ended up working against us," he said.

My father blamed the Bureau of Indian Affairs for much of this because of its paternalistic attitude which caused Indian people to be treated like children, and for the lack of training by the BIA which should have been given to elected tribal officials in progressive government.

He told me, "Back then, we had many of our young men return to the reservation after getting good educations at schools like Carlisle Indian School and other schools, and they ran for public office, hoping to use their knowledge to bring factories and jobs to the reservation, but it seems like they never got elected. Most of the time we voted for people who were the descendants of our former chiefs. Sometimes this worked out, but most of the time, they had the name, but they did not have the talent or experience to do any good for us."

Like many young Indian men of more than twenty years ago, I, too, had been brainwashed by a system that encouraged us to abandon our reservations and make it in the white man's world. The idea of coming back home and trying to work on the reservation of my birth was planted in my head by my father.

He said, "I am an old man, and there are not too many years left for me. Perhaps I would have done things differently if I could have seen what was going to happen, but for me it is too late. Get your education and don't ever be ashamed of it, but don't waste it on yourself."

We used to sit in the kitchen of his tiny trailer home, a pot of steaming coffee on the stove, and we would read by the dim glow of a propane lamp. Although he had been away from the reservation for nearly twenty years, this man with a third-grade education never lost the ways of his people. He still spoke with the broken English and the colloquiallisms he grew up with, and he still injected Lakota words into his conversation.

From him I learned that it doesn't matter how much education you have. He used to say, "Some of the people with college degrees I have known have been the dumbest because they've never listened to the song of a bird, the sound of the wind through the pine trees, or appreciated the beauty of a white cloud floating in a blue sky on a summer's day. They will never be intelligent until they learn these simple things."

He may have been hurt by the system, but he was never conquered by it.

Taxes Create Problems for Indians As Well As Whites

How many times have you heard these tired cliches spoken with tongue-in-cheek, followed by weak, submissive chuckles: "The only thing you can be sure of is death and taxes," or "Taxation without representation," or "Don't mess with the IRS"?

If we are to believe the white man's history books, many Europeans came to this continent in the 15th and 16th centuries to escape unfair and burdensome taxes. They were being imprisoned and enslaved for failure to pay taxes.

Once they settled in the New World, as they called it, even though it was ancient to the original inhabitants, they were subjected to heavy taxation by the countries they had just deserted because of too many taxes. They revolted because they believed they were being taxed without representation.

Taxes! That is one of the most dreadful words in the English language. The Indian tribes of this continent lived in communal settings. Since everything was shared by all, there was no need for taxation. The nearest thing the Indians had to taxes was the toll they charged other tribes or other people to use a portion of their land, either for temporary dwelling places or as passageways to reach a destination that could not be reached without crossing their lands.

Another popular saying of the white man is, "If we don't learn from history, we are bound to repeat our mistakes." Did they learn from the sad history of taxation? Apparently not! Instead, they created the Internal Revenue Service. The IRS is a branch of federal government that rules by generating fear. Immigrants came to this country because they were being jailed for failure to pay taxes. This was the land of the free and the home of the brave. What do you suppose will happen to you if you refuse to fill out tax forms each year? You'll be sent to prison for failure to pay taxes, that's what!

Now you might be asking yourself: "What does the Indian race care about whether we pay taxes or not? They don't!" And you will be fooling yourself once again. We do pay taxes, and what's even worse, we pay taxes without representation or little, if any, compensation.

For example, when we shop in any of the towns or cities off the reservation and pay sales tax for cars, appliances, groceries or furniture, where do you suppose those tax dollars go? They go to the state, the county or the city. We spend millions of dollars each year in the towns bordering our reservations, which amounts to millions in taxes each year, and those tax dollars are used for your communities, not ours on the reservation.

But that's not your fault. The fault lies with tribal governments that have not realized that to keep some of those dollars on the reservations, and put them to work for the people of the tribe, they must institute a form of taxation from a tribal level. Many tribal people are afraid to do this because they have been instilled with the fear common to the white man when it comes to taxes. They do not want to create a tax organization which can become as ruthless and powerful as the IRS.

There is a man named Ken Barney who lives in Hill City who decided that federal taxation was not only burdensome, but illegal as well. He became a member of a very small group of people who are willing to stand up and be counted, called tax protesters. Barney is not a criminal by any stretch of the imagination, and yet when he lost his case against the federal government, he was sentenced to prison. If the federal government says you are a criminal, then by God, you are a criminal. How dare you question the U.S. government?

On the Indian reservations of this land, many Indians who find jobs must share their meager incomes with their families. Now this could include mothers, fathers, brothers, sisters, aunts, uncles, grandparents, nieces and nephews. They are the Tiyospaye—the extended family. What does the IRS think of this tradition?

One young Indian lady earned a whopping $7,000 for a year's work. She claimed a few members of her family because they were not working, and because she helped clothe and feed them. She claimed the huge some of $400 for this support. What did the almighty IRS do? It said, "You do not qualify as head of the household and therefore you must return the deduction you received!" The implications were clear. You must return the money or else!

How could the citizens of this nation create an agency that has the powers of judge, jury and executioner over them?

One young Indian man demanded a hearing from the IRS because he thought the decision it rendered in his case was wrong. Even though he demanded a hearing in writing, three years have passed and he still has not had his hearing. He was told by an IRS agent out of Aberdeen, "Sure, we'll arrange for you to have a hearing, but I'll tell you right now, you don't have a chance."

Nothing gets an Indian madder than to hear a white man say that Indians don't pay taxes!

Professional Advocates Needed in Indian Organizations

There is a feeling of pessimism on the reservations of this country. A recent trip to Washington, D.C. by Arizona State Representative Daniel Peaches, himself a Navajo Indian, caused him to return to Arizona filled with a sense of foreboding.

Peaches found that the feelings of security and bureaucratic smugness are dissipating from the lives and faces of entrenched bureaucrats with each new round of budget cuts.

"I returned from Washington with an uneasy feeling that something bad is about to happen or is happening that will have a detrimental effect on Indian people for many years. The worst thing that can happen, aside from the budget cuts, is that Indians will be made subject to state jurisdiction," Peaches said.

It is his opinion that the new Assistant Secretary of Indian Affairs, Ken Smith, is not a friend of the Indian people. He quoted Smith as saying that the education of Indian children should not be considered a part of the federal trust responsibility. "For the first time in many years, termination may be upon us again," Peaches said.

What is needed in Washington is "a new breed of professional Indians who are committed to Indian sovereignty and Indian self-determination," he said. He believes that high positions in Washington are being filled by "technocrats who have no idea of what Indian self-determination means, or any idea of how Indian trust responsiblities will be protected in the face of budget cuts and trend of policy shift to the states with a new emphasis on the private sector."

This astute assessment of a critical situation by Rep. Daniel Peaches should be applauded by tribal leaders on every single Indian reservation in this country. With straight, yet simple logic, he has gone directly to the heart of a problem which has been growing, like a cancer, for too many years.

The Washington hierarchy has heeded the advice of the "technocrats" over the protest of the tribal people for generations. If these sychophants looked like an Indian or sounded halfway knowledgeable about the needs of the Indian population of the nation, the bureaucrats turned a deaf ear to the real needs of the reservation people. These self-proclaimed "Indian leaders" ensconced themselves in the nation's capital, ready to traipse over to Capitol

Hill at the drop of a hat, to tell the bureaucrats everything they ever wanted to know about the needs of the American Indians.

These "elitists" celebrated their own importance with elaborate conventions each year (and still do), held in the posh surroundings of the finest hotels, in the biggest cities, steeped in all of the trappings that money could buy. At these conventions, they would wheel out the political speakers, garbed in their finest, to tell the conventioneers how much they are helping the Indian people. Heaven forbid that they would hold these affairs on an Indian reservation where they could address the very people they were professing to serve.

To me, the saddest parts of this annual charade were the resolutions presented and passed amidst all of the hoopla of a convention, which carried about as much weight with the White House as the paper they were printed upon.

Rupert Costo, a Cahuilla Indian, editor of *The Indian Historian* of San Francisco, California, has said over and over, "It really doesn't matter who is put into the titled offices of the bureaucracy of Washington, Indian or not. In a very short period of time, their spines turn to jelly."

Indian organizations are started to fill a need. Inevitably, the organization becomes involved in a struggle for survival, and that struggle becomes more important than the reasons for forming the organization. The energies devoted to the organization's survival become the focal point of its existence, and its effectiveness to serve the needs of the Indian people are negated.

The tribal people of the Indian reservations can no longer look to these organizations as their advocates. If lobbying is the name of the game (and it has proven to be very effective in the past), then the tribes themselves must provide the trained personnel from their own reservations, to lobby in their behalf. Then, and only then, will the true and distinct needs of the Indian tribes be served.

Peaches summed up his Washington visit this way: "It is time for the Indian people to fill key positions in the Interior Department, in the Health and Human Services, and other agencies of the federal government with knowledgeable and skillful Indian professionals. Otherwise, the concept of self-determination for Indian people will be only a memory a year or two from now."

Peaches concluded, "We must make that something good happen ourselves because no one is our advocate in Washington. It looks like we are on our own."

BIA Plays Musical Chairs with its Officials

Do the many Indian tribes subservient to the Aberdeen (South Dakota) Area Office have any say in who is appointed director of that office?

Donald Dodge, the new acting director at Aberdeen, was, until last week, the director of the Navajo (Arizona) Area Office. But he made a speech before 950 people at a political rally held in Wheatfields, Arizona. In the speech he endorsed the candidacy of Peterson Zah, the main political opponent of Tribal Chairman Peter MacDonald of the Navajo Reservation.

As a federal employee, Dodge is subject to the provisions of the Hatch Act, which forbids the public endorsement of political candidates by government employees. Zah's election committee issued a press release acknowledging Dodge's support. And MacDonald's campaign committee fired back, criticizing Dodge for "getting involved in tribal politics."

At stake in the political squabble is the office of the chairman of the largest Indian tribe in the United States, 150,000 strong. MacDonald has served as chairman for twelve years. His salary is $55,000 per year, and even if he loses this election, his pension plan based on his longevity, calls for him to draw $41,250 annually until the day he dies. Seven candidates will have a run-off for the chairman's seat in the primary elections scheduled for August 10, 1982.

By the time this article is published, there will be only two candidates left to face each other in the general election to be held on November 2. Coincidentally, on that same day, the elections for federal, state, and county offices will also be held. This arrangement could lead to the largest Navajo turnout for any off-reservation election in the history of the tribe.

Skilled politicians, such as former Senator James Abourezk, have urged the tribes in South Dakota to arrange the dates of their tribal elections to coincide with state and federal governments to ensure maximum participation. The turnout for tribal elections on many reservations runs as high as 75 percent and the turnout for state and federal elections has run as low as 10 percent.

Registering to vote in state or federal elections has been a huge problem. Many tribal people believe that if they are registered to vote in the tribal elections, they are automatically allowed to vote in the state and federal elections. This should be the case, but it is not.

Reports and rumors began to circulate around the BIA offices in Washington, D.C. that Donald Dodge would be transferred from the Navajo Area Office to become the new director of the Aberdeen Area Office, replacing Jerry Jaeger who is being transferred to Washington, D.C., to be acting director of Indian Education Programs. Shades of the Peter Principle! The rumors turned out to be true!

The procession of musical chairs will find Curtis Geigomah, a Kiowa Indian, replacing the Navajo Indian, Dodge, in the Navajo Area Office. Is the immediate transfer of Dodge, for his alleged transgressions, an indication of how quickly the BIA can act when the action is in its own interests? Do the Washington bureaucrats consider Dodge's transfer a form of punishment—such as sending the German soldiers to the Russian front?

Since its inception, the BIA has moved superintendents around like so many pawns on a chessboard with little or no input from the Indian tribes. That attitude toward the tribes seems to be—like it or lump it—we know what's best!

Every tribal chairman of any tribe being served by the Aberdeen Area Office should protest this action. If our marriage to the area office is to be one of convenience, then let us see to it that the convenience is a mutual one. Perhaps

Law enforcement officers on the Pine Ridge Reservation at a training school

Computer courses are taught at Oglala Community College.

An employee at the moccasin factory cuts moccasin parts with this machine.

Tribal officials discuss governmental affairs with John Fritz, assistant to Ken Smith who is a top Department of the Interior official

*Dorothy Black Crow, Alvin Josephy, Robert Burnette and Rob Gay confer about an article for the **National Geographic** magazine.*

the position of the director of the Aberdeen Area Office is not that important to the faceless bureaucrats in Washington, and they believe that they can send their people here for disciplinarian reasons, but they are trampling upon our rights and our integrity in the process.

I, for one, am firmly convinced that the Aberdeen Area Office should be shut down completely and the responsibilities of its personnel should be transferred to the local agencies and to the tribal governments. Since that is not about to happen, the next best thing would be to put happy, qualified Lakota people in charge. When are the bureaucrats going to stop making a joke out of our goals of "self-determination?"

Big Brother Living in Aberdeen

George Orwell's 1984 outlined a fictional totalitarian state where "Big Brother" ruled over thought and deed. Published in 1949, the novel makes one wonder whether Orwell had researched any of his materials by referring to Bureau of Indian Affairs or Public Health Service manuals.

The weekly Pine Ridge Reservation newspaper, *The Lakota Times*, has been printing articles contributed by employees of the Public Health Service Indian Hospital. The purpose of the articles was to open up a line of communication between the IHS and the people of the reservation. The articles were intended to inform, enlighten and educate.

One weekly column addressed the problems faced by women in the area of health and was appropriately titled, "For and About Women." Written by Barbara Criss, a highly respected woman who directs the Mid-Wives Program on the reservation, the series of articles on childbirth, teenage pregnancy and other issues important to women drew wide acclaim on the reservation.

The other weekly column was contributed by JoBeth Adamson, Health Nutritionist, and was called "From . . . Commodity Corner." In this column, recipes were suggested to make the food offered to the reservation residents through the Food Commodity Program more palatable. These articles also were well received on the reservation.

Enter "Big Brother!" On November 16, a memorandum was sent to Service Unit Director of the Pine Ridge Hospital, Terry Pourier. Under subject matter, the memo read, "Writing for Publication by IHS Employees." Signed by Rolland Nielson, Program Management Officer, Aberdeen Area Indian Health Service, the memo begins, "This is in reference to the question raised concerning IHS employees writing articles, upon request, for publication in local newspaper."

The memo continues, "We made a telephone contact with IHS headquarters to obtain some manual or regulation reference point and were referred to the DHHS Standards of Conduct. We also advised that such writing and editing did require advance approval.

Next the memo went on to list "three different approaches" the employee may take to comply with rules and regulations, such as: Make no mention of his or her official title or affiliation with the department, and submit the material for clearance (see attached IHS Circular No. 75-6)."

Then, tossing all three of these options into a cocked hat, the memo reads, "Regardless of which one of the three above options the employee or local management elects, advance approval is required."

A telephone call to Neilsen's office in Aberdeen was answered by Jimmy Johnson. When asked about the memorandum, he replied, "I know exactly which memo you are referring to because I wrote it, and I don't think it says one goddamned thing about any form of censorship." When I asked Mr. Johnson if I could quote him on this, a lengthy silence followed, and finally he responded, "I'll have Mr. Neilsen call you just as soon as he returns." I'm still waiting for that phone call.

If you have ever tried to determine the source of a memorandum issued by any branch of the federal government, you'll know that it is a rough situation. Noting that the memo referred to "IHS Headquarters," I immediately placed a call to that department located in Baltimore, Maryland. Once connected, I went through the usual bureaucratic shuffling, and was finally put in touch with a Dr. Geswalde Verrone of Program Operations.

Dr. Verrone assured me that the same rules and regulations applicable on the Pine Ridge Reservation also applied to the "headquarters staff." The policy in Maryland, according to Dr. Verrone, allowed IHS employees to write articles for publication "if the employees did not use their official titles."

Meanwhile, back on the Pine Ridge Reservation, IHS employees are being asked to do the following in order to get approval to submit articles: "To obtain approval, each employee who writes articles for the local newspaper should complete an HEW-520 per instructions in the Supervisors Handbook." The service unit director is being requested to get a letter "from the editor or manager of the newspaper requesting that members of your staff periodically provide articles in their areas of specialization," and finally, "concurrence of the appropriate tribal authority would be required."

Terry Pourier said, "I must say that I saw no reason why the articles could not be printed. I felt they were beneficial to the health and well-being of the people. I will ask my employees to comply by requesting approval to write articles for the paper. In the meantime, the articles will be discontinued. I regret having to take this action."

Big Brother is alive and well and is living in the Aberdeen Area.

Sovereignty Still Important Issue

What is the meaning of "trust responsibility" held by the federal government over the Indian people and their lands?

Are the solemn treaty agreements, the basis of federal-tribal relations, as worthless as the paper they are printed upon?

Webster's Dictionary has many definitions for trust and responsibility. The one which best encompasses the role of the federal government as regards Indian tribes should read, "something committed or entrusted to one to be used or cared for in the interest of another."

On April 24, 1981, the South Dakota Supreme Court heard arguments in the State of South Dakota vs. Marvin Wayne Janis. This is an extremely important case because it deals with state jurisdiction over highways on Indian reservations.

State Move

In an untimely and unexpected move, South Dakota U.S. Attorney Terry Pechota asked the State Supreme Court to disregard the brief he had submitted in behalf of the federal government supporting the case of the Cheyenne River Sioux Tribe.

Explaining away this shocking breach of federal trust responsibility, Pechota said the move indicated "the new conservatism of the Interior and Justice departments." If the federal government is going to institute a new policy of forsaking the trust responsibility it holds for the Indian tribes, and throw them open to the baying wolves, let the tribes beware. Perhaps it is about time the Indian tribes throw off the yoke of the Department of the Interior and actively pursue the course of true liberal sovereignty entirely on their own.

If the federal government has changed the rules of trust responsibility and it is, at last, revealing its true intentions of abandoning the Indian tribes, then it is about time the rules were rewritten by the tribes to their own best interest. It is time the albatross of the Interior Department is removed from around the neck of the Indian tribes and they are allowed free reign to determine their own fate.

The Indian Reorganization Act of 1934 imposed a supposedly democratic form of government upon most of the Indian reservations. The Inerior Department issued sample tribal constitutions for the tribes to use as guidelines. Many of these sample constitutions were adopted in toto by the tribes.

Puppet Governments

What the IRA did, in fact, was to establish puppet tribal governments that could not pass a single law or enact a single resolution without the express consent and approval of the Bureau of Indian Affairs and the Secretary of the Interior. This stuck in the craw of many Indian people and they refused to recognize the IRA government.

The Interior Department confirmed the darkest suspicions of these dissenters by using its role as overseer to severely hamper tribal independence. Instead, it solidified its dictatorial authority over the tribes by making them totally dependent upon the government. The federal umbilical cord became the sole source of nourishment to the dependent tribal governments.

Time after time, decisions handed down by the Interior Department went against the tribes in favor of big business and actually encouraged state and individual encroachment upon tribal lands. The unsavory dealings of the federal government diminished the land holdings of the Indian tribes while increasing its own. This double-dealing by the government has lent new meaning to the words "trust" and "responsibility."

The colonial status foisted upon Indian tribes, by a nation clamoring to be the greatest on earth, is a national disgrace. The treatment of Indian people has caused even the most sedate of Europeans to raise an eyebrow in shock and sorrow. Has the maniacal pursuit of water and energy resources by the government and big business opened up the floodgates for the final assault upon the Indian reservations?

Melting Pot

As shocking as it might sound to most patriotic Americans, the Indian tribes do not want to be tossed into the great melting pot of this society. Instead, they wish to retain their own status as independent, sovereign nations; free to practice their own religion, speak their own language and maintain their own culture without federal intervention. In no way does this diminish the Indian's love for his land or his country.

Since the treaties signed between the federal government and the Indian tribes were by mutual consent, turning to a "new conservatism" should not be the exclusive right of the federal government. Perhaps it is time for the tribal governments to take a close, hard look at the decision of their "trustees" to abandon them, and to act accordingly.

Bureaucrats Fail to Serve People

George Bush, the vice president of the United States, and all the local politicians have suddenly become very concerned about the poor Indians of South Dakota. Or have they?

Observing the frenzied activities of these politicians in trying to keep the Bureau of Indian Affairs Area Office in Aberdeen and the various Indian schools open reminds me of the skit by the oldtime comedian, Jimmy Durante. He used to shake his head to emphasize his most outstanding feature, his "schnozzola," and say, "Everybody wants to get into the act!"

I'll not go into the pros and cons of keeping the BIA schools open. I'm afraid that I could not render an impersonal opinion on this matter. I attended boarding schools when I was young, and I will never be a proponent of this type of educational facility. I believe that our children should be educated at home on the reservations where they were born and not shipped off to a BIA school.

For more years than I can remember, tribal officials have been expressing their displeasure with the area offices of the BIA. They have condemned them as bottlenecks in the future of the Indian reservations.

Patterned after the "granddaddy" office in Washington, D.C., the area offices across the country soon developed reputations as bureaucratic and impersonal replicas of their master.

Often, fearful of losing their status and their jobs if some of the responsibilities handled by their efforts were shifted to the tribes, area bureaucrats have been guilty of making the efforts of self-determination more difficult. Intentional roadblocks have been stewn across the paths of the tribal leaders in an effort to make them appear incapable of contracting the services provided by the BIA.

The Indian Education and Self-determination Act, Public Law 93-638, designed to give the tribal leaders more say into how the funds for different programs would be utilized on a local, reservation level, has not met with much success. Many tribal leaders blame the BIA for this.

Cities, such as Aberdeen, South Dakota and Billings, Montana, have been notorious for their biased treatment of Indians. Suddenly, with the spectre of millions of dollars flying away, they have made a concerted effort to keep the area offices in their cities.

Where were the concerned chambers of commerce of these two cities when Indians were having such a hard time finding homes to live in because of racial discrimination?

The elected officials of the states of South Dakota and Montana have turned deaf ears to the pleas of the tribal leaders about the incompetency of the area offices. These politicians have never made an effort to visit the Indian reservations of their respective states and find out, firsthand, from the Indian people, themselves, what it is they want to do about the closing of the area offices in Aberdeen and Billings.

Instead, they held their opinions to themselves until they were sure that the political winds were favorable, and then they fell all over themselves trying to appease the non-Indian complainers. I guess most politicians know which side their bread is buttered on.

If the high mucketymucks of the Department of the Interior were genuinely interested in saving the taxpayers of this nation millions of dollars, they certainly would not have recommended keeping the area office in Aberdeen operating. They would have recommended shutting it down completely and allowing the Indian tribes to deal directly with Washington.

I am absolutely aghast at the audacity of our elected representatives for projecting themselves into the center of a very complex issue without once consulting with the tribal leaders elected by the people of their reservations. After all, whose lives will be affected by a decision to keep the area office in Aberdeen or move it to Rapid City? Certainly, such a move would have no impact upon the economy of that city, but the impact upon the daily lives of the Indian people served by this agency is much more crucial.

Elected officials, who wouldn't touch an Indian issue with a ten-foot pole, are suddenly scrambling all over each other to voice their concerns about the future of the Indian people of the state. You don't suppose the sudden concern is evident because it is an election year? Heaven forbid! Perish the thought!

If the statement made by Vice President Bush that the area office will stay in Aberdeen is factual, then I pity those politicians who let the rantings and ravings of a mainly non-Indian chamber of commerce influence them enough to make a decision that will have a profound impact upon the lives of the 45,000 Indians of this state.

Natural Resources
People Compared to Flock of Sheep

It has been many years since I have seen anything like it. Traffic was backed up across the Bay Bridge to San Francisco for several miles. Inching ahead at a snail's pace, caught up in this ribbon of steel, trapped in the midst of four solid lanes of commuters was an experience I will not soon forget.

I took the time to observe the drivers and passengers in the cars, vans and trucks surrounding me. They seemed to be totally shut off from the world around them. With their windows rolled up tightly against the early morning chill, their radios or tape decks at high volume, hunched over their steering wheels, they appeared to me as caterpillars snug in their self-woven cocoons, oblivious to reality, secure in the metal wombs.

Has the headlong pursuit of material wealth, modern technology, and so-called progress reduced us to mindless robots, caught up in a traffic jam, pushed along with the flow, like a flock of sheep? It's a frightening thought and one for which there is no clear answer.

Traffic Jams

Traffic jams are a rarity on Indian reservations. Perhaps in this respect reservations are "islands unto themselves." Several years ago, while traveling across a reservation in the Northwest, a gravel truck overturned and blocked passage of all traffic on the road. Once more, I was unfortunate enough to be caught in this unexpected traffic jam.

Now, this is where the similarity ends. After observing that traffic would not be flowing at a regular pace for a short while, the passengers of the autos and trucks caught in the line began to emerge from their vehicles and exchange conversation. Most of the drivers and passengers were Indians. There was a lot of joking and laughter echoing through the line of commuters. I joined in a light banter with some truck drivers in front of me, and I thought to myself at the time, "This is a pleasant way to make the best of a bad situation."

Are the small communities such as Farmington, New Mexico or Rapid City, South Dakota becoming miniature replicas of metropolitan cities such as San Francisco? Is the slow pace of ten years ago beginning to pick up speed and force the inhabitants of these communities to go in a direction they do not wish to follow?

These are the questions which are being asked on many Indian reservations across this continent. Vital sources of energy, needed more than at any other time in our history, have been discovered upon the distant Indian reservations of this nation. This has brought the tribal officials eyeball to eyeball with a law known as "the law of supply and demand." The supply is there, on the reservations, and the demand is growing with each day.

Unlike the non-Indians, who can pursue whatever course chosen on an individual basis, each Indian is an individual within a tribal structure. The decision an Indian must make is not "what is good for me?" but, "what is good for my tribe?"

The protection of the tribe as an individual entity against outside influences is a concept that is very hard for the average non-Indian to comprehend. The death of the tribe is the death of the people; and this is one of the greatest fears of the Indian. All decisions, from a tribal leadership point of view, must be made to include the continuity and the survival of the tribe. There is no other approach to any dilemma. The survival and growth of the tribe must take precedence over every other consideration. This is the way it has always been.

These are the things that are in the minds of many Indian people as we enter the decade of the 1980s. They are asking themselves and their elected leaders to proceed with caution—to not be caught up in the pursuit of material gains so that they lose sight of their culture, their religion and their heritage.

Many of the elders are inspiring the young with the message that "the energy beneath the surface of Mother Earth will not last forever." It is tansitory; and once it has been removed, it can never be replaced. They are asking the young people to slow down and think of tomorrow. "Do not get caught up in the flow of traffic. You may end up in a huge traffic jam."

Perhaps this is a message for all people of this planet Earth!

Indian Water Rights Must Be Protected

The American Indian Lawyer Training Program conducted a symposium on Indian Water Rights at Oakland, California last November.

The theme of the water conference: "Increasingly, Indian tribal leaders are recognizing that water management and water rights are issues of universal importance and not limited to those regions with arid conditions."

As the mad search for new sources of energy has gripped this country, it has become apparent to the energy companies that water is one of the key ingredients to exploration and development. Mining operations are contingent upon the availability of large quantities of water.

An article appearing in the CERT Report (a bi-monthly news magazine published by the Council of Energy Resource Tribes) took a hard look at the complex issues surrounding Indian water rights. Referring to the symposium held in Oakland, the Report said, "In the Missouri River Region, there are interstate disputes over the apportionment of water between the upper basin states for energy development and the lower basin states for in-stream flows to protect river freight traffic. These disputes may limit amounts of water available to Indian reservations in South Dakota, despite a current surplus of water in that state."

Whether to negotiate or to litigate water rights is a core problem faced by tribal leaders. Many feel that the Indian tribes have always fared badly when they chose to negotiate because they do not have the legal expertise available to them that is available to state governments. Some tribal officials are rankled by the position advanced by the Interior Department which recommends negotiation over litigation.

Oglala Sioux Tribal Attorney Marvin Amiotte, a member of the tribe has been studying the ramifications of a lawsuit brought by South Dakota Attorney General Mark Meierhenry that would attempt to settle the water rights disputes in his state once and for all, at least from the state government's perspective.

Amiotte said, "It has always been my contention that Indian tribes come out on the short end of the stick when negotiating any legal matter with state governments. Of course, state governments are looking to serve their own best interests, and too often, tribal governments are not recognized as viable governments, nor do Indian tribes have the potential clout to use as a lever during the negotiating process."

Many tribal attorneys, including Amiotte, believe that tribal interests are not being protected by the U.S. Justice Department. "There is a definite conflict of interest present whenever the Justice Department becomes involved in water rights disputes. They also are protecting the legal concerns of the Corps of Engineers and the U.S. Fish and Wildlife Service, and when the positions presented by these agencies are in conflict with the interests of the Indian tribes, it becomes very difficult for the Justice Department to remain impartial and objective," Amiotte said.

Amiotte admitted there are definite perils to the Indian tribes by litigating water issues. "Victories by tribal governments in federal courts have been few and far between. The judicial system has not been favorable to Indian tribes, and the very fact that, in most cases involving water, the Justice Department can become the adversary of the Indian tribes makes litigation a fearful proposition, also," he said.

Kenneth Smith, Assistant Secretary of Indian Affairs, proclaimed the position taken by the federal government:

"Since I favor negotiated settlements, I am willing to accept quantification. I know that there are tribes and individuals who want to cling to the open-ended position. However, I believe that quantification is inevitable. Through litigation or through negotiation, Indian tribes are going to have to quantify their water rights. The temendous economic pressure of water will force the end of open-ended rights. Consequently, my recommendation is that tribes focus on maximizing what they can get in the quantification process."

One by one, as the state governments have begun to face the vital concerns affecting their future, they have begun the long, drawn-out legal processes to settle water disputes within their borders. The solemn warnings issued by Rupert Costo, a Cahuilla Indian, more than twenty years ago that "if we do not begin to act now, as Indian nations, to preserve our water rights, our nations will perish for lack of water," fell on deaf ears.

If the Indian nations had heeded the warnings of Costo, and had initiated the legal battles for water rights way back then, they would not be scrambling to survive the many legal battles being thrown at them by state governments over water rights.

The CERT Report summed up the ominous situation facing Inidan tribes, saying, "Tribal leaders must be aware that time and water are running short. Tribal cultures cannot survive without water and an intertribal approach toward achieving a national Indian water policy and projects for Indian water management must be implemented without delay."

State

Many Still Wary of U.S., States

Until the year 1982, the Indian reservations of South Dakota were effectively gerrymandered so that no Indian could be elected to state office. Even in counties such as Shannon County, with an 85-percent Indian population, the Indian vote was diluted to the point of being useless.

The Voting Rights Act changed all of this. The federal government intervened and admonished the legislature of South Dakota to either clean up its act, or face federal guidelines which would reapportion the voting districts to include fair representation to all people of the state.

The Indian voters are not ingrates. There are many untold circumstances which make the Indian apprehensive about participating in state government. Many believe that if we are sucked into the state processes, it is the first step toward allowing the state to assume jurisdiction on our reservations.

Given the past record of state government to usurp Indian lands by whatever devious means at their disposal, outright theft included, is it any wonder that the Indian people have not been clamoring to become a part of something they have no respect for, fear and abhor?

In this regard, one of my favorite sayings has been attributed to General Tecumseh Sherman. When asked by an eastern news reporter to give his definition of an Indian reservation, Sherman is said to have replied, "An Indian reservation is a body of land set aside for the exclusive use of the Indian people, and it is surrounded on all sides by thieves."

The so-called "protectorate of Indian lands," the Department of the Interior, often joined hand in hand with the white squatters, eastern corporations, and land speculators to strip the Indian tribes of land considered valuable. Totally ignoring the fact that they held the "trust responsibility" of the Indian tribes to preserve and protect their legal boundaries, the Interior Department ruthlessly divested the tribes of millions of acres of choice lands teeming with game and plentiful in mineral resources through false treaties, false promises and corrupt legislation.

These devious acts perpetrated upon the Indian tribes by the state and federal government may be ancient history to most non-Indians, but they are not ancient history to the Indian tribes. We can look upon this land that was taken from us illegally, every day of our lives. It is there for us to see, and knowing that it was stolen from us through hook and crook, is a constant reminder of our past dealings with the state and federal government. It is a grim lesson in misplaced trust and it has installed a firm resolve in the hearts and minds of the Indian people never to allow this brand of sanctioned "rip off" ever to happen again.

There never was a poll taken of the people dwelling upon the reservations of this state to determine if we wanted to participate in state government. Once more, it was a branch of the federal government, the Justice Department, that passed the rules and regulations to bring about this change. Is it any wonder that only 10 percent of the eligible voters on the reservation turned out for the primary election on June 1?

Often, I am accused of taking the state media to task for their penchant to look the other way and pretend that there are not racial problems in South Dakota. To the newspaper editors, television and radio station managers of this state, I'd like to ask this one little question. Why did the federal government have to come into the state and force the state legislature to reapportion the voting districts in order to allow equal participation by Indian people? Why wasn't a journalistic cry of indignation raised by the media over this gross injustice?

Well, the laws have been passed and the voting districts have been reapportioned. For the first time in the history of this state, Indian reservations will have Indian representatives working for them in the state capitol. But don't be surprised if we are not jumping up and down with glee.

There are no peoples on the fact of the earth who can be excluded and legally forbidden to share in the elective processes for almost one hundred years who will rush through the door as soon as it is opened.

Whether the Indian people of the reservation decide to become actively involved in the politics of state government is debatable. Total sovereignty is still the major objective of every Indian tribe in this state.

As we have done for centuries, the Indian people will observe, with extreme caution, this latest invitation to jump into the "great melting pot." But don't be surprised if we choose not to take the plunge. Trust, once trampled upon, is almost impossible to restore.

Indian Tribes Contribute to National Economy

Who is reaping the benefits of taxpayers' dollars, the Indian or the white man?

In Arizona, Congressman Morris Udall got a little bit tired of hearing some of his non-Indian constituents complain about the "outlandish amount of taxpayers' dollars for every Indian," so he did a study to determine the validity of these claims.

The data he compiled showed the average per capita government expenditure for all citizens of the United States in 1980 was $3,687.61. In plain English, this means that the government is spending $3,687.61 in tax dollars for each and every citizen not residing on an Indian reservation. The percapita amount spent on Indians from federal, state, local and tribal governments was a mere $2,947.82! Udall concluded, "The Indian people, whom all people generally concede are the most impoverished in this country, have been receiving 20 percent less in governmental services than the national population!" Another myth exploded?

I could not help but be amused at the reaction of the white citizens of Aberdeen, South Dakota and Billings, Montana when they learned they were about to lose the Bureau of Indian Affairs area offices located in their cities. They suddenly realized what an economic impact it would have on their fair cities. Isn't it amazing how the fear of losing millions of dollars can turn the most ardent of bigots into Indian lovers?

The citizens of Rapid City would certainly howl with anguish if the government decided to close Ellsworth Air Force Base. The citizens would be up in arms! Without a doubt, the financial contributions to the city by the air force base is a major portion of the local economy.

It has been said that, although the Indian population of South Dakota is a mere six percent of the total population, the Indian reservations contribute approximately 25 percent of the total state income.

Now if the non-Indian population is becoming upset over the loss of an area office or the closing of a BIA school, how would it react, in these economically depressed times, if all the Indian reservations in the state were terminated? Before some of you non-Indians let out a cheer, seriously consider the financial disaster that would befall the state economy.

The closing of Ellsworth Air Force Base would be a mere drop in the bucket compared to the tremendous impact the termination of Indian reservations would have upon the entire state economy.

David Getches, in his book, *Cases and Materials on Federal Indian Law*, says, "Indian people, tribal governments and reservation economic enterprises generate considerble taxable wealth for the state through government services, mining, tourism, manufacturing, conventions and the like. Most significantly, Indian reservations attract federal funds from almost all agencies of the federal government, and all of this economic activity has a multiplier effect throughout the economy."

To better illustrate the "multiplier effect," let's look at a study titled *Flow of Funds on the Yankton Sioux Indian Reservation* (one of the smallest reservations in South Dakota) for the Ninth District Federal Reserve Bank of Minneapolis, Minnesota in 1976. The study showed that money spent by the Yankton Sioux people is "re-spent by merchants, vendors and their employees. Thus, the effect of original spending is multiplied 3.88 times through re-spending cycles locally and regionally."

In an article, *Notes from Indian Country*, I wrote for the Rapid City, South Dakota *Journal* November 30, 1979, I stated, "One of the most significant contributions Indian people make to the overall economic growth of the state is through the sales tax. Each time we spend money in the cities or towns that border the reservations, a certain percentage goes into the state, county and city coffers. When you consider the goods purchased by Indian people such as cars, trucks, refrigerators, clothing, food and other necessities, the tax dollars paid by Indians are substantial."

Now consider that every single tax dollar collected by the state from Indians spending their hard cash in stores and businesses off the reservation belongs to the state in total. Not one single penny is returned to the economy of the Indian reservations through revenue sharing. Now where did I hear that old saying about "taxation without representation?"

Isn't it about time the state government realized the major finanaical contributions Indian tribes make to the state economy is vital to the future of the state, itself? Wouldn't this suggest that the state government work with us, and not against us?

State-Tribal Adversary Roles Lessening

It is common knowledge on Indian reservations across this land that the tribal and state governments have usually faced each other as adversaries.

Oftentimes, legislation passed by the duly elected officials of the tribal governments is looked upon as inconsequential by state officials. Over the years, as Indian nations have attempted to enact laws that would produce revenues for the reservations, the state government has challenged the tribe's right to do this.

Many state officials are unable to accept the fact that there are nations within their borders over which they have no jurisdiction. Rather than work to open a line of communication between the tribal and state governments, and thereby work cooperatively in an effort to bring benefits to all of the people residing within the state boundaries, a good deal of time and money is wasted by the state in an effort to subjugate the tribal government.

While fighting against what they deem to be state encroachment, some of the smaller tribes have become embroiled in extremely important cases that have had severe repercussions throughout Indian Country. By not informing the larger tribes about legal cases scheduled to go before the U.S Supreme Court, cases that will eventually set national precedents, some of the smaller tribes have jeopardized the sovereign status of the larger Indian nations.

A case in point involves a tiny "ranchero" known as the Pala Band of Mission Indians. Mrs. Eva Rehner, a member of that tribe, owned a general store on the tiny reservation located in San Diego County, California.

When told that she would need a state license to sell liquor in her store, she sued the Department of Alcoholic Beverage Control. She filed her suit in 1977, hoping to get a federal court to rule that she did not need a liquor license to sell liquor in her store.

She lost her first attempt in federal court, but that decision was later reversed by the Ninth Circuit Court of Appeals. The state of California appealed to the U.S. Supreme Court, and that court ruled that the appeals court has misread a federal law. Justice Sandra O'Connor wrote in her opinion for the court, "We find that the Congress has delegated authority to the states as well as to the Indian tribes to regulate the use and distribution of alcoholic beverages in Indian Country."

Justice O'Connor also wrote, "Because we find that there is no tradition of sovereign immunity that favors the Indians in this respect, and because we must consider that the activity in which Mrs. Rehner seeks to engage potentially has a substantial impact beyond the reservation, we may accord little if any weight to any asserted interest in tribal sovereignty in this case."

On July 29, 1983, the second largest tribe in the United States, the Oglala Sioux Tribe of the Pine Ridge Reservation of South Dakota, will hold a referendum election that will address the issue of legalizing the sale of alcoholic beverages on that reservation. The decision by the tribal council to put this question on a referendum ballot was prompted by the restricted economic opportunities on the reservation, and the limited number of ways available to the tribe to raise meaningful revenues.

Because of the moral issue surrounding the legislation of liquor sales on the Pine Ridge Reservation, and because of the volatile controversies evident on the reservation, there is no sure-fire guarantee that the liquor issue will be resolved by the voters in favor of the tribal council. But, if the voters do decide to legalize the sale of liquor on the reservation, the latest ruling by the Supreme Court will come into play. For one, the state will be able to charge the tribe for a liquor license to sell liquor, and the state will have jurisdiction over those sales. With a little cooperation between state and tribe, even this can be done amicably.

As Governor William Janklow told me Friday, "I just came from a meeting between myself and several of the tribal presidents. It was one of the most meaningful meetings we ever held. I realize that we're not going to agree on everything, but I feel that I now have the opportunity to do something constructive for the Indians of this state."

Janklow was quick to point out that he is a "lame duck" governor and is no longer eligible to run for that office. "I point this out so people will not point a finger at me and accuse me of political motivations in dealing with the Indian tribes. I gave my office phone number and my private number to every Indian official at that meeting. I told them to call me, any time and we will try to solve those specific problems where we do agree."

The governor said that the federal government treats each state as an individual entity. "Whether it's Nevada, Iowa or South Dakota, we are treated as individual states. That is what I intend to do with the Indian nations of the state. I will treat them as nine foreign nations, and deal with each nation individually," he said.

Like the Indian tribes, Janklow said he is tired of all the fighting and litigation. "The state and the Indian tribes are spending money in court that could be spent for the betterment of the people. It is costly and it generates friction. We should be able to solve our differences without spending the rest of our lives in court," Janklow said.

Tribal

Reservation Liquor Sales Volatile Issue

Several of the larger tribes in this country are deliberating over the sale of liquor on their reservations. This is a volatile and controversial issue; but one which must be faced within this decade.

Emotionalism and hysteria must not enter into the final decisions by the tribes; but the pros and cons of legalized liquor sales on the reservations must be determined by levelheaded people who are willing to base their judgments on the social and economic realities, taking into consideration the cultural and religious implications.

I believe that one of the key words that should became an integral part of any decision is "self-determination." Are the tribes of this country going to pursue the goals of sovereignty and self-determination or are these words merely being used as window dressing?

Every effort has been made to stamp out the illegal bootlegger; but this has proven to be a losing battle. Hundreds of thousands of dollars change hands daily on the reservations of this country as purchases are made by Indians from the bootleggers. It should be noted that this money is absolutely tax free!

Border Business Booms

Beer joints, cocktail lounges and liquor stores located near the boundaries of these reservations are wearing out their cash registers ringing up sales to Indians. The efforts to legalize alcohol on some reservations are being fought, quite strenuously, by the owners of these establishments. For them, legalizing alcohol on the reservation would be like killing the goose that lays the golden eggs. Many of these liquor dealers have spent hugh sums of money in an effort to prevent the Indian tribes from passing a law legalizing liquor sales.

It is a fact that the prohibition of alcohol by the Indian tribes has not stopped the consumption of alcohol; but, indeed, may have made it more attractive. We know that it has not put a dent in the number of bootleggers. Instead, they have flourished with each passing year. The only real loser in this debacle is the poor victim of the disease. Prohibiting the sale of liquor on the reservations has in no way diminished its availability.

Supposition

Suppose the good people of Farmington, Bloomfield and Aztec, New Mexico were required, by law, to purchase any and all alcoholic beverages at Cuba, New Mexico, and, to add insult to injury, they were not allowed to bring the alcohol back to their respective communities but had to consume it in Cuba, or on the road back home. The people of Cuba would soon believe that there were an awful lot of drunks living in the Farmington area, and the highways between Farmington and Cuba would soon be dotted with little white crosses. Sound ridiculous? Of course, it does; but this is exactly what is expected of the Indians living on reservations.

There are enough valid arguments on both sides to bring this issue to a stalemate on several reservations. Let there be no mistake about it, the question of legalized liquor sales on Indian reservations drew fierce reactions from both factions. There are very few individuals residing on Indian reservations who have not seen the affects of alcohol upon family members of friends,, or who have not shared the consequences of broken homes, accidents, criminal acts, child abandonment, or the proverty of these abuses. These are powerful arguments against legalizing the sale of alcohol.

Weapon Against Indian

The liquor of the white man was used as a weapon against the Indian. Kegs of rot gut liquor were a standard item at most trading posts in the early days, and large quantities of alcohol were dispensed to the Indians to insure a better bargaining position for the white traders.

Many an Indian woke up to find that all he or she had to show for furs or goods was a monstrous hangover.

Even the agents of the United States government were not bashful in using alcohol at the bargaining tables when important treaties were to be settled. Thousands of acres of Indian lands went by the wayside because of "old demon rum." Since alcohol is alien to the Indian culture and to the religion of all Indian tribes, is it any wonder that the opposition is so vehement?

Elgin Bad Wound of Oglala Lakota College
addressing the Pine Ridge Tribal Council at Kyle

General Tecumseh Sherman was thought to have the unscrupulous traders and their tactics in mind when he was asked by an Eastern newspaper reporter to give a definition of an Indian reservation. Sherman said, "An Indian reservation is a parcel of land set aside for the use of the Indian tribes, and it is surrounded on all sides by thieves."

My next article will discuss what is happening on one reservation where alcohol has been legalized. This two-part series is intended to show both sides of the controversial issue.

Results of Tribal Liquor Sales Noted

My last column dealt with the sensitive issues surrounding the legalization of liquor sales on Indian reservations. This column is intended as a follow-up, and is in no way meant to change the minds of tribal officials, one way or the other.

It has always been my contention that the leadership of Indian tribes should always be aware of what is happening on other reservations. Many times, problems confronting one tribe have been attacked by another tribe, and by observing the results, local tribal officials can make decisions based on facts rather than speculation. The similarities between Indian reservations in this country are far greater than the differences.

Several years ago, the Jicarilla Apache Tribe, headquartered at Dulce, New Mexico, legalized the sale of liquor on the reservation. What have been some of the results of this experiment? In discussing alcohol, it is impractical to use the terms "advantages" or "disadvantages." Obviously, the consumption of alcohol has neither. With this conclusion in mind, I spoke with the editor of the Jicarilla *Chieftain*, Mary Polanco, and the assistant editor, Carey Vicenti.

Different Opinion

"First of all," Vicenti said, "We do not operate under the same laws as the State of New Mexico. Our hours of operation are different and we are open on Sundays." He continued, "Many of the elders believe that things are better now than before because they really resented the bootleggers. Now they don't have to put up with them."

Vicenti stressed one fact many tribal officials are reluctant to discuss. "When debating whether to legalize liquor sales or not, you have to be able to admit that a problem does exist, and when we decided in favor of legalizing alcohol sales, we admitted that this problem does exist."

"Like any community, reservation or otherwise, there are always going to be the hardcore, problem drinkers," Vicenti emphasized, "but, by controlling the sales to minors, vagrancy incidents, and the establishments can refuse to sell to those people who are too drunk."

"The money spent at the liquor stores and bars remains on the reservation, and is turned over within the community," Vicenti stressed, "and the revenues collected by the tribe are used for different programs on the reservation, including a strong alcoholism rehabilitation program."

Mary Polanco added her voice to this commentary. She said, "In the past, before we legalized the sale of liquor on our reservation, the people had to travel great distances to drink and, as a result, we had a much higher incidence of vehicular accidents, many of them fatal."

Crime Decreases

Polanco also touched upon the fact that because the people from the reservation had to do their drinking in off-reservation communities, the rate of crime committed by Indians was much higher than it is today. Off-reservation law enforcement officers often over-reacted and, as a result, provoked troubles with Indians who had been drinking. This usually resulted in arrests and incarceration.

The social problems of child abandonment and broken homes also came under discussion. Polanco feels that "before (legalized liquor sales), Indian people from our reservation drove to the off-reservation communities to drink, and quite often, they left their children at home, by themselves, for long periods of time. This amounted to child abandonment."

Of course, the social and psychological effects of problem drinking among Indian people are serious ones, and must be included in any decision made by tribal leaders when discussing the pros and cons of legalizing the sale of liquor on their reservations.

Highway Crosses

A few years ago, I made a business trip to Tucson, Arizona. A young Papago Indian man by the name of Dennis Ortega drove me from Tucson to Sells, Arizona, the capital of the Papago Indian Reservation. As we drove down the narrow, straight-as-ribbon blacktop, I noticed all of the various crosses, wreaths and markers along the highway.

"There are about forty or fifty crosses out there," Ortega said, "that mark the places where Papago people have been killed in car wrecks. In fact, there is one spot where there are about twelve markers where one accident claimed all twelve lives at once."

I can show you a dozen highways leading from many reservation towns to off-reservation communities that are also lined with neat, white crosses. The fact that hundreds of young lives were snuffed out before they had a chance to begin should be considered by the members of the tribal councils before they cast their ballots for or against the legalized sale of alcohol on their reservations.

Tribes Should Provide Accurate
Information on Legalizing Alcohol Sales

The move to legalize the sale of alcohol on the Pine Ridge Reservation in South Dakota appears to be headed toward a decision in the next thirty days. (January 23, 1981)

Some members of the Tribal Council are suggesting that the individual reservation districts hold referendum elections to decide whether to legalize alcohol sales.

The advocates of legalized liquor sales point out that cash revenues of almost $2 million per year could be generated for the tribal government.

A preliminary, proposed ordinance, which will be distributed to the various districts governments, reads:

"1. Thirty percent of all profits shall be restricted for use by the tribal court system, the tribal law and order system, and for use by the alcohol and prevention and treatment programs.

"2. Twenty percent of all profits shall be restricted for use by the tribal governments for general uses.

"3. Twenty percent of all profits shall be divided equally among the community governments for district governmental purposes.

"4. Ten percent of all profits shall be set aside for educational scholarships and loans to tribal members attending schools of higher education.

"5. Ten percent of all profits shall be set aside for elderly and youth programs.

"6. Ten percent shall be set aside for land purchases."

In a telephone conversation with two tribal council members, I was told the council has not made any commitments on the final liquor ordinance yet. They said they are seeking input from all of the districts to help them formulate an ordinance acceptable to all parties concerned.

As I stated in an earlier column, the pros and cons of whether to legalize liquor on the reservation have been argued, quite vehemently, for many years. There is a definite difference of opinion on the subject.

One question asked repeatedly is: If the tribal government cannot operate any business without dragging it into the political arena, how can it expect to operate a tribally-owned liquor business? There is some legitimacy for asking this question. All one need do is to look at the many tribal enterprises that have failed in the past because of politics, favoritism, nepotism and very bad management. The shoddy record speaks for itself!

Anytime the implementation of a new law or ordinance causes an impact upon the moral and traditional values of a community, there is good reason to consider all of the possibilities.

And yet, in the final analysis, the ultimate decision should rest in the hands of the people. Self-government and self-determination have brought certain responsibilities to each reservation community. In order for each community to exercise sound judgment in making any major decision, it should be the responsibility of the tribal government to provide accurate and honest information to the people so they will have all of the facts at hand in making a decision.

An End to National Organizations?

Several tribal chairman attending the Aberdeen Area Tribal Chairmen's Association meeting in Pierre last week voiced strong disapproval of the National Tribal Chairmen's Association and the National Congress of American Indians.

They were very vocal in denouncing ineffectiveness and the "elitist Indian" label of these organizations. One tribal chairman was angry that many key positions in Washignton, D.C., positions very important to Indian reservations, were being filled upon the recommendation of these two organizations. He said that they usually selected people for these key jobs from within their own membership.

The lofty conventions these organizations hold in the major cities are becoming the social events of the year. They are, indeed, turning into gala affairs for the "elite."

Jurisdiction Poses Problem for Tribes

The problems of jurisdiction are not unique to the Navajo Nation. Take a case in Idaho:

Idaho State Representative Ray Infanger is being sued by the Shoshone-Bannock Tribes of the Fort Hall Reservation in Idaho. The suit was initiated because Infanger is extending a trailer park into reservation lands contrary to a tribal land use ordinance.

The *Idaho Statesman* newspaper quoted Infanger as saying, "If those Indians don't stop their interference, I will make life extremely difficult for the tribe."

Infanger's chief supporter, Powers County Deputy Prosecutor Ben Caveness, was quoted in the *Idaho Statesman*: "It's like a master-servant relationship; the Lord giveth and the Lord taketh away. This is the white man's case: There are more of us than there are of them (Indians). The treaties give them rights; but the treaties can be amended."

Liberals Lambasted

Caveness lambasted "liberals like Senator Kennedy who have a kind of cigar store image of Indians—we ought to keep them around because they are nice to look at—but if they keep clamoring for their rights, we will have to look at the Indian picture in a different light."

Another Idaho newspaper, the *Post-Register*, commented on the lawsuit in an editorial: "It is not easy to understand how a lawmaker thinks he is above the law, or a county official thinks he has jurisdiction on the Fort Hall Reservation. Powers County has no more jursidiction on the Fort Hall Reservation than Fremont County has in Yellowstone National Park."

Not Above Law

The article continues: "Rather than simply apply for a tribal permit, Infanger and Caveness apparently want to make an issue out of it. Certainly lawmakers and deputy prosecutors should be able to read the law and not think they are above it. The Indians are concerned about land uses and land use planning. Certainly a lot of counties with these same kinds of officials and legislators are not. It would be better if these men would solve some of the county and state problems and not talk about a 'master-servant' relationship, thinking they can better manage Indian lands."

Many times I have touched upon the adversary relationships between the state governments and the tribal governments. This is one of the major reasosns that talk of a "Sagebrush Rebellion" is so repugnant to the Indian tribes. Most Indian officials feel that if the state governments can gain control over the federal lands within their boundaries, it will be just a matter of time before they try to gain control over Indian lands.

Criticism Answered

Samuel Pete, executive assistant to Navajo Tribal Chairman Peter MacDonald, sent a letter to State Representative Tony Abril of Arizona in answer to a letter that Abril had sent to the *Navajo Times*. Abril had been critical of the amount of money spent by the tribe on legal affairs. Pete's letter said, "A careful examination of the legal affairs of the Navajo Nation would reveal that in almost every instance, the need for lawyers comes from litigation commenced by outsiders against the Navajo Nation and our attempts to improve the lot of our people and enhance our sovereignty. In fact, your own State of Arizona, through the attorney general, is one of the groups suing the Navajo Nation to question our rights to tax, when tax revenues are desparately needed by the Navajo people to improve the deplorable conditions you refer to in your letter."

Why don't the states encourage the Indian tribes to become more financially independent of the federal bureaucracy instead of blocking them at every turn? The states would be the eventual winners.

U.S.-Tribal Treaties Obligate Both Sides

I received an interesting call the other day concerning the five-part series that had just been run in the Farmington, New Mexico *Daily Times* dealing with the realtionship between Indians and non-Indians over the past years.

The caller touched on several points; but I would like to concentrate on one of those points.

The first thing we discussed was the various treaties that were made between the government and the different Indian tribes. The point he brought out was in the form of a question: Why should the government of today feel obligated to carry out the letter of those treaties? Considering the fact that many of the tribes which had signed treaties with the government were not the original inhabitants of that land, but had come to this country across the land bridge between Asia and the North American contient, didn't this fact have legitimate relevancy?

Historians and anthropologists are in general agreement that the Native American reached this continent by several routes. The great land bridge between Asia and North America was one; but there are also some strong theories that many Native Americans reached this continent by boat. Recent studies of the sea currents and trade winds would seem to bear this out. The similarities between some of the cultures of Egypt and the Mayan Indian and Chaco Indian civilizations are too striking to be mere coincidence.

Legal Documents

Ancient history aside, the treaties signed between Indian tribes and the federal government are legal documents. They carry the weight of the law. The government did sign those treaties, in good faith, with the tribes that were the occupants of the land at the time the treaties were signed. The agreements were with those tribes, and those tribes alone.

Suppose you purchased a house. You sign a deed with the party that now owns the house and you have little concern about the previous inhabitants. That is a legal and binding document between two consenting parties. The treaties were the same thing.

Some people will say, "That treaty was signed by people who are no longer with us, and I should not be held responsible for treaties signed by my ancestors."

Ridiculous Arguments

If the white man can use that theory for an argument over the validity of treaties, so can the Indian. The Indian can also say, "Those treaties were signed long ago, by my ancestors, and I should not be forced to abide by them today. Therefore, the land still belongs to us, so give us back our land."

One argument is as ridiculous as the other.

No matter how you look at it, the treaties signed between the government and the various Indian tribes have come back to haunt both parties. Because the Indian tribes of that time had no written language, all of the language contained within these documents was set down and organized by the white man. The conditions and requirements were discussed between the tribal leaders and the government officials and then transcribed. The legal language of these documents is in English! There can be no doubt that the white man knew, exactly, what he was putting down in those treaties. The Indians could only pray that their demands were interpreted properly and depend upon the honesty of the U.S. government to record it fairly and accurately. That trust was often misplaced, and the Indians of today must bear that burden.

Because of limited space, an important paragraph had to be left out in my final column dealing with the termination of Indian tribes, and the abrogation of treaties. The paragraph said: "It would be folly for the opponents of the American Indian to think that a decision handed down by the Justice Department will abolish Indian treaties and rights forever. The legal ramifications over such a ruling, and the many challenges that would be mounted against it by the Indian tribes would create legal battles that could rage for another hundred years. Who's to say that the Indian tribes will not be the eventual winners?"

Treaties, like laws, were made to protect the interests of the early white settlers of this continent. They were made between two sovereign nations acting as equals; and time should never diminish the integrity, or the intent, of those solemn agreements.

Voting Districts, State Jurisdiction, Input Need Attention

The 'one man-one vote' concept of state government (or single-member districts) will come under serious discussion during this session of the state legislature. It is obvious why reform is needed when one looks at the maps showing the legislative district boundaries and sees how the Indian reservations have been effectively gerrymandered these many years to prevent Indian participants as a solid minority voting bloc.

The final apportionment plans may not be conclusive, however, because certain limits have been provided on the actions by the governor and the Legislature.

In a report prepared by the South Dakota Advisory Committee to the U.S. Commission on Civil Rights, it says "The U.S. Supreme Court decision in Baker vs. Carr made reapportionment a justiciable issue; any aggrieved citizen may file an action in court. The Voting Rights Act of 1965, as amended in 1975, also restricts South Dakota's reapportionment by requiring the state to submit its plan for Shannon and Todd Counties to the U.S. Department of Justice for review and preclearance."

The largest concentration of Indians in the state are in Todd, Bennett, Shannon and Washabaugh counties. The Rosebud and the Pine Ridge Reservations are within those counties. Indians comprise almost two-thirds of the total population of these counties.

According to the South Dakota Advisory Committee report, these counties were divided into Districts 23, 24 and 25 by the 1971 apportionment. As a result, none of these districts have "a potential majority of Indian voters." The report continued: "The Task Force on Indian-State Government Relations made it clear that with this arrangement of legislative districts, Indian people in South Dakota have had their voting potential diluted."

At the present time there are no members of the Legislature from Todd, Bennett, Shannon or Washabaugh counties (Districts 23, 24 and 25) even though approximately 62 percent of the total population of those counties is Indian.

The proposal submitted to the legislators by the Rapid City Indian Service Council (partition North Rapid, Sioux Addition and Lakota Homes as a distinct and separate district) is not without its merits. Sometimes it is imperative that state governments take bold actions to insure total equal rights to all of its citizens. As long as the minorities of this state are denied the right to participate in state government, they cannot be chided for turning their backs upon the democratic processes of government.

State Jurisdiction

Perhaps state jurisdiction on Indian reservations isn't all it's cracked up to be. At least, that seems to be the conclusion drawn by one New Mexico legislator. State Democratic Senator Les Houston has suggested that the state look into letting the Navajo Police Department handle law enforcement in the checkerboard areas of McKinley and San Juan counties.

According to the Farmington, New Mexico *Daily Times*, Senator Houston is convinced that the expense of policing these areas is much too great. He said, "It would cost the state $500,000 to hire the forty to fifty additional officers necessary to adequately cover the checkerboard area." He added, "My personal preference is to figure out a way to utilize Navajo police officers by commissioning them as state policemen."

Assistant Secretary of the Interior

There are several names being bandied about the corridors of Washington, D.C. for the position of Assistant Secretary of the Interior. This is a cabinet-level position created in the early days of the Carter Administration designed to coordinate Indian affairs between the tribes and the President.

Incoming Secretary of the Interior James Watt has suggested that he will confer with Indian tribes before making this appointment.

Names suggested so far include Chuck Trimble, originally from Pine Ridge; Terrance Brown, a Karok from California; Alexander "Sandy" McNabb, director of the CETA Indian desk; and Ernie Stevens, currently director of the economic development program for the Navajo Nation.

The one thing that all of these nominees have in common (with the exception of Stevens) is that they are all longtime members of the Washignton, D.C. establishment commonly known (not so affectionately) as the "Washington Reskins."

Secretary of the Interior-designate Watt is looking for input from Indian people, so if you have someone in mind you would like to recommend for this position, send your vote to: U.S. Department of the Interior; Office of the Secretary; Washington, DC 20240.

Take a few minutes and send in a name. Not only can you let the new secretary know who you want, you can also let him know who you do not want. You can always say you tried.

Political Actions Embarrass Residents

The elections had been held. Stanley Looking Elk had been declared the winner and was now the president-elect of the Oglala Sioux Tribe.

There is that period of time between administrations called the "lame duck" period in which the outgoing administration is still in power. It was during this period that the president-elect decided to go to Washington, leaving the chicken coop unguarded. The outgoing administration decided to take advantage of this situation by holding a tribal council session and using this meeting to reduce the salaries of the Executive Committee (president, vice president, secretary, treasurer and a fifth member) to $15,000 annually. They took this same opportunity to increase the salaries of the twenty-seven-member tribal council from $12,500 to $15,000. This meant that the president's salary was reduced from $30,000 to $15,000 or by exactly one-half.

Needless to say, this did not set too well with the new president of the Oglala Sioux Tribe. He wrote a letter to the law firm of Fried, Frank, Harris, Shriver and Kampelman in Washington, and asked for their opinion on this embarrassing turn of events.

The attorney, Richard Schifter, replied to this request by quoting page eight of the minutes of the March 27th council meeting which said:

"Fred Brewer moved, seconded by Newton Cummings to set Tribal Council and Executive Board salaries at $15,000 per annum and salaries for Critic and Sergeant-at-Arms shall remain at $12,500 per annum. Motion carried; 10 for; 8 against; and 4 not voting."

It was the conclusion of Mr. Schifter that the resolution passed by the "lame duck" administration was, indeed, a valid one. It appears that the only recourse by Executive Committee members to get their salaries raised to their previous level is by action of the Tribal Council.

The Scandal Sheets

On more than one occasion I have mentioned those pieces of literary muck that appear periodically on this reservation, always unsigned and usually libelous, that are intended to degrade and smear the individuals who are unfortunate enough to be chosen as the subject matter. In the past few weeks, several of these scandal sheets have appeared, mailed to members of the tribal council and other tribal members, from Rapid City. They seem to have reached a new low, if that is possible.

These smear sheets have attacked Tribal Councilman G. Wayne Tapio and Melvin Cummings with methods that border upon racism. They attempt to revive the hatred born of the strife that followed the Wounded Knee takeover. In the case of the two councilmen mentioned, the muckrakers have attempted to legitimize their accusations by attaching official documents to their libelous cover letters.

It is the opinion of many people on the Pine Ridge Reservation that G. Wayne Tapio and Melvin Cummings were two of the most outstanding councilmen ever to be elected to that office. In my opinion, the unbridled ferocity evident in the scandal sheets that attacked these two individuals says more about the writer of this filth than it does about the people who have been attacked.

Politics

A few weeks back I reported the termination of twenty-three program directors by the new adminsitration. No reasons were given for this wholesale firing of tribal employees except that it would be a matter of policy for the Looking Elk administration.

As I reported earlier, one of the program directors terminated was a tribal elder named Wallace Little Finger. There is now a move afoot to discredit this man by alleging that some of his employees were accepting dual compensation by being paid by the Comprehensive Employment and Training Act (CETA) and also by the program that Mr. Little administered, the Tribal Work Experience Program (TWEP).

Now it has been learned that the new program director of TWEP is Karen Looking Elk, the daughter of President Stanley Looking Elk. Politics, nepotism, or both?

One Day Upsets Reservation Employees, People

There was a song that was popular several years ago that was sung by Dinah Washington that went, "What a difference a day makes, twenty-four little hours. . ." and more than anything else, that song can be applied to the tribal government on the Pine Ridge Reservation.

The first thing the new tribal government did when it assumed offices was to "terminate" twenty-three program directors. Needless to say, there is much anger among those people terminated. Most of them feel it was politically motivated and serves to reinforce in their minds the fact that every single new administration makes the promise that this will not occur again but somehow loses sight of this promise the minute a mantle of power is placed in its hands.

The furor caused by this act forced the new administration to have seond thoughts, and the new president, Stanley Looking Elk, immediately said it was all a big mistake and all he wanted was progress reports from the program directors, and that they could continue in their jobs if they proved to him that they were doing a good job.

The "termination letter" I read states, "Because of a change in administrations, your services will no longer be required" and under the subject matter, the heading read: "Termination."

Wallace Little Finger, one of the program directors affected, called Looking Elk and asked him what it all meant, and was told, "Just exactly what it says: You're fired."

Wallace Little Finger is an elder of the Oglala Sioux Tribe and the cruel way in which he was released has many people on the reservation very upset.

The absolute power each tribal administration has over the future employment of tribal members is awesome. Many of the people who called me to complain asked that I not mention their names because they hoped they could get other jobs with the administration, and they did not want to jeopardize this slim chance.

There is a lack of security and continuity on this reservation that will be one of the major problems to overcome. It could lead to the eventual loss of self-government if it is not solved in the very near future.

If a tribal president is not his own man, and does not make his own decisions, he will only be as good as his advisors. For the sake of the Oglala Sioux Tribe, we can only hope the new president terminated the program directors on bad advice. But if this be the case, then it is imperative that he sit down and study the input from his advisors and determine the long-range effects on the structure of tribal administration.

Imagine, if you will, the problems that would develop in any form of government (Rapid City's included) if every administrator was fired every time a new mayor or governor was elected. The turmoil that would result would be incalculable. Many highly qualified and skilled employees would be very reluctant to take jobs under these conditions and the job positions would soon be filled with people incapable of long-range planning but by those who are able to adjust to short-term employment.

This has been one of the major stumbling blocks placed in the path of effective tribal government since Congress first authorized tribal self-government under the Indian Reorganization Act of 1934. All of the major jobs on the reservation have been used as political plums, and the chaos that has resulted is very evident in the lack of continuity and progress that has hampered true self-determination for forty-six years.

What happens to the Igemu Tonkas (fat cats) once they assume the positions of power that they lose sight of all their campaign promises and resort to tactics that are all too familiar to the long-suffering residents of the Pine Ridge Reservation? As Dinah Washington sang so many years ago, "What a difference a day makes."

Tribal Governments Draw Criticism, Too

I have a very good friend who is an instructor at the Oglala Sioux Community College at Kyle, South Dakota. His name is Mike Her Many Horses. He said something to me one time that made a lot of sense and it is something that is always in the back of my mind, especially when I sit down at my typewriter and write this column. Before I talk about the advice given to me by Mike, let me give you the reasoning behind it.

There are many things happening on the reservations and many of us, as Indian people, would like to see them changed. We live with the conflicts and the pettiness which permeate our tribal governments. We know that, too often, decisions by tribal officials are based upon petty politics and personality clashes, rather than upon the overall and best interests of all the people of the tribe. How many times have I heard members of the tribe say, "Why can't they (the tribal officials) just put aside their pettiness and get on with doing the things that will benefit all of the people?"

Why not, indeed! As tribal members, we know that most tribal administrations have grown top heavy with salaries that far outweigh the responsibilities or the time actually spent on the job. We know that our funds (I say "our funds" because we forget, at times, that the money being spent by the tribal government is really our money) are being wasted to support useless programs, or to pay the exorbitant salaries of the administration, and it makes us angry.

Subjective Report

Perhaps what I am about to reveal now could be misconstrued in many ways, and most likely, could be placed under the category of subjective journalism; but please try to understand my reasons for following this course.

The advice given to me by Mike Her Many Horses was this: "You must be very careful about hanging our dirty laundry out in public. There are those people who would gladly, and gleefully, use the things which are extremely critical of the tribe, or damaging, against us, and reinforce their own misconceptions of Indians."

By this, Mike meant that there are those people in the federal or state governments who would sieze upon controversial issues of tribal mismanagement and waste, and use these things to abrogate our rights and our treaties. They would say, "See, I knew that those Indians couldn't handle their own government, so we ought to abolish it once and for all!"

Many Problems

Yes, we realize that we do have many problems, and we also want, very much to see these problems corrected and changes for the good of all the people to come about; but we must have the time and the tools to accomplish these objectives. Because there are problems in the state government, the county governments, or in the city governments, are the people calling for an abolition of these structures? Of course not. They are seeking to correct these malfunctions through better laws and by electing better qualified officials to administer these laws.

It wasn't until the Indian Reorganization Act of 1934 that tribal governments were fashioned and established to serve the reservations of this country. These democratic governments tried to accomplish, in forty-six years, what it has taken other governments in the United States two hundred years to achieve. During all of these years, the tribal governments have had the "albatross" of the Department of the Interior hanging around their necks, and interfering in every aspect of government, including the administering of the funds needed to make government function. The dictates from Washington, D.C. were so inconsistent that they caused further confusion and chaos. It was like telling the city of Rapid City to function with all of the directives, the constitution, the by-laws and the source of power located in a city 2,000 miles away. It is an impossibility!

Four-Year Terms Recommended for Tribal Officers

The cost of any referendum election on the Pine Ridge Reservation can run into thousands of dollars. The proposed referendum on the legalization of alcohol will be no exception.

Since a referendum election is going to be held anyhow, there are some tribal members suggesting to their councilmen that an addition be made to the ballot: a constitutional change to permit the tribal president, executive committee and the tribal council to extend the two-year term of office to a new four-year term.

No administration can pass such an ordinance in order to benefit its own elected officials. If passed, such action would not become effective until after the present administration's term in office has expired and a new administration has been voted into office.

The reasoning behind this push is obvious to many people who are tired of seeing the Oglala Sioux Tribe march in place while many other tribes are marching forward. Those Indian tribes which have accomplished the most over the past few years are those which have made an effort to turn the corner to progress while maintaining their culture, religion and Indian ways. These tribes had the foresight to set a four-year term in office for their elected leadership. The success they have enjoyed speaks for itself.

The obvious argument against passing such an ordinance is: "We have a bad enough time keeping some of these clowns around for two years. Can you imagine how horrible it would be if we had to keep them in office for four years?"

Perhaps if the people of the Oglala Sioux Tribe had a four-year term for their elected officials, they would be a little more careful about the officials they elect. Maybe we could take elections out of the realm of popularity contests and put them in proper perspective.

It is about time we began to look at the qualifications of the people we put into office. It shouldn't make any difference how popular a person is, but it should make all of the difference in the world as to whether that person has the intelligence and the capabilities to handle the job we are electing him or her to perform.

It is impossible for any man alive to make any inroads into the many problems which beset the Indian people in two short years. He hardly has the time to introduce himself to all of the government officials he will be required to do business with them when his term in office is over.

Costly projects and programs begun during one administration are interrupted or discontinued under another, and we have to begin all over agian every two years. Highly qualified tribal members are fired from their jobs and friends, relatives and cronies of the new president are installed in their place. and in another two years, the vicious cycle starts all over again.

This game of musical chairs has been going on since 1934 and the only real losers are the Oglala people, themselves.

If a tribal administration remained in office for four years, it could be held accountable for the funds placed in its care during that time. Accountability is almost nonexistent when administrations come and go before an accounting can be made.

Perphaps I'm kicking a dead horse by saying this so many times, but I am going to continue to say it until somebody listens—we are heading into some very serious and troubled times. Funds that were easily available several years ago are being curtailed and canceled outright. The dollars coming in to the reservations of this land are drying up.

We can no longer afford the luxury of incompetent, inadequate and narrow-minded leadership. If we continue to put this kind of people into office to govern us, we are leading ourselves down the road of poverty and self-destruction.

We can talk about sovereignty, self-determination and self-government until we are blue in the faces, but that's all it is—just talk. If we do not find the capable leadership to point us in the right direction and help us to cut the umbilical cord of total dependency upon the federal government, we have no future.

Does anyone on the reservation believe this administration is capable of doing that? I am as much to blame as anyone on the Pine Ridge Reservation for helping to elect the present bunch, because in order to remove one leader, I supported and pushed another.

It's not easy to admit you were wrong, face up to it, and hope you never make the same mistake again. I don't believe I will. How about you?

Tribal Officials Offered Pointers Regarding Salesmen

"How to analyze advertising and economic propaganda" was the heading on a Universal Press Syndicate article which listed fourteen points to watch out for when dealing with sales people.

In the past ten years, it has become apparent there are a vast amount of mineral resources lying beneath the surface of the earth on many Indian reservations. As a result, the "snake oil" salesmen have been showing up on the Indian reservations in droves.

Since many of these salesmen are on the reservations with high hopes of making a quick killing—and then returning to parts unknown—it becomes apparent that elected tribal officials must be able to discern fact from fiction when listening to the sales pitches of the various individuals and companies desirous of doing business with the tribe, or, as many of the salesmen put it, "doing the tribe a big favor."

I am going to list the fourteen points brought out by the Universal Press Syndicate survey, revised slightly to fit the Indian reservation perspective, and

I do truly believe that, if every elected tribal offical, regardless of where his reservation is located, followed these fourteen points, it could save their respective tribe millions of dollars lost annually to fly-by-night organizations who prey upon the gullibility of the Indian people.

Here are the fourteen points with added comments:

1. What is the "angle" of the party trying to influence you? (Surely, they didn't travel all the way to your reservation just because they love Indians. Find out what's in it for them!)

2. What is said that's within your experience (In other words, do you know what in the heck he is talking about?)?

3. Is the pitch consistently vague? (Does the salesman say a lot of cloudy things inconsistent with the hard facts of reservation lifestyles?)

4. What isn't said? (Are you reading between the lines?)

5. Are nonsequiturs used? (A non sequitur is a statement of response that does not follow logically from anything previously said.)

6. As far as the tribe is concerned, if action is taken, what will be the effect? (When talking about cutting timber or drilling for oil, are all of the negatives being considered?)

7. Can you get impartial advice? (This point is very important. When you are talking about investing thousands of tribal dollars into a business venture, you are talking about the people's money. Every avenue of comparison should be sought by the tribal council.)

8. What's the track record of the party trying to convince you? (This is one of the easiest things to check out, and yet it is one of the things many tribal councils don't even consider. Has this company or individual established successful business ventures on other reservations? Are they still operating? Did the tribe profit from them? Would the tribe recommend them to other Indian tribes?)

9. Check for a desire to hide facts! (It is imperative that the tribal officals have someone present familiar with the product or services being sold. Until all questions are answered satisfactorialy, no decisions should be made, and no monies allocated.)

10. If you are being rushed, watch out! (If the tribe has managed to survive for the past 100 years without this particular business venture, why get in a hurry now?)

11. Is it too good to be true? (Almost any major improvement on an Indian reservation sounds too good to be true, so there is lots of leeweay here.)

12. Are there any appeals designed to get around your intelligence? (In other words, is the salesman trying to "dazzle you with his footwork"?)

13. Set up a meeting of tribal people before the presentation is made, and come up with a list of questions of your own. This is common business sense!

14. Asking questions is pro-tribal survival! (Don't ever accept anything as fact until you have checked it out. No individual or company is going to do business with an Indian reservation unless there is something in it for them. You will not be dealing with charity organizations, but with very shrewd business people interested in making a profit. Not all of them are crooked!

Some of them may have a deal in mind that will make the tribe a nice profit—as well as themselves.)

Don't jump on the first deal offered. Shop around and, if need be, get a second opinion, or a third opinion. If the deal is a good one, it will keep!

Indian Leadership Must Deal with Austere Economy

This is an election year in many parts of Indian country. It has been my belief, for several years, that the 1980s are the most crucial years to the continued existence of the Indian tribes of this land.

It doesn't take a great mind to analyze the mood of the nation. The excesses of the past have finally caught up with America. The constant monetary demands of the powerful unions, particularly in the auto and steel industries, have all but priced these businesses out of the market. Foreign nations have taken much of the trade from American owned companies through lower prices and better products.

On Indian reservations, privately owned enterprises have had a very difficult time surviving. Lacking the ability to borrow by virtue of location and faced with a dwindling influx of dollars because of the extremely high unemployment picture, many Indian businesses have turned to the federal government in search of financial assistance only to discover that even these funds are no longer available.

This situation did not develop overnight. During those years when America was flexing her affluent muscles, many enterprises popped up in Indian Country constructed on a foundation of benevolence and socialism. The government bureaucrats knew little of sales and marketing, and it has become apparent that many companies were put into operation with an eye toward the endless influx of federal assistance, technically and financially.

Whenever these tribally-owned, federally backed enterprises fell upon hard times, little consideration was given to the fact that much of this was caused by poor management, excessive spending and waste. Instead of determining the root causes of the problems and correcting them with an eye to the future, the federal handouts continued. Money that could have been spent to streamline tribal ventures in order to make them cost conscious and instill the concept of profit motivation into top level management, was pumped into tribal enterprises with little chance of survival.

Mismanagement and waste dragged the tribally-owned enterprise down until even "Papa government" saw the handwriting on the wall and pulled the plug. Always looking for ways to "save face," it was an easy matter to point the finger at the tribe and accuse them of not taking advantage of a golden opportunity. More than once I've heard top-level government officials say "Even when we try to help these Indians, they can't seem to get their act together." Heaven forbid that federal officals take a look at their own policies that pointed the enterprises toward certain failure.

A classic example of this is the millions of dollars wasted by the Economic Development Administration in the 1970s of an ill-fated venture to construct motels and restorts on Indian lands. Many of these resorts were built far off of the beaten path with little thought of accessibility to tourists, hunters. fishermen, or conventioneers. It was a lesson in placing the cart before the horse. The resorts were constructed and then opened for business before management personnel were trained to operate them.

Of the sixteen resorts constructed, only three are now in operation and making a profit. The others have either been torn down or are being used by the tribe for purposes other than those for which they were constructed. Those that have survived did so through the powerful efforts of the local tribal government which put many of the tribe's dollars into the venture rather than see them fail.

It is imperative to the survival of Indian tribes that the voters take a long, hard look at the parade of candidates marching by for review. These are times when those professional politicians who have feasted at the governmental trough for too many years must be cut loose. It is a time to elect tough-minded, educated, knowledgeable leaders with management and business backgrounds.

As America has found itself floundering in its own excesses, it has slammed the door on federal spending. Ninety percent of most jobs on Indian reservations have been provided by the federal government. The move to austerity has been devastating to tribal governments.

We must also be aware that extremism is not the answer. Those radicals who preach the doctrine of running all federal agencies from the reservation have little knowledge of the realities of economics. They are standing on platforms filled with a lot of hot air.

Now is not the time to destroy what little we have. One does not burn down the old neighborhood until a new one has been built to replace it. The voters of most reservations are aware of this.

Finally, as we prepare to go to the polls, we cannot look at those candidates who continue to say, "This is what I am going to do." We must look toward those leaders who have a proven track record—those leaders who can stand up and say with pride, "This is what I have done!"

An elderly Indian man coined a new word for me the other day. He said, "It looks to me that most of the people we elected in the past were CONdidates. What we have to do now is to vote for the real CANdidates."

If we are to survive the turbulent '80s as independent Indian nations, it is our leadership that must pull us through. If we continue to elect those who cannot lead, we are dooming ourselves to failure.

Budget Cuts Punishing to Reservations

There was a priest who taught at the Catholic Indian Mission I attended. He had a favorite expression he used whenever he was about to whip any of the young Indian students. He would scowl ferociously and say, "Assume the position."

Much like Pavlov's dogs, the boys knew what he meant. He was saying, "Bend over and grab your ankles because I am about to chastise your posteriors." And so this short sentence uttered by this priest, "Assume the position," brought an immediate response from the boys, almost by reflex action.

Having to behave like marionettes was embarrassing enough to most of the boys. But, to add insult to injury, the priest demanded that the object of his attention, the boy who had just been administered a severe whipping, respond by standing at rigid attention and saying, "Thank you, Father."

This almost forgotten scene returned to my conscious mind after I witnessed the Navajo Tribal Council agreeing "reluctantly" to support the Reagan administration's budget cuts in order to balance the federal budget.

Every major program on the Navajo Reservation, from health care to housing, will suffer because of those proposed budget cuts. Some Navajos are predicting cuts in the food stamp program that will bring untold hardships to more than 10,000 Navajo people.

Tribal Chairman Peter MacDonald had been optimistic about the budget cuts, believing the cuts "would not affect the Indian people as much as it would the rest of the nation's population."

Most Indian reservations are totally dependent upon federal dollars. Programs such as the Comprehensive Employment and Training Act provide most of the non-governmental jobs on many reservations. I say non-governmental jobs in the sense that these CETA jobs are not deducted from the meager budgets of the tribal governments, but instead supplement the tribe's ability to hire and train Indians on reservations where the unemployment rate can be as high as 70 percent.

The government's theory that the private sector would benefit from the cuts and respond by providing more jobs does not hold water on the reservations to pick up the slack. Conversely, the drastic reduction in funds allocated to the reservations will dramatically reduce the amount of money the Indian people have to spend in the towns and cities which border the reservations. These communities provide jobs in the private sector to Indians because of the influx of dollars from the reservations.

Since the flow of dollars to these border towns will be severely reduced, the few jobs provided by the private sector in these communities will also be eliminated. The diminished purchasing power of the Indian people will have a strong impact upon the economy of the reservations and, ironically, upon the economies of the border towns.

One Navajo man, John T. Yazzie of St. Michaels, Arizona, said, "It was with anger and sadness that I read how our tribal council unanimously endorsed President Reagan's proposed federal budget cuts and sold out the Navajo people." Yazzie asked a question and answered it in the same breath: "What could our council have been thinking about? Clearly, not the interests of their own constituents."

Tribal leaders who claim to be loyal Republicans should never allow blind faith in the party to give them tunnel vision. The passage of legislation which can only bring misery, hunger and sickness to their own tribal people should be recognized for what it is—bad legislation. Whenever they attempt to paint a rosy picture of an intolerable situation, they are only fooling themselves; the finished portrait will still be an ugly one to the average, grassroots Indian.

Most of the reservation-based tribal leadership in this country stood shoulder to shoulder to condemn openly the unfair burden being placed upon the already sagging backs of the Indian people.

Yes, the endorsement given to President Reagan's proposed budget cuts by the Navajo Tribal Council reminded me of the priest who used to ask us to assume the position, whip us, and then ask us to give him a thank you in gratitude for the licking. I wonder if the Navajo Tribal Council said "thank you" to the Great White Father for the licking he gave them.

Oglala Sioux Tribal Audit

An audit released two weeks ago by the Department of the Interior shows the Oglala Sioux Tribe's Special Payroll Account with a negative balance of $223,000. The tribe has had to assign about $100,000 of lease collections per year to the bank to assure payment on consolidated loans.

The tribe is spending $15,000 more per month this year than it did in 1980. On April 24, 1981, the bank refused to pay $39,832 in payroll checks presented. The tribal treasurer had to borrow $100,000 from various program accounts in order to meet the payroll.

According to one tribal official, "This is the worst financial shape the tribe has ever been in as far back as I can remember, and I've been involved in tribal government for many years."

The auditor summed up his report, saying, "I've been told that in the end analysis the Council is ultimately accountable for tribal operations. Since you're accountable, I'm here to suggest you take very prompt action to reduce your expenditures in accordance with your revenue. I am making this suggestion now because from my vantage point, it looks like you are standing on the brink of insolvency."

New Industry on Reservation is Possibility

Much of the research is being done in absolute secrecy. An article in *Business Week* reports, "Union Carbide refuses to comment on a blend of natural and synthetic zeolites that it is supplying to scrub radioactive materials from water at the failed Three Mile Island nuclear facility in Pennsylvania. And Anaconda which claims to have identified 170 potential applications, is keeping mum about its plans for natural zeolites. "We are pioneering a major business," snaps Dennis Leonard, an Anaconda marketing executive. "Why should we tell the competition what we're doing?"

Why concern ourselves with zeolites on the Pine Ridge Reservation? A recent study prepared by the U.S. Geological Survey team of William Raymond, Alfred Bush, and Arthur Gude for the Bureau of Indian Affairs would indicate vast deposits of this mineral on the reservation.

The final paragraph of the geological report reads, "The United States is now on the threshold of developing a natural zeolite industry. Several companies are actively involved in developing markets for natural zeolites for a variety of uses. Deposits are being mined in other parts of the nation, but no others of substantial size are known to exist in the Northern Plains. If the zeolites in the Pine Ridge Reservation have useful prospectives, these deposits will have high commercial potential because of their convenient location to the midwest and their great size."

David Holmes, manager of exploration for Phelps Dodge Zeolites of Lakewood, Colorado, will be addressing the Tribal Council of the Oglala Sioux Tribe in the next few weeks. He said, "Last month we took several samples of the zeolite deposits on the reservation for study. The results of this study have not been released, as yet, but we feel that the potential to develop the low-grade zeolite deposits on the reservation are quite good."

Holmes said that the uses in this area would be primarily agricultural. Zeolite can be used as a food supplement for cattle. "Researchers suspect that the zeolites increase the animal's ability to convert food to flesh either by holding nutrients in the animal's digestive tract longer or by binding up materials such as toxins that might interfere with digestion," according to *Business Week Magazine.*

Zeolites can be used as additives in fertilizers, to replace some of the phosphates in detergents, as coolants in refrigerators, and in recent experiments, to convert hydrocarbon feed-stock, such as vegetable oil, to gasoline. An executive for a Denver-based mining subsidiary said, "Natural zeolites have tremendous potential in end uses from the mundane to the far out."

In the past, synthetic zeolites have been used for much of the research, but the availability of natural zeolites, and the fact that they can be mined cheaper than synthetics can be manufactured, makes the development of natural zeolites very attractive.

Zeolites are obtained through open-pit mining. "Since the largest reserves of zeolites are located in the Badlands, it will be very easy for a mining company to restore the land to its natural state after it has been mined," Holmes said.

Business Week makes this projection: "With potential applications ranging from livestock feed additive to refrigerants, Occidental Petroleum Corporation, Atlantic Richfield Company's Anaconda Copper Company subsidiary, and others are rushing to file claims on the huge reserves of zeolites scattered throughout the western United States. Those companies are betting that the less pure—but less costly—natural zeolites will capture half of a market that is projected to top $2 billion within ten years. The present $400 million market for zeolites is held almost entirely by synthetics."

Oglala Sioux Tribal President Joe American Horse is optimistic, but he said, "There are a lot of questions to be asked. We are looking for a lot of answers about environmental impact, health hazards, and, of course, upon an acceptance by the people living on the reservation."

American Horse will have David Baldwin, an officer with the Energy, Minerals and Resource Department of the Bureau of Indian Affairs, based in Denver, Colorado, address the Tribal Council and the community at large, this week.

If the mining of zeolites is feasible for the reservation, American Horse sees several possibilities. "First of all, we need jobs on the reservation, and, secondly, we need a source of income. Zeolites could provide both. If we entered an agreement as an equal partner and built the manufacturing facility on the reservation, this would provide jobs. A fair market price for the sale per ton of zeolites would provide tribal income," American Horse said.

The tribal president also envisions using the product to establish feeding lots on the reservation and to be used as a source of fertilizer to help develop the agricultural prospects of the reservation. "We'll just have to stop, look, listen, and ask a lot of questions," American Horse said.

Mescalero Orator Warms Audience at Inauguration

Traditionally, because they had no written language, the tribal leaders of long ago became oratorical masters.

Their speeches were performed with a style that would have blessed the finest theater of the arts. A nod of his head could show contempt; a motion of the hand, anger; or a sweep of the arm, joy.

This tradition has been carried on to this day by such eloquent speakers as Frances Freeman, a Caddo woman; Bea Medicine, a Standing Rock Sioux; John Rainier, Taos Pueblo; and last, but not least, one of the greatest orators of them all, Wendell Chino, Mescalero Apache tribal president.

Chino was at his fiery best as he addressed the crowd at the inauguration ceremonies for the newly-elected governing body of the Jicarilla Apache Tribe Friday in Dulce, New Mexico.

"Newspapers across this country are trying to accuse the tribal governments of incompetence and corruption," he almost shouted. "Look at the examples we have to emulate: the federal government is not perfect, the state government is not perfect, because, after all, they had Watergate, Koreagate, Abscam, and then, Billygate." With a frown on his face, and an accusing tone in his voice, Chino continued, "Everybody makes mistakes, so give the tribal governments the opportunity to make their mistakes, also; this is the way we learn."

"So goes the leader, so goes the government; so goes the government, so goes the tribe," Chino said with poetic cadence, "and as I said, none of us is perfect."

Chino paused as his gaze surveyed the assembly, "No—tribal government is not perfect, BUT, it is OUR government." Rapidly, he added, "The outside government will not solve your problems; the Albuquerque *Journal* will not solve your problems; nor will the Santa Fe *New Mexican* solve your problems." Raising his hand and sweeping across the seated dignitaries of the Jicarilla Apache Tribe, he shouted, "Your tribal government must solve your problems."

Chino dropped his voice to a low monotone as he continued, "The most dangerous threat to our existence is the uninformed public. Uninformed and misinformed non-Indians become biased in their attitudes toward Indian people." Chino mused sardonically, "Take a look at the people who call themselves the 'Sagebrush Rebellion.' They say they want all of the federal lands in this state to be declared surplus and turned over to them." He queries the audience, "If any surplus lands are to be turned over to anyone, why don't they give it back to the rightful owners?"

"The efforts being made by the federal government to 'deregulate' tribal governments is one of the things that we must fear in the 1980s," Chino warns.

The audience has become very silent now. Only the sounds of the folded, blue, inauguration programs, beating the air to stir up a little breeze in the hot, sunny afternoon can be heard.

"We are the First Americans," Chino begins very softly. "The Indian people have been meeting and greeting the boat people coming to this country since 1492." Chino now has everyone's attention as he raises his voice to maximum volume, "No tribal government should fear federal 'deregulation,' now or ever. The Jicarilla Tribal government is here to stay because, like every other tribal government in this country, it is older than the United States government. We were first, and we will be here last, because we will survive."

Priorities Differ on Reservations

We are now reaching the part of the year when the politicians are worn out, and the elections are just around the corner. I believe that the voters have more reason to be tired out than the politicians.

Sometimes it is very difficult for the residents of Indian reservations to decide how they are going to vote. In most of the cities of this country, the politicians address the issues that are important to that particular constituency. They talk about jobs, inflation, the economy, taxes and defense spending. These issues have some importance to the reservation people but they are not on top of the priorities, by any stretch of the imagination.

In some states, Indian voters have been neglected and excluded from the voting process for so many years that there is a reluctance to participate at all. Many Indian people feel that democracy is a fine sounding word, but is meaningless to the people of the reservations.

Federal Patronizing

First of all, they are responsible to their tribal government, and as a result, the elections of tribal officials and administrations take precedence over national elections. But even the process of choosing tribal officials has been abused to such a point that many reservation residents feel that they are being patronized by the federal government.

Much of the blame for these attitudes can be placed squarely upon the shoulders of the tribal government While the lifestyles of the elected officials have improved, and, as the old saying goes, "the rich get richer," there has been little improvement in the lives of the grassroots people. Even though the costs of administering services to the tribal people have escalated out of sight over the past few years, there has been no improvement whatever in the lives of the poor people. After awhile, many of the reservation people begin to ask themselves, "Why in the heck should I waste my time voting for these people when they get back into the same rut, and all of their promises turn into fairy tales? It seems that they are only able to help themselves at our expense."

Silent Majority

Who are these grassroots people I always talk about? They are the reservation people who are very seldom seen, and almost never heard. They are the silent majority. They are those people who place their faith in a system, year after year, only to find out that they have been misled. They are the people who have maintained their ties to the land, to the religion and to the culture.

When tribal politicians are accused of "ripping off" the people or feathering their own nest, the people who are the victims of these crimes are usually the grassroots people. They are the poor and the needy for whom every tribal program reaching the reservation has been designed, for whom every single dollar appropriated by the tribal government is intended, and they are the targets of every "do-gooder" and "social worker" with a penchant to save the world.

Sure, we all hear talk of how many millions of dollars are being spent on Indian reservations every single year. We all read about how these dollars are being misspent and wasted.

Nothing for the People

But there is one thing we never read about; these wasted dollars were intended to help the grassroots people, and they are the very people who will never see a single dime of that money. So much of it has been eaten up by the government and administration that by the time it goes through all of the various channels and winds its way down to the people who really need it, there is nothing left!

And yet, maybe the poor people of the reservation should ask themselves some hard questions. Did they vote in the last elections? Do they realize that the politicians who continue to keep their position are there, in that office, because they were elected by a majority vote? And finally, shouldn't the grassroots people begin to assume the responsibility of their own future by seeing to it that the politicians who represent only themselves are voted out of office, and honest, trustworthy, and capable Indian people elected to replace them? Maybe then, and only then, will they begin to share in some of the progress now being enjoyed by the politicians and their families.

Indians Must Accept Responsibility to Change System

One of the most over-worked words of the past decade has been "unity." In fact, one candidate for the office of the Oglala Sioux Tribal presidency used the slogan, "Think Lakota, Think Unity" as his main theme, and won that seat. The slogan of the 1978 National Congress of American Indians Convention in Dallas, Texas in 1977 was "Unity through Leadership."

"Unity" implies common goals, similar objectives and, used within this context, there is absolutely no lack of unity among Indians. All Indian people, the so-called traditonal, the grassroots, Bureau of Indian Affairs employees, tribal employees, the unemployed, urban, reservation, farmers, ranchers, American Indian Movement members, or John Birch Society members, have similar goals.

They want better homes, jobs, a good education for their children, honest tribal government, better health care, respect, better law enforcement, a better judicial system, a sovereign nation, control of their own lives, a return to traditional values, revival of the culture, and last, but not least, better communications with their elected officials. The goals and objectives are the same; so, why the lack of unity?

The Indian people themselves know that there must be change because the present system is not working. Is it the method being used to bring about this change that causes the lack of unity? We learned, or at least we should have, that the violent attempts to bring about change, as occurred at Wounded Knee in 1973, also, do not work. And yet, in order for change to occur, it is the people themselves who must bring it about.

If there is a positive trend facing the Indian tribes of this country for the 1980s, I am hard pressed to find it. But one thing is for sure: we are not going to have our problems solved for us in Washington, D.C., nor are we going to solve them by tearing down what we have without providing an alternate system. If it is an attitude that is creating division amongst the Lakota people, then it is the attitude that must change.

The tribal officials must stop thinking in terms of "what is good for me" and start to think in terms of "what is good for the people." Whether the Indian people realize it or not, the ability to bring about positive change is clearly within their grasp. There are those who have refused to participate in the election process of tribal government because they were against the Indian Reorganization Act, the basis for self-government, from the outset, and they will not bend. Who are they really hurting, except themselves and their families?

They have shut their eyes since 1934, hoping that when they open them, the tribal government will have disappeared. But it has not. As a matter of fact, it is because these good and intelligent people have chosen to ignore it, that it has grown and festered into the unmanageable monster they so resent.

As the world around us has become complex, so has the system which governs us. The fact that someone has a nice Indian name such as "Looking Elk" hardly qualifies him to deal with these complexities. We must begin to search out our leaders because of the capabilities, not because of their names.

The old prejudices which have begun to suppress logic must be stifled.

There are many good things from the past that we want to retain but we must not be afraid to let go of the bad things. The terms "mixed blood" or "Iyeska," "full blood," "AIM" and "goon" should no longer be used to create division. The honorable word Lakota should be used to mean all of the people of the Lakota Nation. In my opinion, it is this internal prejudice which has torn our people apart. The old BIA encouraged it and they fostered it to insure their own existence. The greatest fear the federal government had in the past is that the Indian people would unite in a common cause. As history has taught us, they effectively saw to it that unity never happened.

In 1981 primary elections for a new tribal president and council will be held at the Pine Ridge Reservation. It is now, at the beginning of the year, that the people should be analyzing the performance of their elected officials and looking toward the future. The people of the reservations of South Dakota can no longer turn their backs on this responsibility. We can no longer blame all of our ills on the white man. The day of looking for scapegoats is past. In reality, the future of the Indian people is in their own hands, and whether they can arise to accept this challenge or not, will decide their future.

Unity Necessary on Reservations

On CBS Sunday Morning, a poignant television show about the division on the Mohawk Reservation in New York state was aired recently.

It was the story of two brothers, one a traditionalist and the other the chief of police for the reservation. There was a lot of bitterness and frustration in the voices of the two brothers as they talked about the differences in their approach to life which created mental wounds that could not be healed.

Caught in the middle was their mother, a soft-spoken lady who seemed to be puzzled by it all. She said that she loved them both equally, and she would just have to wait and see what finally happened to solve their problems.

Other Problems

And all the while the Mohawk people were fighting among themsleves, their river was being polluted and the chemicals drifting down in the smoke from an aluminum factory which bordered their reservation was making the fish inedible and slowly poisoning their crops and cattle.

Cases before the federal and state courts which could affect their very lives forever were not being given the undivided support of all Mohawk people and, as a result, the tide was being shifted against them.

The narrator of the program commented that while the Indian people fought among themselves, the white man was, once again, winning the war to have his way. The not-so-secret weapon of the white man of "divide and conquer" is alive and well and living on many of the Indian reservations of this land.

It reminded me very much of the division that almost tore the reservations of South Dakota apart. How much ground did we lose out here, and how much are we continuing to lose, while we square off with each other and ignore the greater dangers from outside the reservation?

A Common Cause

Are the scars so deep that they can never heal? At one time, it would have seemed that this was the case; but in recent years, many brothers and sisters have stepped across that invisible line, made peace with each other and discovered that the adversity between them has strengthened, rather than weakened, their wills to work together as one people for a common cause— the survival of the tribe.

The old saying goes that "those who do not learn from history are bound to repeat its mistakes" and all one needs to do is to look back to see how tribe after tribe went under, some forever, because the Indian leaders chose to fight each other rather than unite in a common cause. Is this the fate that is awaiting the good people of the Lakota Nation?

Many years ago a message was left to the Lakota people and it was intended for all of the people, not just those who chose to interpret it to suit themselves. It was spoken by Back Elk at Harney Peak in the Paha Sapa and it says:

"Again, and maybe the last time on this earth, I recall the great vision you sent me. It may be that little root of the sacred tree still lives. Nourish it then, that it may leaf and bloom and fill with singing birds. Hear me, not for myself, but for my people; I am old. Hear me that they may once more go back into the hoop and find the good red road, the shielding tree!"

All That Remains

The reservations are all that remain to a people who once owned the whole continent, and it is here, on these reservations that the unity to save this last foothold will determine how history will record this period of our lives.

In 1904, a great chief named "Thunder Rolling over the Mountains" by his father, and later called Chief Joseph by the white man, said, "I want to have time to look for my children, and see how many of them I can find. Maybe I shall find them among the dead."

A large tombstone was placed over Chief Joseph's resting place at Nespelem, Washington; but his monument can never tell of the wars he fought to preserve his lands, nor could it ever answer the question he asked of his dying father, Old Joseph: "What kind of animal would sell the land where lie the bones of his fathers?"

Sovereignty Issues Confronting Tribes

Navajo Tribal Chairman Peter MacDonald is urging that there be peace between the Navajo Nation and the State of Arizona. According to the *Navajo Times*, May 22 edition, MacDonald's address to a group of Arizona officials stated, "Time and time again we have had to go to court to protect ourselves from acts of aggresion." The tribal chairman continued, "We have won these lawsuits but each time it has cost us thousands of dollars, and each time it has diverted our limited energies and resources and personnel from the real job at hand—building a future."

Indian tribes across the United States find themselves in much the same position as the Navajo Nation. Time and time again they are forced into state courts to defend or protect their basic rights or sovereignty. This basic right was established by the U.S. Supreme Court in Worchester vs. the State of Georgia when Indian nations were designated as "dependent sovereign nations."

At this very moment many tribes in this country are in court fighting state governments for the preservation of water rights, land rights, mineral rights and for their right to use their natural resources for the benefit of their respective tribes.

South Dakota Case

Last month Attorney General Mark Meierhenry of South Dakota filed a suit in state court against 60,000 land owners in the western two-thirds of the state. The suit will affect individual landowners who live outside municipal limits, Indian tribes and the federal government. Meierhenry said, "the suit is designed to establish who owns the water of the Missouri River and its tributaries." He contends that the suit "isn't aimed against anyone." But many tribal officials in South Dakota believe that the lawsuit is a political smokescreen designed to get at the tribes.

This "water rights" suit brought by the South Dakota Attorney General could cost the state one million dollars and last as long as twenty years before it is eventually decided.

For too many years the Indian tribes and the state governemtns have found themselves in adversary positions. Hundreds of thousands of dollars have been spent in court battles that could have been used to better the lives of the reservation residents and the state residents.

Economic Development

Several years ago the Economic Development Administration funded several projects related to tourism on Indian reservations that cost millions of dollars. After many of these projects failed, the EDA spent several thousand dollars more hiring experts to determine why the projects were not successful. Most of the projects were tourist resort hotels located on remote reservations such as the Chief Gall Inn, located 150 miles from the nearest interstate highway in South Dakota, near a small farming community which had ample accommodations for most tourists.

The EDA study discovered that the agency had: (1) funded these projects without on-going involvement and provision of expertise; (2) emphasized unemployment needs rather than long-range economic benefits; (3) failed to provide a cohesive national program of assistance; (4) made loans and grants without insisting on feasibility studies and marketing analyses; (5) made loans and grants without requiring accounting and management procedures; (6) did not provide for backup capability in terms of operating capital, advertising, marketing and training in all phases of the hospitality industry.

Finally, the EDA study decided that "self-styled experts" in many cases were the major problem. It seems that many overzealous consultants, designers, architects and builders saw these projects as "an opportunity to fulfill impractial dreams" and the "dreamers built without regard to needed attractions for tourists," according to the report. Is it any wonder that tribal enterprises are in trouble?

With friends like this to assist them, the tribes certainly don't need enemies.

Questionnaire Reveals Feelings about Tribal Government

The *Lakota Times* decided to do a survey on the effectiveness of tribal government. A questionnaire was prepared by concerned citizens of the Wounded Knee district. More than 1,000 responses were submitted to the newspaper office!

Approximately 200 Indian tribes in the United States use a tribal council form of government, with a chairman, president or governor seated as the titular head. This questionnaire could have been prepared by the people of any of these reservations, rancheros, or pueblos and the responses to the questions could have, as easily, been the same.

Here are the questions, and the answers broken down to percentages:

1. Do you feel the larger Tribal Council has been effective? 17 percent said yes; 83 percent said no.

2. Do you feel the decision-making process should be at the community or district level? 87 percent, yes; 13 percent, no.

3. Do you feel the Tribal Council representatives express the issues of your district 22 percent, yes; 78 percent, no.

5. Do you know how your representative votes? 39 percent, yes; 61 percent, no.

6. Do your representatives meet with the district people to explain what happened at the last meeting? 22 percent, yes; 78 percent, no.

7. Do you feel a roll call* vote should be exercised in all council voting? (*Roll call vote means each representative must identify himself and how he is voting.) 92 percent, yes; 8 percent, no.

8. Do you feel a small Council could do as good a job as a large Council? 66 percent, yes; 30 percent, no; 4 percent, no opinion.

9. Do you go to your representative and make known your concerns? 66 percent, yes; 34 percent, no.

10. What would you recommend as an effective Tribal Council? (Consider the cuts of federal programs by the Reagan Adminstration.)

The following recommendations were submitted:

1. Reduce the size of the Council.

2. Let the BIA Agency Superintendent become a part of the Council.

3.Let people make decisions at the community and district levels.

4. Do away with the Tribal Council and have one leader, a chief.

5. Require candidates for the Tribal Council to take an intelligence test before they are allowed to run for office so we can be sure qualified people get elected.

6. Stop voting for people just because they are your friends or relatives. This is 1983. We need to elect intelligent, well-qualified people to represent us.

7. Stop fighting amongst ourselves over blood quantum. We have enough troubles wihtout fighting each other.

Under the Indian Reorganization Act of 1934, many Indian tribes chose democratic forms of self-government. On some reservations, traditional Indians opposed this form of government, and in protest, refused to participate in it. For many years they refused to vote—or to run for office.

The IRA governments, as they became known throughout the Indian country, were under the strictest supervision of the Bureau of Indian Affairs. Any resolutions passed by the Tribal Councils had to be approved by the BIA at the agency level, and then submitted to the area offices, and then to Washington, D.C. for final approval. This close control by the federal government created many bad situations on the reservation.

In the 1960s, the Office of Economic Opportunity pumped federal dollars into local governments. For the first time since IRA was instituted on reservations, Indian people at grassroots level had the opportunity to participate in making day-to-day decisions on issues that affected their lives. This was the beginning of the new awareness on Indian reservations and self-determination policies of the Richard Nixon administration.

As more responsibilities have been shifted to the tribal governments, the grassroots people have become more active in tribal politics. Many of the traditional people, who had refused to participate in tribal government, have decided that if important changes are to take place in the structure of tribal government, it must come from within, from policy enacted by the people. The tremendous response to the questionnaire from across this reservation is testimony to that new awareness.

Reservation Enrollment; Prison Overcrowding Considered

There is still confusion over the recent tribal council action regarding the right of non-enrolled members of the tribe to vote or run for office.

Most council members would agree that the confusion stems largely from the council's vacillation. Their voting on this subject ran something like this: first you can, then you can't, then you can, and now you can't. Ultimately they agreed to open the enrollment, and set up a committee to research individual claims. But they did not establish an effective date.

Is there any wonder that so many people on the reservation were uncertain as to the final decision? The council's action has become an embarrassment to many members of the Oglala Sioux Tribe.

The question of enrollment has plagued this tribe for over forty years, and is not to be taken lightly. There are an estimated 17,000 enrollment members—people who were born of Oglala Sioux blood on the reservation.

What worries opponents of opening the enrollment to those born off the reservation is that it could open a Pandora's box because of pending multimillion-dollar claims that would be available to tribal members.

Councilman Garvard Good Plume, Wakpamni, asked me to address the council during the debate on enrollment and tell what happened to the Papagos of Arizona in their efforts to update enrollment on their reservation.

The Papago tribe was awarded $26,000,000 for land claims in 1974. At that time the total tribal enrollment was approximately 7,000. An enrollment committee was set up to bring the tribal rolls current. That enrollment committee has been working steadily now for five years and has received applications for enrollment as Papagos from over 12,000 new applicants, from as far away as Australia and West Germany. They see no end to the new applications for tribal membership, and must set a date to conclude the process so that the tribe can get on with the business of determining the dispensation of these funds.

Hanging over the Oglala Sioux enrollment deliberations is a $105 million claim based on the 1868 Laramie Treaty. Both remain in litigation but if the tribe wins the awards, as many as 24,000 to 30,000 people could apply to be members, to reap part of the awards.

The enrollment committee faces a monumental task: it must determine what blood quantity would qualify, and it must research the background of every individual who claims to be a member.

Imagine if somebody from West Germany called to say his great-grandmother on his father's side was a full-blooded Oglala Sioux, and he only had an Indian name to go on. The committee would have to trace the name through the Bureau of Indian Affairs, enrollment lists in Aberdeen, South Dakota and St. Louis, Missouri.

The Santa Fe Prison Riot

Several years ago, scientists concluded a test using laboratory animals to determine the effects of over-crowding. Animals were added to a small enclosure until they barely had room to move around. The animals, in this case, rats, became so upset that they turned to cannibalism, wanton killing and to catatonic behavior under these conditions. The tests proved conclusively that laboratory animals reacted adversely to extreme overcrowding.

According to Homer Thunder Hawk, a former inmate of the maximum security prison at Santa Fe, New Mexico who served eighteen months for aggravated assault there, the conditions in that prison led to a small-scale riot in 1975 and were destined to lead to a larger riot if they were not improved. Apparently they were not.

Mr. Thunder Hawk said, "We were confined to two per cell in an 8x5 cubicle designed for one person. The man with the most seniority was given the single bed in the cell, and the new arrival had to sleep under the bed on a canvas mattress. Many times there was not enough bedding to go around, so we did without."

"Many of us who had an opportunity to go to work on the outside, were denied work permits because of the nature of our crimes," he said. "When we protested by refusing to go to our prison jobs, tear gas was fired into our cells, and we were driven out with clubs, through a gauntlet of guards armed with night sticks, and severely beaten all the way to the gymnasium area where we were forced to strip, and then driven back to our cells."

Thunder Hawk concluded, "I knew, even after I was finally paroled, that if conditions weren't improved in the next few years, a terrible riot would take place."

Election

The general election on the Pine Ridge Reservation is scheduled for March 11, 1980. The upset victory scored by Vice President Stanley Looking Elk over incumbent President Elijah Whirlwind Horse leaves the outcome very much in question. Looking Elk won the primary by over two hundred votes, which is a significant number of votes when you consider that just over 2,000 voters turned out for the primary.

National Indian Organizations

There is a rumbling among several Indian tribes in South Dakota about extricating themselves from membership in some of the national organizations such as the National Congress of American Indians and the Coalition of Energy Resource Tribes. The tribal council of the Cheyenne River Sioux Tribe decided to stop talking about it and act.

The council voted to withdraw from the United Sioux Tribes Development Corporation and from the National Congress of American Indians. Several weeks ago, the tribe had withdrawn from the Council of Energy Resource Tribes. One councilman said, "These organizations have taken it upon themselves to make decisions, formulate policy and seek out funds for themselves without consulting the tribal members. They are setting themselves up as another Bureau of Indian Affairs, and we certainly don't need two BIA."

Nurses attending the graduation ceremonies at Oglala Community College, Kyle

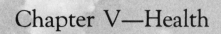

Chapter V—Health

Health

Navajos Reviewing Medicine-Religion

Eddie Tso stood in the center of the room with his foot propped up on a chair and addressed about forty people, mostly women, from the various health programs in Shiprock, New Mexico.

"There may have been a time when we felt ashamed because there were no health programs among us; but the more we investigate it, and look into it, we find that the health programs were here, but they had been pushed aside, and now they are being revived," he said.

In conjunction with the Navajo Health Authortiy and the Navajo Community College his program is designed to review the art of the elder medicine men and try to bring it back, if it is useful.

"There are only two of us working to handle the program for the entire reservations," Tso said. "One of the things we are trying to do is to integrate Navajo medicine with Western medicine and, through the Navajo Medicine Man's Association, protect, preserve and promote Native American medicine.

"According to our Master Health Plan," Tso continued, "we are attempting to detrermine how Western medicine and traditional Navajo medicine can co-exist today, and maybe from this we can cross-reference medication and eliminate some of the myths (a real understatement) that label Indian medicine as 'taboo' or 'witchcraft.'"

"To us, medicine and religion are synonymous, but when the settlers first came here, they told the Indians that their religion was no good, and to forget it," Tso pointed out. "But all cultures have negatives and positives. There is no culture that can say it is perfect."

Tso emphasized that the non-Indian used to laugh at Indian religion and medicine, "but to us, it was no joke because our culture is very important to us."

"Now under the Freedom of Religion Act," Tso continued, "we are bringing back our religion and our medicine, and we are finding out that it is good. Some of the old people cry when they are told that the law is changing these things, and it is allowing us to practice our religion without fear."

There are a lot of questions that have arisen about the Navajo Medicine Man's Association by the medicine men themselves. Many of the approximately 2,000 medicine men scattered across the entire reservation have not joined the organization.

One of the fears is that they demean the traditional art and serve to commercialize it. Another is that by joining the organization, the medicine men will then be held accountable to the Internal Revenue Service, and be forced to declare their fees as income. Tso feels that by getting out and discussing these things with the different medicine men, many of these fears can be alleviated.

According to Tso, there are legal, social, economic and religious ramifications to be considered. "The medicine men need to be protected, too," he added, "just like doctors."

Armed with a stack of literature about one foot high, Tso travels across the reservation speaking to health groups and medicine men, and tries to acquaint them with his program.

"We hope to learn about the medicine of other tribes, also," Tso concluded. "But, because there are only two of us to serve the entire reservation, it is a tremendous responsiblity, but one that is vitally needed." He added, "I wish that I could have spent a lot more time with you, but since there are only two of us to cover the entire reservation, it is very difficult. But if you want to hear more, just call and we'll set up another session at your convenience."

The meeting room was filled with applause!

Fewer Drinkers Found in Navajo Community

This series on alcoholism is not intended to illustrate that there is no problem with alcohol consumption among Indian people, but rather to correct a gross misconception as to the proportion of drinkers to non-drinkers. Philip A. May of the University of Montana undertook a study, using data compiled by other researchers, which questioned the methods of previous study and suggested that a new approach to alcohol-related problems among Indians was needed, and a new method of obtaining data, minus the white, middle-class infusion of thought, was absolutely necessary in order for true statistical figures to surface.

May refuted many of the accepted statistics in his article by saying, "Adult Navajos from two wage work communities were found to have a higher percentage of abstainers, 61 percent, of which approximately 20 percent were lifelong abstainers, while the remainder had given up drinking. When these figures are compared with a rural, conservative and largely Anglo state such as Iowa, the outcome is surprising. Comparison data showed that 60 percent of the Iowa residents drink, significantly greater than the 39 to 42 percent among the Navajo. Therefore, at least among the Navajo, it appears that a smaller proportion of the adult population is drinking at any one time than among the general population."

The study continues, "This is quite a surprising statistic when one considers the typically described image of the 'drunken Indian.' In fact, a study by Levy and Kunitz in 1974 found that a smaller percentage of the Navajo communities drink than any type of community studied by their report."

There are many reasons why the image of "drunken Indians" has spread throughout the United States. Grade B Western movies, television and books have reinforced many of these myths with little regard to accuracy or authenticity.

The article by May, *Not All Indians Drink: Evidence Against the Stereotype*, suggests "When Indians drink, it is many times a highly conspicuous type of group drinking, so that people may feel it is a large social and health problem.

In rural or more isolated areas of the reservations many may be abstainers; but among those who drink, drinking may tend to be more sporadic and group oriented."

In fact, May's study implies, "Further evidence against the stereotye can be found in various existing data sources. Arrests of Indians for alcohol-related offenses (driving while intoxicated, drunkenness, liquor law violtions) in the Uniform Crime Reports, tend to reinforce the old notions about Indian drinking. In 1974, 62 percent of all Indian arrests recorded in Uniform Crime Reports were for alcohol or drinking-related offenses. This data, however, is data from off-reservation sources, which tends to over-represent drinking Indians, who, due to prohibition laws on most reservations, have to migrate to off-reservation towns to consume alcohol."

Implications for Future Research

One of the major findings set forth by May concerned the methods of research and he stresses this point by saying, "The implications of researching the validity of the 'drunken Indian' stereotype are many. First and foremost, there is a sense of 'fair play' and the righting of some of the wrongs perpetrated by the continuance of the gross and negative overgeneralization. In many areas of the United States, all Indians, regardless of their orientation, are treated as if they are, or could behave as a 'drunken Indian.' The implications for self-fulfilling prophecy are strong. If the stereotype is untrue, then more accurate assessments of reality should be attempted by social scientists."

My final column on the "drunken Indian" misconception will deal with the importance of renewed research using updated methods, and open-minded methods geared to accuracy, rather than generalization.

Athletics to Alcoholism to Advisor

I started out to do an article on Glen Three Stars, the former athletic great from Oglala Community High School.

I was going to describe some of his athletic achievements, especially the time in 1948 when he placed second in the 100-yard dash, second in the 220, and set a state record in the 440 that stood for twenty-five years at the State B championships.

But while talking with Three Stars, I discovered a man who reached his apex as an athlete but was just beginning a life in a profession that gives him much more personal satisfaction than his track records.

That profession is in alcoholism counseling.

Project Recovery began six years ago on the reservation. It was a program designed to assist alcoholics in their struggle to conquer alcohol. Before he became a counselor with Project Recovery, he sat on the other side of the desk waging a personal battle with the debilitating devastation of alcohol—a battle that almost cost him his life.

Roy Red Shirt, a recovered alcoholic who is director of the project, remembers what it was like: "My doctor told me, 'Roy, if you want to drink, go off into the hills by yourself so that you can die in peace. Because that way, I won't have to waste my time and medicine on you.' He meant that I was as good as dead if I continued to drink," Red Shirt said.

"Squeak" Herman feels that alcoholics are the most fantastic con-artists around. "They've learned to manipulate people to serve their needs," she said. "Sometimes it gets very discouraging when they call you at four in the morning, and you sit up with them for hours trying to help, and they end up refusing your help, but it's a real challenge."

The counselors from Project Recovery have an agreement with the tribal judges and prosecutors that enables them to visit the jails every day and attempt to assist in the rehabilitation of the prisoners who are suffering from alcoholism.

"It's so easy to get alcohol on the reservation even though it is illegal," said Three Stars. "Usually the reason for drinking is family problems. The next thing you know, even the children are involved."

Three Stars continued, "They find themselves unable to face their problems and so they turn to drink, but they find out that they've only added to their problems."

Counselors are from across the reservation. Garvard Good Plume, Herman, Don Bear Runner, Ben Lovejoy, Doris Hollow Horn, Anna Furman, Virginia Poor Thunder, Jim Rock and Les Lafferty work in the districts and are always on call to assist a problem drinker.

Most of these counselors are taking courses at Oglala Sioux Community College on a variety of subjects that will improve their ability to understand and to assist alcoholics.

Three Stars concluded, "We try to educate the people and we set up Alcoholics Anonymous meetings that encourage the problem drinkers to help themselves.

"So far, we've had about a fifty percent success rate, but I think that if we could get the tribal government behind us, and get them to make our program one of their priorities, we could do much more."

There is a handwritten sign prominently displayed on the office wall that reads, "Success may yet come to those who have failed, but never to those who quit."

Sidney Has No Horse and puppets he created—a new kind of humor for Pine Ridge residents

Humor

Jokes Often Used to Teach Lesson

Whenever Indians gather together for a meeting or a conference, there are usually a lot of new jokes tried and tested, or a few old ones updated and revised. Quite often, the jokes are in the form of a story that teaches a lesson, or one that stresses humility.

Not too long ago, I attended a conference in Denver, Colorado. After the business day had ended, several of us from several different tribes retired to the hospitality room to relax, unwind, and of course, tell a few jokes. A non-Indian man sat very quietly on a sofa, listened, laughed and seemed to really enjoy himself. After a bit, he stood up, shook hands with everyone present and said, "Another myth has just been expunged from my mind; the myth of the stoic, humorless Indian. Thank you for sharing your warm sense of humor with me and removing a stereotype image forever."

Not Sleeping

Commissioner of Indian Affairs William Hallett addressed a large conference crowd recently.

He said, "One time I was giving a speech to a crowd such as you when I noticed an elderly Indian man in the front row with his chin resting on his chest. He appeared to be asleep. I called out to him and asked him if he had heard what I said. The man stood up immediately and said, "My cow died!"

Hallett continued, "Now what in the world do you mean by that?" The man answered, "It means that I don't need your bull any more."

Pickup Tale

One of my all time favorites goes like this: A Texan was driving through the Navajo Nation when he spotted an Indian on a horse watching over some sheep. He pulled over to the side of the road, climbed out of his car and walked over to talk to the man.

He asked the Navajo man, "How much land do you own?" The man answered, "Not much, you can see all of it from where you are standing."

The Texan puffed out his chest and bragged, "Back in Texas I can get into my pickup and drive from sunup to sunset and it usally takes me about three days to reach the end of my property."

The Navajo man listened patiently, paused for a long while, and then replied, "You know, Mister, I used to have a pickup like that."

Strong Words

Another joke making the rounds concerns the old White Sands Proving Grounds in Southern New Mexico. In seems that back in the early 1940s, an

Indian man was riding near the atomic testing area when he spotted another Indian on a horse several miles away. It looked very much like a friend of his, so he waved frantically, but to no avail. The other rider did not see him. Hurriedly he jumped from his horse, gathered some wood and sagebrush, quickly built a small fire, and then threw his saddle blanket over it, and began to send smoke signals. Finally, the distant Indian spotted the smoke, climbed from his horse, and began to build a small fire to answer the signal. The first Indian shaded his eyes, peered into the distance, and waited impatiently for a reply. At that precise moment, the United States government detonated the first atomic bomb. The first Indian rider watched in awe as the giant, mushroom shaped cloud rose into the clear blue skies. Angrily he slapped his leg with his cowboy hat and exclaimed, "Damn it, why didn't I think of saying that!"

Jokes Have Moral

Each tribe has its own jokes, fitted to words that are a part of it own language. If members of other tribes are present at a gathering, quite often, the jokes are changed to apply to them, and everyone has a big laugh at their expense. But it's always good, clean fun, and no harm is intended. The moral is: If we can laugh at others, we can laugh at ourselves.

Scary Incident of '38 Recalled

The year was 1938. The rumblings of war were growing louder with each passing day. A state of near panic existed in Europe.

On the reservations of South Dakota most people were just trying to get by. The devastation of the Great Depression had given White America a small taste of what Indian America had been experiencing for years.

I lived with my parents in a long, duplex type of house, replete with dirt floors, wood burning stove, and kerosene lamps in the village of Kyle, in the Medicine Root District of the Pine Ridge Reservation. My father was a clerk at Kieff's Store and because he was fluent in Lakota, he was kept very busy by the many elders of the tribe who visited the store to make purchases of groceries and other items.

Mr. Kieff had grown very accustomed to approaching the service counter to assist a Lakota man or woman, and acknowledging the inimitable gesture of the Indian of pointing in my father's direction with the lower lip. This silent gesture indicated to him that they would patiently wait for my father to complete a transaction, and get to them, no matter how long it took.

Although the movie industry in America was just beginning to flourish, movies on the reservation were still a very rare treat. Remember that the following year, 1939, two of the classic motion pictures of all time would hit the silver screen: *The Wizard of Oz* and *Gone with the Wind*.

Signs had been posted in the village announcing that a movie, a Laurel and Hardy film would be shown on Friday night at the Kyle Day School gymnasium. The price of admission would be 15 cents for adults and 5 cents for children under 12.

The Christmas holidays were upon us and snow had been falling in huge, drifting flakes all day Friday as most of us busied ourselves in anticipation of seeing our very first motion picture. In fact, many of the adults in our community had never been to a movie and they were as anxious to go as were the children.

Folding chairs had been set up in the gymnasium for the adults. After we had parted with our nickels, grown damp from being clutched for hours in our sweaty little hands, we were directed to proceed to the front of the gym and sit on the floor in neat rows, in front of the motion picture screen. In wide-eyed wonder, we complied without a murmur.

In a short while, all of the folding chairs directly behind us had been filled with adults, and those who were not lucky enough to get a chair, stood along the wall at the back of the gym. All of we children glanced back apprehensively at the movie projector that was resting on a platform in the center aisle.

After what seemed like hours, the lights in the gym went out, and a burst of light shot from the projector and splashed on the large, white screen directly above us. Back in those days, movies consisted of a "newsreel," "cartoon," and then the feature movie.

On this special evening, the night of our first motion picture, the newsreel led the parade of excitement. As the pictures went by in an astonishing blur, a man's voice told us about people, places, and things we knew nothing about. We sat directly below the screen and gasped in awe at the magic that flashed before our eyes.

And then it happened! To our utter amazement, a huge, rattling, noisy, army tank began to roll directly toward us. Even as we drew back in sudden fear, the vicious looking tank continued to approach. They used a trick in those early movie days of having a cameraman climb into a hole in the ground, and a car, or as in this case, a tank, could drive directly over the top of it. Of course, we didn't know this.

Suddenly, the tank was right on top of us. The sight and sound of this monster bearing down upon us was too much! We panicked! The children seated directly under the screen started to rush to the exits, but the adults, many seeing a movie for the first time, soon joined in the headlong rush for the doors.

The movie projector operator suddenly realized what was happening and very swiftly cut off the projector, and flipped on the lights. The sudden blast of lights caught children and adults alike in various poses of sudden flight, and just as in the childhood games we played of 'red light-green light,' we froze in the positions we had assumed in the moment of panic.

For just a moment, there was total silence. And then the laughter started. Even the elders clutched at their sides as the tears of unrestrained laughter rolled down their cheeks. And as friends and family members began to point at each other as their eyes adjusted to the bright lights, the laughter grew and grew.

Before long, we were rolling on the floor as some of the adults braced against each other to keep from joining us on the floor. In my entire life, I have never experienced again the total spontaneity of laughter that enveloped that crowded room of Indian people.

Those were, indeed, the good old days.

"Dogged Out, Skunked Out, Muled Out" Jake Herman

After you pass Three Mile Creek, but just before you get to Kyle, on the Pine Ridge Reservation of South Dakota, you'll come to a blacktop road, the only one that turns off the main road, and if you follow that blacktop, it will take you behind Kyle toward "Spud Creek." Off to your left, you'll see a solitary, white frame church sitting in a large field, with its tall steeple pointing up at the blue, Dakota skies. This is a Catholic Church called St. Stevens.

There's a graveyard in front of that church, and one of the markers in that graveyard says, *Jake Herman, born Jan. 13, 1890—Died Jan. 20, 1969.*

A few years before his death, while a patient at the Veterans Administration Hospital in Lincoln, Nebraska, he told a reporter from the Omaha *World Herald*, "I'm not ready to cash in my chips yet. I have a daughter named Faith, one named Hope, and I still have to have another one so I can call her Charity."

Well, he never did have the daughter named Charity; but his two daughters, Faith and Hope, now live in New Mexico. Faith lives in Farmingtoin and Hope, in Gallup.

Jake was one of the last of a dying breed. Bronc buster, calf roper, bull dogger, fancy rope spinner and all-around cowboy whose serious attempts at rodeoing brought so much laughter to the crowds, he decided to make the most of it by becoming one of the premier rodeo clowns.

He rode with Jack King's Wild West Show and traveled with the Rodeo Royal Circus and Wild West Show clad in his baggy pants, swallow-tail coat, flat derby hat, putty nose and black whiskers. With a trick mule called "Creeping Jenny," a trained dog named "Tag" and a de-fumed skunk named "Stinky" he brought howls of laughter from rodeo crowds from Montana to Nebraska. Many a rodeo bull rider owed his hide to that ridiculous figure in the baggy pants.

Born to Antoine Herman, a round-up foreman, and Elizabeth Clifford, an Oglala woman, Jake attended "more boarding schools and government schools than any Sioux alive." The last school he attended was Carlisle Indian School in Pennsylvania, made famous by the man voted "Athlete of the first 50 years of his century," Jim Thorpe. According to Jake, he quit school "because I didn't want to show up Abraham Lincoln."

Despite his traveling days he found time to marry Alice Janis of Pine Ridge and father six children: Jacob, Grace, Paul, Rex, Faith and Hope.

After Jake's rodeoing days were over, he used his natural talent to write a news column for the *Shannon County News* called "Wa Ho Si" and contributed articles to *True West, Frontier Times, The Western Horseman* and many legends and tales of the Lakota to *The Indian Historian*. This man of many talents began to paint during his retirement and his art work began to be known as "The primitive art of Jack Herman" and was often compared to the works of Grandma Moses.

A compulsive story-teller, most of the tales of humor spun by Jake were on himself. One of his favorites went like this: "This lady was looking at one of the paintings I had on exhibit, a painting of a buffalo. She said, 'I'd buy that painting if you had not made the buffalo's legs so long.'" Jake continued, "I came back real fast with: 'The reason I made the buffalo's legs so long was so that he could reach the ground.'" And Jake would have you believe the lady bought his painting.

In his waning years, Jake loved to talk about the cowboys and cowgirls who traveled the rodeo circuit. He talked about Casey Tibbs, Earl Thode, Leonard Strand, Chet Byers, and one of the top clowns of the day, Benny Bender. He'd remember Oklahoma Curly, Paddy Ryan, Floyd Shilling, The South American Kid and many others, almost forgotten figures from the Wild West shows.

A few years before his death, he summed up his life in an article he wrote for *Frontier Times*: "The rodeo had been good to me. It made it possible for me to build a little home, and, as I've always said, I now live with my memories of rodeo days that once were and that have now faded away. My trick dog Tag is dead, my skunk Stinky is dead, and my mule Creeping Jenny is dead; so now I'm dogged out, skunked out and muled out."

Nothing Can Top Indian Joke Session

There are times when writing a weekly column can become a real chore. This is especially true when the smell of spring is hanging in the air and I would much rather be seated on the bank of a blue lake with a fishing pole in one hand and a cool brew in the other.

There is an old saying hanging on the wall in front of my typewriter, intended to stir the creative juices and to blow away the clouds of writer's lethargy: "Here I sit invoking muses and biting my truant pen."

Or, I am reminded of the comic strip character Shoe perched high in his tree staring balefully at his typewriter while empty thoughts in the form of clouds float above his head. Voila! An ornate "A" resplendent in vines and flowers appears and causes Shoe to snap his fingers as he acknowledges the idea. He turns to his typewriter, taps the letter "A" with confidence, puzzles over it and then tears it from his typewriter in disgust and tosses it over his shoulder. Of such small beginnings are columns created.

Over the past two years, this column has been tacked up on bulletin boards from Window Rock, Arizona to Eagle Butte, South Dakota. Two columns in particular drew several phone calls and letters requesting copies. One on Indian humor and jokes really made the rounds in Indian Country. The other column which drew many favorable comments, particularly from the reservations, was one on the "diploma Indians." One lady told me she clips each column and mails it to Europe. *Notes from Indian Country* now appears in five newspapers and is read weekly on ten reservations.

This brings me to the subject of today's column. A few weeks ago, at the district basketball tournament, I ran into many old friends from the Pine Ridge Reservation. A few of them had some jokes to tell, hoping I would do another column on Indian humor and include these stories. Tribal Councilman "Sunshine" Janis told this one:

"An Indian holy man had an audience with the Pope in Rome. As a gesture of friendship, he presented his holiness with an Indian ceremonial pipe. A few months later, while visiting the United States, the Pope told his entourage he had to visit his Indian friend out on the reservation.

"When he arrived on the reservation, his Indian friend noticed how tired and haggard he looked, so he took the Pope to a small lake—his private fishing hole—to relax away from the crowds. The Pope, clad in his white robe and cowboy-shaped vatican hat, sat in the holy man's boat enjoying the peace and quiet. The Indian holy man needed more bait, so he climbed out of the board, walking on the water to the bank, picked up more bait, and walked on the water once more to the boat. The Pope was flabbergasted.

"The Pope said, 'I knew you Indians had powerful medicine, but I would never have believed you could walk on water unless I had seen it with my own eyes. Well, if an Indian medicine man can walk on water, so can the head of the greatest church in the world.' With that, the Pope stepped from the boat, and sank out of sight. Only his hat was left floating on the water. The Indian holy man helped the Pope from the water and back into the boat. Still spitting water, the Pope said, 'Well, I guess your medicine is much stronger than mine.'

"The Indian holy man sat in the boat and looked at the Pope for a long while; and then he said, 'Not really, Your Holiness. You just have to know where the rocks are to step on.'"

I don't know whether Tony Fast Horse wants to be accused of telling this one, but here it is:

Question: What's the Lakota word for friend?

Answer: Kola!

Question: What's the Lakota word for enemy?

Answer: Uncola!

Garvard Good Plume, a tribal councilman from Wakpamni told a few, but try as I might, I could not clean them up enough to make them presentable to a G-rated audience.

As a parting shot, a Lakota man from Kyle told me this one (I won't embarrass him by using his name):

He said: "Have you ever heard of the disaster that happened to George "Evel Kneivel" Custer? It seems that he tried to jump over the entire Sioux Nation on a hobby horse."

It has been said that humor pulled the Jewish and the Black people through the hard times. It is said they could not have survived without it. Well, the moral of this column is, if you want to see some real survivors, just sit in on an Indian joke session. There's nothing in this world that can top it!

Litigation

Tribe Seeking New Attorney

Can a federal court continue to allow an attorney to represent an Indian tribe after that attorney has been first fired?

Attorney Arthur Lazarus had been representing several tribes of the Great Sioux Nation in cases involving the Black Hills and other cases related to the 1868 Treaty of Fort Laramie.

After the tribes decided to pursue return of the land instead of monetary compensation for the loss of the land, the Oglala Sioux Tribe of the Pine Ridge Reservation of South Dakota refused to renew his contract.

Even after this action, the U.S. Court of Claims is still recognizing Lazarus as the attorney of record in some of the cases. Members of the Oglala Sioux Tribal Council believe that Lazarus was more interested in monetary compensation than in seeking the return of lands lost. Because of these fears, the council refused to renew Lazarus' contract and instead hired a member of the tribe, attorney Mario Gonzalez, to represent the interests of the tribe.

Payment Offered

In a letter dated September 17 to Oglala Sioux Tribal President Joe American Horse, Lazarus wrote, "For your consideration I am enclosing a copy of a letter in which the United States once again has offered to settle the 1868 Treaty case for a payment of slightly less than $40 million. This offer is identical to the settlement worked out four years ago before the Court of Claims had reversed the Indian Claims Commission's favorable decision on the issue of offsets."

The monetary offer involves lands in North Dakota, Wyoming, Montana, Nebraska and northern Kansas. The actual settlement offer is in the amount of $39,749,700, and includes the Cheyenne River Sioux, Rosebud, Oglala, Lower Brule, Standing Rock, Crow Creek, Santee and Fort Peck Sioux tribes. The case, known as Docket 74, is separate from 74B which is the case involving the Black Hills Claims settlement.

Tribal attorney Mario Gonzalez said, "When the U.S. Supreme Court ruled on the Black Hills, they ruled that the taking of the land was an unconstitutional act. The lands confiscated by the United States in Docket 74 were taken by the same 1877 Act. You must realize that the lands in question include the coalfields around Gillette, Wyoming and the Big Horn Mountain Range. These lands are worth billions and billions of dollars when you consider the coal and oil that has been removed."

Carol Dinkins, assistant attorney general for the Land and Natural Resource Division of the U.S. Justice Department, sent a letter to Lazarus on July 27. The letter attached several conditions to the government's offer of monetary compensation in the Docket 74 case.

Condition four of the letter drives directly to the heart of the reasoning behind the Lakota people's refusal to accept a monetary settlement in lieu of the return of the land. It reads: "That judgments entered into pursuant to this settlement shall finally dispose of all claims or demands which the plaintiffs have asserted or could have asserted, in Docket No. 27, before the Indian Claims Commission and the United States Court of Claims."

So, here we have an attorney who is pursuing a course of monetary compensation for lands the Lakota people consider to be "Not for Sale," and although his contract has been legally terminated by tribal resolution, he is still being recognized as the attorney of record by the U.S. Court of Claims and the Justice Department.

Washington, D.C. attorney, Robert Coulter has been hired by the Oglala Sioux Tribe to take over Docket 74 and Docket 117 cases, which had been handled by Lazarus. Thus far, Lazarus has refused to turn over the files on these cases to Coulter, thereby making it very difficult for Coulter to adequately represent his client, the Oglala Sioux Tribe.

U.S. Ignores Attorney

Instead of trying to resolve the matter in the best interests of the client, the federal government is, in essence, obstructing justice by refusing to deal with the attorney, Coulter, hired to represent the tribe.

Lazarus has already been paid more than $10 million for representing the tribes of the Great Sioux Nation in the Black Hills Claims Settlement case even though now one of those tribes, the Oglala Sioux, alleges that he did not have a contract to represent it in these proceedings.

One would think that it is an easy matter for a client to rid himself of an attorney he believed was not representing his best interests. Not so! The Oglala Sioux Tribe has been trying for more than two years to declare Lazarus persona non grata without success.

For the Oglala Sioux Tribe, Arthur Lazarus has turned out to be like a case of "herpes simplex:" easy to get but impossible to get rid of!

Jurisdiction Issue in Accident Case

There is a case now pending before the South Dakota Supreme Court which can have a profound impact upon the Indian tribes and a financial crunch upon the non-Indian residents if the court rules in favor of the attorney general.

Case Number 13237 is the State of South Dakota, plaintiff-appellant, vs. Marvin Wayne Janis, defendant-appellee. It concerns an automobile accident which occurred on Aug. 19, which claimed the lives of two individuals. The accident occurred on the Cheyenne River Reservation on fee patented land, as opposed to tribal trust lands. The defendant is an Indian enrolled on the Pine Ridge Reservation. There are two legal issues involved:

1. Whether the Circuit Court has jurisdiction over the state's second-degree manslaughter charges against the defendant, where the offense occurred in an area within the confines of the original 1889 Cheyenne River Reservation, but also within the area opened by the Act of 1908.

2. Whether the Circuit Court had jurisdiction under SDCL 1-1-18 through 1-1-21 to hear second-degree manslaughter charges arising from an automobile accident on U.S. Highway 212 in Dewey County, South Dakota.

Checkerboard Effect

The trial court ruled in the negative on both of the legal issues, and this is now being appealed to the Supreme Court of South Dakota. If the state wins this case, it will have jurisdiction over fee patented lands, and this will cause a checkerboard effect upon the Indian reservations in South Dakota.

When Congress passed Public Law 280, South Dakota made several attempts to assume jurisdiction on Indian reservations. As a matter of fact, the state once passed a law to assume jurisdiction over "highways only." This was challenged on the Pine Ridge Reservation in a case known as In Re Hankins, 125 NW2d 839. In this case, the South Dakota Supreme Court held that the state had to accept ALL jurisdiction under P.L. 280, or NONE AT ALL. The findings in the Hankins case have been in effect since that time.

By bringing up the two legal issues in the Janis case, it would appear that the state of South Dakota is attempting to get the decision handed down in the Hankins case reversed.

Precedent Exists

There is a precedent to follow in this case. In 1979, the United States Supreme Court ruled that it would follow state Supreme Court decisions in cases such as Hankins, in a case involving the Yakima Tribe in the state of Washington, the Supreme Court allowed the state of Washington to assume partial jurisdiction over that reservation. The main difference here is that Washington State is known as a Public Law 280 state, and South Dakota is not!

In the 1960s, by referendum election the voters of the state of South Dakota defeated the application of P. L. 280. The state of Washington did not. The voters in South Dakota realized that providing law enforcement to all of the reservations would require a tremendous amount of money. If the state assumed jurisdictional control, that money would come from the pockets of the taxpayers.

At the present time, the tribes are provided with federal funds to enforce the laws within their boundaries. The cost of providing law enforcement on the Pine Ridge Reservation alone could amount to over $2 million annually. Take that amount and multiply it times the number of reservations in the State of South Dakota, and you end up with quite a large chunk of money. The voters in South Dakota looked at this huge, addtional cost to themselves, as taxpayers, and decided that this was a financial burden they did not wish to assume.

Adversary Role

Why must the legislators of South Dakota assume the adversary role when it comes to dealing with issues important to Indians and non-Indians alike? Isn't progress best made through cooperation? What is the total amount of taxpayers' dollars being spent in litigation against Indian tribes—dollars which are usually spent on cases the states eventually lose?

In this day of tight money, restrictive budgets and inflation, it is the taxpayers of South Dakota who should be asking these questions. Has any form of the media in the state ever bothered to check up on the amount of money spent by the attorney general's office pursuing cases involving Indian tribes? Has it ever occurred to the taxpayers that negotiation is far less expensive than litigation?

Peter MacDonald, chairman of the Navajo tribe, has stated:

"Time and time again we have had to go to court to protect ourselves from acts of agression by the states.

"We have won almost all of these lawsuits, but each time it has cost us thousands of dollars, and each time it has diverted our limited resources, energies and personnel from the real job at hand—building a future."

Graduates Face Big Assignment

Seniors in caps and gowns are lining up across this country to receive their high school diplomas. It is no different on the Indian reservations, except for the message given the graduates.

I had the privilege of addressing the graduating class at St. Francis Indian School on the Rosebud Reservation and also was invited to address the graduating class at the Navajo Academy in Farmington, New Mexico. The message I had was not a pretty one.

The reservation, the home base of the Indian people, the one thing we have always been able to call our own, is being threatened with abandonment by the Interior Department and by an insensitive Justice Department. Indian treaties, the basis for all the agreements ever reached between the tribes and the federal government, are being ignored or rewritten by misinterpretation to deny the tribes the rights they believed they would never lose.

The repercussions of a recent U.S. Supreme Court ruling are being studied by the Indian tribes and the state governments. In March, the court ruled the state of Montana, not the Crow Tribe, has control of the section of the Big Horn River that runs through the reservation in southern Montana.

Different Cases

One Indian attorney believes the cases cited by the Supreme Court supporting the ruling have no bearing upon the Montana case. He said the cases involved Oklahoma Indian tribes where the land base and the water rights of those tribes evolved under different circumstances and were completely alien to the situation concerning the Crow Indian Tribe.

The Montana Intertribal Police Board drew these conclusions from the court's decision: "That all tribes, especially those whose reservations contain significant energy, mineral and water resources and non-tribal land, are seriously threatened by the case. That Indian tribes involved in land title disputes and other treaty issues should steer clear of the current U.S. Supreme Court unless they are sure they have an airtight case."

Litigation Costly

The various Indian tribes have had to spend thousands of dollars defending themselves in state and federal courts. Money that could have gone to improve the living conditions on the reservations has had to be paid to attorneys. Money earmarked for education, improvement of the tribal courts, law enforcement and economic development has been eaten up by legal fees. Litigation has become a way of life for the tribal governments.

Instead of encouraging the tribes to seek out new sources of revenue to support their governments, the state governments have jealously guarded their rights to levy taxes. Many Indian tribes are tied up in court battles today because they attempted to levy taxes on their reservations in order to raise much-needed monies to help their people.

For many years, the state governments discouraged political participation by the Indian tribes by effectively gerrymandering the voting districts on reservations so it became impossible for an Indian to be elected to state office even from reservation counties with an 85 percent Indian population.

Redistricting

Only the threat of federal action and intervention caused equitable redistricting in states such as South Dakota. In 1982, for the first time in history, the reservation counties of Shannon and Todd will be able to elect Indians to serve in the South Dakota Legislature.

Is it any wonder that Indian people fear state jurisdiction on reservations? Is it any wonder that a move by Western states to assume control over federal lands within their boundaries, under the guise of the Sagebrush Rebellion, is dreaded by the Indian people? Just as Black people have suffered at the hands of state government, so have the Indian tribes.

My message to the Indian graduates of 1981 was this: "Be proud of your heritage. Stand up and fight for the rights of your people. Be aware that the future of the Indian tribes is in your hands and the 1980s may mark a new beginning—or the bitter end—of the Indian nations. Pull together, as one people, and it will be a new beginning."

Good Reasons Seen for Tribal Protection

General Manager Max Sklower of KOAT-TV, Albuquerque, New Mexico, gave an editorial comment on the early evening news on July 17. Here is the entire 50-second editorial:

"I see where the Court of Appeals recently made a ruling that repossessions on Indian lands would be greatly modified to conform with local Indian rules. This case involved repossession of a car on the Navajo Reservation. While some Indian tribes may be hailing this as a victory, stating that their people will not be subject to different laws on repossession of unpaid items, I look at this as just the opposite. What business or bank would now want to sell or finance anything of substantial value to someone living on an Indian reservation when the purchaser can default and the buyer cannot reclaim the collateral? This, in my opinion, defeats both potential purchaser and potential seller, and I hope the Supreme Court overrules this. If everyone is hestitant to sell to people on Indian reservations, I can only see an increase in strained relations and worsening communications as the final outcome."

One-Sided

It should be obvious to most Indian people that this is a one-sided editorial. In my opinion, it is apparent that Sklower did not consult reponsible Indian individuals or officials in an effort to see the other side of the story.

Did Max Sklower utilize the expertise of the station's Indian reporter, Conroy Chino, by seeking his opinion and advice on this matter?

I think not! Most forms of the media, and that includes newspapers, have been doing things their own way for so long, without regard to the opinions of the Indian community, that even if they do not have an Indian on their staff, his knowledge and experience is often totally overlooked or underestimated.

'Expert' Opinion

Instead, most newspapers and television stations rely on the "expert" opinions of their wire services. Nothing bothers me more than to see erroneous stories about Indians come over the wire services, be picked up by hundreds of newspapers, radio and television stations, and repeated as the gospel truth. This lends credence to existing and popular misconceptions about Indians.

I have spent a lot of time and money correcting erroneous press releases by the Associated Press and the United Press International. This persistence caused AP and UPI in the state of South Dakota to take great pains to be certain of their facts before releasing stories about Indians. In fact, quite often, they called upon me and other proven sources to verify the authenticity of many releases.

An Example

Now back to Max Sklower. Let me underline my disagreement with his editorial by citing an example: An Indian lady from an Indian reservation purchased a house trailer in a border-town community. The trailer was set up on her reservation property, and, punctual to a fault, she made her regular monthly payments, which amounted to 75 percent of the total purchase price. A lease check owed to her by the federal government was late in arriving. She immediately notified the bank that she would be a few days late in making her payment. That weekend, while she was not at home, the trailer was repossessed after her personal possessions had been dumped on the ground where her trailer had stood.

The tribal courts have won the right to have any merchant seeking to repossess property appear before the tribal court and prove his case. This is a guarantee that no honest merchant need have fear of a law designed to protect them as well as the Indian consumer. Laws are made to protect the innocent as well as to punish the guilty.

Tribal Land Claims Remain Major Issue

The American Indian Claims Commission was established in 1946 to hear the complaints of the different Indian tribes in the United States about treaty violations, illegal taking of tribal lands and the lack of just compensation as stipulated by the treaties.

The one major drawback in the AICC concept was that it provided for monetary compensation only. Many Indian tribes, upon the advice of their attorneys (usually non-Indians based in Washington, D.C.), fell victim to this concept and accepted monetary compensation for the loss of vast tracts of land. The legal representatives of the tribes concerned did not have the same feeling for "Mother Earth" as the Indian people and assumed, incorrectly, that the only thing the Indians were interested in was the financial gain they could receive for the loss of the land.

Tribe after tribe relinquished title to lost lands by accepting monetary compensation. In many cases, they were never informed that if they accepted money, it would extinguish title to their lands and negate any further claims to the land forever.

Created by Congress

The AICC was an enigma in itself. It was, and is, an organization created by an act of Congress, and it is repsonsible to Congress for its existence and financing. How can an arm of the legislature be an impartial body when it is required to make decisions involving millions of acres of land which was taken, in many cases illegally, by the very government it represents? For many years Indian tribes have been saying that this is a gross example of conflicting interests.

There are very few, if any, Indian tribes in this country that have not had a case involving tribal lands placed before the AICC. In every case, these tribes were told by their attorneys that the only recourse they had was to accept monetary compensation.

The Oglala Sioux Tribe of the Pine Ridge Reservation in South Dakota decided to rebel against this patented concept. In the suit filed with the Eighth Circuit Court of Appeals in St. Louis, Missouri, it states: "This is an action to quiet title of the Oglala Sioux Tribe to seven million acres, more or less, of its original national territory, all of which was confiscated unlawfully and unconstitutionally by the United States of America in 1877, and now is in the possession of the defendants. This action seeks to restore the territorial rights of the Oglala Sioux Tribe to their status had no confiscation occurred and, therefore, plaintiff also seeks damages for waste, severance of minerals, and wrongful exclusion from the use of this territory for religious and subsistence purpose."

Commission Challenged

The Oglala Sioux Tribe, through its attorney, Mario Gonzalez, himself an Oglala, has challenged the legality of the Indian Claims Commission in limiting its remedies to monetary compensation only, and suggests that the return of the land should have been included as a legal remedy.

Gonzalez bases his case on the Fifth Amendment of the Constitution which states very clearly, "No land shall be taken without due process, or unless the land is to be used for public purposes, and without just compensation being awarded."

Tribes Defending Rights in Courts

The war between the United States and the Indian tribes has never ended; it has only changed direction. From the fields, hills and valleys of Indian country, it has moved into the courtrooms of this nation.

Make no mistake about it, the battle is as intense as it ever was; and the Indian tribes are stubbornly defending the last foothold on a continent they once owned, the Indian reservations.

The people of these reservations are slowly beginning to realize they are not "out of sight and out of mind" nor are they "islands unto themselves" in these legal battles. Every single case which reaches the Supreme Court and is eventually decided by the conservative, political appointees serving as judges on that court, has a resounding impact upon every Indian reservation, no matter how large or small.

Two Examples

Two classic examples of Supreme Court decisions, which should have alerted the tribal governments to the impending trend of state governments seeking jurisdiction over Indian lands by attacking them piecemeal in federal courts, were the Oliphant vs. Suquamish Indian Tribe and the State of Washington vs. Colville Indian Tribe decisions.

In Oliphant, the court ruled Indian tribes do not have criminal jurisdiction over non-Indian lawbreakers living on reservation lands. In the Colville case, the court said states can impose cigarette taxes on Indians sales to non-Indians.

Seattle, Washington Attorney Russell Barsh calls Oliphant "a betrayal of Indian tribes that have struggled to Westernize their legal systems." South Dakota Attorney General Mark Meierhenry believes there are much broader issues involved in the Colville decision than just taxes. He said, "Colville is the biggest court case on Indian law in a decade—a case that ties individual Indian rights to membership in the tribe, while diminishing the idea of tribal sovereignty."

While most of the Western states with large Indian populations have joined legal forces to pursue ultimate victory in these cases involving Indian tribes, the same cannot be said of the tribal governments.

Why have the tribal leaders stood on the sidelines, like silent spectators, while case after case went against the Indian tribes? Why haven't the tribal governments banded together in a united effort to combat this legal onslaught by the state governments?

Uncomplicated Answer

Perhaps the answer to these questions is not as complex as one would imagine; and, in fact, can be answered with three uncomplicated words—lack of communication.

Washington, D.C. based organizations designed, in the beginning to serve as informational advocates and lobby groups for the Indian tribes, have failed miserably to do that job. Instead, they became saturated with "fat cats" who lost all day-to-day contact with the tribal governments, and, worse than that, they lost contact with the poor, grassroots reservation Indian in whose name they had gained national support to begin with; and thus their effectiveness.

The minute these organizations began to accept federal dollars to survive, they threw their self-reliance and dedication to a cause out the window. In effect, they became locked into bitter competition amongst themselves to survive. Most of their leaders wanted to be chiefs instead of Indians. The internal power struggles effectively negated their objectives. As columnist Lewis Grizzard put it, "Life is like a dog sled team; unless you're the lead dog, the scenery never changes."

Perhaps national Indian organizations have outlived their usefulness to the Indian tribes. When they fail to keep the tribal governments informed of impending legal disasters, which have begun to fall like sledgehammers on the structure of tribal government, these organizations fail to fulfill the lofty ideals which spawned them.

Assuming Roles

On three separate occasions, I have asked the largest and the oldest Indian organization, the National Congress of American Indians, to "please" put me on its mailing list so I can use this column to convey information to my readers. To date, my letters and phone calls have brought no response. If ever I believed there was a lack of communication between national organizations and the Indian people, this failure to respond has confirmed my innermost suspicions.

Judicial Systems Concern of Tribes

Attorneys Russell Barsh and Jim Henderson wrote an article for the Minnesota Law Review on the jurisdiction case which shook many of the officials of Indian reservations. The review concerned the Oliphant vs. Suquamish Indian Tribe in Washington state.

The Supreme Court of the United States held in this case that Indians do not have jurisdiction over non-Indians in crimes committed on reservations. The decision said, "Absent express congressional delegation of power, the tribes may not try non-Indians."

Barsh and Henderson said that "Oliphant is a betrayal of tribes that have struggled to Westernize their legal systems. Since Congress gave its blessing to Western-style constitutional tribal government in 1934, tribes have largely abandoned traditional procedures, persuaded that adaptation and modernization of their courts would enhance their legitimacy in non-Indian eyes, and hence reduce their vulnerability to federal and state interference."

Judicial Conflict

There is a major conflict shaping up on many Indian reservations over the legal systems now being used by tribal governments. Many tribal leaders feel that their judicial systems are being torn apart by an attempt to conform to an Americanized system or to include within that system traditional methods of justice that have long been a part of Indian lifestyles.

It has been said many times that if the tribal courts are going to emulate the American system, then they should place higher standards upon those individuals chosen to serve as tribal judges. Many people feel that the complex structure of legal interpretation requires expert legal minds.

In fact, some tribal councils have taken it upon themselves to upgrade the minimum requirements of tribal judges to include a provision that those people hired to fill these positions hold a law degree.

Touching upon this subject, Barsh wrote in the *American Indian Journal*, "Admittedly, tribal courts and police have been criticized as inefficient, poorly trained and undisciplined, but tribes have been quick to defend them, and much of the blame must be shared by the federal agencies that supervise and finance them."

Barsh continued, "Admittedly, too, tribal legal systems today embody little that is uniquely tribal, leading to the argument that they add nothing to existing state and federal procedures. But we must remember that imitation of Anglo-American legal forms has been made for generations a condition of federal support and recognition."

Federal Controls

Barsh criticized the tight controls the federal government held for many years, controls which are even stronger today, and suggested that if Indian tribes had been allowed to implement their own judicial systems from the beginning, perhaps this sad state of affairs would not exist.

In this regard, Barsh said, "Were they permitted to evolve under tribal control, tribal law systems would have proved more distinctive, more adapted to reservation sociology and values, and, for those reasons more effective. It is not too late to afford tribes this opportunity."

Too many Indian reservations find that their tribal courts are an extension of the tribal government. They find that there is no separation of powers where the tribal courts are concerned. In many instances, tribal judges serve at the pleasure of the tribal chairman and the tribal council.

The old reservation saying goes, "What the tribal government has placed in power, the tribal government can remove from power."

Separation of Powers

The separation of powers between the executive, the legislative and the judicial branches of government is known as the system of checks and balances.

One Indian attorney addressed the lack of separation of powers by saying "As long as a tribal council is vested with the authority to create courts and appoint judges, this problem will continue to exist. What the council creates, it can also dismantle, and this makes the courts subservient to the governing body."

On many reservations, tribal judges have to be very careful when they make decisions which involve the governing body. If the decisions they make are unpopular with the people who appointed them, they stand a good chance of being replaced.

The main problem here is that if tribal judges must fear for their jobs every time they have to make an unpopular ruling, they cannot continue to be impartial in their decision making.

This is one of the most complex problems facing tribal governments, and it is one that cannot be discussed comprehensively in one column. For this reason, I will leave the continued remarks on the tribal court systems on reservations for another column.

Tribal Water Rights Become Major Issue

As we enter into a new decade, the 1980s, we have to begin to take a very serious look at the hard times ahead. For the Indian tribes of this country, particularly those of the western United States, it will be a time of legal confrontation with the states and the federal government.

The hunger for new sources of energy has created a population boom in the western states, and this increased population, combined with frenetic mining activities has served to point out the ever-mounting need for water. Such a large population consumes water. To produce food to sustain this growth requires more water, and worst of all, in order to mine the energy-producing resources of the earth, requires huge amounts of water. Twenty-five years ago, there were the prophets who predicted that the next major battle between the U.S. and the Indian tribes would be over water rights.

Two men who stood side by side in an effort to alert the tribal leadership of the coming danger, whose early warning fell on too many deaf ears, were Rupert Costo, a Cahuilla Indian man from California, and William Veeder, a former Bureau of Indian Affairs attorney. Because of his vocal support for Indian water rights, Bill Veeder soon found himself on the outside looking in on further BIA employment. One does not criticize the policies of the master without expecting some form of retaliation.

Tribal Rights

Rupert Costo, along with his wife, Jeannette Henry (pen name), have been two of the staunchest fighters for water, mineral and sovereign rights of Indian tribes. His publication, *Wassaja*, which used to be a monthly newspaper, has recently been combined with another publication (another of Costo's ventures), *The Indian Historian*, and has been changed to a quarterly magazine format.

According to Jeannette Henry, "because of our strong editorials against federal ineptitude, federal interference, and federal ignorance of Indian rights, we have been audited by the Internal Revenue Service every single year for the past five years. They have not been able to find a single . . . thing wrong with our bookkeeping records. If that isn't undue harrassment, I don't know what . . . harrassment is!"

Rupert and Jeannette have reached the twilight of their lives on this earth; but have continued to stand their ground against federal and state encroachment upon Indian rights. This has made them many enemies. Rupert, himself, puts it very bluntly, "We aren't looking for friends or enemies; we're looking for justice for our people."

Office Criticized

Wassaja has strongly criticized former Assistant Secretary of the Interior Forrest Gerrard and his replacement, Thomas Frederick. Gerrard earlier this year retired to do private consultation work in Washington, D.C.

Someone asked me the other day what Rupert meant when he referred to "sellouts" working within the federal government as a "fifth columnist." What he is doing is referring to a word which was coined during the revolution in Spain. General Francisco Franco had surrounded the city of Madrid and had it under seige. A reporter asked Franco how many columns of troops he had around the city. Franco replied, "I have five columns of troops. There are four columns surrounding the city and my fifth column is inside."

Rupert Costo said recently, "If the act of breathing is the one absolute necessity for all human beings, the act of going to court, getting into litigation and studying the law as it pertains to their situation is the very act of life itself for Indian tribes. We didn't want it that way. We didn't plan it that way. But there is no different way other than outright revolutionary confrontations resulting in Indian-federal warfare."

Jurisdiction Poses Problem for Tribes

"They sought it with thimbles, they sought it with care;
  They pursued it with forks and hope;
  They threatened its life with a railway-share;
  They charmed it with smiles and soap."
                                  Lewis Carrol, The Hunting of the Snark
"The judicial pursuit of principles in Indian law has been a little like Lewis Carroll's The Hunting of the Snark; an aimless voyage towards an unknown objective."

Thus begins "The Betrayal: Oliphant vs. Suquamish Indian Tribe and the Hunting of the Snark" by Russell Lawrence Barsh and James Youngblood Henderson, Minnesota Law Review, Vol. 63, No. 4, April 1979.

According to the "Betrayal," in Oliphant, the Supreme Court reversed a 1976 Ninth Circuit Court of Appeals decision upholding the power of the Suquamish Tribe to arrest and try two non-Indians under the Suquamish Tribal Code for assault, resisting arrest and reckless driving, crimes that were committed within the boundaries of their reservation.

"Such power was," the tribe argued and the court of appeals agreed, "inherent and retained, having never been ceded by the Indians or expressly terminated by Congress." In the absence of specific legislative action, the court of appeals held, the power claimed by the tribe was assumed to exist. The Supreme Court, speaking through Justice Rehnquist, held to the contrary: "Absent express congressional delegation of power, the tribes may not try non-Indians."

There is an uneasy feeling among tribal officials across this country that various states are using isolated, and seemingly unrelated, cases involving questions of jurisdiction on Indian reservations as test cases in hopes that these cases will wind up before the Supreme Court and favorable decisions will be handed down and state jurisdiction over Indian lands will be enhanced.

"The Betrayal" would seem to substantiate the worst fears of these concerned tribal officials. It says: "In spite of the distinction between the exercise and use of jurisdiction, however, there is some evidence that the opponents of tribal jurisdiction perceived the Oliphant case as providing the ideal vehicle in which to attack the exercise of tribal jurisdiction over non-Indian criminal defendants."

For example, former South Dakota Attorney General (now Governor) William Janklow has been quoted as saying, "South Dakota officials prepared the briefs and other legal material (in Oliphant) which cost the state about $28,000. (*Rapid City Journal*, March 8, 1978, page 2, col. 5) Janklow continued, "Oliphant was a test case from the state of Washington, but it was basically funded by the state of South Dakota . . . it really was our lawsuit." He concluded. "Besides us. eleven other Western states participated in the Oliphant case."

Were these participants a coalition of twelve Western states known as the "Sagebrush Rebellion?"

Authors Barsh and Henderson summed up "The Betrayal" with this warning, "Oliphant is a betrayal of tribes that have struggled to Westernize their legal systems. Since Congress gave its blessing to Western-style consitutional tribal government in 1934, tribes have largely abandoned traditional procedures, persuaded that adaption and modernization of their courts would enhance their legitimacy in non-Indian eyes, and hence reduce vulnerability to federal and state interference."

Land Settlement View Erroneous

Whether the Navajo Nation decides to seek land in lieu of the $14.8 million land settlement is, of course, an internal tribal matter that must be decided by the Navajo people.

But, when one tribal councilman uses another Indian tribe to base an argument upon whether to accept the money or to fight for the land, and the argument he uses as a foundation to support his argument is erroneous, then a correction must be made.

Last Sunday's column had a tail-end paragraph touching on this point, but I believe the entire subject needs further clarification. Let me give a brief recap here. Councilman Harry Tome from Red Valley was a part of a special council task force on the land claims. Tome said in a report issued by the task force that the committee favored accepting the monetary settlement.

He stressed the Shiprock Chapter's resolution asking the tribe to file a suit to regain some of the lands which were taken illegally. In refuting this resolution, Tome said, "Such a lawsuit has already been tried by the Oglala Sioux Tribe. It failed because the federal courts do not have the power to hear such lawsuits."

Dismissal Appealed

Now, as a member of th Oglala Sioux Tribe, I resent such information being handed out to support Tome's argument when the "facts" he presents are not true. Yes, the federal judge in Omaha who heard the case did dismiss the Oglala suit because he believed he did not have jurisdiction to hear the case. The dismissal was appealed immediately by the Oglala Sioux Tribe on the grounds that the tribe is being denied "due process" by not being allowed its day in court. The tribe asks, "If your court does not have jurisdiction to hear our case, who does?" The Oglalas have been trying to get their day in court for sixty years to no avail.

The appeal by the tribe was given to the Eighth Circuit Court of Appeals in St. Louis for consideration, and the court will begin to hear oral arguments in this suit on or about March 9. The suit prepared by the Oglala Sioux Tribe asks for the return of the seven million acres of land in the Black Hills taken illegally by the United States. The taking of the land was declared illegal by the U.S. Supreme Court in July 1980 when the tribe was awarded $17 million plus interest from the date of taking in the amount of $105 million.

Money Rejected

There are nine tribes which make up the Great Sioux Nation and thus far two of those tribes have voted to reject the money and fight for the return of the land. Those two tribes are the Oglala Sioux and the Cheyenne River Sioux Tribes. It is the contention of the tribal attorney representing the Oglalas that the United States violated its own constitution by denying Indian tribes any settlement other than monetary.

That attorney, Mario Gonzalez, is himself an Oglala and he has angered some Washington, D.C. attorneys representing Indian tribes by suggesting that the only thing these lawyers are interested in is monetary compensation because their 10 percent of the total settlement is much easier to spend than land, if it is a part of the settlement. Washington attorney Arthur Lazarus, who represented the Oglalas at the beginning of these long proceedings, has already filed a request for $10.6 million in fees for his legal office against the Black Hills Claims Settlement monies awarded to the Sioux Tribes.

Not only has the Oglala Sioux Tribe appealed its case to the federal courts, but it has also brought suits against the State of South Dakota for illegal occupation of the Black Hills, several individual land owners and several municipalities located in the Black Hills.

Victory Possible

The Oglala Sioux Tribe has gone on record as saying, "We do not want your money. Give us back our land." Maybe, as Harry Tome has said much too prematurely, the Oglalas will lose their case. But then again, maybe they will win and the victory would be for all Indian tribes. All of the sure-fire arguments being used to convince the Navajos to accept the money by Tome have been used "ad infinitum—ad nauseum" to discourage the Oglalas into taking the money; but the Oglala people have decided to see the case through to its conclusion all the way to the U.S. Supreme Court in search of justice.

Perhaps Harry Tome left the theater before the opera was over, because as I said in an article I wrote about the Black Hills Claims Settlement for the national Indian magazine, *Wassaja*, "The opera isn't over until the fat lady sings."

Jurisdiction Key in Oglala Lawsuit

The essence of the case is whether or not the District Court in Omaha has the statutory jurisdiction to hear the claims of the Oglala Sioux Tribe against the United States, the State of South Dakota, and Curtis S. McKee in a suit brought by the tribe in the Black Hills Claims Settlement.

On September 11, 1980, Judge Albert Schatz ruled that district courts do not have jurisdiction.

This decision to dismiss the case because of lack of jurisdiction was handed down by Judge Schatz in Omaha.

Oglala Sioux Tribal Attorney Mario Gonzalez immediately appealed that decision to the Eighth Circuit Court of Appeals in St. Louis, Missouri, claiming Judge Schatz erred in his ruling that sovereign immunity prevents the federal government from being sued in district courts. That appeal will be heard Monday.

One Purpose

In the final reply brief filed by Gonzalez on February 10, 1981, he says, "This appeal has but one purpose, and that is to determine whether the Oglala Sioux Tribe's amended complaint alleges matters within the District Court's nonstatutory jurisdiction. If the tribe prevails here, it still will be required to prove its allegations, succeed in advancing the substantive legal merits of its claim, and persuade the District to fashion the quitable remedies sought."

Gonzalez argues the defendants' detailed attention to the overall picture of the Black Hills Claims Settlement is like "putting the cart in front of the horse." He charges judicial consideration of the defendants' "smokescreen" has no place at this stage of the proceedings.

Gonzalez contends there is "only one issue that must be decided here and now." That issue is: "After more than a century, is the Oglala Sioux Tribe to be given the opportunity to try the merits of its claims, arising from federal actions of which the Court of Claims has said, in another action, 'a more ripe and rank case of dishonorable dealings will never, in all probability, be found in our history.'" The Court of Claims made this statement when it ruled on the monetary settlement to the Sioux Nation, which is now under appeal.

State Concession

The state of South Dakota conceded in the brief it filed "that great numbers of non-Indian United States citizens trespassed on Oglala Sioux tribal land between 1874 and 1877, and the United States failed to prevent them as required by the 1868 Treaty."

Gonzalez answers the argument that the land was confiscated legally and constitutionally with, "Congress confiscated for their use, the very land upon which they had trespassed." He strengthens this argument, saying, "In a government of equal laws it is intolerable to pretend that a citizen may be irremediably deprived of his property by government in order to satisfy the demands of any lawbreaker who covets it."

In a recent interview, Gonzalez said, "It is really important for people to understand that the hearing in St. Louis will not decide on the issues of land or money, but it will decide whether our case will ever be heard. The state of South Dakota, the United States and the individual landholders such as McKee are trying to argue the merits of the entire case before it even comes to trial."

Gonzalez said with conviction, "The issue here is whether Indian tribes are going to be given the same constitutional rights of 'due process' as other United States citizens. We have been trying through every remedy available to us, for over one century, to have our charges heard before the courts of this land. All we ask is we be given that right, and that's what the argument in St. Louis will be all about."

Confidence

Sitting in the crowded, little office he occupies in the basement of the old tribal building, it is hard to believe that this quiet, unassuming man, and his secretary, Theresa Two Bulls, his legal helpers, Robert Fast Horse and Louis Bad Wound, have taken on the United States government, the state of South Dakota, and the attorneys of the SAFECO Title Insurance Co. (representing McKee and the individual landowners) and can still laugh with confidence and self-assurance.

Attending Appeals Court is Awesome Experience

The Eighth Circuit Court of Appeals at St. Louis, Missouri is an imposing structure. Two great statues of stone adorn the entrance depicting liberty and equal justice. They stare with sightless eyes at the traffic hurrying past on Market Street.

Inside the courtroom of Judge Myron Bright, seated high on the bench in long, black gowns, three judges gaze sternly at the tribal people seated in the pew-like benches. Most of the spectators are women, crowded together, shoulder to shoulder, with bright shawls draped over their backs, long braids pulled forward, embracing their countenances.

The strength that can be gained only by surviving hard times, by pursuing a worthy purpose, and by a determination to succeed, is etched deeply into the faces of the women, many of them elderly, some needing assistance to rise when the judges enter the courtroom.

They had come to St. Louis on a bus provided by the Tribal Council of the Oglala Sioux Tribe—from the Pine Ridge Reservation, across Nebraska and Iowa, and finally to the city once known as Cahokia, the largest Indian settlement north of the Rio Grande. Dominated by a sacred temple named Monk's Mound by the white man, a temple rising 100 feet and covering 16 acres, this man-made monument once overlooked a community of over 30,000 Indians.

As we sat in the crowded courtroom, waiting for the hearing to begin, one elderly lady leaned close and whispered to me, "I want you to write something for me when we get back home. Ask this question: Where are our warriors?" She continued softly, "Have they become so busy fighting over petty things among themselves that the women must now lead?"

She grew angrier as she spoke, "Are the roles of the man and the woman being reversed?" The elderly lady tugged at my sleeve as she continued, "Look around you at the men—tribal councilmen—from Cheyenne River, Standing Rock and Rosebud who came to support our lawyers and to learn. Where are the warriors of the Oglala Sioux?"

Tribal Attorney Mario Gonzalez addressed the panel of judges. He questioned the posture of immunity from lawsuits taken by the U.S. government. He hammered away at the violation "of its own constitution" the federal government perpetrated upon the Indian people when it took the Black Hills illegally. He asked why monetary compensataion was the only remedy offered to the Indian people and not to non-Indians if their land was seized for eminent domain purposes.

Gonzalez asked, "Is the Oglala Sioux Tribe the only party here fighting to uphold the U.S. Constitution? Are we the only ones who believe in the Constitution or does the United States?" Gonzalez summed up his opening remarks, saying, "This case is not just for the Indian people. It is a case that affects every American. If the U.S. Constitution is no longer supreme, the law of the land, then that means Congress is now supreme. The decision of the District Court in Omaha should be reversed."

The attorney general for the state of South Dakota, Mark Meierhenry, did not make an appearance. Speaking for Meierhenry, Jeffrey Viken, representing the United States, told the court Meierhenry "decided to let the court make its decision based upon the merits of his brief.'

Viken brought up the subject of "res judicata" which caused many news writers to seek out legal assistance. The term means the case has already been heard and should not be heard again. Judge Bright questioned the validity of "res judicata" at this point in the proceedings. He said, "Either we do have jurisdiction or we do not. If we do, we must send it back to the district court for determination."

Representing the individual land owners, attorney William Finley, Jr. was very concerned about what would happen to those land owners if the case proceeded further. He pointed out that this could become very expensive to the land holders. "The sale of real estate in the Black HIlls could be brought to a halt," Finley said.

Making the rebuttal for the Oglala Sioux Tribe was Russell Barsh, an attorney from Seattle, Washington. Judge Bright asked Barsh where the money awarded to the Sioux Nation is at this time. "It's nowhere," Barsh replied. "The appellees purport the money has already been paid, but the money doesn't exist; it has never been appropriated by Congress," Barsh said.

Judge Bright adjourned the hearing. There was a feeling of success among the Indian spectators, and one of confidence between the tribal attorneys. The decision by the Eighth Circuit Court of Appeals will not be rendered for several months.

As the ladies of the Lakota Nation filed from the courtroom, led by Geraldine Janis, they formed a line, unfurled the hand-painted posters created by them on the long bus ride, faced the television cameras and the flash of bulbs from the photographers, and bravely began to answer the questions fired at them from the assembled journalists.

Oglalas Pursue Case in Courts

Members of the American Indian Movement chose to camp on Black Hills National Forest lands twelve miles southwest of Rapid City. Bill Means, an AIM member, said, "We are trying to show that there are alternative ways to get back the Black Hills besides the courts."

There is not a single member of the Oglala Sioux Tribe familiar with the merits of the case pending before the Eighth Circuit Court of Appeals in St. Louis, Missouri, brought by the tribe, who is not familiar with the alternative methods to be employed if the federal courts refuse to hear the case.

Even faced with the option of having the case heard before a Supreme Court of conservative political appointees who have steadfastly refused to recongnize the validity of the treaties signed between the Indian tribes and the federal government, the Oglala Sioux Tribe and several other tribes have allowed their cases to proceed through the circuitous court system in strict compliance with the laws of the land.

Time Factor

Many of the tribal elders believe time is on their side. After all, haven't they patiently waited over 100 years for their case to be heard?

In its lawsuit, the official government of the Oglala Sioux Tribe is asking for return of the land and financial compensation for illegal trespassing these many years. Aren't these the very same things the American Indian Movement members have been fighting for and demonstrating over these past few years?

The AIM spokesmen say they are occupying the land under the auspices of the 1868 Fort Laramie Treaty. If that is the case, why has every legally elected tribal chairman whose tribes were a party to the signing of that document condemned the occupation and the actions of AIM as unsanctioned and illegal? AIM was not a party to the 1868 Fort Laramie Treaty, but the elected officials speaking out against them represent the many tribes who were and are parties to that treaty.

Russell Means has asked that the organization he represents be referred to as the Dakota American Indian Movement; but there are many people taking part in the occupation who are not members of any of the tribes of South Dakota and who have no vested interests in the Black Hills Claims Settlement case now pending before the courts. In all fairness, I cannot call them Dakota or Lakota, when, indeed, they are not.

Merits Weighed

The three judges of the Eighth Circuit Court of Appeals are presently weighing the merits of the jurisdictional question brought before them by the Oglala Sioux Tribal attorneys on March 9, 1982. One of the questions raised by Assistant U.S. Attorney Jeffrey Viken before that court was the possibility of Black Hills lands being occupied. Judge Myron Bright answered, "You are trying to bring something before this court that has not happened. We cannot rule on something speculative."

The question many Lakota people have uppermost in their minds is this: "Will the actions taken by the American Indian Movement in occupying this piece of land play into the hands of the state and government attorneys and cause the judges to rule against the Oglala Sioux Tribe?"

There are many Lakota people who are sick and tired of wasteful, incompetent and corrupt tribal governments who seem to be leading the tribes down the road of extinction. Has the AIM offered a sensible, viable and acceptable alternative to the governments they have labeled as neo-colonialist and vichy?

Support Dwindles

One does not burn down his house in the middle of the winter without having a replacement. AIM has had plenty of time to work within the framework of the tribal government to bring about social changes, but instead has chosen the route of isolation and confrontation. As a result, its support among its own tribal members has dwindled with each passing year until it has reached its lowest point.

Was the action taken by AIM a sincere effort to help the Indian people or was it an action designed to breathe new life into a dwindling organization?

Tribal leaders who remained silent during the Wounded Knee Occupation in 1973 are now speaking out against this newest occupation by AIM. Chairmen of the Northern Cheyenne, Arapaho, Shoshone and of the Great Sioux Nation condemn the occupation as irresponsible, uncalled for, and not sanctioned by any of the tribal governments.

The question about AIM's actions posed to me by many Lakota people was asked with anger and dismay: "What are they trying to prove?"

Tribal Attorneys Due Thanks for Litigation

Nowadays, at any given date, you can visit the different reservations in the nation and find tribal attorneys burning the midnight oil in an effort to present the Indians' cases to the different courts of this land, all the way from county to state, federal and the highest court of all, the Supreme Court.

Litigation is a word that is becoming as familiar to the people of the reservations as treaties are. Litigation has become a way of life. Every single time a case of major proportions is presented for study or trial involving Indian tribes, the special interest groups and state groups immediately line up in an adversary position and pool their efforts and finances to defeat the cases presented by the different Indian tribes.

Try to put yourself in the shoes of such tribal attorneys as B. Reid Haltom of the Jicarilla Apache Tribe or Mario Gonzalez of the Oglala Sioux Tribe. Both are involved in cases which could affect every Indian tribe in the United States. The decisions handed down in the cases they are being forced to present will be precedent-setting cases and will be used exclusively in the future to either help or hinder the causes of the Indian tribes, depending upon the outcome.

Landmark Case

The Jicarilla Apache Tribe is faced with presenting a landmark case to the Supreme Court concerning the severance tax. The tribe will be defending the "severance tax ordinance enacted by its trbal council four years ago. The Tenth District Court of Appeals ruled that oil companies would have to pay both state and tribal severance taxes.

The oil companies took that ruling to the Supreme Court, and on October 6 the Supreme Court agreed to hear the case. Several states, as well as some of the most powerful oil companies in the world, are expected to join in the case against the Jicarilla Apache Tribe.

In the case of the Oglala Sioux Tribe, the tribe has challenged the constitutionality of the American Indian Claims Commission's right to make monetary awards only for Indian land taken illegally as opposed to the awarding of the land. They contend that under the provisions of the Fifth Amendment they are being denied their constitutional rights of "just compensation."

Justice Ambiguous

Justice has become an ambiguous term when applied to the rights of the Indian people. This is partly due to the federal government's (and the state governments') difficulty in understanding tribal as opposed to individual concepts of thought. When it comes to infringing upon state or governmental rights, the rights of the governments constructed around individualism have taken precedent over the rights of those governments built upon tribalism. The logic seems to be that tribalism is not the "American way" and, therefore, it is categorically wrong. Americans, in general, have always had extreme difficulty in recognizing the rights of others as if in grating those rights, they are allowing an entity to remain outside of the mainstream of the "great melting pot."

By seeking to levy a severance tax upon companies doing business on the reservation, the Jicarilla Apache Tribe is saying, "We are a sovereign nation, and we should be allowed to raise revenues in our own way in order to strengthen our local government. City governments, county and state governments are allowed to raise taxes as they see fit. Why not tribal governments?

"Enough Is Enough"

By trying to have land returned, instead of monetary compensation, the Oglala Sioux Tribe is saying, "Enough is enough; you have violated every aspect of our 1868 Treaty, and now you are trying to ease your collective consciences with the almighty dollar. Well, the land is more important to us than the money."

On more than one occasion I have stated that it is imperative that Indian tribes give each other the moral, legal and financial support necessary to win these important landmark cases. The tribes, large or small, are no longer isolated islands. Each major legal decision handed down by the Supreme Court of this land will have an impact upon all tribes.

The attorneys representing the Indian tribes are facing all of the frustrations, the letdowns, the highs and the lows of any member of the legal profession representing an unpopular client. They need a pat on the back and a nod of encouragement, also. The road to justice is seldom paved.

U.S. in Contempt of Court?

When tribal attorney Mario Gonzalez filed his brief before the United States District Court in the Black Hills Claims Settlement, he had a stipulation order approved and signed by Judge Albert Schatz placing an injunction on the Secretary of the Interior from paying any monies to the attorney who purportedly represented the Oglala Sioux Tribe, as long as the case was under appeals or litigation.

Contrary to this stipulation, the Court of Claims awarded attorney Arthur Lazarus, Jr. and his law firm $10,593.94 on behalf of the "Sioux Nation of Indians" case.

This past week, Gonzalez filed a "Motion for Order to Show Cause" with the district court asking the defendant, the United States, "to show cause why it should not be held in contempt of this court's September 30, 1980 order approving the parties' September 23, 1980 stipulation."

Methods Typical

The methods employed by the federal government in completely ignoring legal documents, signed by their own representatives, whenever Indian tribes are involved is typical of the way they have been handling these matters for two hundred years.

Members of the Oglala Sioux Tribe are occupying lands in the Black Hills right now because they have become thoroughly disgusted with the government's penchant to disregard the laws of its own Constitution or the rulings of its own courts whenever Indian tribes are involved.

Now, the next interesting question is: Can the United States of America be held in contempt of court?

Sioux Tribe at End of Road in Court

Where does justice end and federal self-interest begin? There is very little distinction between the two when dealing with the treaties between the federal government and the Indian tribes.

For instance, the latest ploy by the federal judicial system to duck a controversial court case involving an Indian tribe, the Oglala Sioux vs. the United States in the Black Hills Claims Settlement Case, is simply to deny the tribe its day in court.

This is being done by using the legal system to stymie the tribe by saying the federal courts do not have jurisdiction over land claim cases. They say they lack jurisdiction because the Indian Claims Commission, established in 1946 as an exclusive remedy for the Indian tribes, but limited to monetary settlement only, was the only agency allowed by law to hear land grievances.

The fact that the Indian Claims Commission is now defunct is not relevant, according to the federal government. The Oglala Sioux Tribe argues that the Indian Claims Commission was in itself illegal and unconstitutional because it prevented the Tribe from taking land disputes before a court, a legal right accorded all other citizens.

Well, it appears that the Oglala Sioux Tribe has reached the end of the road in its pursuits to have its day in court. After more than 100 years of chasing justice, the Tribe has filed before the United States Supreme Court—the court of last resort. Filed on August 14—the Tribe's legal battle to gain return of some 7.3 million acres of land in the Black Hills in lieu of monetary compensation—the case has, at long last, reached its conclusion.

It is now up to the highest court in the land to see that the jurisprudence system of this country lives up to its obligations to all of the people. Liberty and justice for all should mean just that.

*Mario Gonzalez, Gerald Clifford, Crow Creek tribal chairman Robert Philbrick and
Rosebud chairman discuss Black Hills Claims Settlement litigation*

Attorney Mario Gonzalez in his office at Pine Ridge

The Termination Period: 1945-1965

The struggles by Indian tribes over the retention of treaty lands is nothing new. One particularly dark period in the relationship between the government and the Indian tribes occurred during the Termination Period. A book published by the United States Commission on Civil Rights entitled, "Indian Tribes: A Continuing Quest for Survival," says of that period:

"The United States Senate in 1943 conducted a survey of Indian conditions and found serious and troubling problems. The Bureau of Indian Affairs and federal bureaucracy were held culpable for these conditions. The administrative and financial costs of achieving slow progress assimilation were viewed as excessive."

The report continues, "Criteria were developed by the Commissioner of Indian Affairs to identify tribal goups that could be removed from federaal aigis. The theory was that some tribes were sufficiently acculturated and the federal protective role was no longer needed. But another development of the same period suggests a less benign interpretation of events—some 133 separate bills were introduced in Congress to permit the transfer of trust land for Indian ownership to non-Indian ownership. There were also pressures to terminate certain tribes, such as the Klamaths, who had valuable timber resources, and the Aguas Calientes, owners of much of the Palm Springs, California area. In 1949 the Hoover Commission (although not established to deal with Indian issues) recommended the full and complete integration of Indians into American society."

The "Termination Era" involved three basic plans of attack upon the Indian tribes. One was the termination of the tribes where federal responsibility was thought to be unnecessary, the second was the transfer of federal responsibility over Indian tribes to state governments, and the third phase was the transfer of Indian people from the reservations to the urban areas.

The report concludes, "The three-pronged policy was aggressively carried out by Dillon Myer, former director of detention camps for Japanese Americans, who became the Commissioner of Indian Affairs in 1950. The BIA, which had been a target of congressional criticism in 1943, grew in budget and staff as it administered terminationist policies. Between 1954 and 1962, statutes were passed authorizing the termination of more than 100 tribes, bands, or Indian rancherias. Most of those affected were small bands on the West Coast, but two sizable tribes, the Klamaths of the Northwest and Menominees of Wisconsin, were also terminated.

"In all, approximately 12,000 individual Indians lost tribal affiliation that included political relationship with the United States. Approximately 2.5 million acres of Indian land were removed from protected status."

Ironically, the Menominees did not roll over and play dead. Instead, they took the United States to court, fought to be reinstated as a federally-recognized tribe, and won.

Indians, Land Status, Reservation, Land Grabs

The construction of dams, the willingness of many tribal members to sell out their allotments, acts of Congress, and unfavorable court decisions, have deprived the Lakota people of much of the land they once owned. And yet, the Indian people still own nearly nine million acres of land in South Dakota and are fighting hard to hang on to it. Here is a breakdown of tribal lands— reservation by reservation—and a brief summation of events leading up to the present land status:

CHEYENNE RIVER SIOUX RESERVATION—Including all of Dewey and Ziebach Counties, the reservation originally covered nearly three million acres. Congressional actions near the turn of the century, plus the construction of the Oahe Dam in 1948-1962 forced 30 percent of the tribe to be relocated and reimbursed. This reduced Indian trust lands to 1.4 million acres. The bulk of this land, 916,000 acres, is tribally owned.

CROW CREEK SIOUX RESERVATION—The 285,000-acre reservation is east of the Missouri River near the Fort Randall and Big Bend dams. 105,000 acres are now in trust status, 69,300 are held by individual Indians, and the remainder is tribally owned. Another 19,000 acres bordering the river are federally owned, but preserved for Indian use. The reservation covers parts of Hughes, Hyde and Buffalo Counties. One hundred fifty acres are in Brule County.

FLANDREAU SANTEE SIOUX RESERVATION—Many Santee Sioux split up and moved, or chose to settle on other Sioux reservations. By the 1930s the Flandreau Santee land base was gone. In 1935-36, 2,180 acres were bought for the tribal government and the area was declared a reservation. The Flandreau Boarding School, a Bureau of Indian Affairs secondary education institution, was located in Flandreau in 1893 and continues as the heart of the reservation's economic life.

LOWER BRULE SIOUX RESERVATION—Its boundaries encompass 235,000 acres. Like its neighbor, Crow Creek, land holdings have been substantially reduced due to congressional acts, land sales, and the building of Fort Randall and Big Bend dams on the Missouri River. Nearly 70 percent of the tribe had to be relocated and reimbursed when the Missouri was flooded to its present state. Approximately 106,000 acres are now in trust status, 76,700 of which are tribally owned. About 13,000 acres of land bordering the river is federally-owned, but reserved for Indian use. Most of the reservation lies in Lyman County; a small part falls within Stanley County.

PINE RIDGE RESERVATION—The Pine Ridge Reservation is the largest reservation in the state in terms of population (Oglala Sioux Tribe) and land holdings. Formerly encompassing Bennett County present reservation boundaries cover all of Shannon and Washabaugh Counties. Of the original 2.8 million acres retained under the 1889 treaty, Indian land holdings include 1,151,000 acres of alloted land, and 432,000 of tribally owned land.

ROSEBUD RESERVATION—The Rosebud Reservation used to include Todd, Tripp and Mellette Counties, and a portion of Gregory County in South

Central South Dakota, an area of 3.3 million acres.

The Supreme Court ruled in 1977 (Rosebud vs. Kneip) that various settlement acts from 1904 to 1910 had diminished the original reservation boundaries to those of Todd County alone. In 1973, Indian land holdings, which extend beyond the present day reservation boundaries, include 439,900 acres which are tribally owned and 439,600 acres of alloted lands.

LAKE TRAVERSIE RESERVATION (formerly), now SISSETON-WAHPETON SIOUX RESERVATION—Located in the northwest corner of South Dakota, the reservation was formerly a triangle covering nearly all of Roberts County, and pieces of four other northeast South Dakota counties. Small parts of the reservation extend into North Dakota. About 10 percent of the land, 118,000 acres, within the original reservation boundaries is now in trust status. Due to recent land-buying efforts, the tribe now owns 12,000 acres.

STANDING ROCK RESERVATION—Approximately one-half of the Standing Rock Sioux Reservation lies in North Dakota. The other half includes all of Corson County, South Dakota. Slightly less than 35 percent of Corson County property is Indian-owned. Of the 2.3 million acres within the boundaries of the entire reservation, 323,000 acres are held by the tribe, and 511,200 acres are allotted trust lands.

YANKTON SIOUX RESERVATION—The first reservation established by treaty in South Dakota, the Yankton Sioux Reservation occupies part of Charles Mix County east of the Missouri River in south central South Dakota. Of the original 431,000 acres within the original boundaries of the reservation, only 8 percent, or 34,000 acres are held in trust for Indians; 8,000 acres are tribally owned, and 26,000 are individually allotted.

The litany of congressional acts used to diminish the land base of the tribes of the Great Sioux Nation reads like a horror story to the residents of the reservations. Bill after bill was introduced, many under the guise of benevolent acts, to steal lands from the Indian tribes. Performed in Washington, D.C., at a time when communications were minimal, these various "land grab acts" were made with little, or no consultation with the tribes affected, and with even less regard for the welfare of the Indian people, themselves.

Is it any wonder that tribal leadership of today is saying, "Get out of our lives, Big Brother. You've done enough damage."?

Martinez Case No Escape Hatch for Government Officials

BIA officials use it when it is convenient; federal judges abide by it in many cases, and the Department of the Interior has found it to be a handy escape hatch. Are these federal employees using it to enhance tribal sovereignty or to side-step controversial Indian issues?

I am referring to a decision handed down by the U.S. Supreme Court in the Santa Clara Pueblo vs. Martinez case. The court ruled that the Indian Civil Rights Act does not subject tribes to the jurisdiction of federal courts in civil actions for the "injunctive or remedial relief." In plain language, the court decided that the federal agencies should not interfere with the policies of an Indian tribe where "internal matters" were involved.

A staff report by the U.S. Commission on Civil Rights published in 1978, explains it this weay: "The Martinez case arose on the Santa Clara Pueblo in northern New Mexico and involved a Pueblo woan married to a Navajo. The tribal ordinance made eligible for tribal membership only the children of the male tribal members married to non-members, but not the children of female tribal members married to non-members. Mrs. Martinez and her children sued the Pueblo and its governor in federal district court, contending that the Pueblo's membership ordinance violated the equal protection and due process provisions of the Indian Civil Rights Act. The Supreme Court's opinion began by reaffirming the theory that Indian tribes possess immunity from suit traditionally enjoyed by sovereigns and that a 'waiver of sovereign immunity' cannot be implied but must be unequivocally expressed.

Because Congress did not waive immunity in the Indian Civil Rights Act, or anywhere else, "suits against tribes under the Indian Civil Rights Act are barred. . ."

Suits against the governor of the Pueblo, however, were not barred and the court addressed the jurisdiction of the federal courts under the act. To determine "whether a cause of action is implicit in a statute not expressly providing one," the court utilized a four-part test:

"First, is the plaintiff one of a class for whose benefit the statute was enacted: Second, is there any indication of the legislative intent, explicit or implicit, either to create or deny such a remedy? Third, is it consistent with the underlying purposes of the legislative scheme to imply such a remedy? Fourth, is the cause of action one traditionally relegated to tribal law, in an area basically of concern to tribes, so that it would be inappropriate to infer a cause of action based solely on federal law?"

The court concluded that "Tribal courts have repeatedly been recognized as appropriate forums for the exclusive adjudication of disputes affecting important personal and propety interests of both Indians and non-Indians, and that tribal forums are available."

At first glance, the Supreme Court's ruling appears to be returning internal tribal decisions back to the tribes, and if the tribal courts and the tribal governments were totally free of political consideration in applying the rulings of the court, this would, indeed, be the case.

As many of us who reside on Indian reservations know from past experiences, this is not always the case. Too often, decisions made by tribal courts can, and do, violate the civil rights of reservation residents. Many times, these decisions are made for political reasons and have little to do with protecting the tribe's rights to make decisions on internal matters.

It does not behoove one to get on the wrong side of the tribal government because the tribal polticians are not one bit squeamish about using the tribal court system to strike back at their enemies, real or imagined.

Because the Interior Department has decided to look the other way in many of these cases for fear of interfering with the internal affairs of the tribe, some tribal officials have taken this indifference to mean that they can declare open war upon their political opponents.

Until there is a true separation of powers on the Indian reservations of this land, the powers-that-be are not doing a great service to the Indian people by imitating an ostrich. If they consider the Martinez decision a convenient way for them to avoid shouldering the responsibility for controversial issues, they are only fooling themselves, because in the long run, these issues will come back to haunt them.

Treaty Relationship With Tribes Unique

What is it that sets the Indian people apart from every other racial minority in the United States? There are several reasons why it is impossible to take Indian tribes and lump them into a category with other minorities; but many of these reasons are unknown to the general public, and ignored by the legislators. Whether the lawmakers react through ignorance or design is debatable.

As a race of people, Indian tribes own more property than any other minority. This property has clearly defined borders and boundaries.

Within these boundaries, Indian tribes have their own governing body, law enforcement department, and judiciary system. These governmental bodies are autonomous.

But the one thing that makes the relationship between Indian tribes and the United States government unique is the treaties. These treaties were made at a time when the struggling federal government was dealing with Indian tribes on a "Nation to Nation" basis. As a result many of these treaties specifically mention the "sovereign status" of Indian nations.

Constitutional Law

As a nation of law-abiding citizens, every non-Indian must understand that these treaties are a part of the constitutional law. Because the world situation has changed drastically, and because the United States has become much more powerful than the Indian tribes it once dealt with as equals, does not change the law. Only an act of Congress can do that.

But even a powerful Congress cannot abrogate treaties out of existence. This was attempted in 1978 by Congressman Cunningham of the state of Washington, and was an abysmal failure. Once again, it was congressional ignorance that tried to find a simple solution to a complex problem.

Each and every treaty signed into law between Indian tribes and the U.S. government was replete with different provisions designed to protect both parties. There are no two treaties that are identical. As a matter of fact, some treaties have clauses which protect the Indian tribe concerned from having a particular treaty diminished, abrogated or altered. Now, how can a blanket law, proposed by Congress to abrogate these treaties, hold up in a court of law when in itself it is illegal?

Web of Deception

If ever there were a classic example of the federal government getting caught up in its own web of deception, it is the case of the Western Shoshone in the state of Nevada and the thus far unsuccessful efforts of the government to extinguish title to eighteen million acres of their homeland.

Using a supposed legal method called "gradual encroachment," the federal government, through the Indian Claims Commission, fixed compensation for the $26 million for these lands. It set the "taking date" as of July 1, 1872, thus placing the value of the land at the selling price of that day, 15 cents per acre. That land is now worth $100 per acre!

The Shoshones have been wondering and asking themselves since the 1950s, why the claims commission set the "taking date" in 1872? There were no meetings, no papers signed, and absolutely no legal negotiation in 1872 to warrant the extinguishing of title to their traditional lands on that date.

Clincher to Case

And then came the clincher to this bizarre case. Two Shoshone women, Mary and Carrie Dann, were judged guilty, and fined, for grazing their cattle on Bureau of Land Management lands, formerly a part of the Shoshone Nation. The women claimed that the land was Shoshone, and the judge ruled that title to the land had been extinguished.

The case was referred back to the federal district court, and federal judge Bruce Thompson delayed his decision until after the U.S. Court of Claims certified the final award of $25 million.

Invoking a section of the Indian Claims Act which read, "Payment of a claim would bar further claims or demands against the United States," Thompson held that, "Until the Indian claims judgment became final, such aboriginal title had not been extinguished." (To date the Western Shoshone have refused to accept payment of the award.)

This ruling is being studied very carefully by the attorneys for the Great Sioux Nation because of the judgment awarding $122 million to them for the Black Hills claim settlement.

Wage Garnishment Issues Discussed

Several weeks ago I wrote a column about repossessing merchandise on the Navajo Resevation and of a court ruling which made it necessary for merchants to go through tribal courts in order to repossess. There were some sharp reactions to this article, both pro and con.

A few months back, another case was heard before the Tenth Circuit Court of Appeals, and its decision regarding the state of New Mexico will probably cause turbulent reactions from the businessmen of this state.

The case in question was called Tom S. vs. Hon. Roy Matcum, et al, and here is how it turned out, according to the *DNA Newsletter*, Volume XIII. The DNA-People's Legal Service of Window Rock, Arizona publishes the newsletter.

The report in the Newletter goes like this: "In the state of New Mexico, garnishment of wages is legal. Garnishment is withholding of wages or property as repayment of a debt. On the Navajo Reservation, garnishment is not legal, but a portion of the Navajo Reservation is in New Mexico. Can the state of New Mexico enforce its laws on the "Navajo Reservation?" According to a recent Tenth Circuit Court of Appeals decision, it can not.

Working on Reservation

Tom Joe is a Navajo residing on the reservation and earning wages on the Navajo Reservation, but working for a company which is based in another state. Recently, Mr. Joe borrowed some money from U.S. Life Corporation, off the reservation, and failed to pay it back. The credit company went to the Magistrate Court of Farmington, New Mexico and had a writ of garnishment issued on the wages of Mr. Joe from his place of employment.

According to the *DNA Newsletter*, "Mr. Joe sought assitance from the Shiprock DNA when he was notified by his employer that his wages were about to be garnished. DNA then filed suit in a federal District Court in New Mexico alleging that the state court had no power to garnish wages of a Navajo who has earned his wages while working on the reservation. The District Court agreed, and orderd that the garnishment issue, in this case, be dropped.

Decision Appealed

The newsletter continues, "The creditor appealed the federal District Court's decision to the Tenth Circuit Court of Appeals in Denver. Additionally, the state of New Mexico, representing the magistrate judge who issued the writ, also appealed. The Tenth Circuit Court of Appeals ruled in favor of Mr. Joe, saying that the enforcement of the state judgment on the wages of Mr. Joe would violate the right of self-government of the Navajo tribe.

This ruling re-emphasized the fact that the Navajo Tribe has its own court system, and any attempts at enforcing judgment rulings must be made by them, and through them.

The *DNA Newsletter* concludes, "It was not done in this case, and instead the Magistrate Court was used, which has no power on the Navajo Reservation. As a result of this case, it is now clear that creditors with state judgments should not attempt to enforce these judgments against reservation wages or property in state court. The Navajo Tribal Courts must be used instead."

Tribal Courts Tough

Rulings which place more power in the hands of tribal courts are not restricted to the Navajo Reservation. Several reservations that have been given the power to enforce certain cases involving offenders find that the tribal courts can be much harder on them than the courts off the reservation.

Tribal courts are enlisting the assistance of highly skilled and qualified attorneys in order to strengthen their court systems, and are training many more tribal members. Since the responsibility of conducting fair and impartial court hearings has been placed in the hands of the tribal judicial system, the Indian people themselves are responding to the challenge by making sure that they provide the most professional, impartial and legally sound system that will leave no doubts as to their competence and determination.

Perusal Yields News on Indian Legislation

From time to time, I will use this column to bring my readers up to date on legislation past or pending that might have a direct bearing upon Indian people. Sorting through the different federal registers of Bureau of Indian Affairs directives is time consuming, oftentimes boring, and sometimes, almost impossible.

Hopefully, by scanning various bills, I can capsulize the contents and make them comprehensible.

Did you know that when the BIA submits its budget for the fiscal year, that budget must be determined by legislation, passed by Congress and signed by the president before the fiscal year begins?

The BIA has asked for less money in Fiscal Year 1981 than it did for 1980. The original budget asked for an increase of only $32.5 million; but has since been scaled down by $40.2 million. The largest reductions will be in the irrigation project funding ($22.3 million) and road construction ($10.8 million). An additional reduction on the proposed budget cuts is funding for the operation of Indian programs, to be cut by $7.1 million.

Closings Proposed

Included in the budget cuts is the closing of Stewart Indian School in Nevada and the Fort Sill Indian School in Lawton, Oklahoma, two off-reservation boarding schools. These cuts in budget are in funding requested, and as I stated earlier, the actual budget will be determined by legislative action.

Senator Larry Pressler, R-S.D., introduced a bill (S-2513) in April that would offer private industries tax incentives for locating on reservations. Pressler lauded the bill as "a new direction for federal-Indian relations." In my opinion, the only thing new about it was that it was being presented by a non-Indian senator for the first time. Native American tribes and business associations have been pushing this "innovative" concept for years, without the instant success of the senator from South Dakota.

Bill Derailed

The bill offers: "1. New and existing businesses on Indian reservations would be exempt from federal income taxes for the first ten years after they qualify for such incentives. (The bill does not guarantee any kind of managerial or specialized postions for Indians and it does not specifically promote training directed at preparing Indians for these higher paid positions.) 2. At the end of the 10-year period, when federal taxation begins, the businesses would be permitted to use favorable terms in computing capital gains. The depreciation on equipment would be allowed on an accelerated basis. 3. During the five years following the 10-year tax period, this legislation would also provide a tax deduction every year in which an Indian employee, who has been taken off the welfare rolls because of the employment opportunities afforded by this legislation, remains continuously employed by the qualifying new or existing private business."

Majority Approval

The Act provides that none of its provisions will be implemented on a reservation unless a majority of resident voters have moved to accept it. But no new or existing business can qualify for the tax incentives without being approved by the Secretary of the Interior as well.

The Act goes into "defrayed corporate obligations, an adequate reserve fund, tribal corporations, etc.," the gist of which is highly technical. Copies of the act can be acquired by writing to the Senate Select Committee on Indian Affairs, or by contacting the office of Senator Larry Pressler in Washington, D.C.

The bill has gone to the Senate Select Committee, which has agreed to conduct hearings on the measure. The Navajo Nation has come out with a strong endorsement for this bill.

High Court Ruling on Jobs Defended

George F. Will and James J. Kilpatrick are newspaper columnists. Both write their columns out of Washington, D.C. and both tend to be a little on the conservative side. This conservatism came shining through on one particular issue.

Will and Kilpatrick took strong exception to a Supreme Court decision, Fullilove vs. Klutznick, which was decided by a vote of 6-3 on July 2. The ruling upholds the Public Works Employment Act of 1977 which authorized Congress to set aside 10 percent of the funding for minorities on a $4 billion national public works program. The law states, "Except to the extent that the secretary (of Commerce) determines otherwise, no grant shall be made under this act for any local public works project unless the applicant gives satisfactory assurance to the secretary that at least 10 percent of the amount of such grant shall be expended for minority business enterprises."

For this particular project, the court identified minority groups as "Negroes, Spanish-speaking, Oriental, Indians, Eskimos and Aleuts."

It is the contention of Will and Kilpatrick that this ruling legitimizes bias against whites, and severely damages the Constitution of the United States. Both writers insist that the "Constitution is color blind" and Kilpatrick further quotes the Fifth Amendment: "No person shall be treated unjustly" and the Fourteenth Amendment which prohibits discrimination against "any person" to strengthen his argument.

Minority View

Reading these columns from a minority point of view, several questions come immediately to my mind. Where were these staunch defenders of the Constitution when black people were being forced to use "separate but equal" schools, toilets, and drinking fountains? Why weren't they pounding out columns of patriotic indignation when a mortician in Three Rivers, Texas, was refusing to handle the remains of Pvt. Felix Longoria because he was a Mexican-American? Where were these Constitutional purists when the Japanese-Americans were being rounded up by the federal government and herded into concentration camps for the terrible crime of being Japanese?

And finally, why didn't these self-righteous columnists raise a clamor when the constitutional rights of Indian tribe after Indian tribe were being flagrantly violated by the Congress of the United States in the name of progress?

Is defense of the Constitution a selective process? Is it only when Will and Kilpatrick feel personally threatened that they strike out?

Competition Possible

First of all, no major catastrophe will befall the United States because 10 percent of the public works contracts are set aside for minority firms. Minority firms will finally be able to compete for contracts which have been denied them for too many years by carefully structured technicalities.

Example: Points are often awarded to bidders for "experience." This amounts to a "Catch-22" dilemma for minority contractors. In order to get the experience, one must get the contracts to gain the experience. But how does one get the experience when one loses vital points on the bidding process because one does not have the experience?

In the long run this ruling will give many minority firms an opportunity to learn how to compete in the bidding process. In this manner they will be able to compete in the open market, against all bidders, without special consideration, when the funds set aside for this experiment are exhausted. This stop-gap measure will enable minority firms to pull themselves up by their bootstraps, generate incentive, and above all, create badly needed jobs for the hard-core unemployed. Over the long haul, America will be the beneficiary of this act.

Religious Rights Key to Claims

The United States judicial system is subject to laws made by Congress and the courts. Louis Bad Wound, a headman with the Lakota Treaty Council, who is now deceased, once said of the system: "They make the rules, they own the court, and they can change the rules to fit their game. What chance do we have to secure justice against a system like this?"

Many Indian tribes were offered monetary compensation for the confiscation of lands considered by them to be religious shrines. When they refused to accept the money for the land (their church), the federal judges ruled, "You will accept the money or nothing at all."

The non-Indian justices making these arbitrary decisions had no knowledge of Indian religion or custom. In most cases, they made their rulings against the Indian tribes using white man's logic culled from their own religious background and environment.

A classic case, one which will soon be winding its way through the courts of this land, involves the Sacred Mountain known as Bear Butte. The state of South Dakota decided to open up this sacred mountain to the general public as a recreation area.

Suit Brought

A suit brought against the state of Oglala Sioux Tribal Attorney Mario Gonzalez in behalf of the Lakota and Cheyenne nations to prevent the desecration of Bear Butte is an example which exemplifies the gross misunderstandings between the courts and the practice of the Indian religion. It is a case which could have profound repercussions throughout Indian Country.

The brief submitted by Gonzalez says: "According to Lakota and Tsistsistas tradition, the Black Hills are the place of origins where the people first came into the world. Bear Butte was the place of their first instructions, and remains the central and most powerful ceremonial site, where they can come closest to the Creator. It is most particularly a place of visions and dreams, where holy men, priests and practitioners of both Lakota and Tsistsistas religions have gone for thousands of years to seek guidance, knowledge and renewal. No other place on earth has this power. Just as the symbol of the Lakota religious unity is the Sacred Pipe kept at Green Grass, South Dakota, and of Tsistsistas religious unity the Sacred Arrows kept at Watonga, Oklahoma, Bear Butte is the central and common altar for both religions, and the most frequent and important place of pilgrimage."

From April to May of this year, the state prohibited all religious use of Bear Butte and advised the Indian people that "religious use thereafter would be limited to five days, renewable to a maximum of ten days, by discretionary permit only."

The plaintiffs in this case see these restrictions as denying their First Amendment rights. Gonzalez believes this is "as if all Catholic churches were closed for a time by the state so that devout worshippers were uable to attend mass, take communion, give confession or celebrate Easter."

What other religious group in this country must obtain permits to attend services, or is limited to a maximum of ten days to carry out religious practices? How would the non-Indian react if he were required a renewable permit, limited to a certain number of days, each and every time he wanted to attend his church or synagogue?

The suppression of Indian religious practices and the destruction of religious sites have not been ucommon in the history of this country. Some Indian tribes, such as the Lummi and Nooksack of Washington state, deliberately deceived the Bureau of Indian Affairs by performing their most important religious ceremonies on national holidays, telling the BIA agent that they were honoring the United States.

The federal government attempted to destroy the sacred Pipestone Quarry in Minnesota by building a railroad through it in 1891. Adhering to the wishes of missionaries and federal officials, the sacred ledges which created the falls, were deliberately dynamited in order to erase all traces of their outlines and to make them useless for ceremonial purposes.

Act of 1978

Finally, in 1978, it was congressional law entering into the realm of religion which prompted the passage of the "American Indian Religious Freedom Act."

The "Introduction—Historical Overview" of the American Indian Religious Freedom Act concludes "with the enactment of the American Indian Religious Freedom Act, our Nation is being afforded the opportunity to correct past injustices and to begin anew with regard to treatment of those who adhere to the tenets of traditional Native religions. In countless ways in the past and present, both our government and our people have proved themselves equal to challenges inherent in new beginnings. This will be no exception."

This act, by law, has established clear-cut guidelines for the education of the judges sitting on the bench to hear cases involving the concepts of Indian religious practices. There should be no excuse for ignorance leading to an erosion or miscarriage of justice. The ball is now in the court of the federal and state judges. What they do with it may have a profound impact upon the future of the Constitution of the United States.

Will Occupation of Yellow Thunder
Camp Extinguish Black Hills Claims?

On April 4, 1981, a group of people from the American Indian Movement settled on eight hundred acres of land in the Black Hills National Forest at Victoria Lake. Several weeks later, the occupiers named the encampment "Yellow Thunder Camp" in honor of Raymond Yellow Thunder, who was murdered in Gordon, Nebraska in 1972.

Much water has passed under the bridge since the occupation of the land at Victoria Lake a year ago. The culmination of the encampment seems to be a bill, H.R. 5664, introduced by Representative Shirley Chisolm, Democrat of New York, which directs the Secretary of Agriculture to issue a ten-year permit to Yellow Thunder Camp for the use of eight hundred acres of land for religious and cultural purposes, "subject to the authority and conrol of the leaders and organizers of the Yellow Thunder Camp community."

Morris Udall, chairman of the Committee on Interior and Insular Affairs, has mailed a letter to the tribal councils of all the tribes of the Great Sioux Nation. A spokesman for Udall said Monday that the pressure has been mounting to pass the bill. He added that those parties urging passage of the bill have indicated it is supported by the tribes and tribal councils of the "Lakota-Dakota Nation."

In his letter to the various Sioux tribes, Udall has asked the tribal councils to respond, "by tribal resolution," to five specific questions. They are:

(1) Is there an entity or body known as the "Lakota-Dakota (Sioux) Nation" or "Lakota-Dakota Nation," as set out in the bill, which is authorized to represent, and bind the separate Sioux tribes?

(2) Do the leaders and organizers of the Yellow Thunder Camp community have the authority to represent your tribe and its members on matters relating to the Black Hills and the Black Hills Sioux Claim?

(3) Do the leaders and organizers of the Yellow Thunder Camp community have the authority to represent your tribe with respect to the religious and cultural activity of your tribe and its members?

(4) Does your tribe feel that the issuance of a ten-year use permit for 800 acres of land in the Black Hills National Forest to the leaders and organizers of the Yellow Thunder Camp community, is in any way, a fulfillment of the desire of the Sioux tribes for the return of some part of the Black Hills for national and religious purposes of the Sioux?

(5) Based upon your answers to the foregoing questions, does your tribe support the enactment of H.B. 5664 for the benefit of the leaders, organizers and members of the Yellow Thunder Camp community?

Udall summed up his letter by advising members of the various tribal councils that their answers to the questions "may well influence this committee with respect to H.R. 5664 and with respect to any further action it may take on the larger issue of the Black Hills claims.

Sisseton-Wahpeton Tribal President Roland Ryan expressed his concern. He said that his tribal council will be meeting June 1, and there is a move to rescind the resolution passed recently advocating support for the Yellow Thunder Camp community.

Pat McLaughlin, chairman of the Standing Rock Sioux Tribe, contacted at Fort Yates, North Dakota, said, "We passed a resolution supporting the people at Yellow Thunder Camp on sort of a 'sympathy' resolution, but we added to the resolution that their efforts to pass H.R. 5664 would in no way jeopardize the larger Sioux claim to the Black Hills."

McLaughlin said he is calling a special session of the tribal council to take another look at the resolution, and if council members determine that it places the Black Hills Claims Settlement case in jeopardy, "we will probably rescind that resolution supporting Yellow Thunder Camp."

Oglala Sioux Tribal President Joe American Horse said, "We generally support any sincere efforts by Indian people to pray in the Black Hills, but the Oglala Sioux Tribe cannot support H.R. 5664."

American Horse said a resolution is being prepared to present to the tribal council at its next scheduled meeting.

The three points to be considered by the tribal council are:

(1) The bill does not give control to the individual tribes.

(2) The Oglala Sioux Tribe fears that if the council supports Yellow Thunder Camp, and then proceeds with its own case involving the Black Hills, Congress may retaliate by claiming that the granting of the eight hundred acres at Victoria Lake extinguishes any further land claims.

(3) Any support for the bill could defuse the entire issue of the Black Hills Claims Settlement Case. It could lead non-Indian supporters of the Sioux Claims to believe that the case has been settled honorably.

For now, the tribes of the Great Sioux Nation seem to be lining up in favor of the larger issue of the Black Hills Claims Case, fearing that H.R. 5664 can be used against them in the long haul.

Oglala Sioux and a Fight for Mecca

Suppose the Lutheran Church has owned a large piece of property for more than one hundred years. Located on this hypothetical property are burial grounds, several shrines, and the land itself holds such religious significance that pilgrims come from miles around to worship there. In short, it is the Mecca of the Lutheran Church.

Curious visitors, non-Lutherans, discover deposits of gold on the land. They illegally trespass on the land and begin to actively mine this precious metal.

In dire need of additional wealth, the government ignores the entreaties of the church, and suggests it is unable to stem the tide of trespassers.

Eventually, the situation deteriorates to the point where violence is imminent. Unable to appease the church or to police the trespassers, the government decides to confiscate the disputed lands, and allows the miners to assume possession of the lands they had illegally occupied.

Many years pass. The miners have built many towns and cities on the land and have extracted tons of mineral wealth and timber worth millions of dollars. During this time, the church has tried every means at its disposal to get its day in court to protest the illegal taking of its religious lands.

Finally, the government decides to quiet title to these lands, once and for all. It sets up a special court called "The Church Claims Commission" where representatives of church groups who believe they have lost lands illegally can go to seek monetary compensation. Payment of money is the only solution offered to the church, and the court istelf is considered to be the "exclusive remedy" for settling church grievances filed against the government for the loss of lands.

At last the church is awarded several million dollars for the land at the going rate of land one hundred years ago. The church protests, saying it doesn't want the money. It wants the land returned. It claims its First Amendment (freedom of religion) and Fifth Amendment (land must be taken for public purpose, due process must be afforded, and just compensation must be awarded) rights have been violated.

The government claims that it lacks jurisdiction to hear this case. It claims the matter has already been decided by the the "Church Claims Commission" and this "exclusive remedy" is the only one available to the church. The First Amendment rights violation charges are not addressed at all.

The church appeals the ruling, saying, "If Congress can abridge the freedom of speech, or of religion, or abolish the right of speedy trial, upon payment of damages to the citizens injured thereby, our entire constitutional framework is destroyed. The First Amendment does not say, 'Congress may make laws abridging the freedom of religion, provided it makes adequate compensation.' It says, 'Congress shall make no law . . .'"

Even though the circuit court upholds the ruling of the district court and says the court lacks jurisdiction to hear this case, the church continues to pursue the course of justice by filing a petition for a rehearing.

Of course, all of the above relates a hypothetical situation; but this is exactly what has happened in the case of the "Oglala Sioux Tribe vs. the United States of America." for the return of the sacred Black Hills.

Unable to comprehend the religious significance of the Black Hills to the Lakota people, the court seems to have decided to duck the issue by ignoring the First Amendment violation with silence.

A portion of the brief for rehearing filed by Oglala Sioux tribal attorney Mario Gonzalez goes right to the heart of the matter when it says, "If Congress were to condemn every church in the land with the intent of suppressing worship, the issue would not be limited to the payment of money damages. If Congress were to take the lands of blacks in a place, and donate them to neighboring whites, on the pretense of alleviating jealousy and conflict, surely there would be substantive issues under the Fifth and First Amendments apart from any consideration of compeensation."

The brief continues, "Such is the case here. Congress confiscated the lands and the church of the Oglala people to donate to trespassers. The issue is the power of Congress to satisfy lawbreakers by dismantling the church of their victims. This circuit dare not rule, sub silentio, that Congress had such powers in its dealings with petitioner. There is little to distinguish this from a case in which, for example, Congress chose to appease marauding neo-fascist demonstrators by giving them synagogues; the constitutional inquiry would not end with the offer of monetary compensation. If there is any distinction between that case and this, it is only in the race of the victims, and surely that cannot be a legitimate constitutional factor."

As Attorney Russell Barsh, co-counsel to the tribe, has said so many times, "There is far more at stake here to the white man than the constitutional rights of the Oglala Sioux Tribe."

Two Wrongs Do Not Make A Right

It shouldn't have taken too much intelligence on the part of the bureaucrats within the Bureau of Indian Affairs to realize their ridiculous, capricious, unconstitutional, and illegal authorization of "forced fee patents" would eventually catch up with them. Did they also take into consideration the fact that their actions could lead to bloodshed between Indians and whites?

An amendment to the General Allotment Act, known as the Burke Act of 1906, set into motion a BIA program that may culminate in violence between Indian and white seventy-seven years after the fact. The amendment reads:

"That the Secretary of the Interior may, in his discretion, and he is authorized, whenever he shall be satisfied that any Indian allottee is competent and capable of managing his or her affiars at any time to cause to be issued to such allottee a patent in fee simple, and thereafter all restrictions as to sale, incumbrance, or taxation of said land shall be removed and said land shall not be liable to the satisfaction of any debt contracted prior to issuing of such patent. . ."

One must understand that this arbitrary act of the BIA occurred before the American Indian was legally a citizen of the United States. Bending to the wills of the settlers and land speculators, the constituency which coveted the land and had the power of the "vote" to wield as a club of intimidation, federal officials began to force fee patents upon Indian allottees without their application or consent.

Competency Commissions were set up to determine if an Indian was competent to be issued a fee patent, and as this procedure dragged on, a faster and easier method was discovered. All Indian allottees of one-half Indian blood or less were arbitrarily issued fee patents.

Historical research by attorneys James McCurdy and Linda Marousek of the University of South Dakota Law School at Vermillion, South Dakota disclosed that "one-fourth to one-third of all Competency Commission patents issued in the United States were forced upon Indian individuals located on the northern plains within the area presently under the jurisdiction of the Aberdeen Area Office."

Competency Commission patents totaled 1,545 and blood quantum patents numbered 1,255. In all, 250,000 acres; one-fourth million acres of Indian land, were removed from trust status. The twenty-five-year guarantee from taxation all Indians with land in trust status were given was wavied time and again in order to make this illegal act work. With little or no knowledge of tax laws, many individual Indians lost their lands to the tax collector.

The fact that all of the Indians about to be issued forced fee patents were not citizens of the United States hardly deterred the BIA. They designed a colorful ceremony that took all of five minutes—and made the Indians United States citizens.

Dreamed up by the then Secretary of the Interior Franklin Lane (1913), the ceremony went something like this. An Indian was asked his Indian name. The Indian said his name aloud. He was then handed a bow and arrow and told to "Take this bow and shoot the arrow." After the Indian shot the arrow, he was told that he had shot his last arrow. "That means you are no longer to live the life of an Indian. You are from this day forward to live the life of a white man," the ceremony went. The Indian was then told that he could keep the arrow. "It will be to you a symbol of your noble race and of the pride you may feel that you come from the first of all Americans," the Indian was told. The presentation of the flag and a badge concluded the ceremony and made the Indian a U.S. citizen.

Now, seventy-seven years later, those forced fee patents, known by the BIA as "2415 Claims," have come back to haunt them. In December of 1982, the BIA hoped to sweep all of those claims under the rug by declaring a final cut-off date on December 31 for the filing of claims, but the U.S. Congress extended that deadline by another year.

Thousands of acres of land purchased by non-Indians, either from individual Indians, or by paying the outstanding taxes on the land, are now being claimed by the descendants of the original allottees as having been taken illegally. Non-Indians have organized to protect their rights to the land in twelve South Dakota counties. They truly believe that the lands of their ancestors purchased forty or fifty years ago is legally theirs, and they are willing to do whatever it takes, legally and physically, to protect their land.

And so, a giant snafu, created by the Secretary of the Interior more than seventy-seven years ago, could very easily cause bloodshed in 1983. One white farmer living in Bennett County told me, "The people are angry. They will lay down their lives to protect their rights to the land they have been living on for the past fifty years. I'm afraid there will be bloodshed over this, and so are a lot of other farmers."

Two wrongs will never make a right and the ultimate consequences of any friction between Indian and white, or any ensuing violence, rests squarely in the hands, and in the conscience of the federal government. The government built the tinderbox that is about to explode into violent confrontation—and it is up to them to solve the problem before this happens.

Force Fee Patents Caused Many Problems

History buffs of World War II will recall a "program" initiated by the Third Reich which became known as "The final solution to the Jewish problem."

Long before the rise of Adolph Hitler, the same terminology was used by the Commissioner of Indian Affairs, Francis E. Leupp. In one of his first reports written to the Department of the Interior in 1905, Leupp stated: "At first, of course, the government must keep its protecting hand on every Indian's property after it has been assigned to him by book and deed; then, as one or another shows himself capable of passing out from under the tutelage, he should be set fully free and given 'the white man's chance,' with the white man's obligations to balance it. In short, our aim ought to be to keep him moving steadily down the path which leads from his close domain of artificial protection toward the broad area of individual liberty enjoyed by the ordinary citizen. If we can thus gradually watch our body of dependent Indians shrink, even by one number at a time, we may congratulate ourselves that the final solution is indeed only a question of a few years."

An amendment to the Dawes Act of February 8, 1877 allowed the Indian commissioner to place the Indian lands held in trust status to be placed into a forced fee patent by using Competency Commissions to establish competency of individual Indian landholders. This arbitrary issuance of fee patents would be forced upon allottees of one-half or less degree of Indian blood.

When an Indian was decided to be "competent" by the commission, he was "to be issued a patent in fee simple, and thereafter all restrictions as to sale, incumbrance, or taxation of said land shall be removed and said land shall not be liable to the satisfaction of any debt contracted prior to issuing of such permit."

Many Indian landowners did not want to have fee patents issued for their lands but they were not given a choice. The superintendent of the Pine Ridge Agency told one allottee, "The issuance of this patent has been reported to the tax collector and, if you do not pay the taxes, whether you take the patent or not, eventually, the land will be sold to satisfy them."

In 1921, newly elected representative from South Dakota, William Williamson, claimed, "These policy patents issued arbitrarily to the allottees without their consent are illegal." Williamson was appalled over some of the problems arising from the forced fee patents. He said, "Many of these patents were issued while the owners were over in France as part of our armed forces there. They knew nothing about the issuance of the patents until they returned to this country, when, in many cases, they found out their lands had been patented and assessed and that taxes had accumulated.

Thousands of Indians lost their lands by selling them, losing them to tax collectors, or by failing to pay mortgages taken out on the land in order to pay the taxes. This vicious cycle soon returned to haunt the Bureau of Indian Affairs.

The BIA was charged with identifying those Indian people who had lost lands under the forced fee patent program, and was ordered in 1966, under the

2415 Claims Act to protect the Indian land interests. All in all, 17,000 individual land claims were identified by the BIA up to the final cutoff date of December 31, 1982.

As the filing deadline date approached, the BIA published a twelve-page list of Indian landowners with possible claims. Many of these individuals had little or no time to file lawsuits to satisfy those claims. In the first place, most cases would have had to be handled by private attorneys, and most Indians could not afford that luxury.

A suit filed by the Native American Rights Fund of Boulder, Colorado saved the day. The filing date was extended for 360 days, depending upon the kind of claim, and was signed into law by President Reagan late in the day on December 30—one day before the deadline.

Although it was the gross incompetency of the BIA, itself, which brought this severe problem to the Indian landowners, they refused to provide legal services to litigate the land claims or to provide funds to the beleaguered allottees.

As a matter of fact, the BIA has done everything within its power to sweep this disaster under the rug.

Only the determination of the Indian landowners has made it possible for many Indians to seek either a return of the lost land, or monetary compensation.

Robert Fast Horse, Pine Ridge attorney

Chapter VIII—Politics

Politics

Anderson Rates High As Rights Advocate

I've said it before, and I'll say it again; the Indian tribes of this country cannot afford the luxury of ignoring the national or state political process. Whether we condone or condemn the political opinions of the various candidates, we can no longer doubt the disastrous possibilities now lurking in ambush, if we do not act to express our displeasure by casting a vote of protest on election day. The next four years could well be pivotal years for all of the Indian tribes in the United States. Look around at the vital issues confronting the tribal governments. The battles to find a solution for water rights, mineral rights, natural resources, treaty rights and tribal sovereignty will be fought in the courts of this land during this time, and it is imperative that we elect congressmen, senators, and a president who will be supportive and knowledgeable of Indian issues.

Several times, in the past few years, I have heard tribal officials comment, "You know, I hate to say this," and at this point they usually glance nervously around to see if anyone is within earshot, "but Richard Nixon did more for the American Indian than any president in the past thirty years."

Blue Lake

The process of returning lands to the Indian tribes, such as the sacred lake (Blue Lake) to the Taos Pueblo, and the Indian Education and Self-Determination Act, P.L. 93-638, are two examples of legislation carried out in behalf of the Indians during Nixon's tour as president. For these things to be achieved during a Republican administration is unheard of, at least in my lifetime. Perhaps Nixon will go into the history books as a villain of the worst kind; but credit should be given where credit is due.

ABC buttons (Anyone But Carter) are beginning to spring up, around the country. What about Jimmy Carter? As an Indian magazine, *Wassaja*, through its editor, Rupert Costo, a Cahuilla Indian man, says about Jimmy Carter, "He has continued the time-worn policy of attempting to buy Indian support by permitting money to be pumped into questionable Indian programs, while cutting back or cutting off funding for needed programs in education and health."

Costo continues, "By a selective elevation of some Indians to leading positions in government agencies, especially in the BIA, he has created a stable of mendacious eunuchs. They are the fifth column in the centuries-old struggle of the native peoples for justice. Carter is no friend of the Indian people. He is probably this era's worst Indian enemy."

Ronald Reagan

Let's take a look at Ronald Reagan. He is a firm supporter of the so-called "Sagebrush Rebellion," a coalition of Western states set up to fight for the return of federal lands to state control, and he is a powerful advocate of states rights. If there is anything minorities fear more than death, it is the thought of having their lives controlled by the state governments. They can still see the specters of Alabama Governor George Wallace standing in the doorway of the state university, blocking the administration of a lone, single, black man. They can still see in their minds the TV commercial of nightsticks falling on the heads of Indian men, while the background voice-over is saying, "When we needed law and order, William Janklow was there."

In my opinion, there is only one true friend of the Indian people running for the nation's highest office; that man is John Anderson. The pundits continue to say, "A vote for John Anderson is a vote for Ronald Reagan," but I can't buy that line of reasoning. As Anderson himself said, I believe that a vote for John Anderson is a vote for John Anderson. In my travels, I have talked with Indians from South Dakota to New Mexico who feel that Anderson is their only real choice. Check Anderson's record as a congressman, and you will discover that he is a staunch advocate of Indian rights.

These are the things which we must weight with extreme care as we step into the voting booths on Nov. 4. Choose wisely!

Tribes' Hopes Unmet by High-Level Post

How effective is the cabinet-level office of the assistant secretary of the interior? The position has the potential to be one of the most productive advocates of Indian rights of any yet established. But, like most offices set up to improve the conditions of the Indian people, it can be only as effective as the individual selected to fill it.

Since its creation at the beginning of the Carter administration, the assistant secretary of the interior position has failed to live up to is expectations among the various Indian tribes. In the beginning, it was intended to serve as a direct pipeline to the secretary of the interior, and allow the tribes of this country the ability to furnish input from the reservation level that could help to bring about favorable decisions in their behalf.

The first assistant secretary, Forest Gerrard, proved to be totally ineffective. He was more of a sycophant for administration policy than a buffer for Indian concerns. The second assistant secretary, Tom Fredricks, was not in office long enough to indicate what his strength or weakness would be. The only thing both of these men had in common was that they were both Indians.

Token Position?

There are those who feel that it really doesn't matter who is appointed to this position. They feel that it is a sop to the Indian tribes and was never intended to be more than a token position with lofty expectations. Many tribal members feel that only those individuals willing to acquiesce to the bureaucratic position of continued domination of Indian tribes, and contribute to the steady erosion of Indian rights, would be considered to fill the job.

The Reagan administration has selected James G. Watt as the Secretary of the Interior, and although it was expected that he would receive some opposition at his confirmation hearings, Senate approval seemed certain. Watt has suggested that he will seek input from Indian tribes in helping him to select a new assistant secretary of the interior.

Already there are several names being bandied about, and there is no doubt that many tribal officials have viewed these potential nominees with trepidation. They are wondering why the old refrain, "It seems to me I've heard that song before," keeps ringing in their ears. Those infamous "Washington Redskins" who have been lurking around and about the halls of Washington, D.C., queuing up whenever the choice jobs are being handed out, are well represented, as usual.

Urban Orientation

For too many years there has been a clique of urban-oriented Indians who have been selected for top positions in Indian affairs and they have leapfrogged over each other so many times that it is impossible to tell where they will land next. It's "Potomac Fever" at its highest temperature, musical chairs at its finest, and the only losers in this charade are the Indians living out on the reservations.

You can take the names of three of those mentioned for this prestigious position, place them in a hat, shake it up, make a selection, and you won't be able to tell who you've picked out of the hat without a scoreboard. They are all clones of one another.

The only one on the list I have seen who has the capabilities of doing this job effectively has said that he would not be interested in it. That man is Ernie Stevens, who is presently working for the Navajo Nation as the director of economic development. As far as I can see, he is the only man around with the experience and the guts to take the bull by the horns and shake it.

Collecting Dust

While he was the executive director of the American Indian Policy Review Commission, he put together a list of recommendations which, if they had been implemented, would have moved the Indian tribes of this country into a new beginning. But, ultimately, many of those very strong recommendations which were taken directly from the people living in Indian Country on the reservations, were too far ahead of their times and are still collecting dust on the shelf of some bureaucrat.

If there is any kink at all in the armor of Ernie Stevens, it is that he was once a very large part of the Washington, D.C. establishment I alluded to earlier; but by shaking the dust of that city from his feet, and moving to an Indian reservation and experiencing first hand the many problems confronting Indian tribes, he has overcome this handicap. If James Watt wants to have input from the Indian people of this country, why don't we give it to him by making our own recommendations for the position of assistant secretary of the interior? Send your recommendation to: U.S. Deprtment of the Interior, Office of the Secretary, Washington, DC 20240.

I also recommend that you send this column along with your nomination (if you feel as I do) and let him know who you don't want.

Reservations Wary of Shift to Right

A gentleman who distributes an underground sort of newspaper called *The Spotlight* asked me what the Indian tribes of the United States are facing over the next few years. He also asked what direction the tribes of this country would be taking.

With the presidential elections behind us, and a lot of new faces in office, particularly within the Senate, it will be a little easier to look at what the future may hold for Indian people.

Whenever there is a shift to the right in politics, it usually means bad news for Indians. President-elect Reagan has been a supporter of the so-called "Sagebrush Rebellion." Cases involving the rights of states to take over federal lands within their boundaries will be winding their way through the judicial systems of this land over the next few years. The quesion of whether Indian reservations are federal lands or the lands of dependent sovereign nations will have to be addressed in order for these states rights cases to have any validity.

It is no coincidence that the "Bertrand Russell Tribunals" are being held at this particular time of year. Correspondence from knowledgeable Europeans has indicated to me that there has been a general feeling that this country would be making a tremendous shift to the conservative point of view. It is no secret overseas that the energy hungry people of America are seeking cheap sources of instant energy within these borders, and it is also no secret that much of the energy producing resources are located upon Indian lands.

Underground Wealth

It takes no genius to put two and two together and come to the conclusion, at least from an Indian point of view, that covetous eyes are, even at this moment, surveying the potential wealth beneath the ground, all the way from Canada to Mexico, that is in the hands of the Indian tribes. Lands which were supposedly set aside for the use of Indian people, barren and arid lands, have suddenly become very valuable.

There is an old Indian joke which goes: "When the white man presented the treaties to the different tribes, they read: 'This land shall be yours for as long as the grass shall grow and the rivers flow;' but what the Indian people failed to realize was that at the bottom of these treaties, written in very small print, it also said 'or 90 days, whichever comes first.'"

The answers of how to deal with the coming onslaught are being discussed and dissected by the Indian people themselves. The entire gamut of reasons to proceed, or not to proceed, must be considered. There are the spiritual, the cultural, and the economic problems to be considered. The white man may scoff and scratch his head wondering how a poverty-stricken race of people can turn down the offer of potential wealth in the face of that poverty, but this is where the different points of view, culturally, are most obvious.

Thanking Mother Earth

My grandmother performed a religious ceremony every time she went to the riverbank to collect leaves and herbs for medicine or tea. She would pray in our native language as she gathered her leaves, and when she was finished, she would leave a small gift on the ground to thank Mother Earth for her generosity. She used to say, "Never take anything from this earth without leaving something in exchange."

The "Russell Tribunals" being held later this month in Rotterdam, Holland, will be attended by many nations of this world. They hope to focus the world's attention upon the mistreatment of native people of the Western Hemisphere. The legal rights of the native peoples will be the major topic; and some of the finest legal minds from around the world will be seeking solutions in behalf of the native inhabitants of North, Central and South America.

The native peoples of these continents know that the drive to find energy-producing resources will result in the final assault upon Indian lands. By seeking the support of the different nations of this world, the Indian tribes are not seeking to deny access to sharing in these resources; but, instead, they are attempting to become active participants in deciding if these resources should be taken from the land, and if so, how they should be taken. They are saying that if the resources are to be removed for the good of all, then let it be done our way, in our fashion.

The Indian tribes will no longer submit to being unwilling victims to insensitivity.

Official Disagrees with News Story

Take a word such as "realistic" and dissect it from a different point of view. What is realistic to one person may not be realistic to another. It may depend upon whether the end result of the realistic act is good or harmful.

South Dakota Attorney General Mark Meierhenry wrote an article in the October 17 issue of the Rapid City *Journal* in answer to a column I had written for *Notes from Indian Country*. The attorney general suggested that I had failed to give the entire context of some quotes attributed to him in the *Rocky Mountain News*.

The interview given to the Colorado newspaper by Meierhenry implied that the Pine Ridge Reservation was "a nothing place" and that anyone who chose to live there was "programmed for poverty."

The quote I did not use stated:

"Most of us in South Dakota agree that when the land was taken from them (the Indians), it was one of the darkest, most dishonest moments in U.S. history. But you can only look back for so long.

"My relatives were chased out of Germany and Russia in the 1880's, but I am not going to go back and reclaim the family plot. It wouldn't be realistic."

Not Relevant

First of all I did not use the quote because I did not consider it relevant. Secondly, I do agree with Meierhenry that, no, it would not be realistic to try to reclaim his family plot in Russia or Germany.

The Lakota people of the Great Sioux Nation are not trying to "reclaim the family plot," as it were. There is a vast difference between lands taken from individual land holders and lands taken from sovereign nations. The Lakota people had a treaty signed by the president of the United States which guaranteed them the lands now known as the Black Hills. The treaty was, and is, a legal and binding agreement between two sovereign nations. Can the attorney general produce a document of equal weight to support any claims he might have over lost family plots in Russia or Germany?

Meierhenry then went on to say, "I do not believe it is racist for a public official to face the economic reality of Indian life on the reservation. The opportunities for economic growth are too limited to provide an acceptable standard of living for the approximately 14,000 residents of the Pine Ridge Indian Reservation."

He then went on to list the much smaller populations of Bennett, Mellette and Fall River counties and suggest that "the poor standard of living on Pine Ridge is a direct result of the strain such a large population places on scarce economic resources."

Implied Solution

Now we get back to the word "realistic" once more. The implied solution of moving several thousand Indian families off the Pine Ridge Reservation in order to decrease the population enough to enhance the chances of "economic growth" may be an acceptable and "realistic" approach to Meierhenry, but I do believe that several thousand Indian families scheduled for removal would not agree with him. If the 60,000 people living in Pennington County experienced a severe economic depression, would Meierhenry suggest that 40,000 of them give up their homes and their land and move to another location in order to improve the economic situation of those who remain behind? Who would make the decision of who is to stay and who is to go?

The Indian tribes of this country find themselves in deep financial troubles because of a governmental system of forced dependency and paternalism designed to eradicate the fierce independence prevalent within the ranks of the various Indian tribes.

Many Experiments

Experiment after experiment was tried and tested in a losing effort to assimilate the Indian tribes into the mainstream. Several billion dollars were spent in this futile effort without once asking the Indian people themselves what they wanted to do to improve their own lives.

If we had been allowed, from the very beginning of reservation life, to take our futures into our own hands, and had been given the opportunity to establish a standard of economic growth in keeping with our lifestyle and traditions, countless millions of taxpayers' dollars would have been saved, and the conditions which exist on many reservations today would be nonexistant.

If the federal government has decided to write us off as a hopeless cause, and has decided that the best way to accomplish this is by cutting off financial assistance, ignoring our treaty rights, and leaving us to sink or swim on our own, it is doing us a grave injustice.

It was not our fault that the policies designed to acculturate and assimilate us failed. It is the fault of a misguided government, and to abandon us now, because of the government's own inadequacies and bad politics, is as wrong as attempting to place the blame upon the Indian tribes.

There is a vast difference between realism and expediency, and for the attorney general to suggest that we abandon our homes, our last foothold upon a continent we once owned, in the name of economic growth, is not only wrong, it is immoral.

U.S. Generosity Draws Criticism

It came as quite a shock to most of the hostages taken at the U.S. Embassy in Iran in 1979 that many countries in the Third World have no love for the United States.

The generosity of the United States in aiding foreign countries is not really the issue. Too many times, that generosity had many strings attached. Along with the financial assistance came unwanted political, ideological and religious interventionism.

Dictatorial and oppressive governments, whose only redeeming value was their loyalty to the United States, were often lavished with financial assistance and military aid which was used to crush any opposition. Billions of dollars in foreign aid never filtered down to the truly needy people. Instead the rich got richer, and much more powerful with their new found wealth, and the poor got poorer.

Class struggles in developing countries were heightened by the continuation and strengthening of the power of the ruling classes. Tyrannical governments, which would have toppled on their own, were given new life by the influx of foreign aid dollars.

Focus on Shortcomings

It was not difficult for the enemies of the United States to bring world-wide focus to the shortcomings of this supposed benevolence. All they had to do was point out the apparent inequities between the very rich and the very poor. The propaganda bonanza provided to the socialist countries by the apparently successful transition of the Cuban government from capitalism to communism had been milked for all it was worth.

As a journalist, I have corresponded and conversed at length with journalists from many other countries. Because the very nature of journalism causes these individuals to be aware of what is happening in their countries and in other nations, and because they must cut through the propaganda to get to the heart of a story, these foreign journalists are, oftentimes, sensitive barometers to the real problems of the masses surfacing in the developing nations.

Psychologists will tell you that it is possible to be so close to a problem, or an issue, that it is quite easy to overlook the cause, which could lead to a solution to the problem. This is where my conversations with foreign journalists magnify one of the major contributors to the tarnished image of the United States and it is so close to the bureaucracy, it is often unseen.

Guidance, Examples

When the leaders of developing nations seek out a form of government which would be suited to the needs of all the people within their borders, they do look to the super powers for guidance and examples. One question they ask themselves is this: Has this form of government worked for all of their people? Keep in mind that they are looking at the governmental successes through the eyes of the very poor. Consequently, the people they are going to identify with are the very poor people of the nation they hope to emulate.

Now, take a look at the track record of the United States in dealing with the poor, who are usually the minorities, within the confines of a democratic system. A classic example of the "out of sight, out of mind" mentality of the government is the treatment of the Native Americans of this country. How can an already poor, oppressed and dark-skinned people of a developing Third World country have any faith in a government which has broken promise after promise, treaty after treaty with Native American tribes of its own country?

Centuries have passed since the white man first set foot upon this continent, and yet he is no closer to solving the conflicts between himself and the American Indian than he was 400 years ago. Consumed with the all powerful urge to make the Indian over in his own image, the white man tried to destroy that which he could not change.

Cruel Failure

Don't doubt for one minute that the cruel failures of the U.S. government to assimilate the American Indian at all costs, even if it meant destroying a culture, a race of people, and a religion, are not well known and chronicled by the poor people of the Third World.

The actions of the government in trying to take what little is left of the Indian nations through the courts, and thereby justify the centuries of avarice, theft, broken treaties, and broken promises have not gone unnoticed in the Third World countries. These things are happening here and now. They cannot be attributed to the trials and tribulations of history.

The Shawnee Prophet, Tenskawtawa, said more than 150 years ago that until the U.S. government learns to deal fairly and honestly with the Indian nations of this land, it will never attain stature in the eyes of the rest of the world.

Occupation of Park Not a Wise Move

Suppose a group of white teenagers has a beer bust in Wind Cave National Park in the Black Hills in southwestern South Dakota. In the process they vandalize several park signs, damage benches and tables, and leave beer cans strewn all over the place.

The newspapers print this story and when the papers are read on the reservations of South Dakota, the Indian people react by saying, "Those damned white people. Don't they have any respect for park property? Is this what they are going to do to the land just because they claim it is a free country?"

Now don't you believe it is a little unfair to blame the entire white race for the actions of a few irresponsible, impetuous, white teenagers? Don't you think it is stretching the blame and overreacting to a situation from a position of racism and ignorance?

I am not going to make any excuses for the Indians who occupied land in Wind Cave National Park and left it in a mess when they moved to Sheridan Lake in the middle of the night. What they did was inexcusable. It was an example of very poor leadership and bad planning. It was a black eye for all Indian people who respect Mother Earth.

I've heard all of their excuses and I'm not buying any of them. If an incident was needed to provide fuel to the opponents of Indian ownership of the Black Hills, a better script could not have been provided by the Indian haters. What makes it all more disastrous to us is the fact that the script was written by the occupiers with little or no concern for the feelings of the majority of the Oglala Sioux Tribe.

What I strongly object to is the animosity and venom being directed at all Indians for the actions of a few. The white media made no distinction between this small group and the many thousands of Indians living on the Pine Ridge Reservation who were just as disgusted by this scene as the non-Indians.

What sort of Indian leadership could not comprehend that you do not give this kind of ammunition to your enemies to be used against your own people? One does not throw a bone to a hungry dog and not expect it to pounce upon it immediately.

If blame is to be placed, don't make the mistake of blaming Wind Cave National Park Superintendent Lester McClanahan for doing his job. Blame Tribal President Stanley Looking Elk, legal advisor Tony Fast Horse, and Tribal Councilman Ivan Starr for not having the foresight to realize the extent of the wrath to be brought down upon the heads of the Indian people because of their inexcusable neglect.

Blame the eleven tribal councilmen who voted for the occupation of federal lands in the first place, or the eight councilmen who sat on their hands and did not vote at all on such a vital issue; but don't blame all Indians or all members of the Oglala Sioux Tribe.

Intuition is a gift usually attributed to women, and in the tribal council meeting authorizing the occupation of federal lands, the insight and intuition of a tribal councilwoman who opposed the action is quickly becoming apparent. Against all odds, Tribal Chairwoman Penny Janis from the Medicine Root district stood alone. She objected to the occupation even though she knew she would be loudly, roundly and angrily criticized. Hiding her fears, she was the only member of that august governing body with the guts to stand up against what she truly believed to be wrong.

There are many tribal members who are fast becoming disgusted with our elected officials who chose to duck controversial issues by either not voting or not showing up for the council meetings when controversy is expected. We did not elect these officials to hide from the issues or to hold secret meetings dealing with events bound to have a profound impact upon the lives of all tribal members.

From the very beginning, I have voiced opposition to the authorization of occupying federal lands by the tribal council, and to the occupation of what is now called "Yellow Thunder Camp" by members of the Dakota American Indian Movement.

It is my contention that we have a case before the U.S. Supreme Court on the Black Hills Claims settlement, and until all of our legal remedies are exhausted, we have no business occupying lands. Now is the time for patience and planning; not for impetuosity and immaturity.

Since June 18, 1981, the day the council voted to occupy lands in the Black Hills, we have not had a legally constituted governing body. The powers of the tribal council have been usurped by an executive committee composed of the tribal president, treasurer, secretary and a fifth member. The only two members of the autonomous committee elected by popular vote of the people are the president and vice president. The others are elected by the tribal council. In a way, it's pathetic that our tribal council has been replaced by a committee it created.

Loss of Fairchild Plant Hurt Navajo People

Through the brown haze that swirls at its base, it juts a couple of thousand feet into the air, like the dorsal fin of a huge shark. The Navajo people named this mountain "Shiprock." The village that lies next to the mountain in New Mexico bears its name.

The brown maze that lies in this valley comes from the Four Corners Power Plant, which is south of this village of 9,000 on the New Mexico section of the Navajo Nation. The plant's gigantic concrete stacks belch smoke into the atmosphere twenty-four hours a day, 365 days a year.

One would think that the pollutants that hang in the air would be one of the major complaints of the area but it is not.

Of several people I talked to, one was a Navajo lady who was ageless. She could have been twenty-five or she could have been fifty-five. She was wearing a purple, velvet pullover that extended to her hips and a purple, cloth skirt that hung all the way to the ground. Around her waist was a concho belt of silver. Her shining, black hair was pulled tightly to the back of her head and held in place with a turquoise hair pin.

The Navajo lady pointed, with her lower lip, at a large building that stood near the main road through town. "That was the Fairchild Plant," she said. "At one time there were over four hundred Navajos working there. I was one of them. We made many kinds of electronic parts for the company." She paused for a long while, as if translating the words she wanted to speak in her head from her native tongue to the English. Then she continued:

"They call themselves the American Indian Movement and they came here to the plant with guns and took over the place. We didn't know who they were or why they were doing this thing to our plant. Before you know it, there are television reporters and cameras all over the place and we can no longer go to work."

There was anger in her voice as she said, "Why did this AIM group do this to us without asking our permission? Now look at that plant. It is closed up tight. The company just locked up the doors and moved away. There are hundreds of us Navajos that are out of work now, with little chance of getting another job. The Fairchild plant was one of the few places to work here in Shiprock."

A Navajo man dressed in faded denim pants, a western shirt, topped by a black cowboy hat who stood near by during this exchange of conversation, stepped forward. "When you go back to South Dakota, tell that AIM bunch that if they want to help the Navajo people to get us back our jobs. It is because of them that we are out of work," he said.

Ed McCabe is the superintendent of the Bureau of Indian Affairs in Shiprock. He is Navajo, and he holds a master's degree from Harvard. His wife, Bella, is the only woman on the 87-member Navajo Tribal Council. "The Fairchild plant has 50,000 square feet," he says, "and this includes office space and the manufacturing area. It has loading docks, receiving docks and is wired for heavy manufacturing."

Ed continued, "When the company locked its doors, it made many of our people very unhappy. Why? Because AIM came onto our reservation, without our permission, and caused the management of the plant to move away. They came here with guns and little else. They had no alternative plans to help the people in the event the plant closed. Now they are all gone but the people must remain here.

"We have been trying to reopen the plant since the takeover in 1974 without success. But we have been unable to get another company to relocate here even though the plant has been repaired and rehabilitated for further use for whoever wants it."

The extreme poverty of the people who live here is obvious and one can understand the anger and frustration that surfaces because they have lost one of the few things that could have brought them prosperity.

Politics is Dominant Factor of Reservation Life

"Politics" seems to be a dirty word in any language. For so many years, "politicians" were synonymous with "rip-off" artists. Just when it appeared that elected officials were gaining respectability, a scandal would shatter the scenario and plunge the political activist back under the quagmire. Reservation politicians are no strangers to adversity.

In order to understand reservation politics more readily one must come to grips with some obvious differences between our form of government and other forms of government.

First, it should be understood that approximately 95 percent of all salaried people are working for some branch or agency of the federal government. Whether you work for tribal government, the Bureau of Indian Affairs, Public Health Service, Housing and Urban Development and so on and on, you are being paid directly or indirectly by the federal government.

Secondly, approximately 50 percent of the reservation population is unemployed. Many of these unemployed own large tracts of land which they lease to farmers and ranchers for a per-acre lease payment that gives them an annual income, once again, administered by the federal government. Those people who do not have lease income or no jobs must draw welfare money of some nature to survive. These are also federal dollars. No people in this area detest this total dependency on federal money more than the Indian people themselves.

When you hear talk of "self-determination" or sovereignty, it usually is because of an effort by Indian people to break this pattern of governmental control they have endured for two hundred years. In other words, the people are saying, "Stop using us as guinea pigs and let us begin to take control of our own lives; we certainly can't do any worse with it than you have; in fact, we might surprise you."

There are several reasons why politics has become such a dominant factor of reservation life. The very survival of an individual and his family can depend upon the political whims of the powers in office at any given time. In other words, if the power structure does not like the way you part your hair, or if the power structure has a relative who needs a job, you can very easily find yourself on the outside, looking in, and for no other reason than politics.

What makes this situation more difficult is that many very qualified Indian people are left without jobs or a future because too many unqualified politicians already have filled the positions. As one lady from Wanblee put it so picturesquely this week, "Many of our elected officials are so dumb that they couldn't find their rear ends if they had an instruction manual and a rear-view mirror." As you can see, it is the entire tribe that suffers in the long run because of this situation.

The situation I have described is not a pretty one. In fact, I can be accused of "hanging our dirty laundry out in public," but I have known for a long time that one of the main reasons these conditions are allowed to exist is because we have no form of news media on the reservations to keep the people informed. The lack of communications; hence, the inability to constructively criticize is one of our major problems.

Many people ask, "Why do you keep electing tribal officials who are not doing the job? It was you who voted them into office, so why complain?"

The blame for this also can be placed on the lack of communications. If we know nothing about the candidates, how can we make an intelligent decision when we vote? If we have no effective means of communication, how do we find out about the candidates' qualifications? It becomes a vicious circle.

It may be many years before "politics" becomes a respectable word. The one consolation we have on the reservation is that this is true of all forms of government throughout this country.

Councilman Newton Cummings and son

Chapter IX—Rights

Rights

Swiss Journalist Questions American Treatment of Indians

His name is Amleto Brunner. He is an inquisitive, sensitive and verbose newsman from Zurich, Switzerland. He asks a question, and like a tenacious English bulldog, hangs on until he gets an answer. He came to the United States to do a television story for the Swiss News Service on Indians in America.

Amleto wrote a letter to me with his impressions of Indians and of America. Here is a capsule report:

"Many people around the Indian Reservation were curious upon hearing of my intentions. Some betrayed fears I would go abroad telling bad news about the United States. Others expressed concern that I was doing a risky job by going to the reservation and spending time with that mean bunch. I think that both sides were expressing what may be a general feeling of uneasiness upon seeing a European coming to check, so to say, on how far Jimmy Carter's policies of human rights are respected within the United States.

"I did not come to the U.S. to tear down any portion of the glorious image the U.S. used to have, and partly retains, among Europeans. I came to verify the stories that were being told of the American Indians; but to do it from the Indian as well as the Whiteman's point of view.

"There are many things that left a profound impression on me. For instance, anywhere I traveled in Indian Country, not only on the Pine Ridge or Rosebud, but everywhere, I felt the quiet reserve of the Indian people. You called it shyness on the part of your people. I found this to be only partly true. Partly, because upon managing to break through that shyness, there was a tremendous amount of information about dissent, factionalism and concern among Indians. Many Indians deplored the fact that it was the government that brought these conditions about; and yet they were perplexed as to what could be done about it.

"It may be just democracy as many well-intentioned white people were inclined to say; but to me, it was democracy at its worst. It was a democracy that crippled the initiative of the minority by forcing them to defend the right to their land and resources against the overwhelming odds of big business and governmental collusion. I had always been taught that democracy meant an equal chance for everybody.

"I was a child of the late Thirties and I lived through the Nazi nightmare and the Allied victory. I was among the many thousands of youth who welcomed the GI's as liberators. I still feel that way! I met many fine war veterans during my stay in the U.S. and I dared to question them about the U.S. role in the world (We depend so much on the U.S. over here with the world split into adversary blocks, and us on the chasm of red slavery.) and I questioned Americans, young and old, on their views on the Indian problem.

"I left the United States after three months of very strenuous work. I investigated openly and honestly, without preconceived notions. I have left it with a deep concern: Is the United States so weak, is my question, that it does not respect the well-confined minorities of Indians as a different people? Can they not see the Indian, not as an enemy, but as an equal partner in human relations, cultural relations and political relations? It is my opinion that if the United States does not (and very soon) outgrow its Indian bias, it will have to face a major crisis, both at home and abroad.

"But I wouldn't be fair if I was to leave out another very important point. There is a readiness to discuss, and to accept even critical views from a stranger. This has amazed me and made my visit to the U.S. a happy one. Discussing issues as sensitive as the Indian issue is difficult even over here in Europe. The spirit of tolerance which is the very basis of democratic opinion, still lives in the U.S., and it has been very hard for me to leave this behind.

"I saw Indian reservations, such as yours, bereft of the media—the Indians having no voice, in a modern sense of the term. Crossing the borders of reservations always struck me as leaving the United States! Why this fearful attitude? Certainly, there must be plenty of news issues that would emerge if Indians were allowed to participate in the media. So many a bias would be broken down, such as the fear that is so prevalent between Indians and Whitemen, and among Indians themselves. I am simply dumbfounded that the United States, the fountain of democracy and free enterprise, has not, to this day, incorporated the Indian people into the concert of voices that comprise the media. How much longer will this be left up to 'others,' whoever they may be?

"These impressions from my visit in 1979 have been buzzing around in my mind since I left the United States and returned to Switzerland. I have great faith in the U.S., and I developed a great love for the reservation and the Indian people. Pilamaya!"

Reservations are Separate Nations within a Nation

So many times as I read about Indians in articles that are very profound and display a knowledge gained through long years of research and communication with different tribes in this country, I think to myself, "Why can't this information be spread across the pages of every major newspaper in the United States to insure that a better understanding between Indians and non-Indians will become the rule, rather than the exception?"

One such article was reprinted in *The Indian Historian* of San Francisco, California. It had been printed at the University of Michigan, Ann Arbor, School of Natural Resources in April of 1979, titled: *Fisheries and Native American and Northwest Experiences.* The presenter was Alvin M. Josephy, Jr., retired editor of American Heritage Books and now president of the Museum of the American Indian, Heye Foundation, New York City, an author of considerable renown.

Josephy is not an Indian, but has devoted his life to study and promotion of Indian culture. He has been a champion of the Indian people's struggle for survival for many years.

The purpose of this column is to provide information objectively about different problems facing Indian tribes in this country and give my readers an opportunity to evaluate that information to develop a better understanding of these problems. The premise is to point out there is a different point of view—the Indian's.

There is an old adage among the Plains Indians that goes: "Do not be my judge until you have walked a mile in my moccasins." Perhaps these "moccasins" can best be fitted to your feet if you can see "the other side of the story."

Over the next few columns, I would like to share from the paper presented by Josephy. I believe it is an important paper and contains the seeds of the historical differences between Indian and non-Indian. Hopefully, a brighter light can be focused on the shadowy areas of some of these differences.

Josephy's text begins: "Recently, I was reviewing the transcript of the hearings before the House of Representatives Subcommittee on Fisheries and Wildlife Conservation and the Environment of the Merchant Marines and Fisheries committee, held at Petoskey, Michigan, January 13, 1978. The following caught my eye—it was just a sentence or two in the testimony of Dr. Howard Tanner, director of the Michigan Department of Natural Resources. Sometimes it is unfair and misleading to quote out of context, but this statement really stands on its own and parenthetical to the thrust and substance of Dr. Tanner's full testimony:

"'Based on an everchanging Indian policy and trust responsibility,' said Dr. Tanner, 'The federal government now is fostering self-determination for Indian people. Put another way, the policy of self-determination translates into the establishment of a separate nation within a nation and superior rights for a small segment of our society.'"

Josephy continues: "There are fundamental errors in that statement, but in many ways it is about as relevant as anything can be to the purposes and aims of this symposium—for it reflects the great need of gatherings such as this one—that can cast light on darkness, supplant misinformation with truth, and, by friendly discussion and exchange of opinions and explanations, erode or eliminate contention and adversary relationships that have been based on ignorance, prejudice or self-interest so strong as to have precluded an understanding of anything save what one has wished to believe."

Next: Josephy's comments on the differences between Indians and non-Indians from the time of Columbus and how varied perceptions affected resource development.

Josephy Explains Indian-non-Indian Differences

As published in *The Indian Historian*, Vol. 12, No. 3 for the summer of 1979, an article by Alvin Josephy, Jr. referred to the historical and cultural context of White-Native American conflicts. Josephy, a longtime advocate of Indian rights, is an author and president of the Museum of the American Indian, Heye Foundation, in New York City.

Josephy began by looking at the problems existing between Indians and non-Indians from a historical point of view: "From the time of Columbus, almost five full centuries ago, until the last few years, very few Whites have either wanted to, or been able to try to see the world through Native American eyes. Very few have had any motive to try understanding, much less appreciating, the relationship of a Native American tribe, community, or family to its own universe, as that group perceived it to be, or its points of view and needs, usually stemming from that spiritual relationship, as they affected the Native Americans' actions and reactions in any particular aspect of their daily life of contact with Whites. Non-Indians, by and large, from 1492 until today, have inevitably viewed Native Americans and interpreted their words, deeds lifeways, and values from their own Euro-American perspective. It has led to endless misunderstandings, frictions, and conflicts, including many that are with us today and continue to plague the relationships between Native Americans and the rest of the American population."

He continued, "Within the present-day United States, such ethnocentricity (if we can call it that), began even before the days of Jamestown and Plymouth. To the Spaniards in the Southeast and Southwest (Ponce de Leon, De Soto, and their successors) the Native Americans were alien, strange, heathenish, and different, and the Europeans equated being different with being inferior. The Indians were to be converted, conquered and impressed as inferiors. If they resisted, they were to be exterminated. The French were more benign. Though many of them also viewed the Indians as inferiors, in fact as children of nature, and converted and asserted dominance over them, the dynamics of the fur trade demanded dependent, but relatively content, Indian fur suppliers. Above all other Europeans, the French made the greatest efforts to see the world as the Indians saw it."

Josephy began to draw a comparison of the treatment of Indians by other Europeans as regards religion and the use of the land: "Along the Atlantic Coast, the Dutch and English traders and settlers carried on the legacy of the Spaniards and immediately established the heritage of misunderstanding, stereotypic thinking, and conflicts that still pervade White-Native American relations within the United States. The first of these, again, was that the Indians, being different, were inferior. But that inferiority often translated into fear that the wilderness man, the Indian, with his free, seemingly simple, and unChristian way of life would corrupt the European settler and the society the European had come to erect in the New World."

Josephy then focused on the land and the resources. "Divine guidance told the settlers that they were to multiply and replenish the earth. If Indians were not physically dwelling on and planting the earth, it was being wasted. The Whites could take it and use it themselves, buying it from Indians, if, indeed, they could find Indians who claimed ownership of it. Or, if the Indians refused to sell it, they could take it by force."

The perceptions of the land were observed in a totally different manner by the Whites and the Indians and so Josephy expounded on this apparent difference: "Much of the land, of course, contained hunting grounds or fishing stations; but the Whites came to regard it as wasteland, and the so-called 'right of the huntsman' became secondary to the right of the agriculturist. So was born the concept of "the highest and best use" of a resource, which is with us yet, especially with regard to the use of water in the arid West of today."

My next column will deal with Josephy's interpretation of the rationale behind the first White and Indian wars.

Puritans Created Incorrect Images

(Third of a series of five columns about Indian-non-Indian relationships.)

At some point in the history of man, there has to be a beginning, a first set of circumstances that set a precedent and, whether right or wrong, establish a policy that will soon be adopted by the many.

In the past two columns, I have been sharing with you the writings of Alvin Josephy, a noted author and longtime advocate of Indian rights.

It is the contention of Josephy, and of many other Indian historians, that the relationships between Indians and whites could have taken a far different turn if a set of occurrences in the 1600s had been predicated by an attempt at misunderstanding.

It was the misfortune of the Pequot Indians, of what is now Connecticut, that the first contact they had with white settlers involved the Puritans.

Puritan Writings

Josephy feels that this was important because "Puritan writings on the Pequot War are not only part of the standard history of the beginnings of New England, but they created images of Indians which, though largely false, were carried westward from frontier to frontier and persist even to this generation."

"As an example of what Puritan history did not bequeath to us, however, is the fact that Massachusetts Bay settlers, in the New World only seven years, began a war against the Pequots without any logical reason by attacking a Pequot village and killing men, women and children," Josephy stated. "When the bewildered Indians, who up to then had not warred on women and children, asked if the English intended to kill their women and children, the English lieutenant, Lion Gardiner, replied fatefully, 'the Indians would see that thereafter.' " From then on it was total war.

Three Options

Also, from then on, the American Indians were given three options: (1) they could be assimilated into the white society and disappear as Indians; (2) they could be relocated or moved much farther westward so that they could have no contact with the whites (out of sight, out of mind); or (3) extermination.

Josephy's transcrit sums up what occurred in the ensuing years because of these three options:

"From the time of the close of the colonial wars, these three threads run through the long course of white-Native American relations. Though it would seem to some that extermination was the strongest of these threads, actually American policy since the founding of the Republic has pursued assimilation unwaveringly as its principal goal. From one administration to the next, changing ideas regarding how to bring about assimilation have caused wild zigzaggings in programs and surface policies. For a long time, the goal was to isolate Indians under agents, missionaries, and educators who would work to assimilate them. The Dawes Act of 1887 hoped to speed the process by breaking up the reservations into small allotments on which individual Indian families would become farmers and live like whites.

Josephy's Analysis

There is no way that I can improve upon Josephy's analysis of the relationship between the whites and Indians during this period in history:
"For decades, repression of almost every sort was visited on the captive and isolated native peoples. Their traditional governmental and religious structures of society were smashed and obliterated. Their leaders were punished, exiled or killed. Their religious ceremonies were banned. Their children were shanghaied away from them, sent to white-run schools where they were punished if they spoke their own language. Rations were withheld on reservations for the smallest sign of opposition. Church and State were combined, possibly the only time in our national history, and missionaries and agents, backed by troops, created tyrannies on reservations, unquestioned and unchecked by any organ of government. Indian arts, crafts, legends, lore, music, dance and other elements of tribal and group culture were discouraged, mocked or proscribed."
In my next column we'll take a look at "termination" and "self-determination."

Reservation Status Cause for Concern

(Fourth in a series of five articles)
Is self-determination a prelude to termination? Many Indians look at the very word "self-determination" and they say among themselves, "If you remove 'self' and 'de' from the beginning of the word, you end up with 'termination.'" This is a genuine concern among many reservation Indians. They look back on the history of the 1950s and compare the mental attitudes of that genertion with those of today and see a striking similarity in the bureaucratic posture of then and now.
Program after program was visited upon the reservations of this country by the faceless and nameless bureaucrats in Washington, D.C., and the attitude seemed to be: "If this doesn't work out, we'll try something else." Through all of this, the Indian people had no voice or representation at the congressional meetings that decided their fate. The input at these hearings was supplied by

white agents, and missionaries. No one ever asked the people whose lives were to be so drastically affected, the Indian people, whether they agreed or disagreed with these decisions.

It was during the Eisenhower administration that termination became the byword. The Klamath Indians of Oregon and the Menominees of Wisconsin were two of the large tribes that had their reservations "terminated." The rich timber lands of the Klamath people were absorbed by the huge timber interests of that state and the Klamath people ceased to exist as a tribe. The Menominees fought the federal government with all of the legal means they could muster, and became the first Indian tribe in this country to regain their status as a tribal entity after they had been "terminated." This victory by the Menominees brought an end to the termination era. Scratch one more government experimment!

Treaties Forgotten

For generations, the Indians were "out of sight, out of mind" on reservations set aside for them. The contemporary generations of white forgot all the legal treaties and promises made to the tribes. They were treaties made by a generation long since dead, was the attitude, and since this generation had nothing to do with the treaties, they would have absolutely no bearing on their present lives. Everyone forgot these dusty treaties, except the Indian people; they never forgot.

Alvin Josephy, noted author and supporter of Indian rights, said in his paper published by *The Indian Historian*, "It was not history to them, not something for the life of a single man. It was for their people, for their children and their children's children."

For many generations the Indian was a captive in his own land. According to Josephy, the Indian was "a helpless and powerless ward, unable to assert his rights, unable to protect himself, or maintain his rights, unable to make the white man carry out the solemn guarantees made to him, but in many episodes the BIA colluded in flagrant violations of Indian rights, ignoring laws that supposedly protected Indians and their property, entering into unjust contracts for Indian resources, and waiving Indian interests in actions and adjudications and illegally appropriated Indian property."

Clearer Understanding

Josephy leads us into the era of "self-determination" by surmising, "The fact that history has come back to haunt the white man of 1980 is not the Indians' fault. We now begin to understand a little more clearly, the move to self-determination. As that drive got under way and gathered momentum in the 1960s and 1970s, the tribes began to push aside their so-called protectors who had failed to carry out their trust obligations, and with the help of lawyers of their own began to act for themselves. Their object was not to assert new rights or expanded rights, but to gain recognition and acceptance of rights that they had always had or that had been promised them and then illegally taken from them. Just because the non-Indian population had forgotten about Indians and their rights did not mean they were dead."

My final column in this series will take a brief look at the volatile 1970s and a glimpse at the promise of the 1980s.

Some Confrontations Result in Violence

(Final of five columns on Indian-non-Indian relationships)

You can still see the bumper stickers on the highway. They read: "Red Power," "Custer wore Arrow shirts," "Hands off my natural resources," or "Remember Wounded Knee."

They are the grim reminders of the confrontations that began in the late 1960s and continued into the middle 1970s.

The occupation of Alcatraz, Wounded Knee and the Fairchild Plant, the riots at the Custer County and Minnehaha County courthouses, culminated by the violent deaths of two FBI agents near Oglala, South Dakota are the legacy of these times.

History Will Judge

History will judge whether the violent confrontations spearheaded by the American Indian Movement, have helped or hurt the cause of the Native Americans.

Alvin Josephy, author and president of the Museum of the American Indian in New York City, summed up his 1979 article in *The Indian Historian* by saying:

"The attorney general is questioning whether the Supreme Court, and the entire United States Government, throughout the two hundred years of the nation's relations with Indians, have been all wrong.

"He has publicly advanced the proposal that the federal government should abandon the trust obligation. That course, on which he is now working, leads in one direction: farewell to treaties, to treaty obligations, to reservations, to tribes and to Indians.

"The White House is silent. There is no Indian policy today. The administration is waiting for the attorney general to make his case.

"It is a case that most directly stems from the backlash against Indians which, in turn, has resulted from the Native Americans' vigorous assertion of their rights. Politically, Indians are no longer 'in.' They are 'out.'"

Two Short Stories

Here are two short stories that lead up to a point:

—In the late 1960s, at a convention of the National Congress of American Indians, several members of that organization were confronted by a young, militant Indian (who would soon become known all over this country) and ridiculed for wearing western, modern attire.

Wearing jeans, a weather-beaten jacket, braids and topped by a beaded headband, the militant proclaimed: "When will you learn to dress like real Indians?" One of the officers of the NCAI listened patiently and then said sadly: "If you want to dress like a real Indian, get rid of that beaded headband, because only the women of our tribe wore those things."

—While campaigning for office, the current president of the Oglala Sioux Tribe, Stanley Looking Elk, was asked by me to appear on a radio show. His reply: "No, I couldn't do that because my people would not want me to; I am a traditional Indian and there were no radios back in the old days."

I asked Stanley a question at this point: "How did you get to work this morning?" He replied: "In my pickup." To which I retorted: "You should have ridden a horse or walked, because there were no pickups back in the old days either. If you're going to be traditional, don't be selective about it."

Indians Differ

My point is this: Indians come in all shapes, sizes and colors. They have hundreds of different beliefs and philosophies. Richard Little, from Oglala, South Dakota, put it this way: "It's not what you have on the outside that makes you an Indian (at this point he swept his hand across his face and over his body) but (placing his hand over his heart) it is here, inside, that makes you an Indian."

Those who profess to be traditionalists can learn much from the Pueblo Indians of New Mexico. You will find, in the center of their villages, the Kiva, a ceremonial house, even to this day. Go back to the ancient ruins of the Chaco civilization, 1,000 years ago, and you will discover that these ancestors of the modern Pueblo Indians had a Kiva at the center of their villages also.

These Pueblo Indians have learned to maintain the strongest ties with their religion and culture, and yet, compete and survive in the modern world.

Travel across this country and stop at any reservation or in any city where there are many Indians and ask: "What will it take for the Indian people to survive? You may get a lot of different answers; but if you listen very carefully, they all will be saying the same thing: "Unity."

Indian Holocaust Began in 1492

An artist from Sioux City, Iowa painted a portrait entitled "The Madonna of the Holocaust."

Dan Paulos said that he did the painting because "it is a sad chapter in human history that none of us should ever forget." The painting shows a beautiful lady superimposed over a swastika, and in the foreground nude people marching to their deaths in the gas chambers.

If you read the history books of this country, you will not find out about the holocaust that has beset the Native Americans of this Western Hemisphere.

The holocaust began in 1492, and if allowed to continue, will have reached five hundred years of unabated genocide in 1992. Did you know that there are Indian people being killed even today in Brazil and other South American countries because covetous eyes have been cast upon their lands?

When the white man first landed on this continent, he estimated the population of the Native Americans to be somewhere around three million. Archaeologists have studied this and placed that number at seven to eight million. At one time the population of Indians in this country was reduced to less than 200,000. What happened to the millions of native peoples that once inhabited this country?

In the name of "Manifest Destiny" bounties were placed on the heads of men, women and children and they were hunted down like animals and slaughtered. Entire towns and villages were pillaged and burned to make room for progress—the white man's progress.

A philosophy developed that was labeled "frontier mentality" by Attorney Ramon Roubideaux. This attitude was that the land was there for the taking and the original inhabitants had to be exterminated at any cost to relieve them of these lands.

A few years back I was reviewing a history book that was being used at Douglas High School. The maps of the United States for the 1700s showed the vast areas of the great Southwest and were marked in several places as "uninhabited." What of the Navajos, the Hopis and the other countless Indian tribes that lived since time immemorial in this territory?

Chief Dan George, an actor, talked about the white man giving gifts of blankets to his tribe. The blankets were laced with a disease which he figures was typhoid, and as a result, more than 2,000 members of his tribe, including most of his direct ancestors, died. This was not an isolated incident; but stories of this nature can be found across this country and repeated by many other tribes.

Was this the beginning of germ warfare?

Mr. Rupert Costo, a Cahuilla Indian, publisher of *Wassaja* and *The Indian Historian* of San Francisco, figures the Indian population was placed much lower than it really was so the tremendous numbers of Indians who were eliminated would not appear to be so high and history would not label this catastrophe so harshly.

In his novel, *Genocide in Northwestern California* published by The Indian Historian Press, Jack Norton, the author, says, "The rape of the environment was the legacy left by these remarkable argonauts of the West, who came to conquer a continent and left a unique and fruitful land a rotted stubble."

It took a few centuries for the white man to include in literature the cruelties of slavery and other gross incidents against the black population of this country; but history books should reflect the bad as well as the good things that occurred in the development of a country.

History should never be slanted to eliminate the "warts."

The young people of this country have every right to know what their ancestors did to the red man and as artist Dan Paulos said about his painting,

"It is a sad chapter in human history that none of us should ever forget."

'Tribunal' to Hear Rights Violations

The Fourth Russell Tribunal will be held in Rotterdam, Holland, from November 24 to 29 this year. The Tribunal is gathering this year to discuss, and present before a 'jury,' the violations of the rights of the Indians of the Americas.

For those of you not familiar with the Russell Tribunals, I will give a little background. This Tribunal was established by Bertrand Russell in 1963. It made headlines around the world in 1967 when it held an inquiry into U.S. involvement in Vietnam. Members of the jury, which condemned the United States, included Russell, Jean Paul Sartre and DeBeauvoir. The Tribunal feels that it was this trial intended to bring world opinion to bear upon this country, which caused the Vietnam War to come to an end.

The inaugural speech given by Jean Paul Sartre for the first Tribunal stated, "We're perfectly aware that we have not been given a mandate by anyone. We are powerless; that is the guarantee of our independence. There is nothing to help us except for the participation of the supporting committees which are, like ourselves, meetings of private individuals. As we do not represent any government or party, we cannot receive orders. We will examine the facts in our souls and our consciences, as we say, or if one prefers, in the full liberty of our spirits."

Evidence Readied

Representatives from Indian tribes and organizations from Canada, America, Central and South America will present evidence of violations "of the rights and autonomy, laid down in treaties, of these people," according to the Tribunal magazine.

Several Indian attorneys will present legal opinions on treaty violations to the Tribunal panel. Tim Coulter, an Indian attorney for the Indian Law Resource Center, Washington, D.C., in an interview with Claus Biegert of Gessellschaft fur bedrohte Voker (Germany) is quoted, "If the U.S. government has the power to take away all of an Indian Nation's land without compensation, then the U.S., having that power, is in a position to force those native people to give up almost anything in order to avoid a threat. The threat is often used. For example, in the land claims situation, the U.S. commonly threatens to simply take away all of the claimed lands, unless the Indians involved agree to give them up voluntarily and accept only a small part of what is rightfully theirs."

Coulter continued, "So, to sum it up, in our view, unless we are able to take away from the U.S. the power that it now has to simply take Indian land, it will be extremely difficult to begin attacking other aspects of the problem of the U.S. dealings with native people. As long as the U.S. has this power, very little else can be done."

What possible purpose do these hearings hope to serve? According to the Tribunal publication, the following results are expected from the inquiry into the violation of the rights of Indians:

1. Better conditions for the Indians to develop themselves according to their own discernments, culturally, politically and socio-economically.

2. More help and understanding in their struggle against colonization, exploitation and extermination.

3. All over the world, more objective information about the situation of the Indians in order to change the biased image created by mass media and "Hollywood."

4. More attention to the rights of minorities in comparable situations in other countries.

International representatives from many countries, including Belgium, Canada, Denmark, Germany, France, Holland, Italy the United Kingdom and the United States, are expected to attend the week-long conference.

Indian Rights Violated

This spring, the Indian Law Resource Center, Washington, D.C., submitted a complaint to Secretary-General Kurt Waldheim of the United Nations on behalf of the traditional Seminoles, Haudinousaunee, Hopi, Western Shoshone and the Lakota Nation concerning the violations of human rights perpetrated against these people by the United States of America.

The complaint charged the United States with grossly violating the Indian people's right to own property, the right to equal protection of the laws, the right to be free from racial discrimination, and the right to an effective remedy for violations of fundamental rights.

Attorneys Curtis Berkey, Robert Coulter and Steven Tullberg submitted the complaint to the United Nations after they had tried to resolve these complaints through all of the remedies available to them.

Redress Attempted

The complaint reads, "All of the victims in this communication have attempted to redress the numerous violations of their human rights by resorting to domestic remedies within the United States legal system. In all cases, these legal and administrative efforts have been futile. All domestic remedies have proven totally ineffective either because no relief was provided or the proceedings were unreasonably prolonged. Instead of vindicating their rights, the United States has ignored their complaints or summarily denied their efforts to obtain relief. No alternative exists but to bring these violations to the attention of the United Nations Human Rights Commission."

One of the major concerns in the complaint is the distinction drawn between Indian lands and non-Indian lands. The lack of protection given to Indian lands is in sharp contrast to the protection given to non-Indian lands.

The "trust responsibility" assumed by the Department of the Interior over Indian lands has become rife with "conflicts of interest."

Opponent's Ballgame

"It's like being in a ballgame where your opponent owns the ball, the court and then officiates the game," comments Louie Bad Wound of the Lakota Treaty Council. He added, "Not only that, but they can change the rules of the game to suit themselves whenever they choose to do so."

For instance, as the power of the United States increased, it began to assume "eminent domain" over the lands. Although there was no legal basis in domestic law or international law for this assertion, the courts of the United States refused to question its fairness or validity. Eventually, that position came to be regarded as the law of the land.

The complaint gives this example of specific violation: "The expropriation of the Black Hills by the United States in violation of the 1868 Treaty constitutes a violation of the right to own property."

Right 'Extinguished'

"The action of the Indian Claims Commission arbitrarily extinguishing the right of the Lakota Nation to recover the Black HIlls constitutes a violation of the right to own property, the right to be free from racial discrimination and the right to equal protection of the laws. The advocacy by the United States of a rule of law which leaves the land of the Lakota Nation legally unprotected against artibrary expropriation by the United States constitutes a violation of the right to own property, the right to equal protection of the law, and the right to be free from racial discrimination."

As a fierce advocate of Indian rights, Louis Bad Wound summed up the complaint saying, "The charges against the United States will be heard by the member nations of the United Nations so that we can let the whole world know that the expression "human rights" means nothing in this country, and if we cannot get justice within our own legal system, we will seek justice in the court of world opinion."

"Frontier Mentality" of Public Officials Noted

The "Frontier mentality" of a United States Senator, governor and attorney general from the state of South Dakota came shining through this past week.

When we studied U.S. government in high school at the Holy Rosary Mission on the Pine Ridge Reservation, we were taught that we elected representatives to the senate and the house to represent all of the people in their respective states, not just their rich and powerful white constituency. There has been no support for the rights of the Indian people by any elected official since James Abourezk decided to resign.

It comes as no great surprise to the Indian people that Governor William Janklow would resort to name calling (he called the Indian people 'pigs') because of his impotency in the face of different sites in the Black Hills being occupied by different Indian groups. Didn't he use the Indian people as "whipping boys" when he campaigned for the governor's office?

Indian people have not forgotten the television commercial he ran statewide depicting law enforcement officers striking Indians with night sticks while a smooth background voice assures the people, "When South Dakota needed law and order, Bill Janklow was there." He was attorney general at the time and instead of trying to ease the tensions between Indian and white, he used the unrest and the backlash to fuel his campaign, and in the process, created a chasm between Indian and whites that has not been bridged to this date.

Attorney General Mark Meierhenry is a willing disciple of Janklow, and although he has not resorted to outright racist attacks upon the Indians of the state, his subtle actions and implications are much more sophisticated, and probably more dangerous.

Why isn't Senator Jim Abdnor, R-SD, working with all factions within the state to alleviate the problems existing between Indians and non-Indians instead of making statements designed to arouse resentment against Indians? He said, "Our patience with Indian groups occupying various Black HIlls sites is starting to wear very thin."

What about the patience of the Indian tribes? Haven't they been trying to get their day in court for over one hundred years? Justice can only be suppressed for so long, and then patience will "start to wear very thin." Patience is not an exclusive property of the white man. Why hasn't Abdnor been fighting to get his Indian constituency their day in court? Maybe the legal questions of rightful ownership to the Black Hills would be answered once and for all if the Oglala Sioux Tribe would be given the opportunity to present its case in a court of law.

Attorney General Meierhenry, in the meantime, has taken it upon himself to ridicule the reservations of this state without reason. In an interview with a reporter from *The Rocky Mountain News* of Denver, he said, "Sioux leaders should forget about owning the Black Hills and encourage their young to leave the reservation and get into mainstream America. There is no hope for the Oglala who insist on living at Pine Ridge. It's a terrible nothing place. It's so damned bleak there. The kids are programmed for poverty."

Meierhenry is ridiculing the home of more than 14,000 Indian people when he talks like this. While many tribal leaders are trying to encourage their young to get an education, stay on the reservation and improve the standards of living, and try to make the reservation a progressive, prosperous place to live, the attorney general insults the intelligence and the integrity of the people of the reservation with his backhanded comments.

Meierhenry's "frontier mentality" becomes obvious when he talks about law and order from his lofty position as the state's number one law enforcement officer. He told *The Rocky Mountain News*, "The state police are ten times better prepared today to deal with violence on the reservation than they were in 1973. They have been trained in riot control and in Indian behavior." He is also convinced the Oglala "don't have the money to act violently."

The offshoot of the negative rhetoric by these, supposedly, responsible officials elected to serve all of the people of the state of South Dakota, is that the bigots are now beginning to climb out of the woodwork convinced they have the blessings of the government to strike out at Indian people.

Indian people leaving the Pine Ridge Reservation to shop in Rapid City via highway 44 are being harrassed by non-Indians who can best be described as "rednecks." They are being called filthy names, and in some case, physically attacked.

Could it be that these "dyed-in-the-wool" politicians are looking down the road to the 1982 political campaign, and in the process are lining up their favorite targets, the Indian people, to advance their political ambitions? For the sake of peace and harmony in this state, I hope not.

I, for one, feel sorry for any politician who would advance his political ambitions by using racist tactics, creating an atmosphere of hate and distrust between Indians and whites, and by laying the groundwork for a violent confrontation.

Athletic Team Names No Honor for Indians

Over seven years ago a movement began at Stanford University, Palo Alto, California, to have the team name, "Indians," removed. For twenty years, a Yurok Indian by the name of Timm Williams, called Chief Lightfoot, romped around on the playing fields at Stanford, his Sioux war bonnet flowing behind him, and effectively promoted the image of an Indian mascot.

The Indian students at Stanford felt highly insulted by this treatment, and so they set out to bring it to an end. They did this quietly, without fanfare, and eventually persuaded the administration of Stanford to remove the name "Indian" from the athletic teams.

Now, it seems, there are those who would revive the idea of Indians serving as mascots. In fact, T-shirts reading "Bring Back Chief Lightfoot" are appearing on the campus. One Palo Alto newspaper attacked this trend to revert to the past by saying, "Native Americans are people, not symbols for athletic teams. To stereotype them, for whatever reason and in whatever manner, is an affront to common decency and courtesy.

The Stanford Indian students got together and issued a statement which was passed out all over the campus. It read in part, "We, the Native American community at Stanford, do not want to be insulted by demeaning caricatures and stereotyping images of us. We do not want our customs and beliefs demeaned through inappropriate and inaccurate use by people who do not understand them."

Human Beings

The statement concludes, "All we want is to be treated like human beings. We had hoped that after seven years, we would have finally overcome this issue. Obviously, we have not. We would like to settle this issue once and for all, but we cannot do it without your help."

I suppose that the only other race of people used as a mascot for a major university is the "Fighting Irish" of Notre Dame. Can you think of any other athletic team named after an ethnic group?

A lot of people fail to realize that it does not end with the Stanford Indians. There are the Washington "Redskins," St. Johns "Redmen," North Dakota "Sioux," Cleveland "Indians," the Utes, Seminoles, and the list goes on and on.

Now one could ask this question: "Why have the Native people of this continent been singled out for this questionable honor? In the name of fair play and equality, shouldn't this special recognition be spread around to other races?

80 Percent Black

For instance: the population of Washington, D.C. is about 80 percent black. What better honor for them than to have the name of their football team changed to the Washington "Blackskins"? Or, perhaps, since the State of Minnesota has such a large Scandanavian population, their team could be called the Minnesota "Whiteskins" or the more colorful "Minnesota Honkies." Using this sort of logic, it is only reasonable that San Francisco, with its large Oriental population, should become the San Francisco "Yellowskins."

When you begin to spread this racial balance of athletic team names around a little, and give all races of people a shot at this special honor, the possibilities become endless. Since individual tribes (Sioux, Seminoles, Utes, etc.) have been accorded the privilege of serving as mascots for college and professional teams, why not let indivdual races of the many immigrants to this country also be included in this array of names?

The Cleveland Indians could be recognized as the Cleveland "Germans," or the Chicago Bears could become the Chicago "Polacks." How about the Los Angeles "Mexican Americans"? As a matter of fact, I think that the New York "Italians" has sort of a nice ring to it.

Many Laughed

Seven years ago, many people laughed at the Indian students at Stanford University for speaking out against such a time-worn tradition as using an "Indian" for a team name and a mascot. The students managed to find a few sympathetic administrators who took the time to put themselves into the shoes of the Indian people, and began to realize that this was not an honor; but a gross insult.

Please do not think that this article is intended to point slurs at any racial or ethnic group of people. Instead, it is intended to show that Indian people have put up with this type of stereotyping and labeling longer than we care to remember. Perhaps it is time that the college and professional teams who have relegated our people to the role of mascots, wake up, and realize that they are not bringing honor to us; but they are insulting us.

As the Stanford University Indian students said, "All we want is to be treated like human beings."

Gunnery Range Taken from Sioux;
Pete Torres Was Friend To All

At the beginning of World War II, the U.S. government decided it needed some South Dakota land close to Rapid City Air Force Base (as Ellsworth Air Force Base was called in those days) for the pilots of the fighters and bombers to practice with live bombs and ammunition.

The closest and easiest land for them to acquire was land on the Pine Ridge Indian Reservation. After the land selection was made, entire families were uprooted from their homes, forced to sell off their cattle and horses, abandon many possessions they did not have the means to move, and left to shift for themselves as best they could.

The land that used to be their home was renamed "The Bombing Range" and young GI's from across this country soon began to bomb and strafe the shacks and cabins that once rang with the laughter of Indian children, blasting many of them from the face of the earth.

Some of those homeless families moved in with relatives on the Pine Ridge Reservation or other reservations, and others migrated to the cities in search of jobs, and a roof over their heads.

The long fight these families have had with the federal government to regain their lost lands after the war ended is one more horror story on a long list. The total disregard for the human rights of the Indian people involved is typical of the extremely shoddy treatment given the American Indian when he has taken the word of Washington, D.C. politicians.

It would be impossible for me to do justice to the details of a story as inhumane and as filled with injustice and intrigue as the acquisition of the "Gunnery Range" lands in this column. It is one story I hope to pursue to the fullest because it is a dark and nasty tale of the dealings of the federal government with the American Indians, which should be reported in all of its grisly details.

The young men and women who had lived on these lands were some of the first to volunteer for the armed forces during World War II, and they fought long and hard to defend this country from the enemy, many of them laying down their lives in the cause. The Indians of the reservations were decorated with more ribbons and medals of valor than any other group in the state of South Dakota.

Rights   319

The Families of Rapid Creek

In the days during the 1940s and 1950s, one could travel the length of Rapid Creek in South Dakota and find the Indians, Mexicans, and the poor white trash families of Rapid City. They lived in tar-paper shacks and clapboard cabins without running water. They heated these dwellings with wood burning stoves, lighted them with kerosene lamps and candles, and kept out the cold winds with rolled up blankets and newpapers stuffed in the cracks.

All the way from Saddle Rock, near the packing plant, past Osh Kosh Camp, by the railroad bridges, and out to the old fair grounds these poor people could be found.

One family, the Torres', had migrated to this country from Leon-Guanijueto, Mexico in 1930. They had one son named Pedro Pasqual Torres, called "Pete" by his friends.

Pete used to say, "When we first came to the United States, we stopped on the Pine Ridge Reservation at a place named Wanblee. An Indian family named Zimiga took us in and helped us until we could get on our feet.

"My father always used to tell us to always respect the Indian people because they were the first, and the only ones to open up their homes to us and feed us even though they had very little themselves."

One thing used to bother Pete, and he spoke about it more than once. He would say, "I came to the U.S. from a foreign country, and yet, for many years, not too long ago, I could walk into any bar in Rapid City and buy a beer. Here were my Indian friends who had lived here long before the white man, and they couldn't even buy a beer because it was against the law to serve an Indian alcohol." Pete didn't like that one bit, and he never got used to it.

Pete passed away eight days before he turned sixty-eight. He was buried in Rapid City October 17, 1980. Although he had moved to Grand Island, Nebraska and had lived there for many years, it was evident he had practiced the advice given to him by his father.

Many of his longtime Indian friends attended his wake, and stood by his coffin with bowed heads that day.

Tony Whirlwind Horse Sees New Attack on Rights

In order to retain his position as the Bureau of Indian Affairs Superintendent of Pine Ridge Agency, Anthony Whirlwind Horse had to take on the entire legal staff of the BIA. When his brother, Elijah, was elected president of the Oglala Sioux Tribe, the BIA ruled that it was a conflict of interest for Tony to stay on as superintendent, and asked him to transfer or resign. Tony decided to challenge this order, fought the BIA in federal court, and won his case. He is still the Pine Ridge Agency superintendent.

In many ways, his job is an unenviable one. Oftentimes he is caught between the tribe and the federal government, and he is forced to take stands that are unpopular. Called a "collaborator" by the more militant Indians, he has had to grit his teeth and make his important decisions the only way he knows how:

fairly and objectively.

Tony was in a reflective mood when I spoke with him last week, and like many of us, he was suffering from a case of the "post-election blues." He predicted that the mood of the country will cause "a total revamping of Public Law 93-638 (Indian Education and Self-determination Act), and this conservative change will cause many hardships and problems for the Indian people."

A pagmatic man with a contagious sense of humor, Tony was very blunt in his assessment of things to come. He said, "We know that there will be changes at the top levels of administrators in Washington, D.C. and we can expect that these new leaders will take a long, hard look at the effectiveness and the progress of reservation law enforcement procedures under the contract method, and this hold true for the two schools (Loneman and Little Wound) which are operating as contract schools. If the problems outweigh the progress, then do you know what they will say?" He continued, "They will say that they let the BIA try it, and it didn't succeed, and then they let the tribe try it and it failed, so now they will let the state of South Dakota try it.

"The trend under Reagan to strengthen state's rights will mean a renewed assault upon the rights of the Indian tribes," Whirlwind Horse stressed, "The tribal leadership has to stop this penny ante bickering over petty things, and start looking at the future on a priority basis. The Lakota people have to stop talking about unity, and start practicing it."

Whirlwind Horse feels that the attorney general and the governor of South Dakota have a strong tendency to take the smallest issues concerning Indian tribes, such as free food offered to voters in this past election and bend these issues to advance and enhance their own political aspirations.

Tribal Attorney Mario Gonzalez put it another way. "Many of our people have to travel great distances to come in to the polls and vote, and it has always been our custom to give a free feed on occasions such as this. If the attorney general has any specific charges to make, then he should quit making political hay with it, file his charges in court, and prove them or shut up about them." He concluded, "Since 1974, certain state officials have been attempting to intimidate Indian voters with flagrant charges based upon scare tactics, and we're getting a little bit sick and tired of this violation of our civil and of our voting rights."

Both Whirlwind Horse and Gonzalez summed up their feelings about the new administration with five words, "Look out for state jurisdiction."

Youths Win

Congratulations are in order for the fine runners of the Little Wound Cross Country Team which won the State B championships for the second year in a row. Congratulations to Myron Ghost Bear who had the "grit" to win his race on a badly sprained ankle, and of course, special kudos to Coach Dave Archambault for the job he has done with this young team.

While I am busy handing out congratulatory messages, I must pay a special tribute to the Lone Eagle Singers of Martin. Headed up by Enos Poor Bear, Jr., with Lemert and Gerard Brown Eyes, Harold Dean Salway and Larry Red Shirt singing and drumming, this group won first prize at the huge Pow-wow held in Las Vegas, Nevada. Competing with singers from dozens of different tribes from all over the United States, these young Oglala singers captured the $1,000 first prize. According to Enos Poor Bear, Sr., "The competition was really tough, and it is a special honor for these boys to come away with the first prize. Hau!"

Wrong Words Used in History Books

In the history books we used at the Indian mission where I went to elementary and high school, there was one word which appeared whenever the books touched upon the subject of warfare between the whites and the Indians. Whenever a battle of historic significance was described (usually called a "massacre" when Indians won) the Indian combatants were refered to as "hostiles."

Surely the authors of these textbooks must have had a vague idea that some of the students learning history in this country were of Indian heritage. This caused me to wonder if the word "hostile" was intended to appease the Indian people by identifying the "hostiles" as a group separate from the so-called "friendlies," another term prevalent in American history books.

Who exactly were these "hostiles" and what made them so different from the "friendlies"? What is revered as "patriotism" in the white soceity; e.g., defense of home and country, giving one's life for a just cause, protecting the defenseless women and children, was not called "patriotism" when the Indain warriors used it as a last resort to save their country from the invaders. If they rolled over and played dead for the white man, surrendered peaceably, and embraced the white man's religion and philosophy, these warriors then became "friendlies." However, if they resisted the invasion, and fought to the death to defend their homelands, the became known as "hostiles." This is what we learned in our American history classes.

Another Misconception

There is another misconception of history which is accepted as fact because it has been taught to many generations of children and is repeated even to this day. Usually, the text book refers to this incident as the time in history when "the Indians" sold Manhattan Island to the "Dutch."

For those of you who are interested, the "Indians" refered to in the history books are the Shinnecock tribe, an easily identified tribe of East Coast Indians, and the "Dutch" were a contingent of settlers headed by Governor Kieft. The selling of land was foreign to the Shinnecock Indians, as it was to almost every Indian tribe residing in this country. Indian tribes often exchanged gifts in order to "use" a portion of land for whatever purpose; but it was understood that the land was just being "used,"not purchased. Actually, the Shinnecocks probably thought they were getting a pretty good deal, letting the Dutch use their parcel of land for what amounted to $24 in trinkets.

The Shinnecock Indians were rewarded for their generosity by Governor Keift by setting his fusiliers upon them and killing men, women and children. If the brutal ending to the Manhattan incident had been printed in the American history books, perhaps it would not have become such a humorous subject.

Reflecting on Heroes

Several years ago, I attended an art festival in Oklahoma City and one piece of art caught my eye. It was titled, "Your Heroes Are Not Our Heroes" and it made me pause and reflect on the merits of that statement. I know for a fact that General George Amstrong Custer is certainly no hero of the Sioux Nation, and that Andrew Jackson is despised by the tribes forced on the death march called "The Trail of Tears." I have heard that there is no love for Kit Carson among the Navajos.

Even a supposed sainted man such as President Abraham Lincoln is not regarded as a hero to many Sioux Indians. In 1862, in an action which became known as the "Minnesota Outbreak" for want of a better description, the Santee Sioux under Inkpaduta rose up after the government had confiscated their treaty funds and refused to distribute provisions, as per the treaty to the hungry Indians, and in one week they destroyed almost every farm and settlement in southern Minnesota.

On December 23, 1862, on an order from President Lincoln, thirty-eight Sioux leaders were hanged in a public execution at Mankato, Minnesota, one of the largest mass executions in American history.

Lawyers Must Learn Treaties, Students Do Not

One time an attorney told me that several non-Indian lawyers-to-be were having a difficult time preparing for the bar examinations because the state in which they filed was known for including several questions on "Indian law."

These prospective barristers looked upon the inclusion of those questions as one would look upon the laws of foreign nations. It should go without saying that the laws written to govern Indian tribes by the U.S. government are laws drawn up and prepared by the non-Indian jurisprudence system.

They are the laws written to coincide with the lifestyles of the non-Indian community and slightly revised for the Indian population to fit into a pattern designed to emulate the white man's version of law, and nothing more or less. Left to their own devices, most Indian tribes would have trashed these contradictory and complex laws generations ago.

When William the Conqueror defeated the Anglo-Saxon Harold, at the Battle of Hastings in 1066, one of the first things he set about doing was changing the structure of the legal court system in England. This is reflected to this day by the fact that much of the terminology used in English and American courts has a Normandic flavor.

In an effort to totally assimilate the people, William brought about drastic land changes, removed most of the religious leaders and installed his own, and attempted to make French the national language. As one Anglo-Saxon of that period put it, "Maybe little Eric had to learn French during the day and obey all of their laws, but when he came home at night, if he needed discipline, he was corrected by a few good old Anglo-Saxon swats across his behind."

I use this analogy to point out the similarities between the assimilation attempts upon the Indian tribes of this land using many of the same methods employed by William the Conqueror many centuries ago. Death and destruction were also a part of the methods used. The fact that questions on "Indian law" would present such an extreme barrier to the bar for the young attorneys would seem to reinforce this analogy. Legal documents, such as treaties and agreements, approved by the Congress of the United States, were treated as meaningless pieces of paper, to be thrown out or withdrawn as the occasion demanded.

Why is it that few, if any, of these legal treaties signed between two nations, the United States and the Indian tribe, are not a regular part of the history texts used to teach the non-Indian children of the nation? An entire continent was acquired using the treaty method and yet, extremely important treaties, such as the 1868 Fort Laramie Treaty, are not included in the American History school books.

Perhaps there are those who would imply that support for the American Indian Movement by such men as Marlon Brando comes about as a result of publicity seeking. I, for one, believe Brando is sincere in his feelilngs about the Indian people, and although his learnings may be misguided at times, he is a complete student of Indian history from the Indian's point of view.

Speaking through his anger at the federal government and the treatment of the American Indian in an interview with *Playboy Magazine*, Brando said, "When the government didn't do it militarily, it did it with doucments and papers. We lied, we chiseled, and we swindled. And now we say we did not swindle."

He went on, "We did swindle, we did kill, we did maim, we did starve, and we did torture. We did the most heinous things that could be done to a people. We will not admit it, we do not recognize it, it is not contained in our history books. I want to pull my hair out when I read high school textbooks that deal with the destruction of a people in two paragraphs."

Brando continued, "Our relationship with the American Indian is unprecedented in history. There's no country in the world that has mde as many solemn documents, agreements, treaties, statements of intention as the United States has, and broken everyone of them. No group of people has ever so consistently and cruelly suppressed another group of people as the Americans have the Indians. There were some four hundred treaties written— and not one was kept. That's a terrific record—not one treaty.

"It is outrageous; it is shocking and unfair—and a lot more important than whether or not I like to get up in the morning, put my Equity card in my pocket, go to the studio, put on my makeup, and do my tap dance of going through a day of let's pretend. There's something obscene about that."

Racial Prejudice is a Learned Trait

A letter which crossed my desk has caused me to reflect on the meaning of racism in the state of South Dakota.

The letter began, "The Lakota and Oglala Sioux are the lowest primates on the evolutionary scale. I have yet to see a squaw over 15 who is not grossly misshapen and greasy. What is the deal with the squaw bellies? Is it from breeding all of those little red dogs? Squaws are simply obese lice bait!"

Such unbridled hatred against people of another race goes against everything I was taught in school about this land of equal opportunity, "the land of the free and the home of the brave."

I have to ask myself, is this attitude indicative of the feelings about Indian people by the majority of the white people—or is this but the ramblings of a very sick mind? For the sake of everything that is good in this country, I pray it is the latter!

Russell Means once said the American Indian Movement is the most hated organization in South Dakota. Did he say this as a boast or a statement of fact? If the incidents surrounding the occupation of the land known as Yellow Thunder Camp and the subsequent bad publicity heaped upon the heads of the Indian people of this state have contributed to this hatred, then another question arises. Why must the majority of the Indian people of South Dakota pay for the misguided actions of a few?

For many days, the supposed return to South Dakota of AIM leader Dennis Banks was bandied about by all forms of the media. How many of the journalists compiling these reports bothered to do a survey among the Indian people themselves to find out whether we even wanted Banks to return?

In the beginning, the American Indian Movement had the very best of intentions. Many Indian people welcomed AIM members and cheered their bravado. They opened up many channels that heretofore had been closed to the American Indian. But, somewhere along the line, they began to lose that support.

The fact that only a handful of Lakota people turned out to participate in the protest march in Rapid City two weeks ago is indicative of that dwindling support. I am not anti-AIM. I am pro-Indian.

Just like members of AIM, I, too, have been critical of the tribal governments. But I have witnessed a sincere effort on the part of many tribal officials to bring about drastic changes within the governmental structures. In my mind, changes—meaningful changes—can only be brought from within. If our tribal governments are to be restructured to serve the best interests of all the reservation people, those changes must come from the people most affected by the incompetence: the reservation people themselves.

The Oglala Sioux Tribal Council voted NOT to support the Yellow Thunder Camp. Council members were fully aware of the fact that by so doing, they could be labeled by members of the AIM as "sellouts," a puppet government, or—as Means is fond of saying—"a Vichy government."

In the face of this, they held to the courage of their convictions and voted the way a majority of the people on the reservation wanted them to vote.

The days of violent confrontations between Indian and non-Indian, and of Indian against Indian, are over. These bitter days are now behind us. Much to the credit of the Lakota people, the bitterness and hatreds fostered in those hectic days has been set aside or overcome. The one overriding factor which contributed to the healing of old wounds was the people's concern for each other. In the long run, the future and the survival of the tribe outweighed all other considerations.

Everything in this world is neither all red—nor all white. There are many shades in between. We are all members of the human race, placed upon this earth by the Great Spirit. We are not born with racial prejudice in our hearts. This is something that must be taught.

There are many people on the reservations of South Dakota who believe that many of the racist attitudes now surfacing against the Indians are because of bad publicity surrounding Yellow Thunder Camp. There is one question we should ask ourselves. Is the racial hatred against Indians a direct result of Yellow Thunder Camp, or is it an attitude that has always been lying just below the surface in the minds of South Dakotans and is beginning to rise to the top with Yellow Thunder Camp as a catalyst?

I began this column quoting from a letter postmarked Rapid City. The letter was signed, "One mad white bitch." She concluded her tirade against Indians with, "God is white and the devil is red! Take your pick and may you all choke on your port wine puke!"

No one knows better than I that we have a long, long road to travel before the racist problems in this state are resolved. It will take much cooler heads than those of the provocateurs who would foment racial conflict between Indian and non-Indian. We can only hope that those people with wisdom and understanding will speak out before it is too late.

Discrimination is not Entertaining

This isn't the first time I brought this up, but since little seems to be happening to solve the problem, I will bring it up again.

A few months back, a commercial on a Rapid City radio station used a voice imitating John Wayne. The voice said, "After a tough day of fighting savages. . ." I made it a point to call the radio station and point out that this commercial was an insult to the Indian people. I said, "In South Dakota, where there is a very large Indian population, this would be the same as running a commercial in Georgia with a voice saying, "After a hard day of lynching niggers . . .""

The radio station dropped the commercial and wrote a letter of apology to the Indian people which was published in *The Lakota Times*, the weekly newpaper of the Pine Ridge Reservation.

Was a commercial of this nature run because of insensitivity to the Indian people or ignorance—or both? It is very important that we find out.

There seems to be an undeclared state of war existing between the non-Indian and the Indian in South Dakota and the bordering states. For instance, in Kaycee, Wyoming, a young Indian hitchhiker is handcuffed by two white teenagers, and his throat slashed. Near Sturgis, South Dakota, an Indian hitchhiker is smashed by the open door of a pickup containing white people, and dies from the injuries. There have been reports of other Indian hitchhikers being assaulted in other areas of this country. If you are an Indian, you cannot help but fear for the safety of your people.

Several years ago, in the 1970s, the mutilated bodies of three Navajo men were found near Farmington, New Mexico. A lengthy investigation turned up evidence to convict three white teenagers for the various crimes. A state law in New Mexico protected the assailants so that they were sentenced to reform school, rather than prison, for these heinous acts of murder.

In Hot Springs, South Dakota, a young white man fires a shot from a hunting rifle into the trailer home of an Indian family. A young Indian man is struck in the neck and dies. The shot could have, just as easily, killed a brother, sister or the mother of the victim. The killer is sentenced to prison but serves less than one year for this act of violence. A local newspaper does a front page story in its Sunday edition explaining the "life of hell" this man went through because of the crime, and detailing how his new "commitment to Christ" had made him see the errors of his ways.

As I read this article, I could not help but wonder why the non-Indian reporter never bothered to interview members of the family of the murdered Indian man to find out what sort of "Life of hell" they had endured since this senseless, mindless murder.

An Indian who has returned to the teachings of the ancient religions of his tribe, and as in the case of the Lakota people, has returned to the teachings of the Sacred Pipe while serving time in prison, faces an insurmountable task in trying to convince the warden, usually a non-Indian, that his Pipe is as sacred to him as the Bible of the Christian Church or the Koran of the Muslim is to those devotees. I have been told by   former inmates that most wardens consider this conversion to be a step backward, a return to the 'savage ways' rather than a true religious awakening.

Perhaps the reasoning behind these vicious attacks upon Indian people has deep psychological roots. But I believe that there is a very simple explanation for this phenomenon. I lay much of the blame on Hollywood.

For many years, Hollywood cranked out movies about cowboys, Indians, settlers and the cavalry, full of the supposed vicious acts committed by the howling savages. These movies, replete with prejudice and hatred, are being recycled for a new generation of white Americans through the medium of television.

An entire generation of white children has been indoctrinated through these erroneous movies, to hate and fear the Indian people. Killing an Indian was of no more consequence than killing a coyote, according to these grade B westerns.

It is quite possible that many of these vicious attacks upon the lives of Indians were hatched in the minds of the young, non-Indian in front of his television set.

Every responsible program manager, in every city in the United States, should take a long, hard look at the plot of these terrible movies. They should not be televised if they continue to spread the filth of racial prejudice and hatred. These movies do a grave injustice to the Indian people of today.

The responsibility of bringing this renewed cycle of hatred and fear of Indians to an end is in the hands of the executives of the television networks and local stations. Just as these program managers are very careful about television programs maligning black people, they should be as careful about programs dealing with Indians. It is time to bring about serious changes when the entertainment industry harms an entire race. Discrimination and hatred are not entertaining!

Indians Applaud Affirmative Action

Vernon Jordon of the Urban League, a black organization, has said repeatedly, "Congress cannot pass a law that will make you love me. But, by God, it can pass a law that says you must give me equal treatment." Therein lies the foundation for all of the civil rights laws and affirmative action laws passed by Congress over the past several years.

Midge Decter, senior editor of Basic Books, Inc., wrote an article for the Saturday Forum of the Rapid City (South Dakota) *Journal* which was published August 30, 1980. He said: "Affirmative Action is held in disfavor by an overriding majority of the American people." Minorities have known this for many, many years and most members of minority races would have been very happy to see equal employment, equal housing, equal opportunities and equal education made available to all citizens of the United States without having laws enacted to force compliance.

The States of the Union had every opportunity to formulate equal rights policies on their own, without federal intervention. Most states chose to sit on their collective duffs and do nothing to correct acts of outright discrimination against members of minorities residing within their boundaries. As the Reverend Jesse Jackson told Ronald Reagan, "States rights has always meant wrongs to minorities."

Perhaps it is true, as Decter states, that "The main groups at whose behest quotas have been instituted are, of course, blacks and women," but they are the most numerous and numbers have always made the deepest impression upon the lawmakers. But somewhere along the line, laws were passed to create an atmosphere of equality for blacks and women, and those laws have served to filter down some equality to other minorties.

Although politically weak, Indian tribes of this state have benefited in many ways from the passage of affirmative action laws.

One of the most outlandish statements of Decter's article says, "Even the qualified, insofar as they know themselves to have won a competition through the added benefits of a special allowance, sooner or later undergo crises of self-doubt." Self-doubt? What about the years of deprivation which brought loss of self-respect, humiliation and second class status?

As recently as the 1950s, not so very long ago, Indians traveling off the reservation to the border towns, made sure that they had plenty of food, bedding and a tent, because they knew that they would be denied these basic needs at most restaurants and motels. Scholarships for bright and gifted Indian students, who wished to pursue a higher education, were unheard of. And what was even worse, the available institutions of education on the reservations were more interested in assimiltion than education.

Indian people, as a whole, have never asked for any special treatment or consideration. All they have ever asked for is the opportunity to compete fairly and openly. All they have ever asked is that the white man respect their way of life, their customs and culture, without feeling the need "to make them over in his own image." If it took an act of Congress to accomplish this objective, so be it.

Finally, Decter says, "Affirmative action is not simply a legal or administrative arrangement; it is a frame of mind—a frame of mind best characterized by the term 'double standard.'"

Double standard? Is something considered a "double standard" only when it affects or inconveniences the racial majority? Why didn't these defenders of the American way of life speak out as vehemently when the blacks of this country were being forced to accept "separate, but equal" schools, toilets, drinking fountains and were being pointed toward the back of the bus?

Where were those scholars who find it "chic" to speak out against affirmative action, when Private Felix Longoria (killed in action) was refused funeral servcies at a mortuary at Three Rivers, Texas because he was a Mexican-American? Were they concerned about equality and justice when the Japanese-Americans of this country were being rounded up, their properties confiscated, and were herded into concentration camps for the heinous crime of being Japanese?

The Indian people of South Dakota know all about double standards, Mr. Decter. And as for our feelings about affirmative action, we applaud, and say "It's about time!"

Hate Letters Show Writers to be Bigots

There is one feature about writing a weekly column that can best be described as an occupationl hazard. Expressing a point of view in a public forum such as a newspaper, especially if that point of view espouses Indian advocacy, leaves one open to criticism or praise.

In the four years I have been writing this column I have received many letters that begin, "I read your column every week and enjoy it very much, but I don't always agree with what you say." If there are specific points of disagreement, most writers explain why they feel a certain way, and then usually request additional informatin or sources for research. By causing a reader to go beyond my column and seek out other sources of information, I have accomplished one of my primary objectives.

A letter I received in the mail on Monday is a grim reminder of the other side of the coin. There are minds that are closed, saturated in racial bigotry, and filled with loathing and hate. Usually, the letters I receive along these lines are grammatically deficient and juvenile. They usually tell me more about the writer than the subject.

The last time I shared a letter of similar nature with my readers, I was amazed at the out pouring of indignation from Indian and non-Indian alike. I excerpt these hate letters for one reason only. I wish to remind decent people of this country that there are many sick minds in our midst. Their comments would be laughable if they did not present a danger to all mankind. We should acknowledge that there will never be racial harmony as long as there is one such person wandering about and sowing the seeds of racial prejudice.

The letter to which I refer was datelined Rapid City. It began, "I was amused at your article in regards to your upcoming elections. A true leader doesn't get up and say—quote: 'This is what I have done.' If you would worship God instead of the stuff you worship, God will know and judge what a leader has done."

The writer went on to say that he had recently moved to Rapid City. "I am sick and tired of what I have seen the Indians do. I was not born or raised around them, so I don't buy the actions they seem to enjoy in harrassing whites." The letter continued, "I saw three of them going through my apartment complex garbage gathering cans and bottles. A dirty habit. For what? More liquor for another drink? I saw an Indian so drunk that he was staggering out on a four-lane highway. If a white man had run over him, God only knows whose fault it would be. I called the police."

The letter writer supported his bigotry with further examples of bad conduct on the part of Indians he had observed. "I was up at the Black Hills National Cemetery when I saw an Indian couple sprawled on the grass. This is no park. It is a place to be respected. If they want to sprawl on the grass, let them do it on the reservation."

The letter went on and on about seeing Indians loitering in the post office, on street corners, etc., and concluded, "From what I have observed, you Indians do nothing to rise above things, and I, for one, don't want to be dragged down to your level by your conduct or your harrassment of whites. Why don't you write about those filthy Indians living in Rapid City and tell them to cool it. I know you won't do that, cause, brother, you're way out in left field with your stories."

Summing up all his bigotry in the final sentence, the writer said, "The manager of the garage where I take my car told me that I should see the restrooms after a bunch of filthy Rapid City Indians have used it."

Perhaps if the writer had taken the trouble to walk around the Black Hills National Cemetery and read the names on some of the tombstones, he would have been amazed to see how many American Indians were buried there. They gave their lives fighting for this country so that people such as he would have the freedom to write hate letters without the fear of being locked away in a dungeon.

Indians observe, almost every day, on the evening news, some of the most atrocious acts of violence committed by white people. However, we are objective (and intelligent) enough to realize that the actions of a few do not relegate the whole to a derogatory place.

Let it suffice to say that we have our drunks and we have our criminals, just as the white race has theirs, but we know that they are not the majority. Most Indians are hard-working, religious and dedicated to preserving a way of life and a culture.

Last week we saw two congressmen stand before their peers and confess to performing sex acts with minors, one with a young lady, and the other with a young man. Both of these gentlemen were white. Wouldn't it be ridiculous and presumptuous of us to accuse all white people of such actions because of the moral laxity of these two? Of course it would! And yet, most Indians have met white bigots who would do this very thing if the two congressmen had been Indian or black.

Racial prejudice is not something we are born with; it is something we are taught. In my mind, anything that is taught can—in most cases—be untaught. The ideal situation would be for the human race to accept the differences of each other. Maybe then I wouldn't be getting these hate letters to spoil an otherwise beautiful Monday evening.

Humor Was Inappropriate in Legislative Action

Unquestionably, the relationship between tribal governments and state governments has been that of adversaries, not only in South Dakota but in every Western state with large Indian populations.

As a result, many Indian tribes have been very reluctant to particpate in state government. It was only after continued threats by the federal government to take action (under the Voting Rights Act) against those states that did not reapportion their voting districts to include participation by Indian tribes that the state governments enacted legislation diminishing gerrymandering.

Passing legislation enabling Indian tribes to elect representation to state government in no way assures the construction of a bridge between the tribes and the states. Too much water has passed under the bridge of misunderstanding and too many illegal acts have been enacted to endanger the existence of the tribes as sovereign nations.

State lawmakers should remember a very simple truth when dealing with Indian nations. Indian tribes do not want to become counties or colonies subject to state jurisdiction. The Indian reservations are the last foothold left to the Indian people on a continent they once owned and encroachment upon those lands is verboten no matter the circumstances.

Many elected officials serving on the legislative bodies of states wherein the largest minority population is Indian are ignorant of Indian thought and of

Indian law. Furthermore, these legislators will not take the time to study and learn about the Indians of their states.

Two attempts aimed at memorializing Lakota leaders by state legislators point out the wide communications gap between the non-Indian lawmakers and the Indian tribes.

January 3 of this year, 1982, Elijah Whirlwind Horse, former chairman of the Oglala Sioux Tribe, died tragically of cancer. He was only forty-six years old. A resolution was introduced in the South Dakota House and Senate to memorialize him. The resolution passed the Senate by a vote of 33-0, but had one dissenting vote cast against it in the House, where it eventually passed 61-1.

Representative K. C. Marsden, Republican of Rapid City, cast the one vote against the resolution. In part, the resolution commended Whirlwind Horse as "an honest, progressive, forthright and a super good man. He probably mediated more of the differences between the races just by things he'd done than anyone in the entire area."

My telephone conversation with Marsden went something like this:
"Why did your vote against the Whirlwind Horse resolution?"
"What's the big flap? The resolution passed, didn't it?" Marsden went on to say that he had never heard of Whirlwind Horse.
"Do you read any of the local newpapers?" I asked.
"Rarely," he replied.
Marsden said he did not believe in eulogizing people he had never heard of, and besides, "I just wanted to poke a little fun into it and humor Gene Christenson." (Representative Gene Christenson, Republican of Kadoka, was one of the resolution sponsors.)

In my opinion, there is a time and place for humor. I believe the resolution to memorialize Whirlwind Horse was introduced out of respect for a great Indian man who did much to improve the relationships between Indian and non-Indian during his short lifetime. To taint this resolution to honor him by injecting sick humor into it is shameful and childish. This sort of juvenile behavior has no place in the halls of the state legislature.

The next incident involves our esteemed governor, William Janklow. Janklow issued an executive proclamation honoring sculptor Korczak Ziolkowski, the man carving the giant figure of Oglala Chief Crazy Horse in the Black Hills. The proclamation mentions that the carving will "depict the story of Indian civilization at its zenith." It then goes on to say the statue will tell mankind that the Indian is saying, "I was here, on this land, and I was a magnificent man."

Who is in a position to say, unequivocally, that the Indian nations have reached their "zenith" and have been on the decline ever since? To add that "I was here" and "I was magnificent" is to pretend that we are no longer here and less than magnificent.

Just like the white race, the Indian tribes have reached different plateaus at different times in history. That itinerary is still being written. Just as there has not been a "zenith" for the non-Indians, there has never been a "zenith" for the Indian nations. Like you, we are ever growing and ever changing.

Perhaps Janklow would like to believe that the Indian "was here on this land," but make no mistake about it, we are still here on this land. Our history has varied since the advent of the white man, but we are here, on the land of our ancestors, and we will continue to live here. We are not past history.

Perhaps it is this sort of blind reasoning that has contributed to the communications gap between Indian and non-Indian. The major difference is this: We, as Indians, have made an effort to learn about the white civilization through your history books. Why can't the non-Indian make a similar effort to learn about Indian civilization?

Federal Dominance, Paternalism Suppresses Indians

Walking down the street in Window Rock, Arizona, a reservation-based Indian from South Dakota or Montana will notice the striking similarities to their reservations.

If the reservation has an Indian Health Service hospital, the neat rows of houses or trailers built to accommodate the medical staff stand out like sore thumbs. Neat homes operated by the Bureau of Indian Affairs for its employees also stand out in sharp contrast to the usually substandard homes housing the grassroots people.

The few paved streets are usually pock-marked with potholes and the gravel roads are as bumpy as washboards. Litter is scattered everywhere and the bodies of abandoned autombiles stand as mute decorations in the driveways and yards of the battered homes.

Visiting journalists usually focus their attention on these eyesores and build their stories around them. In most cases, they never attempt to find out the reasons behind these conditions. It is so easy to write about the obvious. It takes a real journalist to dig at the root causes of these highly visible conditions.

Winos wandering aimlessly through the dusty streets are obvious targets of visiting reporters. Most of the winos have allowed life to pass them by and have found some semblance of solace in a bottle of cheap wine. They would be derelicts in any society, but to a passing tourist, they are just another "drunken Indian."

If one were to get up at the crack of dawn and drive to the center of the town, at first light he would see these lifeless forms climbing from the back seats of abandoned cars and buildings, shuffling toward the busy sections of the community, hoping to catch a stranger or a friend and induce them into coughing up a quarter, or a half-dollalr toward the purchase of the next bottle of wine. As they stagger back toward town, the morning sunlight at their backs, it is almost like a scene from the motion picture, *The Night of the Living Dead*.

Years of federal dependence that furnished just enough funds to hang on and survive, of govenrment experiments that changed with the seasons, of do-gooders extending a hand-out instead of a hand-up, of program after program intended to assimilate rather than preserve, and of faceless bureaucrats ensconced in Washington, D.C., a million light years from the Indian reservations, seeking out senseless solutions to the "Indian problem," have reduced many Indian nations to poverty and near destruction.

Suppose the educational systems in your home town conditioned the young to get an education and then abandon their home. Leave the old and infirm to shift for themselves, without a hope for a better life. Suppose they taught their young that the only way to succeed was to put as many miles as possible between the place of their birth and themselves. Such has been the lot of the Indian people.

The root problems on most Indian reservations can be traced directly to more than one hundred years of federal dominance. They can be traced to a paternalistic approach that considered the Indian lifestyles to be infantile and expendable. Sever the roots and destroy the culture and religion and force them to join the mainstream was the code of the bureaucracy. What does it matter if you destroy a race of people in the process?

With a land base that could not be self-sufficient, could not levy taxes for the simple things common to any self-government, such as raising revenues to clean the streets, repair the roads, or construct new buildings, the Indian nations were reduced, one year at a time, to total dependence.

It wasn't until 1974, just nine years ago, that a goal of self-determination for Indian tribes was instituted during the Richard Nixon administration. It wasn't until 1978, just five years ago, that the American Indian Freedom of Religion Act was passed during the Jimmy Carter administration.

Corruption has not been uncommon to tribal governments, just as it has not been uncommon to the role model, the United States of America. In many cases, it was not uncommon for officials sent to the reservations to lend a helping hand, to rip off the very people they were supposed to assist. They knew they had no longevity on the reservation nor did they have a vested interest in the people of the community. Grab the money and run!

All the while state governments and major corporations fought for the territorial rights to Indian Country. Tribe after tribe saw millions of acres of land handed over to these two entities by the very agency set up to protect the Indian nations, the U.S. Department of Interior, through its agent, the Bureau of Indian Affairs.

When you non-Indian reporters travel to our reservations to do your great humanitarian articles on the down-trodden Indian, take the time to look past the ends of your noses. Don't settle for the obvious things that startle the eye.

Always bear in mind that the problems are deep seated and extremely complex. In order to understand our major problems on the reservations, travel to Washington, D.C., the seat of our problems, and begin from there. Then—and only then—will you begin to realize, albeit it quite vaguely, what Indian Country is all about.

Jeanne White has Struggled for Self-Help Programs

A few weeks ago Senator Larry Pressler announced the introduction of a new bill that would grant special tax considerations and other benefits to businesses on or near Indian reservations.

The purpose of this bill is to induce businesses already existing to continue their operations and to encourage new businesses to locate on or near reservations. This would provide jobs and increase tribal income, encourage self-sufficiency on reservations and take up some of the slack that the loss of funding to reservations will cause because of the many budget cuts by the government's new austerity programs (Spring, 1980).

A new idea? Not hardly. Several years ago Jeanne White, an Oglala woman, had the very same idea. She was the owner of a company, TP Construction, that ran into all sorts of problems competing on the open market, getting insurance and qualifying for bids on government contracts because of the built-in failure factors that most minority businesses face in their first year of operation. Frustrated and angry, she formed the South Dakota Indian Business Association in an effort to unite all of the Indian business people into a single force that would be able to fight for survival with a united effort.

She hired Cleveland Neiss (now a tribal councilman from Rosebud Reservation) and they set about their business of trying to convince the U.S. government that progress can become a reality to many Indian people if they are assisted technically and financially in starting their own businesses. The logic was very simple; if Indian people could get into business for themselves, they would hire other Indians, increase employment for their own people, and by selling goods and services on reservations, they would keep some of the millions of dollars spent off reservations at home and the dollars would turn over within the Indian community and generate economic progress on the reservations. This same formula would be used in the urban centers that borderd the reservations. It would provide jobs and income for those Indians who had relocated to the cities.

Cleveland Neiss had worked in Washington, D.C. and had many connections there. He flew there and met with members of Congress, people from the Ecnonomic Development Adminstration and the director of the Office of Minority Business Enterprises. He presented his proposal, both in written form and verbally. He was lauded and encouraged, but in the long run, Cleve found that it was very difficult to take these promises to the bank. Perhaps the solution Mrs. White and Mr. Neiss suggested to the government to solve some of the problems existing on reservations were much too simple.

It is very difficult for the bureaucracy to look for simple solutions to complex problems. Perhaps the reason for this is because most simple problems suddenly become very complex when they are placed in the hands of the federal government for solutions.

The idea of self-help through self-employment never died in the heart of Jeanne White. Although her organization, SDIBA exists in name only, the dream is still very much alive.

Mrs. White has been very vocal in her challenge to the various governmental agencies that blocked her path. As a result, she has been criticized and maligned by many of these agencies for daring to question their capabilities and ridiculing their lack of competence. She has discovered, as many of us who dare to challenge federal or tribal competence have discovered, that it is not easy being in the public eye when you question the powers that be. The easiest way for state or federal government to quiet dissenters is to discredit them. This tactic has been used against Mrs. White on several occasions without success.

Those of us who know Jeanne White know that she will never compromise her ideals no matter what the circumstances. It is ironic that the ideal she has fought for these many years may become a reality and a success because a non-Indian, who also happens to be a powerful United States senator, chooses to expound on their practicalities. But, knowing Mrs. White, I'm sure she could care less who gets credit for the idea just as long as it succeeds in fulfilling her lifelong dreams of helping her people to help themselves.

Blood Quantum is a Degree of Discrimination

Several weeks ago, I wrote a short article in *The Lakota Times*, the Pine Ridge Reservation weekly newspaper, addressing the prospects of a radio station being established on this reservation.

I was concerned that most of the people involved in the radio station were very strong in their political beliefs. All of them are devout members of the American Indian Movement. As a matter of fact, the original organizers of the radio project included Ted and Russell Means.

My commentary was intended to stress the importance of utilizing the radio station to reflect the views of all the people of the reservation. In the article I said that if the radio station were to truly reflect the attitudes of all the people of the reservation, regardless of political beliefs I would support it 100 percent.

The day the newspaper hit the streets, I received an anonymous phone call from a woman who concluded her tirade against me with, "Go back to Mexico."

One of the underlying problems on this reservation, the second largest in the United States, is the thread of racial prejudice existing among our own people. Granted, we are faced with the mindless discrimination from the communities bordering our reservation, but we are also very guilty of practicing bigotry on our own reservation.

Like many, many Indians on the Pine Ridge Reservation (Eagle Bulls, Two Twos, Bad Wounds, Cedar Faces, Big Crows—and on and on), I have the blood of the Mexican Indian flowing through my veins. But like all of those mentioned above, I also have the blood of the Oglala Lakota.

Tribal Attorney Mario Gonzalez (descended from the Quiver family) also has Mexican Indian blood. At a convention last year in Pierre, one of the tribal councilmen from Crow Creek said, "What kind of name is Gonzalez? Sounds like Mexican to me."

Gonzalez, who was on the podium speaking at the time, responded calmly. "It seems to me that there are many Indians in the audience with French or English surnames. Does that make you French or English? In the same manner, there are many Indians with Spanish surnames. The main thing to remember is that Mexican is Indian. We did not come to this country from Europe. Our ancestors greeted the boat people. We are 100 percent Native American Indians."

Don't we have enough problems trying to unite without creating additional headaches? Why must people be categorized as full-bloods, mixed-bloods, etc.? Many years ago, the Bureau of Indian Affairs decided to establish blood quanta for the purpose of enrollment. At that time, blood quantum was set at one-fourth degree for enrollment. Unfortunately, through the years, this caused the Indian people on the reservation to be categorized and labeled. Many of the good jobs on the reservation went to the mixed bloods and this created a division by blood degree.

This was a situation created solely by the BIA, with the able assistance of the Department of the Interior. It is not indicative of the existing job situation now prevalent on the reservation, and to use this outmoded concept to propagate internal discrimination is contributing to one of our biggest problems.

How many times have you heard a Norwegian refer to himself as a "full-blooded Norwegian" or a person half-French and half-Irish as a "half-breed?"

When I witness organizations spring up on our reservation that will accept "full-bloods" only, I realize that we cannot continue to point the finger of racial discrimination at the white man, if we cannot bring ourselves to clean up our own act. In my mind, there is not room for "All Iyeska" or "All full-blood" organizations on this reservation. As I have stated so many times in the past, it doesn't matter what our degree of Indian blood if our reservation is terminated. We either fight for our rights together, or we will surely sink together.

We are fortunate to have a tribal president who believes as I do, in this instance. Although I did not endorse Joe American Horse when he ran for the presidency, I am very impressed with the many positive things he has started to get us back on the road to recovery. American Horse believes that we are one people. We must heal the wounds dividing us, and get on with the future security of the reservation. This is the sort of leadership needed in these troubled times.

Internal discrimination is pettiness. Pettiness is a detriment to our future. Even our young people are confused by this pettiness that is dividing us. It is not their way, nor is it the way of their ancestors. It is something created by our generation, and it is a problem that can be solved—by us.

Parable Explains Indian View on Land Claim

Sometimes the easiest way to get across a point or to try to explain a controversial matter is by use of the parable or comparison story.

It is very difficult for an Indian to explain why regaining some of the lost land of the Black Hills is so important, especially to most non-Indians who simply refuse to hear what we have to say on the subject. This was brought home to us when Senator Larry Pressler said publicly that he would actively oppose any return of federal lands to the Lakota people while speaking out against a bill being prepared by the tribes of the Great Sioux Nation which will be introduced in Congress later this year.

Most reservation people are quite concerned because Pressler is deathly opposed to a bill he has never read. We wonder if the Senator would speak out so strongly against a bill about to be introduced by his white constituents—if he had never read the bill. Has Pressler finally discovered that supporting Indian causes in South Dakota is political suicide?

A white rancher left his house and land for a few days. Upon returning home, he ran into a police patrol and was told that he could not return to his land. The patrol officer said, "While you were away, a very powerful family moved into your house and began to work your land. Since our department is too weak to make them move off the land, we are going to prevent you from returning to the land so that there will not be trouble."

The county commissioners called a special session to hear the complaints of the irate rancher. Knowing they did not have the courage or the numbers to move the trespasser off of the rancher's land, the commissioners passed a special law awarding the rancher's land to the trespassers. "That is like telling a thief that he can keep that which he has stolen," screamed the rancher.

Since that county had little money, they told the rancher they would be unable to reimburse him for the loss of his home and land. "Serves the renegade right," thought one of the county commissioners whose son had been horse-whipped by the rancher for illegal trespassing on his land. (The 1877 Act to take the Black Hills from the Sioux was passed one year after Custer and his Seventh Cavalry were horse-whipped at the Little Big Horn.)

The rancher went from court to court in an effort to regain his home and ranch. Every place he sought justice he was told the court did not have jurisdiction to hear his case. After many years of trying, tired, old and dejected, the rancher passed the fight for his land on to his children.

Finally, sixty-nine years after his land was illegally taken, the county commissioners set up a special court, called the Ranchers Claims Commission to listen to the arguments presented by the rancher's sons. The special court made it very clear that they could not, and would not return the rancher's land. The court was set up merely to determine the amount of money to be paid to the family of the rancher for the theft of his land.

The court also informed the family of the rancher that they would not pay the current dollar value of the land but instead would try to pay them for the value of the land at the time of the illegal taking.

While the rancher and his family had lived in poverty fighting for the return of their home and land, the thieves of the land had prospered. They had discovered valuable mineral deposts and had made a fortune working the land. The thieves had also sold large tracts of the land to so-called honest people, who, in turn, had built valuable ranches and towns on the stolen land.

338   Rights

Afraid that the rancher's family would try to get back the land they had purchased, the honest people said, "What does it matter if the land we purchased was stolen land? That was a long time ago, and we can't be held responsible if our parents bought stolen property."

The rancher had long since died. At last his family was awarded $1.00 per acre by the Rancher's Court of Claims for the land that was now selling for 100 times that amount per acre. The fact that millions of dollars in minerals and timber had been removed from the land was not even considered by the claims court. One hundred three years had passed since the land was stolen.

One day the county commissioners were at a meeting, sitting around complimenting each other for finally clearing title to the rancher's land, when in marched the descendants of the rancher. Weary, poverty-stricken, but proud, they informed the commissioners they would not accept any money. They intended to continue fighting for the land.

"Not accept the money," exclaimed the commissioners in unison. They were appalled—shocked. How could these poor people turn down good American greenbacks?

"It's the principle of the thing," said the family of the deceased rancher. "The land is like our Holy Land. It is where the bones of our dead lie buried. Yes, it's the principle of the thing."

Genocidal Policies Raged for Two Hundred Years

After more than forty years, a U.S. government Commission has decided that there was no military necessity for the internment of 120,000 people of Japanese ancestry during World War II. The report called their uprooting a "grave injustice" brought about by war hysteria and racism.

All dark-skinned people residing in the United States are painfully aware of the dual standards existing side by side with the patriotic slogans of "Liberty and Justice for All." In the case of the Japanese, we saw American citizens rounded up like cattle and shipped to detention centers simply because they were of a different color. Although this country was also at war with the Germans and Italians, no effort was made to round them up and incarcerate them.

"That's because the Italians (pronounced Eyetalians) and the German looked like what real Americans are supposed to look like," mused one cerebral red neck serving with me in the U.S. Navy.

After the Japanese-Americans were moved to detention centers, they came under the supervision of Dillon Meyer. He apparently did a bang up job of detaining the internees because he was rewarded by being made Commissioner of Indian Affairs in 1950.

It was during his term as commissioner that two programs came into being that almost totally decimated the Indian nations. They were known euphemistically as "termination" and "relocation." During his tenure approximately 2.5 million acres of Indian land were removed from protected status.

I draw the analogy between the Japanese-Americans and the American Indian because both races of people suffered greatly at the hands of Dillon Meyer, and also because of the undisguised racial hatred directed at them for simply being born of another color.

During World War II, an Indian man from the Pine Ridge Reservation, a man decorated with many medals, including the Nation's highest honor, the Congressional Medal of Honor, walked into a bar and restaurant in Nebraska and orderd a meal and a beer. He was told he could have neither. Instead, he was approached by the manager and told unceremoniously, "I'm sorry, but we don't serve Indians in here. Woud you please leave quietly?"

I should add that this man, this American Indian, was wearing a United States military uniform. He had just returned from overseas where he had risked his life to protect the rights of the restaurant manager to deny service to American Indians.

A Japanese-American I knew in San Francisco told me of how he joined the U.S. Army in order to get out of the internment camp. He was assigned to a Japanese company with white officers. This Japanese unit eventually became one of the most celebrated and decorated outfits in the European theater.

My friend said with a laugh, "When we got a chance to go to town, even though we were wearing U.S. Army uniforms, many of us told the civilians—and other GI's—that we were Chinese. We did this to avoid trouble."

Executive Order 9066, signed into law by President Franklin Delano Roosevelt, just ten short weeks after Pearl Harbor, gave the Japanese-Americans a small taste of what the Indian people had been subjected to for more than two hundred years. The loss of freedom, property and personal dignity through executive order is nothing new to the American Indian.

More than 120,000 American citizens were put behind barbed wire fences because of political pressure and fear. Hundreds of thousands of American Indians perished because of those same two reasons—political pressure and fear.

The white man feared that which he could not undertand, and yet he coveted the land. Pushed on by political pressure, the federal govenment began a systematic destruction of the American Indian. Fueled by fear and greed, the genocidal policies of the United States raged for more than two hundred years.

For the Japanese-Americans it is over. They have been vindicated. For the American Indian the final battle has yet to be fought. Greedy eyes are once more cast upon Indian lands because of the resources, and in the minds of many Indians on the reservation, the final assault is about to begin.

Passing on the Stereotypes of Indians

Many years ago a story made the rounds of Indian reservations. It usually evoked a short chuckle from the Indian people, followed by a note of quiet acknowledgement that there's more truth than fiction to the ridiculous tale.

In Rapid City, South Dakota on the corner of St. Joe and Sixth streets is a Western wear store called Duhamels. Several years ago, an attraction for tourists guesting at the famous Alex Johnson Hotel or the many other motels scattered about the Black Hills occurred on the sidewalk outside the store. Indian children from the several reservations in the state would dance for enjoyment of these tourists. Accompanied by a drum and a singing group, they did their fancy and traditional dances decked out in genuine American Indian regalia. As the last beat of the drum ended a dance and the haunting thunder of the beat diminished to a feeble echo, the early evening air would be filled with a harsh clinking as coins tossed by grinning tourists struck the hot pavement. This was the scenario that prompted the story. It goes like this:

"The sun had just reached the peaks of the western Black Hills and the air was heavy with the hot, summer dirt. The beautiful evening had brought an exceptionally large number of tourists outdoors to observe the young Indian dancers performing on the street corner.

"Following the routine taught to them by their elders, the dancing children had frozen in various positions, timing the final beat of the drum with perfect precision. There was that slight pause as the final thump of the drum faded into the approaching darkness and the first coin, tossed by an eager tourist, drifted lazily through the heavy air.

"The comment, made by a white lady in a floppy, straw hat, her face enveloped by huge, dark glasses, a camera at the ready, seemed perfectly timed to split the eerie moment of silence. 'How old do these Indian kids have to be before they grow their feathers?' she asked in all seriousness."

Recent articles printed in national magazines and metropolitan newspapers carrying inaccurate, erroneous and degrading stories about Indian people are a reflection of this general attitude of ignorance common to white America. Horrendous articles, which could have been authenticated by an astute reporter with a simple telephone call, have been published as fact.

These respectable publications are feeding the fire of racial ignorance, reinforcing the image of the commonly stereotyped, primitive savage, passing this misinformation on to a new generation of non-Indian readers.

Perhaps the worst enemy of the modern Indian is the TV set. The networks think nothing of running old cowboy and Indian movies so saturated with erroneus information about Indian people that they are a disgrace to any self-respecting human being.

Does this vicious circle of misinformation, sustained by the media, feed upon itself?

Every journalist should use one basic rule when writing about Indian people. You are dealing with human beings. We live in houses, drive cars, send our children to school, attend church service, fall in love, weep at funerals, laugh at jokes, cheer at basketball games, watch television, read books and newspapers. In short, we have feelings.

There are more than three hundred different Indian tribes in this country with different cultures, religions and lifestyles. Please don't lump us all together as "Indians." For every "drunken Indian" you see staggering down Main Street, there are one hundred Indians who don't drink at all, and other Indians working hard to cure those who embarrass all of us.

Rights   341

Maybe life hasn't treated us all that well, but there are many good, hard-working Indians who aren't sitting around crying about it. They are trying to make the reservations of this land better places to live for themselves and their children. You don't hear about these good people too often because they are not out making the news headlines.

Finally, every journalist assigned to write about Indians should remember that you will be doing us a terrific disservice if you blame the majority of Indians for the misguided actions of a few.

Columnist Tells Why He Writes

There are those who believe that every time an injustice against Indian people is pointed out, they are being singled out as the guilty parties. And there are others who believe that all is now fine and dandy in Indian Country, and any charge of misconduct on the part of the non-Indians is unfounded and refers to the days long gone by and not to the present.

Usually, I do not dwell too much on past injustices, but I am very aware of the things happening on many reservations and within the urban communities of this nation at this time. If there is a single reader out there who can prove to me, and to the Indian people, that there is no longer injustice, that the federal and state governments are not trying to impose their collective wills upon the Indian people, abolish treaties, and terminate reservations out of existence, then I will stop writing about these things once and for all.

Discrimination

If there is any individual in Farmington, New Mexico who can prove to me that racial discrimination in housing, jobs and fair treatment in the business establishments and bars of this town do not exist, I will quit writing about these things also.

How many of you realize that for countless years the Indians had no voice whatever in the media to express these things most people pretend did not exist? How many times do you think Indian people picked up newspapers, watched television or listened to the radio and read or heard things that were an insult to all Indians, and yet could not respond?

Did we cancel our subscriptions to newspapers, throw out our TV sets and radios, and close our eyes, ears and minds to the racial slurs and the media inaccuracies surrounding us? No, we did not! Instead, we tried to confront this injustice by becoming a part of a system, to a point, which enables us to have a forum for our own opinions.

Point of View

Granted, I do not speak for the Navajo or for any other tribe of this nation through my columns. But I do speak from a point of view that has been garnered because I was born and raised on an Indian reservation, my skin is brown, and I have experienced many of the injustices I speak of on a first hand basis.

If in writing this column, I happen to express a point of view that is contrary to the non-Indian's in some respects, and that point of view does not correspond with the opinion of the majority, does that make me radical? Is the non-Indian afraid to see some of his "sacred cows" tarnished by an Indian with a different point of view?

Many of my co-workers within the news media know that I have strong opinions on certain subjects, but I don't think they would classify me as radical. I have never advocated the violent overthrow of the United States government, but in fact, have spoken out against those who would resort to violence.

The many letters I receive from the Navajo community and from many of the non-Indians living in Farmington, Bloomfield and Aztec, New Mexico would indicate to me the support I get for writing my column is far greater than the criticisms I receive. These letters are a source of inspiration to me and without this support I would not have the courage to continue writing about injustice, discrimination and the destruction of a way of life.

Demanding Job

One of the main reasons I reduced my columns from three per week to one per week is that I have been writing fulltime on the staff of another newspaper, and as any journalist will tell you, it is a demanding and time-consuming job. I wanted to keep my column going in Farmington because many Indian and non-Indian people had requested that I do so.

I thank the fine editors of the other four newspapers who carry my column, Notes from Indian Country, and I also am grateful to the editors of the Farmington Daily Times who saw a need for a column such as mine, and had the courage to carry it.

As we say in Lakota, "Pilamaya." (Thank you.)

Native Americans Denied Liberties

An ABC presentation entitled I Love Liberty aired on March 28, 1983. In my mind, it turned out to be a dramatic showing of flag waving, patriotioc rhetoric and varnish.

In attempting to show America as the land of the free and the home of the brave, warts and all, the show bit off more than it could chew in the brief time allotted. Two hours are hardly sufficient to allow adequate coverge of such a diverse, complex and immense subject.

A very brief appearance by Jane Fonda addressing the intricacies of the First Amendment to the U.S. Constitution (freedom of speech, religion, etc.) could have been expanded to include the ongoing struggle by the Indian tribes of the state of South Dakota regarding the Black Hills. A clear violation of the First Amendment rights of the Indian tribes is most evident and could have served as an example to all Americans, freedom loving or not.

Courage Admired

Perhaps, in the past, I have disagreed with some of the actions taken by Russell Means concerning the Black Hills but I have always admired his courage, and the courage of the people occupying Yellow Thunder Camp.

Patriotic Americans should ask themselves this question: Why have members of the American Indian Movement found it necessary to forcibly occupy lands in the Black Hills? Is it because all attempts to receive justice through the U.S. court system have been thwarted in a maze of federal rulings?

If there had been fair treatment of Indian people by the courts, the federal government or the local media (particularly television), there would be no organizations needed to confront the injustice.

How many times have I heard Indian people say that they agreed with the early concepts of the American Indian Movement but did not like the methods used?

The impressions I get from many residents of Pine Ridge Reservation I interview week after week in pursuing my job as a journlist is that any movement seeking liberty and justice for the American Indian should be purely from the perspective of the American Indian. Granted, the situations in Central America involve many Indian peoples of those countries, but the situation, in total, is decidedly different.

Indians Patriotic

For one, the populations of Nicaragua and El Salvador number in the millions as opposed to the small numbers of American Indians populating our reservations.

Number two: too many Indians served with honor and pride in the armed forces of this country, and are not prone to follow the Marxist leanings of these South American leftists, but, instead, are willing to see changes made which will improve the economic and governmental structures on the reservations, but remain patriotic Americans. Radical change based on revolution is contrary to their inherent beliefs.

The word liberty, as applied to the American Indian, is at best, transitory. In seeking liberty, the American people have often found it necessary to trample upon the rights of the Indian people because the Indian's sense of liberty did not coincide with their own version of liberty. The Indian stood in the path of the "Manifest Destiny" of the founding fathers and, therefore, was not entitled to the same liberties.

It is this version of selective liberty that has alienated the Indian people, and has caused organizations opposed to the hypocrtical espousal of "Liberty and justice for all" to form and take angry exception to this sanctioned tyranny.

To say, "We've given the American Indian everything they want—food, housing, schools and hospitals" is a cop out of the greatest magnitude. The treaties signed by the federal govenment and the Indian tribes guaranteed these necessities of life in exchange for land. These items are not gifts. Instead, they are governmental obligations.

There are two other items found in almost every single treaty between the U.S. government and the Indian nations which are very conveniently overlooked and ignored. The treaties also guaranteed the Indian tribes "liberty and self-government."

There are no peoples on the face of this earth who love liberty as much as the American Indian. And yet, we were the last people to be granted American citizenship and the basic right to practice our religious beliefs without federal or state intervention.

Perhaps there should be a total re-evaluation of the priorities of the United States in dealing with the Indian nations and, possibly, a re-evaluation of the methods being used by Indian protest groups to attain the goals we are seeking.

One thing is for sure. Until America learns to deal fairly and objectively with the First Americans, there is no such thing as "liberty" in this country.

Some Rejected by Melting Pot

One day, several weeks ago, a resident of the Pine Ridge Reservation was a guest on a local radio talk show. One of the questions asked of him is one we hear quite frequently. "Why can't you Indians quit considering yourselves different and just be plain Americans?"

It would take much more space than this column to fully answer that question, but I will make an effort to hit upon some of the more important reasons why most Indians have not been integrated into the "great American melting pot" these many years.

An Indian man left his family on the reservation and moved in with his in-laws in Rapid City to search for a job. Since the unemployment rate on the reservation is catastrophic (estimated to be 80 percent), he was unable to obtain employment at home.

Seeking Work

First of all, he began the difficult task of seeking work in a city with a depleted job market and he ran into all the racial problems most Indians confront when seeking employment. He had to answer the questions dealt to him from a position of gross ignorance. "Do you drink? Will you show up for work every day? Are you a member of any radical organization?" These are questions that would never be asked of a non-Indian, but desparate for work, he submitted to this unfair interrogation without complaint.

Although he held an associate degree in business, he accepted a position as a custodian, glad to find this job. He worked at this task diligently for one month, sending most of his income home to his wife and three children, and setting aside a small sum out of each week's check toward renting a house or apartment in order to move his family from the reservation to join him.

Savings in hand, he set about trying to find a place for his family. Every evening, after work, he would check the "For Rent" ads in the newspaper, and then he would visit the landlords who had advertised the vacancies. Time after time, he was told that the apartment had just been rented or that the newspaper had printed the cost of the apartment erroneously. The landlord would say, "That was supposed to read $300, not $200!"

At long last, he found a small rundown house in the north part of the city, paid a rather large deposit, the first month's rent, and then visited the various utility companies to see about having the gas and lights turned on. He was not at all surprised to find that there are some rather healthy deposits required by the utility companies before they will provide service.

Eternal Optimist

The young man was an eternal optimist. He shrugged off the obvious attempts at discrimination as "one of the hazards of being an Indian" and moved his family to Rapid City.

Now it was time to celebrate the family reunion. The young man took his family to a fast food restaurant for treats. Seated directly behind his family, in an adjoining booth were four non-Indians. Speaking just loud enough for the Indian family to overhear him, one of the non-Indians said, "I wouldn't rent any of my houses to an Indian. A friend of mine felt very sorry for one of them one time, and he rented them an apartment. The next thing he knows, the whole damned Indian reservation moved in."

The young man's wife was livid with anger, but he motioned her to remain calm. Quietly, they finished their meal—which was no longer very enjoyable—and left the restaurant.

The next day was Saturday. He cashed his paycheck, and took his family to a large department store to purchase clothing and shoes for his children. A store clerk lurked behind the rows of shelves keeping a wary eye on the young Indian family. Every time a non-Indian entered the department store, the clerk rushed over to ask, "Can I help you?" She completely ignored the Indian family.

When they selected the merchandise, they took it to a checkout counter. Without a word, or a smile, the clerk hastily added up the total, and stuffed the goods into a brown bag, applying several staples to close off the opening in the bag.

Still Cheerful

Still cheerful, the young Indian family headed out to the parking lot. As they were depositing their merchandise into the trunk of their car, a non-Indian family (woman and four children) were getting out of their car. As the non-Indian children began to race about playfully, their mother shouted, "You kids better start behaving yourselves. You're acting like a bunch of wild Indians!"

Welcome to the land of the "plain American!"

The point I am trying to make by this factual story is this: Many many Indians have tried to become a part of the system, but they found out that they were never allowed to forget they were different. They were never permitted to join the mainstream, but, instead, they were discriminated against, excluded, isolated, and made to feel they did not belong.

The majority can put the minority down for only so long. Then the time will come when that minority will turn their backs on the hypocrisy and return to the lifestyle in which they feel comfortable. How would you, as non-Indians, react to the same kind of biased treatment?

Opposition Voiced on Radical Groups

An angry lady called me at the office the other day. She said, "I am a Navajo woman, and I have a few comments to make." She continued, "The other night on the evening news, they carried a story about the American Indian Movement using vehicles to remove the Iranian students from a building in New York, and transport them to Washington, D.C., so that they could continue to demonstate against this country."

She concluded emphatically, "I do not wish to be identified in any way, shape or form with these radicals. They do not represent me, or anyone that I know, and yet, when they do things like this, it reflects upon all Indian people."

Not long ago, I asked the vice president of the Oglala Sioux Tribe what he thought about AIM involvement in Iran, and he replied, "We have enough problems on our own reservation without sticking our noses into international problems. I am aware of all the complexities of the problem, but I think that we ought to let our government handle it without our interference."

Of course, I realize that there are two sides to every story, so I spoke with a longtime member of AIM. Although he did not wish to be identified, he did make these comments, "The United States government has been abusive of many other nations. They made treaties and they broke those treaties, they took their lands and their minerals. Many of the things they did in Iran, they did to the Indian people in this country." He continued, "As an informed member of a large Indian tribe, I know for a fact that much of our wealth was taken illegally, like the cream off the top, and yet we are still poor people. I believe that the U.S. government and the big oil companies used the Shah of Iran as a scapegoat to cover up their own excesses."

That brings us back to an important point. Is it necessary to support the cause of a band of international terrorists and kidnappers in order to prove a point? In the long run, won't this approach do more harm to the Indian cause than good?

Over the past few years, organizations such as AIM have found that the initial support they received form the Indian people, and from church groups who supplied funding, is dwindling to the point of being non-existent.

My criticisms of AIM members for their inability to pursue any consistent pattern of support for Indian causes, and of their penchant to go off on "wild goose chases" that reveal these inconsistencies, and further alienate other concerned Indians from voicing their support for these "unrealistic" causes, have brought sharp attacks upon me from Russell Means and other AIM leaders.

I was moved to answer one of these attacks in an editorial which ran in another newspaper. My contention is this: Anyone who chooses to criticize the American Indian Movement is not criticizing the Indian people. AIM and the Indian people are not one and the same, as Means and others would have the American public believe. Even in South Dakota, where AIM originated, and where its strength is centered, it has only one percent of the total Indian population as followers. Since the Great Sioux Nation is comprised of seven reservations containing about 60,000 residents, you can see that AIM has failed to enlist a large following.

Radical organizations such as AIM have failed to get the support of the majority of Indians because they chose to run "rough-shod" over anyone or anything that questioned their tactics, including their own Indian people. Like the Black Panthers, they attempted to get the attention of the American public by committing acts of violence.

There is not one single, peace-loving Indian nation in this country that will condone violence, no matter the cause. Violence begets violence, and it is the elders, the women and children who suffer the most.

Indian tribes will continue to use the remedies provided for them under the Constitution of the United States to correct past wrongs. Only if these remedies are denied to the Indian nations, and only then, will other methods be employed.

Woman Encounters Bias of Landlord

There are waters that are best left undisturbed, or so say some critics. If one involved in journalism begins to wade into these waters, it is often with extreme care and trepidation. From past experiences, I am aware of the consequences of pointing out things that are unpleasant, but which are also illegal.

The subject of this column was prompted by a discussion I had recently with a young, professional Navajo woman. It deals with discrimination in housing.

Fair housing is described in the American Civil Rights Handbook this way: "The right of all people to equal housing opportunity, known as 'fair housing,' is a broadly protected right. Discrimination in the sale or rental, financing and advertising of real estate and housing is illegal. It covers all housing EXCEPT rental housing with fewer than five units one of which the owner lives in, and single family, privately-owned houses are covered by the act. This law prohibits refusal to sell or rent a house or discrimination in terms or conditions of sale or rental because of a person's race, religion, or national origin.

As I stated earlier, the case in point concerned that of a young Navajo woman who moved to Farmington, New Mexico recently because of a job offered to her. After she was interviewed for the position, and accepted, she began to search for an apartment for herself. She asked her new boss, a non-

Indian man, to keep an eye out for an apartment for her, and in the meantime, she would use the advertisements in the newspaper as another source of housing.

Her boss, who was also new in Farmington, discovered that there were several vacancies at the apartment house where he dwelled, and he verified these vacancies by speaking directly with the landlord. The Navajo lady went immediately to the landlord of the apartment complex, and was informed that there was only one apartment available, and it rented for X number of dollars, which proved to be far more (twice as much) than her boss was paying for the same type of apartment. The exorbitant rental cost was far out of her price range.

The next day, at work, she informed her boss of the situation, and he, in turn, confronted the landlord with his obvious case of racial discrimination. Her boss was told, quite bluntly, "We have had a number of problems in the past in renting to Indians, so we try our best NOT to rent to them. When you rent to one Navajo, it seems like the whole reservation moves in with them!"

One would have a very hard time convincing most Indians that the flagrant violation of the law in the case described is an exception to the rule; but, in fairness to those people who own rental property, there are many fine, law-abiding citizens who would never resort to such tactics. These are the same people who did not need a law to tell them about fairness but acted out of consicence and a sense of fair play. Are they the exception to the rule, or is it the other way around?

There are legal remedies to this type of discrimination. If you feel that you have been discriminated against in the sale of a house or the rental of an apartment, you should file a complaint within 180 days of the act with: Director of Equal Housing Opportunity; Director of Housing and Urban Development; Washington, DC 20410.

Oh, yes, the Navajo lady of this column DID find an apartment, and has settled into her job, and her life, as a new resident of Farmington. She decided not to make waves!

Hatred, Prejudice Seem to Increase

There is an ugly mood spreading within this country. Even those famous "halls of ivy," the institutions of higher education, are not immune from this resurrection of a violent past.

This mood has manifested itself in cross burnings on the campuses of several colleges, hate graffiti scrawled on dormitory walls, and in the form of venomous letters.

Are there people living in this country who are so naive as to believe that because there has been a sudden shift to conservatism nationally due to the election of Ronald Reagan as president, open attacks of racism will be tolerated? Do certain individuals misread these signs and now believe that racial intolerance is now respectable?

Dangerous Concept

Whatever the causes for this resurgence of prejudice, it is a very dangerous concept and one which portends an ominous future. It is my belief that the many giant strides made by the minorities of this nation will not be jeopardized. There are far more good people in this country than bad, and these people are actuely aware of the severe consequences that can befall this great nation, if those people attempting to spread hatred are allowed to gain the upper hand.

One can pick up a newspaper and read about activities involving the Ku Klux Klan or the American Nazi Party and realize that even these despicable organizations are gaining strength. Most of us can thank God that such groups are detested by the majority of the people.

The tremendous influx of Third World refugees into this country has contributed to this mood. It began with the immigration of the Vietnamese, and came to a head with the acceptance of Cuban citizens by the Immigration Service. One elderly Indian man said to me, "I wonder if the non-Indian would have raised such a ruckus if these immigrants would have been white?"

Make no mistake about it, many Indian people were as intolerant of these refugees as non-Indians. Some said, "We are having enough trouble surviving ourselves. Now these people will be getting millions of dollars, money we have been fighting years to get, and it will make our situation even worse."

Open Borders

There seems to be a general feeling that this country can no longer open up its borders to anyone who wishes to enter. There are those who believe that the time has come to re-evaluate our immigration laws, update them, and to drastically reduce the number of applicants allowed into this country.

Third World Nations such as Iran, which take hostages with a total disregard for international law or human decency, and then taunt this country with a carrot and a stick approach to politics, have further served to infuriate the citizens of this country, and undoubtedly have caused some bitter feeling among some extremists against all people with dark skins.

One contributing factor to this uneasy mood which cannot be overlooked and, in fact, may be the biggest villain of all, is the sorry state of the economy. Those who "have" are losing ground with each passing month, and they are in no mood to lose more. Some of these people may even look upon progressive strides made by the "have nots" as threats to their own security.

Indignant Lady

People are angry and they are striking out, sometimes blindly. One indignant white lady said, "I raised three children by myself, without food stamps or welfare, and they all turned out just fine. Now, if I can do it, why can't all of those people on welfare, those bloodsuckers and parasites, do the same thing?"

Yes, the mood of the country is an ugly one. It is imperative that cooler heads take the reins and keep this nation on the right path. So many barriers have been broken down by the minorities of this country over the past twenty years, and it is a frightening prospect to imagine that this mood, brought about by a forecast of hard times, can rebuild those barriers, and throw us back into the dark ages of intolerance.

No, the leadership and the citizens of this country should not be looking for scapegoats to punish for their own excesses, which caused many of these problems; but instead, should be seeking solutions for the benefit of all.

Approaches Vary, But Goals Similar

Those of you who are regular readers of this column will recall that I have had a running battle (verbal) with Russell Means of the American Indian Movement for the past few months. An incident occurred which I believe will bring you up to date on that situation.

Last week, I had occasion to visit Farmington, New Mexico on business, and on the return flight to Rapid City, South Dakota, we had to change planes at Stapleton International Airport in Denver. As I walked toward the end of a long line of airline passengers to board that plane, I ran smack-dab into Russell Means. Means stands about a head taller than I, and with a red bandana wrapped around his forehead and his long hair hanging loosely over his shoulders, he is a fearsome figure, indeed.

We spotted each other simultaneously, and Means held out his hand, and said "Hello, Brother," to me in Lakota, and burst out into laughter.

We both acknowledged that we had a colorful exchange of opinions in the newspaper, and Russell asked, "Did you get the last letter I sent to the editor?" I admitted that I had not. He said, "It was a very short note. It said 'You took the bait hook, line and sinker. . . HA! HA!'"

The reason I am taking the time to relate this incident to you, is because I believe that it says something for the Indian people, and for the cause many of us are fighting for.

Many of us who grew up on Indian reservations have lived with the double standards applied to Indians. One incident in particular has always stuck in my mind. One day, my father and I visited a town which bordered our reservation in South Dakota. After taking care of our business, we stopped at a local restaurant. We took a table and waited, and waited to be served. After a very long wait, the manager of the restaurant came to our table and said, "I'm going to have to ask you to leave, because we don't serve Indians here."

If this had happened to you, what kind of an impression would it have left on your mind about the white establishment? My first reaction was humiliation and then anger. I was very young at the time and I asked my father why they did this to us. In fact, I urged him to do something about it. He replied, "There is nothing I can do, and maybe when you get a little older, you'll understand."

Emma Hollow Horn, a Lakota grandmother from White Horse Creek

352   Rights

I resolved at that time to do something about this kind of blatant injustice. The route I selected is a route which many Indians follow. It is one of working within the legal structure of the country to bring about changes peaceably. There are many of us who do not believe in violent confrontations, but who will pursue every legal remedy available in order to insure justice for all Indian people.

Russell Means encountered this kind of injustice; but he reacted in a different manner. Perhaps there are many of us who cannot condone the manner in which he carried out his revolution; but we must admit that he is a man of courage. He has been imprisoned, he has been stabbed, he has been shot and he has been viciously beaten, but he has remained resolute in his beliefs.

Since his release from prison last year, he has taken a more peaceful approach to attaining his goals; but his objectives are still the same. He believes in tribal sovereignty and the restitution of the sacred Black Hills to the Lakota people. In this pursuit, he has remained adamantly sincere.

I chose the field of journalism in order to open up a line of communications between people; others have chosen medicine, education or law to accomplish their objectives for their people, and Russell Means chose the route of confrontation. There was only one purpose behind our motives and it is best said in my own language, "Hecel lena oyate kinnipi kte." ("That these people may live.")

Grassroots People Often Overlooked

Over the past two decades, a trend has developed among national Indian organizations that many reservation-oriented Indians find disconcerting. It has become the policy of these organizations to hold gigantic conventions in metropolitan areas which makes it impossible for the poor, grassroots Indian to attend. What is even more discouraging is that these conventions are turning into social affairs for the upper middle-class urban Indian.

This unfortunate situation was set in motion by the National Congress of American Indians, one of the oldest Indian organizations, and it has been heralded by the National Indian Education Association, and refined by new organizations as the Native American Public Broadcasting Consortium.

It is beoming apparent that the very people in whose name these "elite" organizations flourish, the average, reservation-based American Indian, is being totally excluded from participating. After all, how many of the very poor Indians can afford to attend these extravagant and costly affairs, even if they wanted to?

Voices Unheard

Why haven't these organizations seen fit to hold these conventions on a different reservation every year so that the average Indian they are purporting to help will be able to attend, and perhaps, have a say in the decisions that are being made in his behalf?

An unkown Indian poet, reflecting on this unfortunate situation, composed this poem, which made the rounds; but had no apparent impact on the convention "trendies." It goes like this:

The Holiday Inn-dian

Author Unknown

Pack your bags, boys, we're catching the plane,
For Denver, or Tucson, or Bangor, Maine.
Get your per diem 'cause we've got to have cash,
We're holding a meeting on the great White backlash!
Call Frontier, or Western, and Hertz Rent-A-Car,
And be sure that the hotel has got a good bar.
Get in your car, or you'll miss the last flight,
We're dancing the boogie in Denver tonight!
Why are we going? Well, who the heck cares?
It's got something to do with Indian affairs.
Our assistants are welcome, we'll take the whole pack,
We'll decide why we took them—when we get back.
We'll boogie and dance—maybe take in the sights,
As we travel United, for your Indian rights!

Social Events

This poem, or many versions of it, has been posted in offices or on bulletin boards all over Indian Country; but the conventions continue, getting bigger and costlier every year. As I said, they are becoming the social events of the year.

It is my contention, and I am not alone in my feelings, that every Indian man or woman who is selected to work for any Indian organization or governmental agency which administers to the needs of the Indian people, should be required to return to his or her reservation for at least two years. This would bring them back to reality.

What is even more improtant than that, it would give these individuals the opportunity of familiarizing themselves with day-to-day problems that exist on reservations, and at the same time, enable them to get an education in tribal government.

For too many years, the politics of hiring these individuals has been left up to the Washington, D.C. bureaucrats. As a direct result we have many Indians holding important positions who cannot relate to the very people they are being paid to represent.

Racism Dispelled Through Indian Youth Events

It all started back in 1951, in the days of the "Dark Ages" for Indian people.

In many towns of the West, signs were posted in restaurants and bars that read: "No Indian Trade Allowed" or "Indians and Mexicans Not Served Here." Sheridan, Wyoming was no exception.

Sheridan's annual rodeo was called the Bots Sots Stampede and Indian dancers often entertained the audience. Every year a rodeo queen was chosen to represent the city of Sheridan.

In 1951, a young Crow Indian named Lucy Yellow Mule entered the competition. Her courage and determination impressed even the crowd. Standing tall and proud, Miss Yellow Mule was astounded to hear the tremendous applause that rang out in the arena as she stepped forward to be acknowledged. She won the competition and broke down many racial barriers in the process.

A journalist named Howard Sinclair, who wrote under the pen name of "Neckyoke Jones," was in town that year. The morning of the rodeo he met a young Indian Marine, a veteran of the Korean War, walking around the town. The young Marine was in uniform but could not find a place to eat breakfast. All of the restaurants were off limits to Indians.

Sinclair became very angry at this gross racism and made a silent vow to do everything in his power to fight racial discrimination against the Indian people.

From this small beginning was born the All American Indian Days celebration that has become an annual event. The climax of the event is the National Miss Indian America Pageant.

Donald Deer Nose, a Crow Indian from Lodgegrass, Montana, became the first chairman of the Indian Executive Committee. He helped organize Indian participation in the annual event, traveling to many reservations promoting the show.

The articles of incorporation for the All American Indian Days celebration outline as one of the major objectives a policy "to foster and promote better understanding between the Indian and white races; to support the American Indian citizens' effort to better the condition of the Indian race politically, socially and economically."

The very first Miss Indian America, chosen in 1953, was a Yakima girl named Arlene Wesley. In 1981, Jerilyn LeBeau, a Miniconjou from the Cheyenne River Reservation, was crowned.

Miss LeBeau, who lives in Eagle Butte, has traveled across the United States representing the Indian people. She has made many TV appearances, and has been a frequent guest speaker for civic groups and conventions. Miss LeBeau has been a welcome visitor to many Indian schools throughout the year.

This year the Miss American Indian Pageant begins with Sheridan's Indian Awareness Week, July 26. The pageant concludes with the coronation of the new Miss Indian America on Saturday, July 31.

Athletic Scholarships

Two great all-around athletes from Red Cloud Indian School have been offered college scholarships. Melvin High Hawk, who led the state of South Dakota in scoring percentage this basketball season, has been offered a scholarship by Chadron State College at Chadron, Nebraska. John Paul Iron Cloud may be attending Huron State College at Huron, South Dakota, if he accepts the scholarship offered to him.

Principal Chuck Cuny of Red Cloud Indian School said, "Coach Rol Bradford sent many letters to different colleges, and spoke with many college coaches in order to promote the Indian athletes on his teams."

Many of the Indian schools do not get the publicity of the schools located in other parts of the state, and Cuny believes that it is imperative that the coaching staff and educators of the reservation school "take the bull by the horns" and actively promote Indian students who have excelled athletically and academically.

Joe Swift Bird, one of the finest all-around athletes to come out of Oglala Community School at Pine Ridge (he holds the regional long jump record and won the state long jump title this year) was offered a full scholarship at Haskell Indian Institute in Kansas. Swift Bird, who wants to pursue an art career, has not made up his mind about whether to accept the scholarship or not.

A few years back I wrote about many great Indian athletes of the past who never had the opportunity to go to college because they were never offered athletic scholarships. I'm happy to see that, as Bob Dylan said, "Times, they are a-changing."

Chapter IX—Religion

Overleaf:
The buffalo is important in Lakota religion

Religion

Religious Freedom Act Two Years Old

Several weeks ago an article was sent over the wires of the Associated Press which was picked up by many newspapers, including this one, that was guilty of containing a very serious, erroneous assumption. The article stated that the date the Indian people of this country were granted religious freedom under the American Indian Freedom Act, P.L. 95-341, was 1936.

Actually, President Jimmy Carter signed P.L. 95-341 into law on August 11, 1978. There is a slight difference of forty-two years involved in this major error. At first I thought that it had been a printing or typographical error; but the more I looked at it, I could not see how a 1936 could be, inadvertently, written in place of 1978.

Why is it important that this error be pointed out and corrected? By using the date, 1936, it is made to appear that the Indian people of this continent had religious freedom for the past forty-two years, not just the last two years. Even though the ancestors of the white settlers came to these shores over four hundred years ago, in search of religious freedom, it is tragically ironic that the original inhabitants of this nation did not receive their religious freedom until two years ago!

Many people wonder why a special law had to be passed in order to give religious freedom to the Indian people. As a matter of fact, one of the chief opponents of this bill was U.S. Representative Jack Cunningham of the state of Washington who kept asking, "Why do Indians have to have a special law passed granting them religious freedom? Are they not covered under the Constitution of the United States?"

Freedom Restricted

As a matter of fact, they are not! Many of the places in this country that were sacred to the Indian people (such as the Black Hills of South Dakota) have been made into national or state parks, and in many intances, they have been made into military bases, and for these purposes they are posted with no trespassing signs, or if they are parks, the freedom to practice certain religious rites has been restricted or forbidden.

As a comparison, this is like making the holy city of Jerusalem "off limits" to all Christian or Mecca "verboten" to all Muslims. If you are not an Indian, you cannot imagine the years of misery the holy men and women have endured trying to get Congress to pass a law guaranteeing them their basic religious freedoms, freedoms that are taken for granted by the non-Indian population.

Many of the ceremonies, so important to Indian religions, in fact, an integral part of the ceremony, were outlawed by the federal government and the practitioners of these rites were arrested and often imprisoned. It seemed that in order to enjoy religious freedom, you had to practice a religion approved and sanctioned by the white man. What the white man could not understand, he banished.

Items that were essential to the rituals involved in these religious ceremonies became unobtainable. In fact, obtaining and possessing some of these items became a crime and, once again, Indian people were punished and imprisoned for practicing their religion. A good example of this occurred just a few years ago when Indian people were being arrested, tried and convicted for acquiring eagle feathers for these ceremonies. Eagle feathers are as important to many of the Indian tribes in practicing their religion as holy water and incense are to many Christian denominations.

The sacred Sun Dance, an important part of the Lakota religion was forbidden, by law, and the Lakota people had to practice this rite in secret for over one hundred years. But many of the religious customs endured and survived the laws and the attempts at destroying them, and were kept alive by the elders of each tribe. Didn't the Christians learn anything from their own holy Bible about the suppression of religion? It never works!

Speech Explains Need for Law on Religion

While gathering information from different Indian tribes which would be used to enlighten members of the "Consultation Task Force" for the American Indian Religious Freedom Act committee, ten meetings were held on different Indian reservations throughout this country, and religious leaders from the different tribes were encouraged to address the task force.

One consultation was held at Zuni Pueblo, and at that meeting Bernice Yucos of the Mescalero Apache Tribe gave a strong speech in behalf of ratifying the act. She said:

"What I have to put before you, is the right that the Indian people have to have religion wherever they want and wherever they meet, because to a white people, religion is open to them. Wherever they go, there's a church. There's the Bible; the Bible is open to them in public. And our Indian people are set back; they would not let us go to the mountains to worship as we want: to the federal land, it is restricted to us. They have restricted us from entering the state and federal lands to get our food and to practice our religious ways."

She continued:
"There are four mountains that represent the Mescalero Apaches. This is our freedom of religion before the white man came. We are there, praying for our people, not only for our people but for the whole United States so that we have freedom, that there will be no war, that we'll have peace. That's why we have these four mountains and they are all sacred to us."

Yucos went on to describe some of the plants and herbs that were an integral part of her religion, and upon the restrictions placed upon her people in trying to gather these plants.

She continued:

"And for the White Sands, this is going into the medicine part . . . We need the sage that we use for our religious medicines. We have to steal that and that's not fair. We have to go behind the bushes to get it and there's other medicines in the federal land that we should get free, as an Indian, because God gave us a different religion. God gave us different medicines to live by, to 'live by' means to help people, our people, to go on. This is our strength. This is our belief. We should keep it. That's the way we Apaches look at it. And there's the dirt and rocks that we need to get outside of our reservation, but there's the gun to stop us, against us, too. We need, our people need it. We feel that we should be free to get it."

Power to Act

Yucos was one of many Indian religious leaders from many Indian tribes who were given the opportunity to address a body, or a committee, with the powers to act in their behalf. This was one of the first times in the history of religious conflicts between the white man and the Indian in which the Indian people were treated as equal religious partners in the overall scheme of things, and their views were treated with respect and dignity.

Needless to say, there were skeptics among some of the Indian tribes, and some religious people felt that this Act would bring a new wave of religious persecution; but the majority of the people felt that it was a good thing.

Cheyenne Sacred Arrow Keeper, Edward Red Hat, summed it up: "I knew that it was supposed to help the people . . . and now—I still have my ceremonies. I hear lots of people talking. That's real good talk they make. I was thinking all the time, they are getting help. That was the first time I know that people are listening about Indian religion. I was up to Washington last summer and I made a speech over there, and that's how this religion came up. They passed on it, and now I feel good."

Religion Debate Has Its Pitfalls

The young Indian woman said, "I will not enter that church because it is where they worship the white man's God."

This comment made me realize what a no-win, combative, controversial, emotional and endless argument arises whenever organized religion is the subject matter. Witness the havoc being wrought in the name of religion in Northern Ireland and in the Middle East.

It is not the Spiritual Being, whether Wakan Tanka, Allah, Buddah or Jesus Christ that is the purveyor of this turmoil, but instead it is the human element.

If one is to believe in a God, then surely there can be no white man's God, black man's God, yellow man's God and on and on. If there is a God, and this

God is spiritual, He cannot be identified with any single race of people.

It is only when the human mind begins to interpret the adaptation of God, and begins to create the theological opinions to support his own interpretations, that God becomes identifiable with one person, one race, and one religious ideology.

Written Scriptures

Out of this state of mind comes such written scriptures as the Christian Bible and the Koran of the Muslims. Now we have the thought process of man, with all of his human frailties and fallibilities, recorded as the word of God. Man can do strange things in the name of a God he himself has created.

Today, no one can doubt the religious fervor of the Muslim sect, and yet, during the Crusades of the 11th, 12th and 13th Centuries, Christian armies attempted to win, what they called the Holy Land, from the Muslim armies in the name of God. They called the Muslims "heathens" because they were not Christians, and in turn, they were called "infidels" because they were not Muslims.

When religion becomes a mass psychologism that will sweep aside another religion as inconsequential because it is different, it then becomes a tool of the human mind. It then takes on the human characteristics of its practioners.

Since the coming of the white man to the Western Hemisphere, the Native people of the land have become objects of religious conversion by many church organizations. It has been said that there are as many as five hundred churches on the Navajo Reservation alone. In the late 1800s and early 1900s, the Indian reservations of the land were divided like so many pieces of pie, and certain sections were assigned to different religious organizations.

Assimilation

With the full assistance of the federal government, the churches set about the task of educating and converting the Indian people in order to acculturate and assimilate them into the mainstream.

Never mind that every single Indian tribe that stood in the path of manifest destiny already had a deep religious belief which was probably much older than the beliefs of those who would destroy it.

The religion practiced by the Indians of North and South America was of the spirit and of the mind. The white man could not grasp the psychology of a religion which was not recorded in books or scriptures. He had to have something tangible to hold in his hand, to read and digest. How could anything have value or substance if it were not recorded?

What mankind cannot, or will not, try to understand he will eventually try to destroy. The religion of the Indian people was not an organized entity. It was not a religion of congregations or church structures. Instead, it was a religion of the mind and soul which considered all living and growing things as a part of a natural order. When a white minister saw an Indian spiritually communicate

Pete Swift Bird

with the sky, the sun, trees, or the four-legged, he immediately assumed these to be religious objects, and accused the Indian of idolatry and paganism.

The intolerance of the white man for anything different, and the attitude of superiority attached to that intolerance, almost brought about the destruction of a religion, and with it, a way of life.

Seeds of Ignorance

There is a return to the religious ways practiced by the ancestors by many Indian tribes. But along with that revival, there are also the seeds of intolerance for those who choose to maintain the status quo. It has never been the way of the Indian to force his beliefs upon another. This is the influence of the Christian concept of conversion.

As Indians, we cannot become intolerant of those who do not believe in our ideas of spiritualism, because in so doing, we are unconsciously imitating a system of religion which attempted to engulf the beliefs of our ancestors because they did not conform.

If an Indian chooses to worship a God, it should not matter how he goes about performing that ceremony, whether on the top of a mountain or in a church, because the Great Spirit of his visions is in his mind's eye and, therefore, accessible to himself and to himself alone. There is no such thing as "a white man's God."

Swift Bird Warns Indians to Revere Sacred Pipe

Pete Swift Bird, Sr. is convinced that spiritualism is being misused against Indians and by the Indians themselves.

"There used to be an old horse and buggy priest called Father Placidas Sialm. He would travel around the reservation telling our parents they were devils for not taking the children to church. And then a Father Zimmerman would follow behind Father Sialm and console the parents who had been called devils," Swift Bird said.

"I realize the harsh discipline used against us in those days at Holy Rosary Mission is no longer used by people such as Brother George, but it was a sad experience for me."

Swift Bird told about hearing old Peg Leg (Jim Red Cloud) speak for the last time before he died. "His voice was shaky with age, but his humor was as sharp as any razor. He sang, 'Red Cloud, you asked me to learn the white man's ways, and I am having a difficult time. Red Cloud, now you are asking me to be an Indian, and I am having a hard time.' He ended his song by warning the treaty council, 'Reorganize this group, and always remember that Red Cloud's people are spiritually guided. Don't ever mock them, or bad things may befall you.' And here I was so brainwashed, I didn't understand what the old man was trying to tell us," Swift Bird said.

"I left the reservation and moved to Kansas City, and then to Chicago. In Chicago I met people like Bennie Bear Skin, Helen Peterson and LaVern

Madigan, and all of those people were trying to tell me that they were Lakota. They formed an organization called the American Indian Center and helped to push the Public Health Hospitals onto the reservation. The reservation Indians never had any say in the matter."

Swift Bird told about seeing many reservation Indians come to the ghettos while he lived in Chicago. "The BIA was sending families from the reservations to the cities in large numbers. It was called 'relocation.' And when the poor reservation Indians came, the city Indians were using them for all of their own causes.

"Drugs and alcohol got the best of me at that time, and so I returned home to the reservation licking my wounds. Nothing had changed. The same old problems were here, only worse. This time it was Charlie Red Cloud trying to unite the people. He had little success because everybody wanted to be a chief and nobody wanted to be a plain Indian," he said sorrowfully.

Swift Bird described how he decided to move to California for one year. He wanted to prove to himself that he could hold a steady job, pay his bills, stay sober under any condition and pray without doubts. "I knew if I could do these things, I would be worthy of the pipe I intended to carry and pray with. I returned home to the reservation the day that President Kennedy was killed."

He paused, as if to let the things he had been saying register on the listener. "Well, I am home now. Too old to run, and nothing to prove to myself anymore. And this time it is Oliver Red Cloud trying to warn the people, just as his forefathers did. He is trying to make his people understand that the Sacred Pipe is being abused and mocked. There are too many pipes and too many shallow ways to use the words "grandfather and Lakota," and so many of our relations with no spiritual values. We have so many sun dances we begin to look like used car lots, banners and all. We have some of our people running here and there, just like looking for new customers.

"What has all this go to do with baptism and a radio program? Swift Bird asked. "Well, I am still a Catholic, but the last time I went to church in Rapid City, I saw a priest dancing down the aisle with two women to the music of rock and roll. On the reservation, I saw a priest offering the peace pipe. So, if the lady wants her child baptized, she should be very careful about where she takes it, because how can you tell if you are speaking to a nun or priest any more?

"As for the radio talk show, I would tell Russell Means: 'There are so many young people confused about religion and spirituality, their traditions and culture. Send them home to their parents and let the elders teach them. And, above all, Russell, watch for the signs that are telling you things, and remember that Red Cloud warned us! There are no books, no Yellow Thunder Camps, or any Black Hills Alliance clubs that will ever help you find Red Cloud's prayer grounds or his medicine. Only Red Cloud and Sitting Bull know the secret of the Black Hills and the Treaty,'" Swift Bird said with finality.

After a long pause, he added, "And, finally, Russell, there is so much hatred and confusion on the reservation, and we are all trying to make amends and unite, so please don't make the job more difficult for the Red Cloud Band of

Indians."

Freedom of Religion Prevails in Spite of Setbacks

A tourist visiting the reservation told me that when one entered the borders of the reservation, "it was like entering a foreign country." I would imagine that driving into a country where people are a different race, where even the language is different, a place that bares all of the scars of an impoverished nation, and realizing that this country is within the boundaries of the United States of America, could generate quite a cultural shock.

I am reminded of the generations of "volunteer missionaries" who came to our reservation to teach at the Indian missions and formed many lifelong friendships with their fellow "volunteers," but never made an effort to become closely acquainted with the families of the Indian children they had come to teach. Exceptions notwithstanding, most of these "volunteers" did not have the courage to try to understand, or to bridge the cultural gap.

One such person was a Jesuit priest named Michael Steltenkamp. He came to Red Cloud Indian School on the Pine Ridge Reservation in 1974 to teach, took an interest in "Native American religion and its practice today," and wrote a book about it entitled, *The Sacred Vision*. In the final chapter Steltenkamp wrote, "One of the prevailing themes worthy of attention is religious consciousness itself. As mentioned earlier, Native people are (like non-Indians) sometimes not very familiar with their own tradition. At other times, their knowledge is reflective and implicit. By contrast, religious specialists who devote their time to such thought are more articulate."

There are thousands of Indian people who experienced the articulation of "religious specialists" who came to the reservations as missionaries and under the guise of religion attempted to destroy the culture, religions, and traditions of the Native peoples. Throughout this book, Steltenkamp draws analogies between Christianity and Native religion and almost backhandedly, postulates over what he perceives to be a certain amount of confusion in the minds of some Native practitioners of the traditional religion.

Has the near fanatical fervor so prevalent at the Indian missions of this land over the first sixty years of this century become so obscure, a fervor dedicated to assimilating the Indian people and erasing all memories of a traditional belief from the core of the mind, that Steltenkamp failed to see it? Or has it been so neatly swept under the Christian rug that it is no longer considered as a part of the Jesuit history that spawned it?

After more than one hundred years of mental and physical indoctrination of Indian children by dogmatists every bit as dedicated and determined to destroy alien thought and practice as the Soviet Union has done in countries it has occupied, is it any wonder that there is some confusion in the minds of Native people turning back to their own religion? The real miracle is that we have survived this assault upon our culture at all. The Indian religion was never destroyed; it only went underground.

There are thousands of us who can recall, with vivid clarity, attending church services seven days a week at the Indian missions. We can recall kneeling in hardwood pews until our young knees ached with pain, knowing that anything less than our reverent attention to the services would bring us a rap on the head with a key ring or knuckle.

We can recall attending classes in American history and being taught that our ancestors were blood-thirsty savages with no higher ambition than to rage, pillage, and kill the white settlers. We were taught that the religions of these heathens were paganistic. The clear implication was that if we did not embrace Catholicism, we would be doomed to the same destruction as our ancestors.

Early this summer I participated in a traditional naming ceremony performed by my good friend and medicine man, Grover Horned Antelope. The name *Nawica Kjici* was bestowed upon me by former Oglala Sioux Tribal President Enos Poor Bear. As the mroning sun climbed high in the deep blue sky, four eagles had soared and swooped above us. Flying in pairs, they had gracefully turned and flown away in the direction of the good red road. My Lakota name was now *Defender*.

As we stood and prayed, I could not help but think of those days I spent kneeling in the Catholic Church. I could not help but compare it to the beauty of the traditional church, the grass and earth upon which we stood, at the foothills of the Sacred Black Hills, under a clear blue sky, feeling the gentle breezes of the early summer, and listening to the music the wind made as it rustled the leaves of the tall cottonwood trees. The gentle fragrance of the smoke drifting upward from the burning sage was of another world, a world far apart from the pungent odor of the oil used to preserve the wooden pews of the church at Holy Rosary Mission.

Why would a nation that preached freedom of religion make such a concerted effort to destroy this beautiful religion? Was it because they believed they would destroy the people if they destroyed the religion? Or was it that they could not tolerate anyone or anything that was different, that did not jump gladly into the great melting pot called America?

Father Steltenkamp has much to learn about Indians and the Native religions. Perhaps his book would be more meaninful if he had not become an "Indian expert" before his education was completed.

Traditional dancers

People

Priest's Death People's Loss

Even the huge gymnasium in Rapid City was too small. The crowds overflowed into the corridors and people lined the walls. The late arrivals had to stand outside the building watching and waiting for the services to end; but they stayed.

Indians and whites seated side by side, many with tears flowing unashamedly down their faces, had come to pay their last respects to a man who had been labeled "radical" by some because of his pointed and vocal efforts to uphold the human rights of the Indian community.

Television cameras, manned by the local news people, roamed the aisles like obtrusive spectators, panning the mourning audience and searching out the grief-stricken faces. "My God! Is there no respite for him, even in death?" one lady uttered aloud to no one in particular.

Anger Magnified

The Indian people of the city were outraged. Their anger at the assailants magnified by the announcement that the suspects were "two Indian males, 17 to 25 years old with ponytails" and their shock was heightened by the possibility this heinous crime could have been committed by two of their own people.

The Reverend James O'Connor, S.J., was due to celebrate his twenty-fifth Jubilee on June 28. He had come to this city eight years ago and had quickly squelched any doubts about his sincerity by rolling up his sleeves and dedicating his every waking hour to standing up for the basic dignity of the Indian people and the poor of the parish.

The burglars, who interrupted the slumber of Father O'Connor and his good friend and compatriot, the Reverend Richard Pates, S.J., showed no emotion or compassion for their victims. As O'Connor lay dying from a fatal heart seizure, compounded by an apparent blow to the back of his neck by one of the assailants, Pates tried desperately to go to his assistance. He was rewarded for his heroic efforts by the bark of a handgun which sent a bullet crashing into his body. Fortunately, Father Pates will survive this violent act.

"Wicasa Wakan" the elders of the community called them, "Holy Men." O'Connor and Pates were cut from a different mold. The chemistry between the two priests, the ability to interpret the Bible with a good dose of common sense, and the respect they both held for the Indian religion and its practitioners, gained them in turn, the respect of every Indian who took the trouble to get to know them.

Holy Men Targets

It should not matter whether one is Catholic, Protestant or a traditional Indian who practices the teachings of the Lakota ways. A deep respect for the

Holy Man is common to all. The violence that is ripping the very fabric of the white society and the Indian reservation community apart is sinking to its lowest depths when the Holy Men become the targets.

I would venture to say that the root evil behind this mindless and aimless violence is drugs, and taken in conjunction with alcohol, they are destroying our way of life.

An elderly man from the Medicine Root District of the Pine Ridge Reervation told me recently, "Did you know there are no words in Lakota language for key or lock?" He continued, "When I was a young man, we had respect for each other's property and rights. We didn't need keys or locks to tell us that stealing from each other was wrong."

And so the huge gathering sat in silence, heads bowed, witness to the mounting tragedies they endured. "How could it happen?" Each and everyone of us, from the Indian reservations of this country to the cities, are asking that question.

Indians Lose Friend

The sad—no, the tragic—consequence of the untimely death of this dedicated and unselfish man, is that, by his passing, the Indian community loses an irreplaceable friend. Father O'Connor was not a talker—he was a doer. He did not consider the Indian people converts—he considered them his friends.

He was simple and direct—quick to smile, to laugh or to joke. It was these special qualities, truly gifts of the Great Spirit, which endeared him to the poor and the minorities.

If his passing causes us to pause and to reflect upon the violent ways which have become the rule, rather than the exception, and inspires us to bring back the beauty, the trust, and the kindness which seems to have left us many years ago, then Father O'Connor will not have died in vain.

Coach Bob Clifford Deserves Honors; Primaries Make Reservation Rife with Scandal Sheets

You won't find his name listed among those in the South Dakota Coaches' Hall of Fame even though his accomplishments were equal to or even superior to many of those enshrined in this exclusive fraternity. His achievements were even more remarkable because of the built-in failure factors he had to overcome.

His name is Bob Clifford, but he was known simply as "Coach" to the many hundreds of boys and girls he coached for over three decades at Holy Rosary Mission (now called Red Cloud) on the Pine Ridge Reservation.

You'll find his name on the statistics sheet of South Dakota traffic fatalities because he lost his life in one at the age of seventy-one but he deserves to be remembered for much more than this.

He coached at a time when Indian coaches in the United States could be counted on one hand. His teams were often short of equipment; but they never were short on spirit and talent.

Last Friday, between games at Holy Rosary, he was honored by the school he loved. His accomplishments as a coach are too numerous to mention in this short column, but they were astounding. Many of those present gasped aloud when told his girls' basketball teams were undefeated for an unbelievable fifteen years!

Many of the former athletes he coached were present that night as two of his sons, Lennie, a teacher and counselor at Red Cloud, and Gerald, president of a consulting firm, accepted the plaque in his honor.

The trophy shelves are filled with the evidence of his coaching talent, awards for many Catholic state championships and Indian tournaments his teams won. But this is hardly the true measure of the man. There is another quality he provided for all to share, an intangible aura that revealed the real essence of the man; that rarity is called "inspiration."

It is our hope that some day, when those people who place the names of great coaches on lists to be considered for the Coaches Hall of Fame, the name of Bob Clifford will be added to it, and that this great individual, an American Indian, be awarded the honor he so richly deserves. His name is already enshrined in the hearts of the men and women of the Pine Ridge Reservation.

Primaries and the Scandal Sheets

The Oglala Sioux election primaries are just a scant twelve days away. As we approach this deadline, the anonymous journalists begin to distribute their wares across the reservation. These journalistic tidbits have one thing in common: they are unsigned. This gives the author the ability to take libelous pot shots at their adversaries from the safety of anonymity.

For the most part, these "scandal sheets" have lost their shock ability because of their outrageous statements. They are, nonetheless, read with voracity by the news-hungry residents of Pine Ridge.

They are copied and recopied, passed from hand to hand, and are the subject of much conversation. Usually these "rags" are read with an unabashed glee by the general population. Of course, the exceptions to this mirth are those unfortunate individuals who have been singled out for such recognition.

The wide circulation of these "scandal sheets" brings into sharp focus the desperate need for an established form of news media on this reservation.

Optimism Displayed by LaDonna Harris

The last time I saw LaDonna Harris was at a convention held in Dallas, Texas. I was working as the producer of a television special for the ABC affiliate in Rapid City, South Dakota, and my cameraman and I had set up our lights and equipment in the lobby of the gigantic convention center in Dallas.

We were busily buttonholing potential guests for the television special when Mrs. Harris came flying through the lobby, her dress flowing gracefully behind her, with several people almost running to keep up with her. I had to smile to myself, because this is the way she always moves about, as if there weren't enough time in the day to reach her objective.

The first time I met Mrs. Harris was in Washington, D.C., in 1974. She was, and still is, the president of Americans for Indian Opportunity, an offshoot of Oklahomans for Indian Opportunity; the wife of former U.S. Senator Fred Harris; and a longtime advocate of Indian rights.

A Comanche Indian woman, Mrs. Harris had established her office in Washington, D.C., after her husband and high school sweetheart, Senator Harris, had been elected from the state of Oklahoma. On any given day of the week, Indians from several tribes, or many organizations could be found in her spacious, upstairs office. In fact, after Mrs. Harris had made the acquaintance of the visitors from the many reservations, she often used her staff to assist in setting up appointments with the "powers that be" and her office became a home away from home to the Indian representatives visiting Washington, D.C. Mrs. Harris opened many doors, from her many political contacts, for the people from the various tribes and, quite often. she used her considerable influence and expertise to assist them in solving special problems and her staff contributed the legwork and paper work to help get projects and proposals off the ground. LaDonna's office was a godsend to the weary travelers, usually suffering from jet-lag, and it was a very popular gathering place for tribal officials visiting that cold and hostile city.

As they say in politics, LaDonna "threw her hat in the ring" and became a candidate for the vice presidency of the United States on the ticket with Barry Commoner. The party they belong to is brand new, and is called the Citizens Party. They have no illusions of grandeur and, therefore, they entertain no notions of winning; not by a long shot. But they do feel they have a message to bring to the people of America, and they do hope that the small beginnings of the Citizens Party will catch on and grow.

Operating out of her AIO office located in Albuquerque, this sometimes flambouyant, but thoroughly likable and believable Indian woman exudes optimism. Candidate Harris will tell anyone who will take the time to listen, "It's time to start a discussion on issues because the other parties are playing dead and refusing to talk."

It is the contention of the Citizens Party that, "The nations's problems are rooted primarily in the greed and growing incompetence of the massive corporate and bureaucratic institutions that dominate both political parties, and the lives of all Americans." They believe that these culprits "have made a mess of things, and it's time to call them to account."

Perhaps there will be those skeptics who will say that LaDonna is doing this to promote her organization, or herself, but they would be dead wrong.

Mrs. Harris has been a dedicated advocate of Indian rights far too long, and she has experienced, firsthand, the prejudices of the majority felt by the Indian people of this country to let her ideals be tainted by personal ambitions.

Her upbringing as a Comanche taught her that all men and women have not only the right, but the duty, to use their powers and talents in the best way they know how.

"Never Let Your Dreams End"

When the Lakota holy man, Johnny Fire, called Lame Deer, gazed into the eyes of the first white man he had ever seen, he described it "like looking into the eyes of a dead owl." The blue eyes of the white man had always struck the Indian as being cold and indifferent. But there are exceptions to everything.

Ruth Ziolkowski, wife of sculptor Korczak Ziolkowski and mother of his ten children (Korczak called her "Fertile Myrtle") is a small, gentle woman with graying hair. There is a softness in her blue eyes which belies the myth of hardness and indifference, and a glowing warmth replacing the legendary coldness perceived by the Indians.

"It is he, the sculptor, whose story must be told, not mine," she says. "It is his project, his dream, and his driving ambition which has sustained us as a family."

"Let me tell you an ironic thing," she adds. "Korczak had to buy this mountain from the federal government in order to carve a monument to the Indian people, who had it stolen from them in the first place. We have not, nor will we ever, accept federal or state dollars to complete this project."

Ziolkowski was born 72 years ago on September 6, exactly thirty-one years to the day that Chief Crazy Horse was killed. Oglala Headman Henry Standing Bear considered this to be prophetic and asked the sculptor to carve a monument to the Red Man so that the world would know that "we also have our heroes."

By nature, the Indian people are not pessimists. There is no race of people on the face of this earth with more reasons to distrust the white man. There is an underlying skepticism among many Lakota people about the sculptor and the monument. A young Lakota woman on the Pine Ridge Reservation said, "I really find it hard to believe that this white man has dedicated his life to carve this mountain for our people, but then again, we've been ripped off for so long that after awhile, you get so that you don't trust anyone."

Ziolkowski didn't blame the Indian people for being skeptical. "Why in the hell should they trust any white man after what we've done to them?"

A few years back, he established the Crazy Horse Memorial Scholarships Program to provide financial assistance to Indian students seeking a higher education. Funding for this, and all of the monument projects, is provided by the thousands of tourists who visit the Black Hills each summer and pay a a carload fee to visit the museum and to watch Ziolkowski work on the gigantic carving on the hill called Thunderhead Mountain.

"The scholarship fund we set up is more than that. It is a quest for a new beginning for the Indian students; a statement of faith in the future," Ziolkowski said.

Located near Custer, the monument itself stands 563 feet high and is 600 feet long. Since a small beginning in 1948 when the first dynamite blast lifted 10 tons of earth from the mountain, more than seven million tons of rock and earth have been blasted and bulldozed from the mountain. Ziolkowski has devoted 32 years of his life to the project.

Plagued by failing health brought on by a heart condition, he refused to abandon his project. Five months before his death, he could still be seen perched on the seat of a bulldozer, pushing the loose granite down the side of the mountain.

"It may take the Crazy Horse National Commission, my family (his sons are helping to shape the statue) and the engineer another 100 years to finish it, but it will be here long after we're gone for the world to see and remember," he said.

In May of 1981, Ziolkowski was honored by Black Hills State College at Spearfish, South Dakota with an honorary doctor of humane letters degree. College President Dr. J. Gilbert Hause, introduced the sculptor, saying, "He is a man whose mark will be felt by civilization in the centuries ahead. This honor is not given to you only because of the massive mountain carving known as Crazy Horse, but because of your unselfish efforts in behalf of the human race and particularly in behalf of the North American Indian."

Addressing the graduates, Ziolkowski said, "It is said that when the legends die, the dreams must end—when the dreams end, there is no more greatness. My friends, never let your dreams end."

Casey Crossed Cultural Gap with Smile on his Face

There is a lot of difference in laughing at someone and laughing with someone.

Tom Casey is an instructor and public relations expert for the Oglala Sioux Community College at Pine Ridge. He is a non-Indian who came to the Pine Ridge Reservation about fifteen years ago in 1967, married a Lakota woman, settled down and made the reservation his permanent home.

An educated, articulate man, Casey is noted for his hasty dashes to and fro on this large reservation. There are those who say that no matter how fast he runs, he is always a little bit behind himself.

One of the annual events organized on the reservation by Casey, a former long distance runner, is the Wounded Knee Run, a 15-kilometer event now in its fifth year. The run will be held this year (1982) on June 26.

Casey is the one responsible for laying out its course. He usually begins very early in the morning the day of the race, takes his flags and markers out into the fields and valleys, and posts the course.

Last year Tom had been missing all morning, and it was assumed, quite correctly, that he was out on the course laying out the markers. At the prescribed time, the eager runners lined up, the gun sounded and the race was on. It wasn't long before the more experienced runners had taken a good lead and were loping easily along the grassy hills and knolls around Wounded

Knee.

About the 12-meter mark, the lead racers rounded a bend in the course and there stood Tom Casey. Hammer and stakes in hand, Casey was still in the process of laying out the course when the racers caught up to him. It was a sudden end to a good run, and Casey had to pick the winners from those who reached him first.

Casey has a gleam in his eye, a long beard and a mischeivous smile. He wears a bandana across his forehead, and can usually be seen hurrying from one place to another weighed down by about three elaborate cameras. There is no finer photographer on this reservation, or any place else, for that matter.

His battered green van is held together by bailing wire and masking tape. One headlight points down at the ground and appears to be suspended from springs, like the eye of a ventriloquist's dummy that has popped from its socket. Every letter he has received or newspaper he has published for the College Center over the past five years is crammed into the back of that van. Ask him to find something for you in that mess, and he'll come up with it.

One Indian gentleman told me a story about driving to Porcupine one windy day. He spotted a green van alongside the road, and this wild-looking white man, beard flying in the wind, chasing various and sundry papers across the grassy plains. It seems that Casey stopped to get something from his van, opened the side door, and a sudden gust of wind snatched a ton of papers from the interior of his van and scattered them across the reservation.

Casey's van is so battered because of his nocturnal dashes across the plains. Thus far, he has rammed into two horses, one cow, two deer, many skunks and several unidentified night creatures. He has been advised to paint the symbol of the animals he has demolished on the door of his van, like the ace pilots of World War II.

There are many non-Indians like Tom Casey who have made their homes on the Pine Ridge Reservation and on the many reservations of this country. They live in peace and harmony. They consider the reservation their home.

I think of wonderful women such as Barbara Criss, who served the people on the reservation for many years as a midwife at the Indian hospital. A sincere, dedicated woman, she was much loved by the Indian women she assisted in their hour of need. She left the reservation to further her education, but she hopes to return some day to take up where she left off.

These people have crossed the cultural gap. They share in the hardships of the Indian people without complaining. They are accepted as "one of us" and they wouldn't have it any other way.

They have taken the time to get to know the Indian people. They are welcome into our homes and to the gatherings and commuity activities out in the districts. They are an important part of our daily lives.

Tom Casey may have done many things to provoke laughter from the people who are often accused of having no sense of humor, but through it all, we are laughing with Tom, not at him. As I said, there is a difference.

Three Stars Found Personal Satisfaction in Helping Alcoholics

He used to have a sign hanging on the wall behind his desk that read: "Success may yet come to those who have failed, but never to those who quit!"

Glen Three Stars was a counselor for a reservation alcoholism treatment program called Project Recovery. He became a counselor because he had waged a personal battle with this devastating disease for many years. In the end, he lost, but he had waged a glorious fight, and in the process, he had been instrumental in saving many lives. In the final analysis, he couldn't use the quiet persuasion, determination and advice he had given to so many others to save himself.

Three Stars was not a quitter. The final years of his short life revolved around helping alcoholics. Only forty-seven years old, he had a difficult time separating his personal life from those of the people he counseled. His clients knew they could depend upon him to come to their aid, day or night, seven days a week. They knew he would come and sit by their side, comfort them, talk to them, or just hold their hand, if that's what it took to settle them down. This total involvement was a heavy mental burden and only a super human being could have remained untouched by the degradation and sorrow. Three Stars was only human.

In his youth, he was one of the finest athletes the Pine Ridge Reservation ever produced. In 1948, while competing for the Oglala Community High School in the State B Track Championships, he place second in the 100-yard dash, second in the 220, and then set a record in the 440 that stood for twenty-five years.

Three Stars died February 10, 1982, a victim of the product he had strived so hard to save others from—alcohol.

I interviewed him for the Rapid City *Journal* exactly two years ago, February 8, 1980. He told me, "I am proud of the things I accomplished as an athelete, but I am prouder of the things I am trying to do as a counselor. The satisfaction I get is much deeper and more personal."

Perhaps we'll never understand the stresses that can cause a man to embrace alcohol even though he knows it will destroy him. Three Stars had said to me, "My doctor told me if I ever decided to drink again, I might as well take a gun, go out into the hills and shoot myself in the head. He said the results would be the same."

In 1951, three boys—Ray Briggs, Richard "Sonny" Torres and I— ran away from the Holy Rosary Mission at Pine Ridge. It was Three Stars who "hid us out" and fed us until we could find transportation to reach our destinations. That's the kind of person he was.

Even though his job was helping alcoholics to recover, he was not against the legalization of alcohol on the reservation. He'd say "Prohibition never worked on a national scale, and it sure as hell isn't going to work on our reservation. We're not children to be told what we can or cannot do, and trying to keep alcohol out of our reach isn't going to solve the problem."

Long before it appeared on a recent advertisement, Three Stars used to say, "Being given the right to drink is also being given the right not to drink. Every reservation in this country has a very serious alcoholism problem, but forbidding people to drink only makes it much more inviting."

He was very concerned about the low priority given to programs such as Project Recovery, and he resented having to beg for funds to keep the program going. "All of the money spent on traveling by the program directors and tribal councilmen would make a tidy sum to help us fight alcoholism, but each and every year we have to practically get down on our hands and knees to get money to keep operating."

There are many people on the reservation alive today leading productive lives because one man cared enough to help them. He surrendered his free time to a cause and his working hours to a project he truly believed in.

Like many Indian men and women, he had to walk through hell before he found peace. "I'm not an angel, nor have I ever claimed to be. Like many Indians, I did a lot of things in my life that I'm not too proud of, and I don't blame anybody but myself for those things; but I learned from those mistakes, and now I'm trying to use that experience to help others, and to keep them from making those same mistakes," Three Stars told me on that day two years ago.

Saturday, Three Stars was buried at Wounded Knee, on the reservation he loved. Project Recovery will miss the steady hand, but largely through his unselfish efforts, it will continue to do the job he worked so hard to do. There are many people on the Pine Ridge Reservation whose lives are much better for having brushed against his. His life was a success.

"Diploma Indians" Need Humility

Several years ago the conservative politicans were referring to the educated elite of the East Coast as "pointy-headed liberals." This was probably an updated version of the "egg-headed intellectual" label given to these same individuals years before that. Did the philosophies or methods of change sought by these individuals have an impact upon the social, moral or political future of this country?

If the conservative mood of today is indicative of the whole, then the answer to that would have to be a resounding yes! Intellectualism for the sake of intellectualism; misguided, misdirected and totally subjective, can be as severe in its extremism as total ignorance. Erudition of itself is not a panacea. But it can become a "bitter medicine" when it is not blended with a liberal dose of common sense.

Perhaps this column can be misconstrued as "anti-education." It is not! It is intended to point out a phenomenon which has become increasingly obvious to many Indian people over the past ten years. For want of a better description, I will use the term "diploma Indian" when referring to the subject of this column.

The "diploma Indian" is the one who returns to the reservation, or to the cities with his or her college degree flapping from a flag pole. Usually he is determined to save his people using the same techniques taught to him by the white man. If you think "white paternalism" is bad, you've never experienced "red paternalism."

There is an entire colony of "diploma Indians" lurking in and about the governmental offices of Washington, D.C. Either they have never lived on an Indian reservation, or they have been away from the reservation for so many years that they have forgotten what it is to be Indian. Too many of them have become sycophantic elitists, ready to sell out to their own brethren in order to keep their high-paying jobs, and continue to live in the high style which has supplanted their heritage. These are the Indians referred to by Rupert Costo, publisher of *Wassaja*, as "mendacious eunuchs."

The "diploma Indian" is an expert at writing proposals for funding in order to sustain reservation or urban programs. Never mind that 80 percent of the funding for the self-styled programs are eaten up by administrative salaries and costs. His battle cry is "keep the money coming" and the crown he has placed upon his head has given him a title: "Executive director."

You cannot tell a "diploma Indian" by his or her attire. The best way to spot him is by the "diploma" which is usually Scotch-taped to his forehead. Another dead giveaway is by the way he begins each sentence with "when I was in college" or "when I got my degree." The reason I say that you cannot spot him by his attire is because he tends to go to both extremes. He dresses in the finest of Western style (or Eastern style) clothing, or he looks like he had just stepped out of a John Wayne movie, draped with baubles, bangles and beads.

Recently a Washington, D.C. Indian woman lectured at one of the schools on the reservations. Clad in dark buckskins, frills, fringes, and beads, she was given the name of "Clay Basket." The name was taken, of course, from the television mini-series, *Centennial*. The young man who christened her said, "Can you imagine this woman coming from back East, to our reservation, and trying to tell us how to be Indians? Hell, none of us dress like that out here!"

There is nothing that turns off the elders of any Indian tribe in this country faster than an Indian who wears his diploma like a badge, and expects the less fortunate to pay homage to it.

It was those Indian people labeled as "uneducated" who made it possible for the "diploma Indians" to get an education. They fought for the future of the tribe when it was not a popular cause. They took their "lumps" in silence, but tenaciously hung on to a past that would have been forgotten, trampled into the dust of so-called progress.

As for myself, I would much rather sit upon a tree stump, next to the warming campfire, and listen to an elder of my tribe talk about the "people," than sit in a plush conference room, in a plush hotel, and listen to a "diploma Indian" talk about things he knows nothing about.

Yes, we need educated Indians to fight for our rights using the same tools that were once used to deprive us of those rights; but these Indians must never forget two basic Indian traits: humility and unselfishness. As an elderly Indian man said, "You don't have to have a degree to be smart."

Curse of Shawnee Prophet Recalled

Is there such a thing as a curse? Perhaps you may not believe it, but there are many believers among the Indian people.

The curse many speak of was placed upon President William Henry Harrison by the Shawnee prophet Tenskawtawa in the year 1840.

The Shawnee prophet was the brother of Chief Tecumseh. Tecumseh died in a battle in 1813, but this was not the reason for the curse, because the prophet considered his brother's death the fortunes of war.

The federal government passed a law called the Indian Removal Act of 1830 which required the forced removal of Indian tribes from Georgia, the Carolinas, Tennessee, Alabama and Mississippi. The Cherokee Nation took the government to court and ended up before the Supreme Court of the land. The court ruled (Worcester vs. State of Georgia) that the Indian tribes could not be forced from their ancestral lands. They ruled the act to be illegal and unenforceable.

Ruling Challenged

President Andrew Jackson challenged the ruling by saying, "Let them (the Supreme Court) enforce it." He then ordered the removal of the Indian tribes of the region and began an exodus known far and wide to all Indian people as "The Trail of Tears."

Tenskawtawa, the prophet, watched in anger as thousand of Indians were driven from their homes, allowed only the possessions they could carry on their backs, and prodded at the points of bayonets, toward Indian Territory in Oklahoma.

Led by pitiful bands of Choctaws, followed by the Chickasaw, Creeks, and finally, the Cherokee Nation, they began this death march in the winter of 1834. The Potawatomi and the Shawnee followed in the spring of 1838. One-third of the Cherokee Nation perished along the trail. Some 3,500 of the original 15,000 Creek Indians died of disease and exposure along this trail.

Curse Uttered

It was amidst this death and destruction of his people that the prophet uttered his curse. He said, "Every president elected to office, beginning with the year 1840, will perish. This will occur in twenty-year intervals, so that those presidents elected from this date on, will have the opportunity to correct these wrongs. Unless the Indian people begin to see justice, the acts of greed, deceit, dishonesty and broken treaties will lend strength to this curse."

William Henry Harrison was elected president in 1840. He died in office on April 4, 1841.

Since 1840, here is how things have happened: 1860, Abraham Lincoln is elected and is assassinated in 1865; in 1880 Garfield is elected and killed in office by Charles Guiteau in 1881; in 1900 William McKinley is elected and assassinated in 1901; in 1920 Warren Harding is elected and dies from a stroke in 1923 (although rumors persist that he shot himself); Franklin Roosevelt became president when he was re-elected in 1940, but he died in office in 1945. Finally, John F. Kennedy was elected president in 1960 and was assassinated by Lee Harvey Oswald in 1963.

Conditions Fulfilled?

If you were a betting person, what would you say the odds were that this cycle would repeat itself, without fail, for the past 120 years? Also, have the conditions set down by the prophet to end this curse been fulfilled? Will the cycle continue in 1980, 140 years after the curse was pronounced?

Thus far, only one president has died while in office, outside this twenty-year cycle. President Zachary Taylor died in office on July 9, 1850.

We are are now approaching the 140th anniversary of the curse, and there is one ironic stituation that needs to be mentioned.

The "Trail of Tears" began because Andrew Jackson ignored the Supreme Court and had the Cherokee people forcibly removed from their homes in the state of Georgia. Herein lies the irony: President Carter is from the state of Georgia, and as the incumbent, he has a very good chance of being re-elected. Will the curse make the full circle, and return to the land where it began?

A Salute

The ladies of St. Isaac-Jogues—There are no people on the face of this earth more generous with their time and their money than the American Indian. The women who volunteer their services to help those who have just lost a loved one by cooking and serving meals following funeral services, who dedicate their time and efforts to make it just a little bit easier for the grieving families, deserve a commendation.

They call themselves the Jogues Ladies and they include Vera Drust, Edna Valandra, Leatrice Mills, Donna Anderson, Ramona Sanovia, Mildred Stinson and Rita Wilson.

These fine ladies deserve a pat on the back and the highest commendation for a job well done! Keep up the good work, ladies; this world would be a darker place without you.

Simplicity, Integrity Key to Charlie Red Cloud's Character

Last summer at the Red Cloud Art Festival held at Holy Rosary Mission, Pine Ridge, a water color painting by Don Ruleaux of Lead won second prize. It was purchased for the mission school and became a part of its permanent art collection.

The painting showed the inside of a simple reservation cabin with a view through a window, a part of an old bed, and on the top of a beat-up old chest sat a greenish colored, battered hat. The painting was entitled, "Charlie Red

Charlie Red Cloud

Cloud's Hat."

The scene was a reflection of the personality of the man. Charles Red Cloud died last week. He was five years old in 1890 when Sitanka and his band of Miniconjou were massacred at Wounded Knee. He was a lineal descendant of the famed Red Cloud, Chief of the Oglalas, and spent most of his ninety-five years preaching the philosophy of peace and progress.

Charles Red Cloud never wanted material gains for himself. He declined offers of a new house for himself and chose to live in the old log cabin that had been his home since boyhood. He would say, "Give the houses to the young people because my needs are few, and I am accustomed to this way of life."

He was an elder of the tribe and was given the respect of all the people of the reservation. Charles Red Cloud was present at most of the cermonial functions that took place on the reservation up until the last year of his life.

He sat on the podium at the presidential inauguration two years ago, dressed in traditional regalia which included a splendid feathered headdress, and waited patiently for his turn to welcome the new president and present him with a headdress as the newly elected leader of the tribe.

In his later years he was a frail man with failing eyesight, but his voice remained strong and resonant. At ninety-five his memory was keen and he could talk at great length about the history of the Oglala Sioux Tribe, about the treaties that affected all of the people and about the course our leaders must take in order to solve the many problems existing on the reservation.

Two summers ago I saw him sitting under a large tree letting its shade protect him from the heat of a scorching day. The place was Three Mile Creek near Kyle, and he was to speak on the Treaty of 1868.

Charles Red Cloud never spoke in English. The speech he gave that day was in his native Lakota tongue. I recorded his words for KINI-FM radio, Rosebud, and the radio station gave him a special half hour show that week.

When I heard of the passing of this great man, I thought back on that day and wondered if KINI had filed that recording away for posterity.

In a day when many of our leaders are ignoring the needs of the people and are serving for their own personal gain, it's a shame that men such as Charles Red Cloud are no longer with us to serve as a conscience to our elected officials.

Here we had a man who, because of his station in life, could have acquired many material things; but instead chose to live a simple life, bereft of personal wealth, and dedicate himself to the improvement of all the Oglala people. It is a rare quality and is reflected in the water color painting of his hat.

It should be the hope of every member of the Oglala Sioux Tribe that his simple philosophy remains alive and is instilled in the minds of the younger generation. His preachings against alcohol and drugs are a strong indication of his personal beliefs, and should not be taken lightly.

The next time you are at Red Cloud Indian School, named for his grandfather, take a long look at the painting, "Charlie Red Cloud's Hat," and know that this humble man was a great leader in his own way.

Reservation Lost Good Friend When Bad Wound Died

Television producer David Wolper (*Roots* and *Roots II*) referred to him as "a unique diplomat. able to carry his message about the Indian people across many cultures, and one of the finest gentlemen I have ever known, bar none."

Louis Bad Wound was a headman with the Lakota Treaty Council, and he was my friend. No matter where he traveled, I could always expect a short telephone call from him, bringing me up to date on his adventures. Louis died at age 54 on Thursday, June 10, 1982.

His friends remember him like this. Larry Red Shirt, a member of the Lakota Treaty Council said, "It is my belief that Louis Bad Wound was one of the few remaining die-hard, traditionalist Oglalas who was totally committed, uncompromisingly and relentlessly, in his efforts to bring back full sovereignty and international recognition for the Oglala people as a separate and independent nation as guaranteed by treaty. Wherever our inherent treaty rights were trampled upon, he was there to offer his wisdom, knowledge and unique talents as an organizer and negotiator."

Red Shirt continued, "Throughout the time I knew and worked with him, he would never complain of his health, the long grueling hours, or the pressure and demands put upon him. He was criticized, verbally assaulted, and even threatened with violence, but he continued. He put the welfare of the people above his own personal needs."

Friends and companions, Red Shirt and Bad Wound had traveled over half of the world seeking justice for the Lakota people. Red Shirt reflected with sadness, "Louis could have had a much easier life, maybe as a contractor or a carpenter, and yet he chose to fight in this political battle to regain what is rightfully ours."

"The death of Louis Bad Wound reminds me of the words spoken by one of our Lakota elders: 'Takoja (Grandchildren), some day, in the future, you will be able to count as many Ikce Wicasa (in this context, "Indian people") as there are fingers on one hand.'" Red Shirt said with a mixture of anger and sorrow.

Throughout the years, Bad Wound counted Tribal Attorney Mario Gonzalez as one of his closest friends and confidants. Gonzalez said, "One of the hardest things about living on the Pine Ridge Reservation is seeing people you are close to die, and Louie Bad Wound will be missed, very much. When you look at his achievements of the past years, it is easy to see that we have lost a great man."

Gonzalez believed that Bad Wound brought Indian Nations of this country into the "international arena." He said, "As a headman in the Lakota Treaty Council, he was involved in many issues, including the Black Hills Claim. He attended the first Human Rights Commission meeting in Geneva, Switzerland, and gained the support of many different groups in Europe for the cause of the American Indian. Louis organized the tour we made of Europe last fall."

One of the major efforts to reach fruition this summer was a project to send four Oglala Lakota students to Austria as official guests of the Austrian government. "Louie engaged us in this 'ping-pong' diplomacy in order to set the stage for the Lakota people to eventually file the Black Hills Claim in the World Court, and in other international forums," Gonzalez said.

Gonzalez shook his head with deep sadness and said, "It is my firm belief that we will get land back in the Black Hills, and when we do, I hope that the Lakota people remember the sacrifices, the unselfish efforts, and the many personal contributions made by Louis Bad Wound. In a way, he gave his life for the survival of the Lakota Nation."

Louie sat with me late last week, just a few days before his death, in the office of *The Lakota Times*. He talked about the efforts he had been making to get the film, *The Mystic Warrior*, adapted from the novel, *Hanta Yo*, into production. "The people who are making the film are professionals. They would never put their signatures on anything that would hurt the Lakota people, or any Indian people, for that matter," Bad Wound said.

Louie had worked long and hard to make this film a reality. He had put his reputation on the line. "I have taken much abuse because of my faith in this project, but I firmly believe that this production will open the door for the Indian people with the national television networks. I have placed my faith in David Wolper and Stan Margulies as honorable men. They have allowed us to read the scripts and to offer suggestions. Anything we found objectionable, even borderline, we asked them to remove, and they have complied."

Bad Wound believed that location producer Paul Freeman ("The Chisolms") and director Richard Hefron ("I will Fight No More Forever") had the unique qualities to bring humanity and sensitivity to the lifestyles of the Lakota people of two hundred years ago.

In a telephone conversation today with producer Stan Margulies of Warner Brothers Studio, Burbank, California, I suggested that the production of *The Mystic Warrior* be dedicated to the memory of a great Lakota man, Louis Bad Wound. Margulies replied, "I think that is a terrific idea, and we will discuss it at our meeting this week."

There is no Lakota more deserving of such an honor than my Kola, Louis Bad Wound.

Military Veterans of World War II Praised

When we were young boys on the reservation going to school at the Holy Rosary Mission, many of us idolized the older classmates of ours who returned in their sharp-looking uniforms and told us stories of the countries they had visited during those days of World War II.

Many of us remember when Clement Crazy Thunder came home in his Marine uniform. He brought a pickup-load of five-gallon containers full of ice cream to the children at the mission. Clement said, "When I was a student, we never got any ice cream, and it is something I always used to dream about. I promised myself that if ever I could afford to do it, I would see to it that all of the mission kids shared in my dreams."

Louis Bad Wound

Eager Youngsters

I will never forget Clement, in his Marine greens, standing by the tailgate of the pickup, and scooping out ladles of ice cream to the happiest bunch of kids in the world. He laughed at our eagerness, probably remembering his own Mission days, and he laughed with us, as we savored this unbelievable good fortune which brought this gentle Marine back home to us.

That was the last time any of us ever saw Clement again. He was killed in action at Iwo Jima Island in the Pacific. When the word was given to us one morning at Mass, many of us could not hold back the tears for the Marine who kept a promise to himself, and brought a little happiness to our dismal world.

Conditions Worse

The veterans began to return home shortly after this. They came home to find the conditions on the reservation were worse than when they left. The poverty and the disease had continued unabated. The shortages of gasoline, food and other necessities, which were hard to come by before the war, were impossible to get now. While much of the country had enjoyed prosperity during the war years, the conditions on the reservations rivaled the Depression years.

Many of the young Indian men and women had stepped forward patriotically and volunteered to defend the United States against the enemy, even with their lives, although they were still considered second-class citizens in the land they once owned.

Honor and Valor

They served with honor and valor, and I would venture to say that if the number of awards, ribbons and medals handed out during the war could be broken down by race, the American Indian would stand proudly at the top of that list.

The novel, *Devils in Baggy Pants*, praises the fighting ability of the Indian paratroopers of the 82nd and the 101st Airborn battalions—men such as "Buddy" White Eyes and Jake Herman, both Lakota who participated in the invasion of Europe. "Buddy " came home but Jake gave his life taking a bridge in Belgium.

There are Indians like Ira Hayes, a Pima, who gained immortality when he raised the flag on Iwo Jima. A Marine named Louis "Piggy" Tapio, an Oglala, stood on the beach and watched Ira raise that flag on February 23, 1945.

Code Talkers

When the Marines were looking for a code the Japanese would not be able to decipher, they turned to the bilingual Marines of the Navajo Nation and the Navajo Code Talkers were born. Peter MacDonald, chairman of the Navajo

Nation, was only fifteen years old at the time, but he wore the uniform of the Marines, and he was the youngest of the Navajo Code Talkers.

These Indian veterans returned to their reservations only to find there were no jobs. The skills they had acquired in the service could not be utilized. They found the racial prejudice in the towns bordering the reservations had not diminished, but because they were more aware of it, it seemed to have increased.

The federal government, glad to have these men and women risk their lives to defend it, now turned its back on them. Some reenlisted in disgust, and made a career of the armed forces, and others rolled up their sleeves and began to fight for a change in the reservation system of suppression, total federal control and paternalism.

No Back Seat

They had discovered in basic training and in combat, they were as good as any white man. No longer would these veterns take a back seat to anyone. They were impatient for changes in a bureaucratic system which had kept them in a position of servitude for too long. Many of the non-Indian soldiers, sailors and Marines who had fought side by side with them and had called them "Chief," derisively in the beginning, had begun to call them "Chief" with the utmost of respect when they saw they could place their lives in thier hands without fear.

These veterans were the original perpetrators of the movement to improve the lives of the Indian people.

When the college Indians are busy counting their credits and hanging their degrees on the wall, they should say a little "thank you" and perhaps a small prayer for those brave Indian men and women, veterans of World War II, who made it all possible.

Red Army Made Friends out of Korean Prisoners

There are times when the word "friendship" is not strong enough to express the feelings between individuals who have shared a deep and emotional experience. A special Prisoner of War Reunion was held in Muskogee, Oklahoma in August, 1983, attesting to this fact.

For Eugene Rowland of the Pine Ridge Reservation in South Dakota, Virgil Rutherford and Jesse McCray of Muskogee, it all began on November 18, 1950 near the 38th Parallel in North Korea. On that day in history, the Red Army of China stormed across the border, killing or capturing many men of the U.S. Army. The three close friends were captured.

This day marked the beginning of a three-year nightmare for them. They were placed in a compound called "Camp Number Five" and for the next thirty-three months they were silent witnesses to the deaths of many comrades. Rowland said of this sequence of events, "I guess we'll never foget our buddies—black, white, red and brown—who gave their lives during this time. They were buried in shallow graves, dug by us, on a knoll we named

Eugene Rowland (Photo courtesy of **The Lakota Times***)*

'Yonder Hill.'"

It was last year that Rowland discovered his old friends from "Camp Number Five" were still alive. In spite of his illness, his physical disabilities, and the fact that he is now almost blind, Rowland vowed to travel to Muskogee to see his buddies once more. "I had always believed that I would never see them again," he said.

The harsh conditions of the prison camp, the near starvation, and the physical abuse and torture had taken its toll of the three men. Each of them discovered they had been fighting for years to regain their health.

July 22, 1953, in a village called Panmunjom, an armistice agreement was signed by General William Harrison for the United States and by Nam Il for the North Koreans. On August 8, Rowland, Rutherford and McCray were set free.

"We were told to go home and resume a normal life. Here we were, broken men, beaten mentally and physically. We had shared loneliness, starvation and torture. When it had become too much to bear, we turned to God together, and prayed for freedom. And now we were being told to go live a normal life," Rowland said sadly.

Each discovered in time that for them there would never be a so-called normal life. The things they considered normal before they were captured were not that important to them any longer. Their health had been destroyed. The extreme abuse had taken a toll upon them. Captured as young and healthy soldiers, their bodies were now diseased and tired.

To these survivors of Camp Number Five, the occasion of their reunion was one of more than a handshake or a time for reminiscing. "There are no words in the English language or Lakota language that can describe the things we felt, or the things we shared with each other on that special day. The emotions cannot be described," Rowland said.

Rutherford recalled, "Over there, 6,000 miles from home, it didn't matter if you were white or Indian. You went through the same kind of hell every day. You learned to rely and depend on each other. Otherwise, we could never have survived. We didn't just become friends. We were closer than brothers, even."

Each felt the same way about the thirty-three months they spent in captivity. To them, it was as if the world stood still for three years. There was a daily routine that kept them regimented, and before long, the prison camp became a little world for them.

As the days dragged into weeks, the weeks into months, and the months into years, they saw many of their companions wither and die. The will to live, to face another day, became too much of a burden and they gave up their spirits.

There are two human emotions they all share and feel deeply about: a feeling of eternal gratitude, and an empty sense of loss. They share a common gratitude at having survived the ordeal of captivity, torture and degradation. "I think that we thank God each and every day that we are alive," Rowland said.

"There is one thing that haunts each of us. It is the fact that so many of our buddies lie dead and buried in North Korea," Rutherford said.

Rowland shares that empty feeling, saying, "Our fellow GI's were laid to rest in unmarked graves. There were no caskets or crosses to mark the spot where they were buried, or markers to identify where they were buried. It has always bothered me that most of our friends were buried without a bugle call, without the beat of the drum to sound retreat. I believe that they still lie buried up there on Yonder Hill in North Korea, but Virgil, Jesse and I will never forget them."

The reunion was a time of happiness, and a time of sadness but most of all, it was a celebration of life, a time to reminisce about the bad, and be thankful for the good. A time when two white men from Oklahoma and an Indian from South Dakota realized the bond that holds them together cuts across all racial barriers.

"We are closer than brothers can ever be, and we will never let thirty years pass before we get together again. A lot of tears fell when we had to split up, but it was good—real good—to see them again. I prayed for this day," Rowland said with a smile.

Anthony Whirlwind Horse Tempers Life with Laughter

"My grandpa used to tell us Whirlwind Horse boys that we were a special cut," Anthony Whirlwind Horse said with a smile. His grandpa told him in halting English, "You are Mexican Indian and Sioux. You don't stand around and take that cheat—you stand up and fight."

Whirlwind Horse, superintendent of the Pine Ridge Agency, Bureau of Indian Affairs, will retire after thirty years of service June 3, 1983. From his grandpa, he learned to be a fighter.

"When I joined the Navy in 1945, my little brother, Elijah, told all of his friends at school that the war would be over pretty quick because his big brother had joined up," Tony said. Seated at his desk in Pine Ridge, clad in a black vest, a beaded choker adjusted neatly at his throat, Whirlwind Horse reminisced. "A few weeks after I joined up, they dropped the A bomb and the war ended. Elijah told his little friends, 'Didn't I tell you?'"

Tony became the BIA superintendent in 1976. Two years later, his little brother, Elijah, was elected to the presidency of the Oglala Sioux Tribe. The powers-that-be in the BIA attempted to transfer Tony, charging him with conflict of interest. He took them to court. The Eighth Circuit Court of Appeals in St. Louis, Missouri ruled in favor of Tony, and he was allowed to remain as superintendent.

Born on the Pine Ridge Reservation, Tony attended elementary school in Wanblee. His father, Louis, was a career BIA man and worked as an assistant farm aide at Wanblee. Louis was transferred to Bacone, Oklahoma where Tony attended high school and later, two years of college at Bacone College. "I started college under the GI Bill and it lasted long enough to get me through Bacone College and one year at Northeastern State College at Tahlequah, Oklahoma, before the money ran out," Whirlwind Horse said.

Tony rejoined the Navy in 1952 and stayed long enough to get his GI Bill reinstated. "I came back to South Dakota and finished up at Black Hills State College where I earned a BS in education." While working as a teacher on the Pine Ridge Reservation, Tony earned a master's degree in elementary education. "I wanted to get so qualified that they couldn't dummy up the qualification requirements for advancement and keep me back," he said.

By this time he had married, and he and his wife, Eileen, were trying to raise five children. "I applied for my Sioux benefits that they used to give out back then in order to continue my education, but I was told I wasn't qualified. I went to South Dakota Congressman Francis Case, and he fought for me, and we won. That's where I learned that you had to be stubborn and determined if you wanted to fight the system and win," he mused.

Whirlwind Horse reflected on the many changes he has seen in his thirty years with the BIA. "When I was replaced by Ray Pentilla as the education program administrator on this reservation, I broke the white barrier. I think Ray always looked at me as a potential trouble maker because at the ceremony we held to change commands, he said, "The bad penny returns." Tony added quickly, "At least it's an Indian penny, Mr. Pentilla."

Whirlwind Horse said that in the past the responsibility of running the reservation was in the hands of the Aberdeen area office. "The Agency Superintendent had little to say in how the reservation was run. Nowadays, many of those responsibilities are coming back to the superintendent. We're getting more local control. Eventually, the area offices, if they continue to exist, will be support offices for the reservation dealing mostly in technical services," Tony said.

Last week the Oglala Sioux Tribal Council passed a resolution calling for the abolishment of the Aberdeen area office. They charged it with being a bottleneck for funding and services. Tony said, "I approved that resolution because I believe in the sovereignty of the Tribe. I believe our elected Tribal Council should control most of the services provided to the people."

There has been talk of Tony running for the presidency of the Tribe after he retires. He puts these rumors to rest with, "Heck no! The way things are going right now, I just want to stay out of tribal politics and enjoy my retirement. I've been caught between the Bureau and the Tribe for so long that one week I'm the good guy and the next week I'm the goat. It makes you pretty weary."

His wife, Eileen, says, "Oh, he'll lay around for a few weeks, and then he'll feel like he's getting moldy. Tony's an old war horse. You can't expect to keep him out of the battle for very long."

Tony just laughs at this. "You know, I've been thinking of going back to school and getting a doctorate. How does Dr. Whirlwind Horse sound?"

Tony is shaking with laughter now. "I'll never forget when this white lady called up from back East and asked for Mr. World Wide Horse," he says, hanging onto his desk.

Whirlwind Horse gets a very serious expression on his face and says, "I'll probably go back to school and major in horseshoe throwing or in how to become a successful tribal chairman—just joking, just joking." He bends forward with laughter.

Tribal Leader's Job Not Easy

When he became president of the Oglala Sioux Tribe on the Pine Ridge Reservation in 1978, Elijah Whirlwind Horse was awed by the scope of demands placed upon that office. He said, "Even the janitors are coming to me and asking if they can keep their jobs. I never realized the power the tribal president had."

Former U.S. Senator James Abourezk corroborated this first impression in a message he sent to be read at the inauguration ceremony for the new president. It read, "There are two jobs I would not wish on anyone. One of them is the job of the president of the United States and the other is the president of the Oglala Sioux Tribe—but not necessarily in that order."

Recently, I saw a portrait of a group of students from the Oglala Community School at Pine Ridge, and seated there in the front row, his scrubbed face unsmiling, sat the smallest boy of them all. He was a boy who would grow up to become the tribal president in 1978.

Untiring Efforts

That tiny boy grew into a large man, with a lot of drive and determination. He fought his way through college and earned a degree in education, and

Elijah Whirlwind Horse

returned to the reservation of his birth to become teacher and principal at Crazy Horse School in the Eagle Nest District of the Pine Ridge Reservation. It was largely through his untiring efforts that the new multi-million dollar school was constructed at Wanblee (Eagle Nest).

At his inauguration he smiled and waved to the crowd, but there were those in the audience who knew he was in great pain. He had been struck with a strange illness that caused him to lose the feeling in his legs and to have excruciating pains in his lower back. Some said it was caused by the bite of a spider.

He went to visit a wicasa pejuta (medicine man) and was told that someone had placed bad medicine on him. A ceremony was held to combat the bad medicine, and everything seemed to get better after this.

His two years in office went swiftly, and his dreams of uniting the people, and bringing some prosperity to the tribe, were still unfulfilled as he left office. Perhaps he had discovered like so many tribal presidents before him that the burdens placed on his back were too great, and the two years in office were far too short.

Disagreements

We didn't agree, politically, but on the reservation, it is very difficult to separate politics from personal differences because they seem to be interwoven. And so, the heat of the campaign to get re-elected in 1980, took us down different roads, and we didn't see too much of each other after that election.

When I heard that he was seriously ill, and possibly dying, I felt a great sadness for his wife and for the eleven children he was trying to raise. The youngest, a baby girl, was born during his campaign in 1978, and was wrapped in blankets that day at his inauguration.

There were things accomplished during his administration which can best be described as intangible. Many of the bitter feelings between tribal members in the aftermath of the Wounded Knee Occupation began to dissipate. People who had been on the opposite side of the fence began to communicate once more. He brought former enemies together to discuss their differences, and in this manner, eased the tensions on the reservation.

Elijah Whirlwind Horse planted the seeds of peace and unity during his two years in office. Now, more than two years later, they are beginning to grow and bear fruit.

I remember Elijah standing behind a long table, covered by white linens, raising a glass of champagne as he proposed a toast. Dressed in a black tuxedo with a ruffled white shirt and black bow tie, he was the picture of health. As the best man at my wedding, and as a friend, his toast, "I wish a long and happy life to you and your bride," meant much to me.

Belief in Miracles

There are those of us who still believe in miracles, and we hope and pray that the cancer that has attacked Elijah's body will depart as swiftly as it struck.

Maybe the monster called tribal politics has caused us to take different roads, Elijah, but in the long run, we were both working toward the same goals, the preservation and the unity of the Pine Ridge Reservation.

It is possible to reach the same destination by taking different roads, and I hope that the road we have traveled is the "good red road of the Lakota."

The toast I propose to you, Elijah, is this: I hope you win this, the biggest battle of your life, and the hopes and prayers of the Lakota people are with you. Oglu Waste, Kola!